Quakers AND Nazis

Quakers AND Nazis

Inner Light in Outer Darkness

Hans A. Schmitt

University of Missouri Press

Columbia and London

Copyright © 1997 by
The Curators of the University of Missouri
University of Missouri Press, Columbia, Missouri 65201

Printed and bound in the United States of America
All rights reserved
5 4 3 2 1   01 00 99 98 97

Library of Congress Cataloging-in-Publication Data

Schmitt, Hans A.
    Quakers and Nazis : inner light in outer darkness / Hans A.
Schmitt.
        p.   cm.
    Includes bibliographical references and index.
    ISBN 0-8262-1134-8 (alk. paper)
    1. Germany—History—1933–1945.   2. National socialism and
religion.   3. Quakers—Germany—History—20th century.   4. Society
of Friends—Germany—History—20th century.   5. Germany—Church
history—1933–1945.   I. Title.
DD256.5.S3356   1997
289.6'43'09043—dc21   97-18914
                                                              CIP

∞™ This paper meets the requirements of the
American National Standard for Permanence of Paper
for Printed Library Materials, Z39.48, 1984.

Text Design: Elizabeth K. Young
Jacket Design: Kristie Lee
Typesetter: BOOKCOMP
Printer and Binder: Thomson-Shore, Inc.
Typefaces: Bodoni and Bodoni Condensed

This book is dedicated to **Florence**

" . . . let Eternal Light penetrate the darkness . . . that surrounds us."

—**Hans Albrecht** addressing the
1933 German Yearly Meeting of the Society of Friends

Contents

Preface

Most of the people discussed in this book belonged to a Christian sect—the Quakers—that claims slightly more than three hundred thousand members throughout the world. Until the mid-twentieth century, the majority were American or British. Despite their modest numbers their influence has been vast. When the Amsterdam historian Ger van Roon wrote his dissertation on the relations between Dutch Protestantism and Nazi Germany, he decided to omit the "smaller sectarian and mystic tendencies" in his country, but did include the Quakers whose Yearly Meeting counted a minuscule dozen members in 1933. He believed that their work on behalf of German refugees put to shame the hesitant commitment of major Protestant churches to that cause and therefore justified their inclusion.[1]

Such reasoning also speaks from the words of Helen Bentwich, a pillar of the Jewish relief effort in Britain, when she wrote to George Bell, Anglican bishop of Chichester, on June 23, 1934, to enlist his assistance, notably on behalf of German Jewish converts to Christianity. "Of the Christian bodies," she explained, "the Quakers alone have made a continuous and sustained effort in England, France, and other countries."[2]

I intend to tell the story of this "continuous and sustained effort," especially in Germany, in order to discharge an overdue debt of personal gratitude. Quakers enabled me to complete my secondary education after leaving Germany in 1934, and Quakers helped me obtain access to a college education after I came to the United States four years later. I have told the personal side of that story in a volume of reminiscences that was published in 1989.[3] As I was writing these memoirs, I came to realize that I knew nothing about the context in which my benefactors toiled. I knew why I had left Germany, but I really had no idea what efforts and what larger resources had been mobilized to rescue many more like me.

After haunting libraries, archives, and importuning with my questions a diverse aggregation of aged survivors, I am now able to provide a reasonably complete chronicle of Quaker efforts to lead to safety countless victims of ethnic, religious, and political persecution from the relentless grip of National Socialism. Gaps remain, due to the fragmentary and elusive nature of the sources. I hope that my work will prompt others to close those in due time.

Mine is a story of decent men and women, "do-gooders" in a time that accepted them as exemplary Christians, but also in a time in which such

individuals courted dangers and, above all, profound and lasting discourage-
ment. Certainly no amount of individual or collective Quaker beneficence saved
more than a small portion of the vast array of victims.

Obscure, few in numbers, my heroes—and that grandiose attribute fits many
of them—made a difference to the contemporaries they helped. They could
not prevent disaster, but they could help contain it. They demonstrated that
individuals who stay on the path mapped by their conscience do change history.
I knew some of them when I was quite young, and I can testify that they brought
light into a darkness that surrounded both me and others they were destined to
guide. To the world at large most remain unknown, and few were ever rewarded.
All too often, their virtue was their only recompense.

In the course of my inquiry I have accumulated many debts to archives as well
as to individuals. Some of them must be mentioned at the outset. The archives
of the library of Friends House in London and the archives of the American
Friends Service Committee in Philadelphia were a rich mine of information.
Both are well organized and blessed with helpful and efficient staffs. Without
Rosamund Cummings and Josef Keith at the first, and Jack Sutters at the latter,
this book could not have been written. Users must, however, gain permission in
writing before using the Philadelphia archive and certainly make sure that their
project does not transgress the fifty-year limit that generally applies to holdings
at Friends House.

In the Netherlands I owe a solid debt to Mevr. A. van Bockxmeer of the
Rijksinstituut voor Oorlogsdocumentatie and to Mevr. Ijzerman of the International Institute for Social History, the latter holding a rich collection of papers
deposited there by a member of the Dutch Society of Friends.

Germany constituted the most difficult terrain. The German Society of Friends
is not large. For obvious reasons Quakers there kept few records during the
Nazi years, and whatever is left remains scattered. Here I was fortunate that the
formidable Quaker Collection at Haverford College contains not only complete
sets of German and Dutch Quaker periodicals but also the papers of Thomas
Kelly and Rufus Jones. Both Elizabeth Brown and Diana Peterson were generous
hosts on whose kindness I have subsequently imposed all too many times. Other
providential discoveries, detailed in the bibliography, helped me fill additional
lacunae in the German side of the story. Most important among these remains
Prof. Hildegard Feidel-Mertz's collection illuminating the history of German
boarding schools that fled the Nazi onslaught. Her archive at the University
of Kassel contains precious information on the Quaker school Eerde in the
Netherlands and was generously opened to me. Anna Halle in Berlin, a survivor
of these times of trouble and the best informed person on German Quaker history,
went far beyond the call of duty not only in sharing her knowledge and her own
private archive with me but also in locating important documents in the Prussian

State Archives in Dahlem and at the archives of the Catholic diocese in Berlin. I cannot express warmly enough my ongoing indebtedness to her help as well as to her own seminal writings on the history of German Quakerism. Nor can I resist mentioning here my old Eerde roommate, Johannes Lüdecke, and his wife, Erna, who offered me unbounded hospitality while I pursued additional research at the Evangelische Zentralarchiv in Berlin, and to Elisabeth and Kurt Reinhuber, who sheltered me as generously while I was working in the domain of Professor Feidel-Mertz.

Many individuals, finally, on whom I called for specific pieces of information answered my inquiries, not just once, but repeatedly. Most of them will be mentioned throughout the notes wherever their assistance provided the desired answers. A few, however, must be recognized here: Roger Carter, the last British representative at the Berlin Quaker Center; Inge Pollatz, the last surviving child of Manfred and Lilli Pollatz; Etta Mekeel, the daughter of the *spiritus rector* of German Quakerism, Hans Albrecht; Brenda Bailey, the daughter of Leonhard and Mary Friedrich; and Tessa Cadbury, the lone survivor of a brave band of Friends fighting the discouraging battle against Nazi brutality in Vienna and Prague. Finally, my most profound gratitude is due Peggy Myers and her staff at the Inter-Library Loan Office of the University of Virginia's Alderman Library and to Annette Wenda of the University of Missouri Press for her peerless editorial work.

In conclusion, let it be remembered that none of these Friends and friends bear any responsibility for the use to which I put the evidence they placed at my disposal. The shortcomings that the observant reader will no doubt discover in the following pages are the exclusive property of the author.

Quakers AND Nazis

Introduction

Quakers Seeking God, Peace, and an End to Human Suffering

When the Puritan victors in the English civil war of the seventeenth century replaced Anglican orthodoxy with an equally rigid code of their own, they set the stage for more dissension. Many devout revolutionaries rebelled against this new tyranny. Notable among them was a group of seekers after God who came to call themselves Friends and who met in silence, waiting upon the Lord to reveal himself. Judge Bennet of Derby has been credited with calling them Quakers because they trembled at God's Word.[1]

These sectarians recognized only the Almighty as their spiritual guide. Like the Hebrew prophets, they saw God reaching out to the "sensitive, seeking soul," considered all humans to be equal in his sight, and denied any need for scriptural or pastoral authority to make their case.[2]

To claim, however, as some authorities in our century have done, that Quakerism was "a bold application of democracy to religion"[3] constitutes a secular distortion of its purpose. Fundamentally, Quaker worship precluded all hierarchy and transcended principles of political governance. The primary quest was for divine enlightenment, not secular liberty, the overriding belief being that the divine spirit can touch and communicate, ending any separation between the individual and God. Without sermons or sacraments, without clerical intercession, each participant in the silent meeting speaks in his heart to God and, at the same time, to his neighbor. Quaker theology begins and ends as personal experience.[4]

In practical terms this has meant that Quaker meetings choose only one official, the clerk, a recording officer who presides when members convene for purposes other than worship. The extent to which this person becomes a leader—and clerks may be male or female—depends on personality and circumstance. Here, as elsewhere, no dogmatic decisions are made, and no permanent rules are laid down. In fact, nineteenth-century meetings in the American Midwest often reversed traditional practice by calling clerks pastors again.[5]

George Fox (1624–1691), the founder of the Society of Friends, was a weaver's son from Leicestershire who believed that God had called him to urge his neighbors to follow him into a living experience of Christ. His strident conduct, including the violent interruption of services of conformist as well as dissident clergy, seems today far removed from the pacific tolerance of Quaker conduct that speaks from the unhistorically sweet-tempered expression of the statue of the New England Quaker martyr Mary Dyer, which adorns the entrance of the Quaker center in Philadelphia. It earned Fox sentences of imprisonment for disturbing the peace and for blasphemy.[6] Yet, his obvious purity of character, as well as his manifest lack of interest in gaining personal power, made a deep impression on thousands of his contemporaries and endowed him with an authority that officers of an established church could rarely equal. In 1669 he married a widow, Margaret Fell, whom he had converted in 1652 and whose estate at Swarthmore became a physical center of the movement. There the inherited wealth of this "mother superior of Quakerism" lent prestige to the Society in ways that portended the role subsequently played by another socially prominent convert, William Penn. Quakerism, in turn, provided Fox's wife with the opportunity to escape the traditional social mold to which women were then confined. Her role and her influence on Fox must be credited with launching a Christian community in which women were not subservient. It has been estimated that there were no less than fifty thousand Quakers in England at the time of Fox's death, when many thousands followed his bier to the burial grounds.[7]

Though the Society of Friends would always remain true to its antihierarchic, egalitarian heritage, the founder did leave the rudiments of an organization: local meetings adopted the habit of monthly conclaves devoted to communal concerns, while larger entities assembled quarterly or annually, reaffirming and reassessing their goals and purposes. These practices never modified significantly fundamental principles, even in a time when thousands of Friends, besides Fox, saw the inside of English prisons, both before and after the restoration of the monarchy. Hundreds died in confinement before the Toleration Act of 1689 drastically reduced both the brutality and the extent of religious persecution. Many Quakers also escaped this scourge by emigrating to the North American colonies. Before the seventeenth century had run its course they had established meetings, first in New Jersey, then in New England, Pennsylvania, New York, Virginia, and North Carolina.

Less persecution, however, resulted in diminished ardor. In the eighteenth century British membership declined significantly, reaching a low of seventeen thousand by 1750. Times of struggle were succeeded by a time of evolution during which Quakers recognized that their religious stance forced them to view critically, and then attempt to remedy, a varied agenda of shortcomings in society. They were among the first to raise their voices against slavery: first in England by none other than Fox, and then by John Bellers (1654–1725). These men believed that one could not defend the servitude or the killing of fellow humans, who were as much God's creatures and as accessible to divine enlightenment and salvation as their masters. Furthermore, how could Christians justify violence? George

Fox rejected "all outward wars and strife and fightings with outward weapons for any and under any pretence whatever."[8] Death itself was not evil and not to be feared, but the taking of life was. A soldier who died in battle suffered in body only; a soldier who killed put his soul in jeopardy.[9]

From the very beginning, embracing nonviolence and rejecting dogma left some room for compromise. During the Jacobite rebellion against the house of Hanover a number of Quakers in the north of England supported the Hanoverian cause with financial contributions. The Society of Friends by and large rejoiced in the victory of the German dynasty, at the same time expelling members who had joined the fighting.[10] In the colonies, William Penn refused to condemn men for bearing arms. But he, and most Quakers, held to the belief that it was better to suffer than to fight. This did not, however, rule out paying taxes that supported armaments. In 1711 Pennsylvania's Quaker-dominated assembly voted two thousand pounds "for the Queen's use," which thenceforth became a standard maneuver to disguise military appropriations as a gift to the sovereign. In 1754 the same body appropriated funds "for the relief of friendly Indians and distressed frontiersmen." The money was actually used to build fortifications. The unease generated by these maneuvers prompted Pennsylvania Friends in the colonial assembly to resign their seats, which helped end their ascendancy in the colony's political life. Characteristically, Friends never formulated a dogmatic consensus. Some pointed to the legitimacy of Old Testament wars, presumably ordained by God. Others upheld the primacy of the Inner Light and the dictates of their conscience over Scripture.[11]

Nonviolence in time became more than refusing to bear arms or to pay taxes. Friends rejected cruel treatment of prisoners, of the mentally ill, and of other religious dissidents. While governor of Pennsylvania, William Penn reduced "the number of crimes which could be punished by death from two hundred to two; . . . treason and murder."[12] Penn's ubiquity in the early history of Quaker peace testimony is, furthermore, affirmed by his advocacy of a European parliament that would represent peoples rather than princes. It was echoed by his coreligionist John Bellers, whose similar blueprint divided Europe into one hundred constituencies, each sending one member to a European senate.[13] Here we see at work not only nonviolent beliefs but also the refusal to recognize the primacy of dynastic interests. In the Quakers' egalitarian universe kings had no right to pursue or preserve their power at the expense of their subjects.

In America, the Revolutionary War accelerated Quakers' withdrawal from political life. In the New World they concentrated on opposing slavery and the mistreatment of Indians. They now refused to pay taxes designated to reduce military deficits. Such civil disobedience still did not shield them from contradictions and perplexities. Prominent Quakers such as John Whittier (1807–1892) and the abolitionist suffragette Lucretia Mott (1793–1880) deplored John Brown's violent descent on Harper's Ferry while admiring his motives and his readiness for self-sacrifice. They favored not only abolition but also the preservation of the Union and kept their distance from Copperhead Democrats. Southern Friends paid fines rather than enter the Confederate ranks and generally refused to provide substitutes. At the same time, many meetings refused to expel young Friends who chose to serve in either army.[14]

Great Britain depended on a professional army that Friends naturally did not join. But with the adoption of conscription during World War I, that conflict, which furrowed so deeply the continuity of history in so many regions of the globe, also became a trial unprecedented in the history of the Society of Friends. As it turned out, they had time to consider their choices until the actual enactment of universal service in 1916. Some enlisted, some joined the Friends' Ambulance Corps in France, others volunteered for alternate service, while an estimated 250 rejected all compromise and went to prison. During an average detention of two years, they could receive neither letters nor visitors for the first two months and were not allowed to speak to anyone during their entire incarceration.[15]

Corder Catchpool (1883–1952), who was one of those prisoners, left a full account of his wartime experience as well as his imprisonment. At the onset of fighting he volunteered for the ambulance service, spending most of the next twenty months in France. The introduction of compulsory military service brought to a head his doubts about the propriety of his choice. In May 1916 Catchpool finally decided that duty to the state was incompatible with service to God, "to whom loyalty is supreme." He returned home and was arrested in January 1917. At his first court-martial he declared that he had "enlisted in the highest service, the . . . world-fellowship of men and was prepared to die rather than take part in war." He was twice released after serving six months performing hard labor. His third trial brought him an eighteen-month sentence. Mentally and physically debilitated after his release in April 1919, he overcame the resulting feelings of depression by pledging "one day to crush Prussianism the Quaker way." He was to live up to that promise, and we shall meet him again.[16]

Quakers constituted only a tiny portion of sixteen thousand British conscientious objectors, of whom sixty-nine died in prison while thirty-nine went insane under the cruel regimen of total silence. Some of them, such as Clifford Allen (1889–1938), who was subsequently the chairman of the Independent Labor Party, emerged broken in body, if not in spirit, and died before their time.[17]

Friends also joined the opposition to other aspects of war government. Most vigorous was their fight against censorship, and in England they continued to issue broadsides against the conflict without prior submission to the censor. More prison sentences did not abate their belief that this campaign for spiritual liberty served the interests of their country more truly than did the policies of the government.[18]

During the United States' relatively brief involvement in the war, a total of 2,743 young Friends completed military service. The Furlough Law of 1918 made possible alternative service, either as noncombatants or in Friends Reconstruction Units. Only 13 went to prison, while 49 were assigned to the newly formed American Friends Service Committee, or AFSC, for relief work in France.[19]

In the midst of these battles, waged on so many fronts and in such diverse international and domestic contexts, the London "Meeting for Sufferings" urged its members to prepare "for the day when once more we shall stand shoulder to shoulder with those with whom we are now at war, in seeking to bring in the Kingdom of God."[20]

This exhortation paralleled, and in some instances initiated, benevolent acts in behalf of war victims among allies as well as adversaries. But such efforts had long been a Quaker tradition whose roots go back to the very origins of the Society. The Meeting for Sufferings had first been organized to aid persecuted Quakers but soon branched out to succor other Protestants: German Pietists and Mennonites, as well as French Huguenots. Eventually, it became the Executive Committee of the London Yearly Meeting and a powerful representative of Quaker continuity. In North America, meanwhile, Anthony Benezet, a Friend of Huguenot antecedents, inaugurated a relief effort for Acadian refugees fleeing Canada in the 1750s, and during the American and French Revolutions the Society sought to relieve sufferings on both sides of the conflict. Civil War in Ireland and Napoleon's campaigns in Germany witnessed the continuation of these nonpartisan efforts. After the battle of Leipzig in 1813, Friends raised seven thousand pounds, and while that sum was overshadowed by the one hundred thousand pounds appropriated by Parliament for the same purpose, the Society was asked to administer these funds. Three Meissen vases, gifts from the king of Saxony to the Quaker Luke Howard for his part in this operation, were subsequently sold by his descendants in 1918 to raise money for Quaker relief work after World War I.[21]

Need and concern persisted during the nineteenth century. In the 1830s Quakers raised considerable sums to help Greek refugees and Poles at war with their Russian overlords. But nowhere was the depth of Quaker commitment more clearly and continuously demonstrated than in prolonged assistance to the starving Irish. They recognized from the outset "that disinterested investment in Irish development was the key if the alleviation of Irish poverty was to be more than . . . momentary." They also acted on the assumption that material betterment would increase respect for law and order. They began with soup kitchens—some credit Quakers with the invention of that emergency device—

and then worked to improve productivity in such sectors of the Irish economy as fishing and the manufacture of linen. Their effectiveness was heightened by their respect for Irish traditions. They deplored London's support of alien Anglicanism and enlisted Catholic clergy in their relief committees. Nor did they spare themselves. Some Friends in Ireland literally worked themselves to death. Their example melded a variety of private efforts, and Quakers were once again entrusted with funds from many sources outside their own Society.[22]

Friends' estimates of their achievements remained modest and realistic. No matter how hard they tried, they could not end the famine. Eventually, some of them, led by James Tuke, became convinced that many of their Irish charges could be saved only by finding homes in the New World. Vested interests— local business, the Catholic Church, and Irish nationalism, to say nothing of American opposition to emigration—fought him every step of the way, but he persevered until funds ran out in 1884. By that time his committee had brought ten thousand Irish refugees to America.[23]

Before the outbreak of the Crimean War in 1854, three English members traveled to St. Petersburg and secured an audience with Nicholas I to plead the cause of peace. Although this most autocratic of nineteenth-century czars received them courteously and listened to their message, he rejected it. Because they did not wish to get involved in the fighting, Quakers focused their aid on Finland, a territory of the Russian Empire that was only peripherally involved in the war. After coastal raids by the British fleet had all but paralyzed Finland's local fishing industry, Friends raised thousands to replace equipment, and after the Russian government ceased to obstruct their work, fearing a famine, they developed a modus operandi that became their standard: a British committee would raise the money, but a Finnish central committee would disburse it to suppliers and local distribution committees that were organized, in this case, within parish boundaries by ministers of the Lutheran church.[24]

Two other major projects ran concurrently with the last phase of Irish relief. The first, during the Franco-Prussian War of 1870–1871, took Friends to the most ravaged regions of France. This time, too, the work was entirely supervised by the Society of Friends, though the finances came from a variety of sources. The Society also furnished three-fourths of the field workers. The administering committee included such Quakers in Parliament as John Bright and Edmund Backhouse. The first contingent left England on October 22, more than a month and a half after Napoleon III's capture at Sedan but almost a week before the equally important surrender of Metz by Marshal Bazaine. Quakers, having established a supply depot at Arlon in Belgium, actually entered Metz two days after the surrender and provided food for a civilian population of forty thousand and distributed clothing in advance of the approaching winter. But here, too, the soup kitchen phase quickly gave way to long-range assistance to the surrounding farm country of Lorraine. Steam ploughs with a daily capacity of twenty acres were brought in, followed by a distribution of seed corn and potatoes to prepare for a timely harvest. These noble efforts, it should be recalled, took their toll. When the Arlon depot closed on April 10, 1871, twelve Friends had died of disease, including one case of smallpox that took the life of Ellen Allen of Dublin.

Elsewhere in Alsace-Lorraine, Quaker money helped rebuild Fontenoy near Nancy, and until 1875 a nonmember, James Long, headed Quaker aid in Belfort, a city almost completely destroyed in a siege that lasted three weeks beyond the armistice of January 28, 1871. Other major areas of Quaker operation extended throughout a territorial triangle whose apex stood at Le Mans and whose base extended from Orleans to Tours.

In the French capital, Friends, endowed with monies from London's Lord Mayor's Fund, began their work a week after the armistice and labored unceasingly through the ensuing civil war known as the Paris Commune. On the last battlefields, south of the city, they toiled well into 1872, distributing tens of thousands of bushels of oats, barley, and other seeds and two thousand tons of potatoes. They bought cattle in Spain and Switzerland to restock the herds of the Loire valley and the environs of Belfort.

While the adversaries of this war came to look upon each other for generations as "hereditary enemies," German and French authorities alike welcomed and supported these selfless helpers from the British Isles. From German commanders to French village mayors spontaneous expressions of gratitude greeted them wherever they went. And well they might. The men among them were, without exception, on short "holidays" from their regular employment. One-third of them were older than fifty. Their only remuneration was their subsistence and the elusive spiritual and psychological rewards of helping fellow humans.[25]

For a few of them the job was not over after the wounds of France had been healed. Turkish persecutions in Bulgaria prompted the Meeting for Sufferings to appoint yet another committee in 1876 to distribute aid to 250,000 refugees, and in October of the same year James Long brought his experience to bear on this more distant theater of anguish. With a contingent that included six carpenters from Alsace-Lorraine, he directed the construction of two hundred dwellings and seven schools. By the following spring almost 5,000 persons were able to take shelter in these buildings, while the now customary distribution of seed produced harvests on ten thousand farms in the surrounding countryside. Quakers recognized no religious distinctions. Jews, Moslems, Christians: all benefited equally. In Bulgaria, too, the rescued constituted a small percentage of the mass of uprooted mankind. At the same time, working among the destitute was, in this instance, not only unhealthy but also dangerous. James Long and his crew had to be on the constant lookout for bandits.

By the time the Congress of Berlin convened in 1878 to impose a definitive settlement on Europe's restless southeast, Long was once more on the scene as member of a Quaker delegation of abolitionists. They managed to see the German crown prince but received no support for their cause. Long died in 1895 in very straitened circumstances. His will not be the last instance of virtue going unrewarded, among both Quakers and their allies in charity.[26]

After Bulgarians came Russians, Armenians, Macedonians, and finally victims of the two Balkan wars that immediately preceded World War I. Meanwhile, Friends had also heard the call for help of dissenter sects in Russia, both Doukhobors and Mennonites. Quakers both in England and in the United States raised funds to finance the emigration of these antiauthoritarian and pacifist Christians and helped negotiate their settlement in Canada and the United States.[27]

But the most difficult and controversial Quaker interventions resulted from direct British involvement in imperial and international conflicts of the twentieth century. In December 1899, Quakers formed the War Victims Relief Committee to mitigate British retribution against the Boer levies of able-bodied men known as "commandos." Boer farms and fields were burned, and women and children related to commando members were herded into "concentration camps" whose primitive accommodations led to a high death rate from disease. Various Quakers and the Anglican Emily Hobhouse visited the camps and aroused public concern back home for the deplorable conditions in which the inmates lived. While Hobhouse was deported from Cape Town on her second visit, Friends were allowed to remain as long as their work was done without publicity. The efforts of their relief workers were soon supplemented by additional nurses and teachers who did yeoman service in arresting this human disaster.[28]

The year 1914 brought national involvement even closer to home. From the outset, the Society of Friends declared that it had a clear duty "to be courageous in the cause of love and in the hate of hate."[29] This high-minded pronouncement was quickly implemented. Germans stranded in London, especially families whose breadwinners had been interned, became the Society's first beneficiaries. Belgian refugees were next, both in Britain and in Holland, where an estimated half-million sought sanctuary, including a large part of the populace of Antwerp. The autumn of that first year of war also witnessed the return of relief teams to some of those same regions of France where their presence in 1871 had not been forgotten and where their work once again continued amid unprecedented devastation long after the last shot had been fired. Still others went to Russia and Poland.

Some of the work, notably "hun-coddling" of enemy nationals, was unpopular. But Quakers had been inured to criticism and controversy too long to be discouraged by such hostility. Too many among them, furthermore, bore with quiet pride names that had become synonymous with the Quaker presence in extremity in many lands and many conflicts. World War I mobilized three female descendants of Elizabeth Fry; a great-granddaughter of Luke Howard; the grandson of Thomas Harvey, the leader of Finnish relief; and the more immediate issue of the generation that had served in France: Rowntrees, Cadburys, and Sturges among them.[30]

World War I also led to the establishment in the United States of a Quaker organization that would gradually assume a preeminent role among the worldwide Quaker efforts to relieve human suffering. As in Great Britain, some young Friends had joined an ambulance unit, recruited in 1915 by the Quaker philosopher and Haverford professor Rufus Jones. Meetings began to collect money to support relief work in Europe. In April 1916 American Friends visited Russia to study conditions, especially the plight of war orphans. Later that year they opened a hospital in Samara and two medical centers in the surrounding countryside. In the midst of the 1917 revolution a group of social workers, some of whom made Omsk their base of operation, widened the radius of Quaker impact and began an interesting, frustrating, and controversial relationship with Soviet authorities. This effort persisted until the last Quaker worker was expelled from the USSR in 1931.[31]

These scattered enterprises received a firm corporate basis when a committee, headed by Jones, met on April 30, 1917, to bear testimony against war "and to do a constructive piece of work in an area which had been used as a battlefield." At the same time, the participants insisted that they were "united in expressing their love for their country and their desire to serve her loyally." The immediate major purpose of this founding of the American Friends Service Committee was to support the relief work of their British brethren in France. Indeed, it was not long before young American Friends departed to do just that, and by December 1917 they were deeply involved in the work of reconstruction around devastated Verdun. Among the participants were individuals whose later work in Germany we will discuss: Eleanor Cary as well as Howard and Catherine Elkinton.[32]

By the end of World War I history had drawn a Quaker portrait whose major features are a personal relation with the Creator free from scriptural or hierarchic mediation, the advocacy of peaceful conflict resolution, and a commitment to abate human suffering wherever it may be found. While these postulates are easy to express and understand, it has always been difficult to live by them. The absence of dogmatic practices has tended to undermine Quaker unity. It has led to at least one significant schism among American Friends in the first half of the nineteenth century, but, more important, it burdens the individual member with a perpetual search for God from which no momentary contact, in meeting or in solitary prayer, will ever relieve him. No one intercedes for the seeker, no one prays for the worshiper, no word and no tradition assures the

Friend that once God has been touched everything will fall into place forever after. Every day begins a new search for divine enlightenment. No wonder the Quaker community has always remained small: being a Quaker is difficult.

If the importance of individual experience governs the relationship between Friend and God, the same is true of the application of Quaker principle in the secular sphere. Confronted by the democratic institution of the national army, Quakers as a rule resolved to let the individual conscience decide how to respond to the challenge of mobilization. On the one hand, this has forestalled an otherwise inevitable conflict between generations, because the responsibility for the decision whether or not to bear arms invariably rests with the youngest members. On the other hand, it has deepened the feelings of guilt that assail Friends whenever the outbreak of war confronts them with their failure to prevent it. The widespread humanitarian exertions of the Society of Friends constitute, in their own eyes at least, partial atonement for that failure.[33]

Living in a world that concedes so little to the best human intentions, even when these intentions have been reinforced by unreserved self-sacrifice, has tended to cast a pall over Quaker culture. The absence of music and art from their meetings of worship has tended, at least until the nineteenth century, to limit their cultivation in Quaker lives and communities. In Britain, exclusion from the universities, and until 1828 from political office, added to this isolation from pleasure as well as influence. Commerce and manufacture, however, were open to Quakers in a changing society, and innovators in new nonacademic areas of science included a disproportionate number of Quakers; one of these innovators was Luke Howard. Quaker poets and musicians, on the other hand, have been few and far between.

The configuration of lights and shadows, of triumphs and of failures, as outlined in this Introduction, reflects what Quakers themselves have reported about their past. They have produced in their own behalf no chronicle of saints, no book of martyrs, no history of miracles. Their records are to a remarkable degree lacking in self-glorification. Knowing their duty, but realizing how little their efforts availed, they faced the end of World War I certain that they must thenceforth try harder rather than compromise. Nonviolence would remain their creed and was no better affirmed than by the American Friend Elbert Russell, who reminded his coreligionists that both early Christians and early Quakers "won without fighting," a belief also asseverated by the London Yearly Meeting that aspired to "a fuller expression of the Quaker mystical conception of religion in international life."[34] The struggle must and would continue everywhere. It would be fought with particular tenacity in Germany. To that battle we shall now turn.

1.
Quakers and Germans, 1919–1932

THE QUAKERS COME TO GERMANY

In a novel published three years after World War I, Aldous Huxley observed that the recent conflict had wrought a dismal change in European consciousness. Until the war erupted, he claimed, tidings of wholesale brutality anywhere in the world caused outcries of distressed amazement. But since the war, he continued, "we wonder at nothing. We have created a Caesarian environment and a host of little Caesars has sprung up," each one a threat to civilized behavior.[1]

In no European country did this analysis of political and moral disorientation fit reality more closely than in Germany after 1918. The kaiser (whose dynasty had only three years earlier celebrated five hundred years of rule in Brandenburg— Prussia, and eventually the Reich), suddenly and ignominiously fled to Holland. Left behind was an orphaned nation, unprepared for defeat and continuing isolation. The election campaign for a national assembly that was to draft a new constitution was accompanied by fighting in the streets of Berlin. After that gathering convened, violence continued, and tensions increased after the provisional government, on June 20, 1919, signed a harsh peace treaty. To the majority of Germans this first historical result of the revolution was an act of treason.

Less than one year later a monarchist countercoup, the Kapp putsch, drove the government from Berlin. Shortly after its failure, parliamentary elections, held on June 6, 1920, resulted in the defeat of the liberal and socialist coalition whose principles had shaped Germany's first democratic basic law, the so-called Weimar Constitution.

The confusion and anguish that was both cause and effect of the republic's birth pangs extended to the area where a hungry and baffled citizenry might have expected to find refuge from these trials: the churches. Twentieth-century Germany counted roughly two Protestants for every Catholic. About half a million Jews constituted less than 1 percent of the population, while the number of individuals who had left their church had since 1910 increased from two hundred thousand to 1.5 million.[2]

Protestants provided the most volatile element in this mixture. Of their roughly 40 million, 98.7 percent belonged to state churches, which had until

11

1918 been headed by the princely sovereigns of the individual states of the federal empire. The republic, therefore, left these establishments leaderless. Material uncertainties, added to the resulting spiritual chaos, blighted the lives of pastors, their families, and their flocks. As a body, the numerous and influential Protestant clergy rejected the postmonarchical order, and a vast majority either supported a restoration or joined the search for a charismatic secular savior who would reimpose "traditional values."[3]

Catholics, who had often been at odds with an imperial government headed by a Protestant dynasty, had less reason to mourn the past. Their political ramparts, which defended their interests against both government and the rising socialist movement had, since 1871, been manned by the Center Party entrenched in Prussia's Rhine Province, Bavaria, Baden, Silesia, and Alsace-Lorraine and had been supported by a broad social spectrum, from Catholic magnates to industrial workers organized in Christian, rather than socialist, labor unions. In 1918 some of the party leaders, such as the Württemberg schoolteacher Matthias Erzberger (1875–1921), supported the Weimar Constitution and provided a disproportionate number of chancellors and cabinet ministers to the fragile political order. The Catholic hierarchy, like the Protestant, rejected Marxism outright, but, unlike their counterparts, considered membership in the Nazi Party equally incompatible with Catholic principles. Strident anti-Semitism of the radical right tended to dampen traditional Catholic hostility to Jews as "Christ killers." Only monarchists in Catholic Bavaria and Austria clung to such time-honored prejudices.[4]

There is no indication that Friends in Britain and the United States understood the extent of the role played by religion in Germany's turmoil. Even if they had it would not have affected their own course of action. They had never allowed other Christian dilemmas to deflect them from their self-proclaimed duties and purposes. In 1918 they believed themselves called to counteract the evils of a war their endeavors had failed to prevent. Thus, they felt an immediate obligation to succor the defeated enemy. Their swift response yielded two results: an involvement beginning in 1919 that would extend over the next twenty-two years and the establishment of a German Yearly Meeting, the latter to represent in these hostile surroundings the search for peace and brotherhood that had distinguished Quaker history in Britain and the United States.

Both developments constituted a second attempt to secure Quakerism a foothold in the heart of continental Europe and illustrated significant changes in the modus operandi of the Society of Friends. Initially, George Fox and his immediate followers had wanted to "let all nations hear the word." Fox and William Penn had been the most famous members of a band of missionaries that had visited both the Low Countries and Germany and had founded some ephemeral Quaker communities, notably in the regions along the lower Rhine, the coastal towns of Emden and Hamburg, as well as in Schleswig-Holstein. But in the eighteenth century proselytizing came to be confined to the sect's countries of origin. This is confirmed by the fact that there are no records of German Quaker communities after 1848. As Quakers developed an increasing tolerance toward other faiths and other cultures, rejecting the assumption that damnation was the inevitable lot even of non-Christians, devotion to humanitarian service took precedence over the desire to convert.[5]

It was affirmed that such service would not be limited to the material sphere. Even before the end of World War I a conference of British Friends had established three goals for their activities abroad: enrichment of the spiritual life of recipients of Quaker charity, participation in the life of the people aided, and reconciliation of conflicting national and ethnic interests. This was to be the trinity of the Council for International Service, later renamed the Friends Service Council.[6]

This triad resulted in the establishment of a series of Quaker embassies, a concept formulated by Carl Heath (1869–1950), a past secretary of Britain's National Peace Council and member of the Fellowship of Reconciliation, an ecumenical Christian body, and the Central Committee of the Union for Democratic Control, whose membership included H. G. Wells and George Bernard Shaw. Heath's uncompromising opposition to the war had made the Peace Council uneasy, and since "the only support . . . for his position came from the little group of Quaker members" he was irresistibly drawn to the Society of Friends. In that congenial company he drafted his Quaker embassy scheme for centers of Quaker activity, designed to set forth "Christ anew in the largeness and strength of that *applied mysticism*[7] which is characteristic of the Quaker Society." In January 1920 Heath became secretary of the Council for International Service, with Frederick J. Tritton as his deputy, and quickly set up centers not only in Paris, Warsaw, Moscow, and Geneva but, above all, in suffering enemy communities in Berlin, Frankfurt-am-Main, Nuremberg, and Vienna. Before long, representatives of the Friends Service Committee expanded the staffs of the centers, notably in Berlin. Four of these—Berlin, Vienna, Paris, and Geneva—would operate well into World War II and would leave a record of Christianity-in-action for future generations to emulate. Carl Heath's leadership of British Friends abroad continued until his retirement in 1935, but he remained active and in August 1939 would be the last foreign Friend to address the German Yearly Meeting before the outbreak of another war.[8]

In spite of their altruistic goals, British and American Friends often met distrust when they arrived in Germany in 1919, where they were the first "enemies" to visit the defeated country. They came, as Joan Mary Fry explained, to help realize what their faith taught them, that "all men are brothers under God" and that "no human being may be viewed as an enemy." Quakers, she affirmed, did not worship and serve within dogmatic limits but in the "large, wide world of God, where his law of love works on forever."[9] Few German Christians, especially among the emotionally devastated Protestant clergy, were ready for such moral disarmament, and one of the most important Quaker contacts, the Fellowship of Reconciliation's "man in Germany," Pastor Friedrich Siegmund-Schultze, recognized an immediate need to remove barriers of suspicion that might endanger the entire enterprise of rescue. His initial search for persons willing to guide Friends' inquiry into local and national penury encountered both hostile silence and outright refusal. Siegmund-Schultze, therefore, took a more aggressive tone when he explained the motives behind the Quaker presence. "These people do not come to satisfy their curiosity, but they come to get a firsthand look at German distress and to initiate a large aid campaign in England, since they cannot—to their sorrow—change the measures of the English [sic] government." He concluded: "They are not only Friends, but brothers and sisters."[10]

Such hostility was not confined to German circles. Joan Mary Fry, departing from Charing Cross Station on July 3, 1919, accompanied by J. Thompson Elliot, the clerk of the London Meeting for Sufferings, and Mary Bellows, who supplied a knowledge of German to this small delegation, arrived the next day in Cologne only to find that "the British military would have nothing to do with us." The British transport officer did, however, issue them tickets, refusing payment because there was "no need to pay the enemy" for a seat on the train to Berlin. On July 5, Fry and her companions arrived in the German capital "with no one to meet them, nowhere to go, not knowing of a single hotel, and rather afraid of making themselves too conspicuous." In desperation they telephoned Elisabeth Rotten whose war relief work among British civilian internees, organized almost single-handedly, was gratefully remembered across the Channel. Rotten responded immediately, came to the station, and found them lodgings with the Lichnowskys, the family of Germany's last prewar ambassador in London—Prince Max Karl (1860–1928)—who had vainly struggled to prevent war in 1914.

After determining the conditions in Berlin, Joan Fry's team crisscrossed Germany, investigating material circumstances and making sure that their presence and purpose became known to public officials as well as to private groups ready to resume friendship with the outside world. At a student rally in Frankfurt a local reporter, watching Fry in action, came away with the feeling of having listened "to a pure soul glowing with the ideal of all-absorbing love."[11] In time, however, this Quaker angel of mercy realized her love for the suffering had to be tempered by a degree of skeptical restraint. At first she listened with uncritical sympathy to a catalog of complaints, particularly about the imperfections and misdeeds of her own country: everything from Britain's entering the war against Germany in 1914 to current delays in train service. But by 1923, when visiting German detainees in the Ruhr, in part responding to German complaints about the conditions of the prisons, she came to realize that these installations had, after all, been built by German authorities. All their defects could not be laid at the door of the occupiers.

Nor did every contact with like-minded Germans bring unalloyed satisfaction. Following Sunday worship in Berlin in 1921, Fry complained that it was "by no means easy for the few of us to sit in the middle of a very heterogeneous crowd and endeavor to hold a real Meeting for Worship. The most diverse cranks found it a convenient opportunity for airing their special views." On another occasion she noted the German resistance to cutting long speeches and dreaded "the rising demand in Germany . . . for a freedom that is not far removed from license," no doubt a result, she hastened to add, of past oppression. Englishmen, she asserted, knew they were free without constantly having to assert it. Finally, acquaintance with Germans who considered themselves conscientious objectors in the 1920s prompted Fry to reflect that antiwar demonstrations after a war constituted no discernible contribution to the future preservation of peace.[12]

Such misgivings adhere, of course, to the worthiest enterprise, and in this instance they did not for a moment interfere with the feeding of the hungry. What a grateful recipient of such assistance recalled later remains the hallmark of the Quaker presence in Germany: "They were there, talking little, but helping wherever they could." A cousin of Joan's, A. Ruth Fry, describes the same scene from the giving perspective: "The hungry were fed, the naked were clothed, the sick were visited, and the prisoners were ministered to, not for any elaborate reasons, but because they were utterly miserable and needed help."[13]

Soon relief work in Germany included American Friends as well. Only days after Joan Fry's arrival three AFSC representatives—Jane Addams (1860–1935), one of the founders of modern secular social work at Chicago's Hull House; her sometime associate Alice Hamilton; and Carolena Wood—began the first extensive feeding of German children, financed with $3 million contributed by Herbert Hoover's American Relief Administration. In 1920 no less than twenty American Friends worked in Germany. They also joined the feeding of students, initiated by their British coreligionists, a second undertaking that eventually included all German universities. Finally, Quakers from both nations opened depots for the distribution of food and clothing to adults in cities such as Breslau, Leipzig, Nuremberg, and Frankfurt. These major campaigns were supplemented by other efforts, such as the fourteen clinics providing special diets for persons afflicted with tuberculosis and the feeding of twenty-seven thousand school children during the Upper Silesia plebiscite that preceded the final drawing of the German-Polish border.[14]

Best remembered are the "Quaker feedings" *(Quäkerspeisungen)* that touched the lives and empty stomachs of hundreds of thousands of young Germans. This operation began in Berlin on February 26, 1920, and by the summer of that year provided a daily meal to 630,000 mothers and children. Thanks to the Hoover funds the dispensation of nourishing food, initially confined to towns with populations in excess of 50,000, could be expanded to include smaller localities, and at its height in June 1921, Quaker food provided meals for more than 1 million individuals in 1,640 feeding centers, concentrating on children between the ages of six and fourteen.

At that point the entire venture involved not only the expenditure of millions but also a workforce of thousands. Replicating the patterns established during the Finland relief of the 1850s, German government agencies paid for unloading, storing, insurance, and transport to various centers. Localities assumed the costs of food preparation and distribution. The cost of maintaining the relatively small flock of 177 British and American Quaker volunteers was assumed by the Society. The larger available resources defrayed the expense of maintaining an army of 40,000 German helpers. These included school physicians who examined the children and determined who merited supplemental nourishment. Local committees, including magistrates, nurses, and representatives of welfare agencies, administered their share of funds and supplies. At each school, principals, teachers, and community volunteers actually fed the children. At the beginning of the summer vacations of 1922, when the entire project was turned over to a German committee, half a million children still lined up to receive their daily Quaker portion.[15] It should be added that Friends established a similar service in Vienna, where 64,000 benefited at the peak of that operation, in this case mostly toddlers below school age. In the Austrian countryside Quakers negotiated the importation and distribution of cattle from neutral countries, including 6,500 from the Netherlands alone. This program continued until 1933.[16]

After the food shortage abated, Quakers felt that they could turn to other tasks. But the memory of this largest effort the Quakers had ever undertaken continued to be evoked during the Nazi years. This time Friends could derive an unaccustomed degree of satisfaction from having met most of the demands exacted by a crisis. How far their reach extended was brought home to this writer when he discovered the unpublished memoirs of a German social-democrat refugee from Nazism in a storage warehouse in Charlottesville, Virginia. That chronicler, too, recalled that "without the midday meal at the University [of Berlin] dining hall, distributed free of charge by the Quakers, I would not have survived these hunger years."[17]

Ruhr invasion and inflation arrested the Quaker exodus and revived the *Speisungen,* though not quite on the previous scale. In the Ruhr, as we have already seen, special efforts were made to improve the lot of German protestors arrested by French authorities. That latter undertaking became more effective after the Friend Gilbert MacMaster told the local French commander about Quaker relief in invaded France, both in 1871 and after the first Battle of the Marne in World War I. In October 1924, German authorities once more began a gradual takeover of residual Quaker enterprises, and feeding by foreigners was discontinued altogether the following year. Only the care of tubercular patients continued, primarily at a facility supervised by the medical faculty of the University of Freiburg.[18]

BEGINNINGS OF THE GERMAN YEARLY MEETING

While initiating and supervising the feeding of hundreds of thousands of Germans, Quakers worried that a grateful German public appeared to be forgetting that the Society of Friends was not an auxiliary of the International Red Cross but was primarily a religious organization. This would be their constant concern until the last foreign Friend left German soil in 1941. Actually, Quaker religion did leave its mark on Germany, but, in a time when Hitler's following increased by tens of thousands, Quaker recruits could at best be counted by the dozens. Still, it was enough to lead to the establishment of a Yearly Meeting in 1925.

In that context, it should first be recalled that the main reason for the disappearance of earlier German groups was the kind of persecution English founders had endured, which was frequently followed, as in the English instance, by communal flight to America. A meetinghouse, built in Germantown, Pennsylvania, in 1686 remains the earliest trace of a German Quaker presence in the New World. Flight by entire communities continued in the nineteenth century.[19]

When English and American Quakers arrived in 1919, therefore, they found no coreligionists and held meetings of worship among themselves. Gradually, German associates from pacifist and ecumenical circles were drawn to these meetings. In August 1919 the Florence Nightingale of the civilian internment camp at Ruhleben, Elisabeth Rotten, actually organized a meeting to bring together these two elements. It convened in the cathedral city of Wetzlar, and its records indicate that the German audience was mostly made up of teachers, types who would predominate in the German Society of Friends throughout its subsequent history. Meanwhile, regular Quaker meetings had come into being, not only in Berlin but in Frankfurt and Königsberg as well. Foreign Friends dominated the first two—Joan Fry and Corder Catchpool in Berlin, Bertha Bracey in Frankfurt—but in distant Königsberg the guiding spirits were Fritz and Martha Legatis. Fritz was a railroad official, and both he and his wife were active in civic affairs and were leaders in the unpopular pursuit of reconciliation with neighboring Poland. Their example revealed that from the very beginning Quakers pursued more than silent communion with their Inner Light.[20]

The first official gathering of "German friends of Friends" took place in 1921 at Dillenburg, birthplace of William the Silent of Nassau-Orange, the leader of the seventeenth-century revolt of the Netherlands against Spain. During the three-day meeting British and American Quakers spoke about their practices, from both a historic and a theological point of view and explained the rejection of sacraments and the communicative functions of silent meetings. On the second day German participants joined a discussion of related spiritual attitudes and traditions in their country, including a spirited exposition of the relevance of socialism to practical Christianity. The last gathering before adjournment was devoted to a consideration of "the tasks which the crisis of the present assigns to German friends of Friends." The report of these proceedings confirms Joan Fry's conclusion that many Germans viewed discussion as therapy rather than as a search for constructive solutions. The chronicle nevertheless concluded that the forty participants, including eleven British and American Friends, had, in the end, been reconciled by the divine spirit that "hovered over the gathering."[21]

The Dillenburg conference took steps to organize like-minded Germans and expressed the hope that attendance at future conclaves would not be confined to "intellectuals." A planning committee succeeded in finding some two hundred individuals willing to join an association that found in Quaker ways the concrete expression of their own often vague and inchoate humanitarian yearnings. This groping initiative tapped no new social circles but led to the establishment of the Exchange for Quaker Work in Germany *(Mittelstelle für Quäkerarbeit in Deutschland);* their first conference at Wilhelmshagen near Berlin in July 1922 coincided with the termination of the first major Quaker feeding. As a result, the Berlin Center now assigned one staff member, the American Gilbert MacMaster, to the task of interpreting "the ideals of the Society of Friends to the people of Germany." The exchange supplemented this effort by preparing lectures, mostly—but not exclusively—delivered by foreign Friends to a variety of audiences throughout the country. The exchange also sought to implement the work of conciliation by finding families willing to invite foreign "friends of peace" to their homes. It projected the founding of a publishing house that would translate and disseminate Quaker writings.[22]

An incomplete file of exchange reports reveals that foreign Friends explained the Society's modus operandi at numerous meetings, usually with the assistance of an interpreter, while several German spokespeople advocated conciliatory solutions to a host of contemporary problems. In Frankfurt, for instance, a gathering in January 1923 ended in a spirited discussion of the question: "How would a Quaker concretely respond to an event such as the occupation of the Ruhr?" In Nuremberg, one month later, the locale was the "English Club," founded in 1921 by Leonhard Friedrich and his English Quaker wife, Mary, for former German civilian internees in Britain and their English wives. On this occasion Alfred Garrett, a visiting American, established rapport with his audience by praising the Ruhr population for the dignity with which it bore current trials and then by paying tribute to the Nuremberg Anabaptist Johann Denk (1495?–1527), whom he called "a Quaker before the Quakers." In Berlin, Heinrich Becker, who became the first clerk of the German Yearly Meeting, addressed an audience on "Quakers and politics." He affirmed that political activism was the inevitable consequence of Quaker service to their fellow humans. At the same time, he warned that such commitment must be an uncompromising search for truth rather than devotion to the program of a particular party.[23]

In July 1923 a national conference of Quaker sympathizers attracted more than three hundred people to Eisenach in Thuringia. It was "a rather colorful mixture of the most diverse opinions and factions," according to one observer; it was "a strangely mixed company some of whom had only very sketchy ideas of what a Quaker meeting should be like," according to another. By that time ten German towns had regular local Quaker meetings, and Quaker sympathizers had begun to publish a newsletter, *Mitteilungen für die Freunde des Quäkertums in Deutschland.*[24]

Two years later a similar assembly at the same venue called for the establishment of a German Yearly Meeting. This decision was made in full consciousness that it was but a "first, feeble beginning," whose success would depend on the support of the Society of Friends "in England and America."[25] From a band of 40 founders, membership grew steadily but modestly, reaching 199 by 1932. Despite these unimpressive numbers, these pioneers were convinced they were engaged in a significant enterprise. In 1929 the Magdeburg elementary school principal William Hubben claimed that "after the frightful experiences of . . . [the war] and the immeasurable suffering each of us has undergone," German Friends were uniquely prepared to build a new and better society.[26]

In 1927 the fledgling Yearly Meeting elected a new clerk whose leadership reinforced this optimism. He was Hans Albrecht, son of a Mecklenburg pastor and head of the safety inspection service in the port of Hamburg. He discovered the Society of Friends when the "enemies" fed his six-year-old daughter, Etta, and he was to lead German Friends for the next twenty years through a succession of trials no one could have foreseen at the time of his election. Albrecht was by no means certain of the extent to which the practices of a primarily Anglophone religious society could be transplanted to German soil. From this skepticism was born an ambition to become more than a mere colony of older yearly meetings. Like Rufus Jones, the great investigator of "mystical religion," he believed, however, that Quaker thought and practice harmonized with certain traditions of German mysticism, that the revival of the German branch of the Society of Friends constituted, in fact, an overdue return to the "original habitat of central Europe's spiritual . . . religiosity." Claiming that German impulses had played an important role in shaping seventeenth-century Quaker principles, he cited in particular Fox's contemporary John Sparrow, the English translator of the German mystic Jacob Boehme (1575–1626). It is also noteworthy that joining and leading the German Yearly Meeting created no personal conflict with the clerk's own evangelical heritage. German Friends decided not to require new members to sever previous religious affiliations, as they did in yearly meetings elsewhere. In a time when the increasingly tolerant attitude of Friends toward non-European cultures and non-Christian beliefs gained momentum, Albrecht also emphasized a Quaker mission that transcended dogma and an ethic individuality in tune with all religions.[27]

In Albrecht's eyes, the Society remained a voluntary community of seekers. Each Quaker, he affirmed, exemplified Christ's words from John 15:15, "I have called you friends, for all I have heard from my Father I have made known to you." To be a Quaker meant "devotion, readiness to sacrifice, and eternal watchfulness." Quaker piety demanded "readiness to suffer and courageous witness."[28]

Such commitments became more than Sunday-meeting exhortations. In the early years of his stewardship, Hans Albrecht did not hesitate to speak out and act on a host of issues. One such position was adopted even before his election by the Eisenach Assembly of July 22 and 23, 1925, when it protested the increase of German import tariffs on the grounds that this measure would increase the price of necessities. It affirmed traditional Quaker opposition to "those acts of privilege, by means of which the few gain advantage at the expense of fellow citizens who owned no property." For a religious group in Germany to take so emphatic a stand on a socioeconomic issue was unprecedented.[29] German Friends also demonstrated repeatedly that they took their role as mediators seriously. They were active participants in meetings between German and Polish academics and teachers who were attempting to liquidate an enmity that was even more deeply grounded in historic precedent than the post-Napoleonic alienation from France. Another example of Quaker intercession was represented by Albrecht's visit to a group of 130 German-speaking Mennonite refugees from the Soviet Union who were on their way to permanent asylum in North and South America. While the material needs of this group were supplied by the international Mennonite network, "Brothers in Distress" *(Brüder in Not)*, and substantial German government subsidies, Albrecht nevertheless urged that Quakers in countries of destination use their influence to overcome the reluctance of governments, notably in Canada, to issue immigration visas to these displaced persons.[30]

Before turning to Quaker positions taken on domestic German issues, one example of Friends *refusing* to join a polemic campaign, which likewise served to illustrate their fidelity to principle, should not be overlooked. Early in its history, the German Quaker publishing company was approached to print the German translation of a work by a British sympathizer of the Indian independence movement, Jabez T. Sunderland, titled *India in Bondage*. The offer was tempting, since the level of hostility to Great Britain on the German political right promised a far brisker sale of such a volume than was achieved by Quaker tracts. But the Quaker leadership feared that potential buyers would be recruited among Anglophobes rather than among partisans of Indian liberation and refused to include Sunderland's polemic on its list of publications.[31]

No inhibitions of any kind, however, restrained Quaker involvement in Germany's "Jewish Question." Anti-Semitism struck German Friends as being a problem of sufficient urgency to warrant the appointment of a special committee by the 1930 Yearly Meeting. This concern passed beyond the confines of internal discussion after the members of a Jewish congregation in Berlin, upon leaving New Year's services in 1931, faced a gang of Nazi storm troopers shouting obscenities. Friends immediately dispatched a letter to the victims, registering "pain and shame for the suffering which these undignified incidents" had inflicted on them. The remainder of the letter illustrates the Quaker sense of responsibility and the degree to which it leads to the identification with suffering fellow humans of any faith: "We, too, feel responsible and guilty [for this act], because we have not done enough to decontaminate a hate-filled atmosphere. We therefore ask your forgiveness for what has been done to you."

Then German Friends went a step further. In October 1931 a circular of the German Yearly Meeting addressed the "churches of all Christian confessions in Germany," warning that political rivalries in Germany had risen to levels that demanded the intervention of "all believers in the Gospel of Jesus Christ." The message dwelled at length on the "pogrom-like" events of the preceding month. It cautioned that the guilt accumulated by Christian indifference increased with every such incident and would soon make the name of Christ an object of mockery and derision. The missive was sent to 190 destinations, including all Catholic bishops and a large number of hierarchs in all Protestant state churches. Among the former only the archbishop of Cologne responded, also expressing outrage over recent desecrations of Jewish cemeteries. Most answers from a mere eight Protestant pastors derided the Quaker position and insisted that the events described in the circular were trivial compared to the wrongs inflicted upon Christians "by largely Jewish-led Bolshevism."[32]

Such disappointments could not deflect the Society from the path of duty. At the same yearly meeting at which it urged "all Friends to commit to the proposition that all men were brothers, regardless of race," it also addressed to Chancellor Franz von Papen a protest against the death penalty. This was an appeal on behalf of an entirely different set of victims. On August 9, 1932, five storm troopers in the Silesian village of Potempa entered the house of a communist and beat him to death. They were apprehended and tried, then condemned to die. Now Friends petitioned not only for a commutation of the sentence but also for the abolition of capital punishment.[33]

The misgivings raised in many minds by the perpetual divergence between Christian teaching and practice caused Hans Albrecht to involve the German Society of Friends in yet another public controversy. The expressionist painter and graphic artist George Grosz (1893–1959), spokesman of a "new objectivity" lambasting the sacrifices imposed by war and its profiteers on Germany's lower classes, exhibited a crucifixion in which Christ's face was covered by a gas mask. Grosz was tried under a provision of the German Penal Code of 1872 that punished blasphemy and the verbal abuse of any legal religious corporation with a prison sentence of up to three years. Although this statute conflicted with Article 118 of the Weimar Constitution, which expressly forbade censorship of theatrical performances and art exhibits, Grosz was tried under the old imperial law. On December 3, 1930, however, Hans Albrecht presented a brief that was concerned not with the artist's civil rights but with the question of whether the very nature of God justified such an indictment. He expressed the Quaker view that there was only "one God for all human beings, only *one* conception of God which is absolute truth, though expressed in different ways by different people." Next, he asked whether any human act could affront God and on what basis any secular authority could decide that such an affront had taken place. Grosz's Christ, he continued, was no less a redeemer than the Christ of other images. In this presentation the Savior cried out: "What have you done to me?" This was the very antithesis of blasphemy; rather it was an indictment "of the blasphemous actions of Man." Albrecht's brief also contained obvious contradictions, and its impact on the proceedings remains unknown. Grosz was, however, acquitted, and a delighted Hans Albrecht told Friends at the 1931 Yearly Meeting that the episode demonstrated how Friends must seize every opportunity to witness their convictions.[34]

Defending the freedom of expression of all individuals, the right to worship of all religious groups, and opposing the infliction of cruel and unusual punishment, even if meted out to perpetrators of criminal perversion, was, however, not the only way in which German Quakers sought to defend liberty in Germany. Friends also ascribed the rising levels of political intolerance spreading across Germany to a peace settlement that Germans considered intolerable. In this instance the historian must disregard later, more balanced analyses of the "war guilt" controversy and the Versailles treaty and see Germans, as well as sympathizers among British and American Friends, as denizens of a postwar decade permeated by the disappointments and sufferings resulting from repeated failures in international policy. Here Quaker views were part of the mainstream of public opinion. At the same time, German Friends expressed their opinions in far more constructive ways than did the majority of their countrymen. Their specific position emerges from Hans Albrecht's report on the German condition, written in 1931, in which he blamed the economic crisis on the reparations settlement as well as on the lack of German business support for social justice and free trade. In political terms he echoed the views of Social Democrats and the bourgeois left, while charging conservatives and radical right-wing groups with advocating a violent removal of Germany's burdens. His solution was to end reparations, followed by an international commitment to disarmament under U.S. leadership. German governments, he insisted, must make their contribution by improving relations with France and Poland and by putting an end to demands for the return of economically useless colonies. He concluded that Friends must advocate all this for the sake of preserving German democracy, because "if democracy in Germany fails, the other democracies will fall as well."[35]

Universal disarmament was a major constant of the German Quaker position. This concern also figured on the agenda of the 1931 Yearly Meeting in Dresden-Hellerau. That conclave concluded that "even a conquered and disarmed people is not defenseless as it opens itself to the influx of the divine power of love and readiness for reconciliation." The participants sent a message to their coreligionist, President Herbert Hoover, in appreciation of his initiative for a one-year moratorium on war debt and reparations payments. "For the first time in history," this message exulted, "a responsible statesmen has moved his people to a great sacrifice in the interest of world peace." A copy went to Germany's embattled chancellor, Heinrich Brüning, a devout Catholic, exhorting him "to continue in the path of peace and understanding."[36] On January 28, 1932, Hans Albrecht and two members of the Berlin Center staff, Corder Catchpool and the Berlin correspondent of the *Baltimore Sun*, Richard Cary, delivered to Brüning a letter urging his support of the aims embraced by the Geneva Disarmament Conference. "Offer the world total disarmament," their communication counseled, "other states will follow, for mankind awaits the nation that places love of God above self-love."[37]

In every instance of an action, the record identifies Hans Albrecht as the chief spokesman, even if not necessarily its author. There is no way of knowing to what extent every member of the German Yearly Meeting accepted every position. Quaker minutes merely record consensual decisions, and opportunities to glimpse what preceded the achievement of unanimity are few indeed. A lonely exception are the protocols of the Berlin meeting, whose evidence parallels the Yearly Meeting's readiness to speak on contemporary issues. Here anti-Semitism appeared on the agenda as early as 1926, as did discussions on Christian communism, the relations between Quakers and bolshevism, and the concern that Friends emphasize their identity as a religious society.[38] It is also possible to validate Albrecht's representative role by examining the lives of a few other members of the German Yearly Meeting who were of sufficient prominence, beyond the confines of their religious association, to have left footprints in the sands of history.

EMINENT GERMAN QUAKERS

Possibly the most visible Friend before 1933 was the poet, writer, and journalist Alfons Paquet (1881–1944), who descended from a family of glove makers that had migrated from Grenoble, first to Luxembourg then to Cologne, birthplace of his father, Jean. When Alfons was born his father had moved the business to Wiesbaden, where he expected his son to continue the family enterprise. But after an apprenticeship in the store of an uncle in London, the youngster decided on a different career. The publication of his first poem, celebrating the five hundredth birthday of Johannes Gutenberg, convinced him that he was a writer. In 1901, when Paquet was barely twenty, a Berlin publisher, specializing in the work of "new poets" (Hermann Hesse among them), accepted a volume of his verse, and before the year was out a Cologne house brought out a collection of his short stories. The advances from these books enabled him to enroll at the University of Heidelberg. But his studies were to be frequently interrupted when a variety of reporting assignments earned him a new reputation as author of travel books: one on the new Trans-Siberian Railroad, another on a visit to the 1904 World's Fair in St. Louis. A second volume of poems earned him more fame, and after the appearance of a third account of travels across Central Asia, Paquet went to work for the prestigious *Frankfurter Zeitung*, an association that ended with that paper's demise in 1943.

During the war Paquet put his journalistic skills at the disposal of his government, and as press attaché of the German legation in St. Petersburg he became an eyewitness to the Russian Revolution. It was here that he first met Quakers on relief assignments and recognized them as "an order of kind human beings, making no fuss about themselves." What further impressed him was their imperviousness to the disappointments they encountered daily in their violent surroundings. He wrote about this encounter after his return to Germany and became one of the first German converts. Well before Hans Albrecht, Alfons Paquet identified German mysticism as a precursor of the Society of Friends and expressed the conviction that Quakers were as exceptional in their original Anglo-Saxon surroundings as they no doubt were in Central Europe.[39] In 1927 he sought to give expression to these views in a play about the life of Penn *(William Penn, Gründer von Pennsylvanien)* that enjoyed, however, only a brief run at the Frankfurt municipal theater. But Quaker activism strengthened his commitment to the Society, whose gospel of social equity harmonized particularly with his own Christian socialism. As he put it in an essay on the "nature of the Quaker spirit," published in 1928: "It is in their nature to attempt heroically the possible best, and to overcome all opposition, whether secular or philosophical, with the logic of their courage."[40]

Two Protestant pastors who considered the fight against social injustice a necessary first step on the road to salvation also found their way to the Society of Friends. The first, Emil Fuchs (1874–1971), was a descendant of Huguenots who left Valenciennes in the 1560s to settle in the Palatinate. His forebears had been pastors since the beginning of the eighteenth century, and he grew up in a Lutheran manse in the Hessian Odenwald, entering the University of Giessen to prepare for the same calling. There he became friends with Eduard David, a future leader of the Social Democratic Party, or SPD, who was to rise to the chairmanship of the Weimar Assembly. He also made the acquaintance of the educational reformer Paul Geheeb and became a partisan of Friedrich Naumann (1860–1919), another rare German Protestant cleric with a social conscience, whose National Social Society sought a fusion between socialism and the political status quo.

Fuchs began his pastoral career in Lampertheim, a large Hessian village whose labor force depended heavily on jobs in neighboring Mannheim's growing chemical industry. In this environment "he began to sense that human beings are not wicked, merely helpless."[41] After a stint as vicar of the German parish in Manchester and one year as a tutor in Giessen, he became pastor in Rüsselsheim, another community reeling under the impact of rapid industrial development, in this instance the manufacture of bicycles, sewing machines, and cars. Here Fuchs began a lifetime of swimming against powerful currents of religious, political, and social conformity. He first rattled the doors of orthodoxy when he requested a female assistant—unthinkable at the time—who could work more closely with the wives of his parishioners. His own willingness to address worker gatherings disquieted both hierarchy and government. His support of other clerical nonconformists closed avenues to promotion.[42]

Emil Fuchs nevertheless supported Germany's war and as late as 1917 described the invasion of Belgium as "justified self-defense." During that year he lost both brothers in action and watched in helpless sorrow as four hundred of Rüsselsheim's young men shared the fate of his siblings. With growing anger he observed the sons of the Opel Automobile Works management escape a similar fate through successions of inexplicable deferments, while the firm harvested record profits.

On Palm Sunday 1918, Fuchs became the shepherd of another working-class parish of some six thousand textile workers in Eisenach. Three years later he added to his scandalous reputation by joining the Social Democratic Party, and in 1922 he met Joan Fry and attended his first silent meeting of worship. The spiritual substance Friends provided him came none too soon, for he found his dissidence on religious and social issues far more difficult to maintain after the war than had been the case before 1914. His position as founder of a small group of religious socialists in Thuringia not only made him persona non grata with his clerical superiors but also exposed even his children to so much abuse in school that he decided to board two of them with Paul Geheeb's *Odenwaldschule*. Only Fuchs's second son, Klaus, of later "atom spy" notoriety, was so outstanding a student and so much in demand as a tutor of less talented peers that he remained unmolested in this hostile environment.[43]

Two associations seem to have preserved Fuchs's mental equilibrium in bleak years that drove his wife to suicide in 1931 and three of his four children into the ranks of the Communist Party: one was with a socialism "that marshalls the most profound spiritual resources to renew society"; the other was an ever closer relationship with the Society of Friends. In 1931 an offer from Prussia's social democratic minister of education, Carl Heinrich Becker (1876–1933), of a professorship in religious education at Kiel's pedagogical academy transferred him into a more congenial circle, though not in time to save his wife. Nor did it insulate Fuchs from continued controversy, especially not after he accepted the presidency of the local Republican Club. Still, as he recalled in his memoirs, "it was a joy to work there," and he even established good working relations with numerous Nazis in his lecture hall. These included, according to his testimony, "splendid human beings" and some excellent students.[44]

A friend of Friends since 1922, Emil Fuchs did not join the Society until 1933. By then he had become an influential presence in its ranks. His Quaker membership came at the end of a long spiritual journey that began with his immersion in the work of early nineteenth-century reformers of German Protestantism, particularly Friedrich Schleiermacher (1768–1834). Two monographs, published in 1901 and 1904, established him as an authority in this field before he became known and distrusted as a gadfly. Almost a quarter-century later a large essay titled "From Schleiermacher to Marx" illuminates for historians the road Fuchs had traveled since the turn of the century and the impasse at which the republic, to whose preservation he was dedicated, had arrived. Here Fuchs pointed out that German Lutheranism, placing a premium on obedience to dogma and established authority, addressed a declining audience as did liberal laissez-faire. Neither set of convictions provided convincing answers to a nation rendered rudderless by the war. Advocates of both lived comfortably while surrounded by misery. Meanwhile, the masses, though revolutionized by Marxism, aspired to more than material comfort. They sought "a new world of justice, liberty and brotherhood." That new order, according to Fuchs, could be attained by recognizing the consonance of Schleiermacher's and Quaker assumptions that faith in God was the base of all knowledge and that confrontation of the fundamental mysteries of existence was the basis of all piety.[45]

The other Protestant clergyman to play a leading role in the German Quaker movement was also the son of a Hessian pastor. Rudolf Schlosser likewise followed his father's vocation. He, too, recognized early in his career that his church was helpless in the face of a changing society and became an acolyte of Friedrich Naumann. He served in the First World War and after his return home felt a call "to build a new national community based on the powers of the gospel." He accepted a pastorate in Chemnitz, a city of two hundred thousand inhabitants and a center of textile production since the fourteenth century, sometimes referred to as Saxony's Manchester. Like Fuchs, he joined the Social Democrats, at whose meetings he rubbed shoulders with many a parishioner, and like Fuchs, whom he met during his Chemnitz tenure, he was relatively isolated from his fellow clergymen. But unlike his older and more learned colleague, Schlosser soon concluded that his conflict with church practice imposed on him the duty to go beyond mere dissidence. He resigned from the pulpit and left the church. His intention was to become a hospital nurse, but when the social democratic city government appointed him head of the municipal orphanage, he abandoned that more humble calling. It was at the beginning of this second career that Schlosser began to attend the annual meetings of the Society of Friends, where he found the spiritual moorings his church had failed to provide.

In 1925 Schlosser accepted the headship of a reformatory for boys near Lübeck. He turned this penal colony into an educational institution with classrooms and workshops and acquired a farm that provided both food and agricultural instruction for some of his charges. Three years later he was appointed director of the largest Saxony reformatory at Bräunsdorf near Dresden, selecting as his deputy Clara Schwanke, a well-known and experienced administrator of reformatories for girls. With mixed results he struggled to convert his staff—largely recruited from the state corporation of male nurses—to his conviction that spiritual and vocational education, rather than a diet of beatings and sermons, rescued juvenile delinquents from a life of crime. At the German Yearly Meeting in 1932 Schlosser decided to end his isolation from organized religion and joined the Society of Friends. He quickly became a pillar of German Quakerism, and in that environment he exhibited the same uncompromising adherence to his convictions that had characterized his conduct after his return from the trenches.[46]

Another Protestant cleric, Wilhelm Mensching (1887–1964), experienced a conversion from orthodoxy to nonconformism in the course of his service as a missionary in Africa from 1912 to 1917. During these years he evolved from a "nationalist, conservative pastor" into a religious pacifist. After the war he became a leader of the German branch of the Fellowship of Reconciliation, and in 1928 he attended the Friends adult education center at Woodbrooke near Birmingham. While I have not been able to establish when he joined the Society of Friends, Mensching became, by action and example, another faithful guide to the persecuted during the difficult years ahead. His thought and his principles were shaped by a heterogenous set of models that included the industrialist and social visionary Walter Rathenau (1867–1922), who vainly pleaded after the war that "the souls of the slain do not demand revenge"; the graphic chronicler of Berlin working-class life, Käthe Kollwitz (1871–1945); and the Norwegian explorer and recipient of a Nobel Peace Prize, Fridtjof Nansen (1861–1930), who counseled Europeans that "we must destroy the bridges behind us that lead back to the old politics and the old system."[47]

Another charter member of the German Society was the Freiburg political scientist Gerhart von Schulze-Gävernitz (1864–1943), whose father's accomplishments as professor of public law at Heidelberg had earned him elevation to Baden's hereditary nobility. Gerhart chose the career pursued by his father and grandfather but found the academic environment more accommodating to his liberal views than the pastorate had been to Fuchs's and Schlosser's. After receiving his doctorate at Göttingen with a dissertation titled "Thomas Carlyle's Attitude toward Christianity and Revolution," he added postdoctoral studies on Russian politics before receiving an appointment at Freiburg, where he was to remain until his retirement in 1929. He, too, did not confine himself to the secular pulpit of the lecture hall. In 1912 a committee that included the historians Friedrich Meinecke and Veit Valentin persuaded him to run for Baden's fifth Reichstag district. He represented that constituency until the end of the war, under the banner of left-liberal progressivism. In the Weimar Assembly he belonged to the minority of German Democratic Party deputies (fourteen out of seventy-five) who voted for the ratification of the Treaty of Versailles. Although his parliamentary service ended in 1920, the nature of his profession prevented retirement from political controversy. In company with Georg Bernhard (1875–1944), editor of Berlin's oldest newspaper, the liberal *Vossische Zeitung;* Johann-Heinrich Count Bernstorff (1862–1939), German ambassador to Washington during World War I; Walter Schücking (1875–1935), the first German appointed to the Permanent Court of International Justice; and the author of the Weimar Constitution, Hugo Preuss (1860–1925), he agitated for Germany's admission to the League of Nations as early as 1923. Schulze-Gävernitz was known beyond the boundaries of Germany. In 1924 he lectured at American universities and then served as chief of research for the Institute for Intellectual Cooperation of the League of Nations before Germany became a member. The following year the newly founded German Yearly Meeting asked him to represent them at the London Yearly Meeting. In 1930, English Friends invited him to give the annual Swarthmore Lecture, named after Margaret Fell's manor house. The title of his speech, "Democracy and Religion," reflected Schulze-Gävernitz's vision of a future state "in which the freedom of every citizen is only limited by the requirements of everybody's freedom."

Just as Fuchs and Schlosser aspired to create a German society where Christianity directed the secular order, this Freiburg professor sought to promote, in secular terms, a similar harmony in international relations. It may well have been Schulze-Gävernitz who provided Hans Albrecht with the appealing formula that tied revision of the Treaty of Versailles to the survival of German democracy. To a German-Polish conference of reconciliation, convened in Berlin in April 1927, he pointed out that dissatisfaction with Germany's eastern border was driving the young into the arms of chauvinism. As a first arena of compromise, he pointed to the need for a reduction of economic barriers. "The creation of larger economic entities" on the Continent "might not move borders, but it could render them unimportant." As a Quaker and as a liberal he also joined sixty prominent fellow citizens—including all liberal members of the Reichstag, the mayors of Dresden and Nuremberg, as well as a dozen Catholic and Protestant theologians—in signing a protest against the anti-Semitic demonstrations that led the German Yearly Meeting to declare its solidarity with Berlin Jews.[48]

Another German Quaker pioneer, Wilhelm Hubben, published in 1929 a history called "Quakers in the German Past," one of the most readable and incisive contributions to Quaker historiography. Born into a Catholic family of marginal farmers near the Dutch border, between Krefeld and Venlo, he grew up in a household in which religious beliefs rested on two assumptions: God was German, and Jesus was Roman Catholic. Before he entered school his parents abandoned their meager acreage for equally precarious industrial employment. His father became a janitor, his mother a seamstress. Hubben's earliest childhood memories included recollections of the visit of his maternal uncle Henry from America, who told his parents that Americans ate better than Germans but lived without the benefits of sickness and old-age insurance. Hubben's elders were shocked to learn also that their relative attended services of non-Catholics, including "silent meetings of the Quakers, where men and women speak whenever they feel God's spirit in them." No less disturbing to the boy's inherited faith was the splendor attending an imperial visit to Krefeld in 1902. After this experience he "realized that the radiance of the Catholic Church had found a most important rival in this new religion of patriotism and emperor worship."[49] Attendance at the local gymnasium further eroded confidence in familial traditions. The talented son of a mere janitor was a social outcast among the sons of industrial managers and civil servants, and the confessional mix represented by his classmates, coupled with a predominantly Protestant faculty, exposed him to influences from which he had theretofore been shielded. He graduated in 1912 and went on to the teachers college at Kornelimünster near Aachen.[50]

Before Hubben could receive his teacher's diploma, war broke out. He entered the army as a volunteer stretcher bearer, an occupation that taught him to see friend and foe as part of one tortured humanity. One year after the war he finished his professional training with a group of rebellious fellow veterans who forced the resignation of the college principal and chose their readings from the Catholic Index of Prohibited Books. His first position as schoolmaster of a one-room school ended in conflict both with his superiors and with local parents, who objected to his pacifist and ecumenical views. He returned to Krefeld and faced more professional harassment when his principal discovered that he had quietly left the church. Involvement in local child feeding brought him in contact with Friends, whom he found "catholic because [they] embraced all living souls, sacramental in [their] active spirituality, and priestly in dignifying our everyday lives." Hubben joined the Society at its German founding, and in due time his talents, so effectively displayed in his history of Friends in Germany, led him to the editorship of the Yearly Meeting's monthly, now renamed *Der Quäker*.

In Weimar Germany, Hubben, like Fuchs and Schlosser, found that religious nonconformism did not close all doors to careers in education. Like Fuchs, his advancement to the headship of an elementary school at Magdeburg yielded both professional satisfaction as well as conflict on many levels in this heterodox environment. The head of his nondenominational school's parents' association was a militant communist. Many of the pupils were underfed and ragged. Administrators at a neighboring Protestant school shunned him with "pharisaic disdain." An ever growing number of his faculty joined the Nazi Party. His attendance at international Quaker meetings in Paris, London, and Amsterdam made him the object of derisive suspicion. He, too, drew the necessary strength from his fellow Quakers, another witness to the power that radiated from a gospel of peace and tolerance.[51]

Hertha Kraus was the youngest among this group of distinguished and visible German Friends.[52] Five years after her birth in 1898 to Jewish parents in Prague, her father Alois (1863–1953) became professor of economic geography at the Academy of Commerce in Frankfurt, which became a full-fledged university in 1919. She grew up in the birthplace of Goethe and attended the new local university named after him. After receiving her doctorate in social economy and public administration, she joined the staff of the British child-feeding mission, rising to district director in 1923.[53]

The following year, to "her own surprise" and that of her parents, Konrad Adenauer, the mayor of Germany's third largest city, Cologne, appointed her head of the municipal welfare office, a position that carried with it a seat on the executive magistrate. This appointment elicited loud protests in the local press, which considered the selection of a twenty-five-year-old "girl," who was neither Catholic nor a native of Cologne, "completely inappropriate." Years later Adenauer told Alois Kraus why these complaints left him unmoved. He had observed Hertha at work in a variety of settings and was certain that she would measure up. She was to fill this position until 1933, and the quality of her performance is perhaps best reflected by an invitation from the University of Chicago in 1932 to give a series of lectures on German welfare practice. Among Friends her eminence was recognized when she was asked that same year to take charge of the faltering Cologne meeting.[54]

GERMAN AND FOREIGN QUAKERS

These biographical sketches reveal that German Friends were largely recruited from the ranks of educated professionals who occupied positions of distinction, despite their constant readiness to battle conventional prejudice. They also show that the German Quaker community did not include persons of wealth. Its work was generally the result of American and British initiatives and depended on continued substantial foreign financial subsidies.

Establishing contact with Friends abroad was, therefore, another important task that fell to the leadership of the young Yearly Meeting. In 1931, Hans Albrecht addressed a convocation of Scandinavian Friends at Helsingør in Denmark. That same year British Friends invited Alfons Paquet to report on "the situation in Germany." The clerk, in turn, attended the London Yearly Meeting, while Irene Helbeck from Elberfeld represented German Quakers at the annual gathering in Paris.[55] The extent of foreign financial support is reflected in the budget adopted by the German Yearly Meeting in 1931. Of its total expenditures of 19,765 reichsmarks, 15,573 came from British and American sources. Without this support, neither the publishing house nor the repossession and restoration of the eighteenth-century meetinghouse in Pyrmont would have been possible.

The publishing activity of the German Yearly Meeting produced the monthly that claimed fifteen hundred subscribers, but no profits, and the translations of British and American Quaker literature, none of which turned into best-sellers. As a result, the venture received in 1930 a foreign infusion of 2,676 reichsmarks. To maintain this subvention Albrecht addressed a steady stream of pleas to the donors. Quaker literature, he pointed out, could not be sold at a profit in depression Germany. On the contrary, some free distribution of such material was indispensable to any effort to spread the Quaker message.[56] Any decline in current subsidies, he warned, would terminate Quaker influence on spiritual life in Germany, at a time when it appeared to be making a perceptible difference. It was not a plea to subsidize the German Yearly Meeting, but a plea to promote the dissemination of Quaker thought in central Europe.[57]

The restoration of the Pyrmont Meeting House caused further substantial expenses requiring another special effort of salesmanship, especially after an appeal to American Friends had fallen flat. Hans Albrecht asked Clarence Pickett, secretary of the American Friends Service Committee, whether his community could raise 35,000 reichsmarks required to buy the dilapidated building and its surrounding land from the city. Pickett replied that "when there is such great demand for contributions for immediate needs," he could not support purchase of "a building that would only be used once or twice a year."[58] However, among British Friends, who had built the house as a gift to the Pyrmont group in 1800, the appeal met with instant approval. The edifice had remained British property until British Friends sold it in 1890, long after the demise of the local meeting. The sale price, it turned out, was still held in trust and was immediately put at the disposal of the new venture. At this point the city administration of Pyrmont remembered the child feedings and offered a plot next to the old Quaker cemetery, at a "nominal rent," on which a replica of the old building could be erected. The German Yearly Meeting seized the opportunity, accepted the offer, and began building under the aegis of an ad hoc committee that would advance the project as funds became available. Another 10,000 reichsmarks raised by British Friends, and a more modest 1,500 reichsmarks from the German membership, provided sufficient immediate capital to enable the Germans to negotiate some substantial loans. At the 1932 Yearly Meeting the roof was raised, and after the completion of the house it became the permanent site of the German Yearly Meeting.[59]

THE INTERNATIONAL QUAKER CENTER IN BERLIN, 1925–1932

We have seen that the Quaker conscience was disquieted by the fear that their feeding of Germany's hungry had established the Society of Friends in most German minds as a charitable, rather than a religious, organization. British and American Friends agreed, therefore, to maintain in Berlin an international center whose task would be to "nurture the infant Quaker movement in Germany." An American historian of German Quakerism has described the resulting activities as depending "almost entirely on the inclination of the representatives. Some meddled in international crises, some sought to improve German society, some sought to nurture the German Yearly Meeting as best as they could."[60] Its condescending tone notwithstanding, this statement does indeed summarize foreign Quaker activity in Germany after the founding of the Yearly Meeting. The first American Friend to come to Germany in 1925 was the Quaker mystic, and subsequent professor of philosophy at Haverford College, Thomas Kelly (1893–1941), who approached his work in a spirit of great humility. Kelly described German Friends as more deeply religious and less encumbered with the "dead wood of tradition" than their American coreligionists. In Germany, he wrote an acquaintance, "I had little to give, but much to learn," because he found a degree of dedication he had not seen elsewhere.[61]

Kelly's successor, Gilbert MacMaster, brought a different background to the Berlin office. At the turn of the century he had come to Hamburg to open a branch plant for an American shoe manufacturer. Subsequently married to the daughter of a local merchant, he was forced to close shop when the United States entered the war in 1917. He returned two years later to supervise the feeding program, first in Munich, then in Frankfurt. During the last phase of that operation in 1923 he moved to Berlin where he joined the center's staff in 1926. Here he became one of those "meddlers in international crises," referred to above, especially committed to the protection of ethnic minorities. To this end he coordinated activities between the Berlin and Warsaw Centers, and attended meetings of the European Nationalities Congress, convinced that this work would have been infinitely more fruitful had the United States joined the League of Nations.[62] That the "international work" took away time from the important task of making Quaker converts only increased MacMaster's frustrations.[63]

German Friends were no less troubled by this lack of focus in the activities of the Berlin Center. In 1930, coincident with MacMaster's retirement, the British member Albert H. Bayes departed after only one year's service. Hans Albrecht feared that the center would languish unless the choice of successors was guided by two considerations. The first was that the appointees must commit themselves to a prolonged term of service, the other that they know German—Bayes had not—so as to increase their effectiveness with German audiences. Both of these conditions were met by the American Richard L. Cary, who agreed to stay three years, doubling as Berlin correspondent for the *Baltimore Sun.* They were likewise satisfied by Corder Catchpool, the British conscientious objector, who had begun the study of German while in prison as part of his personal preparation to become a future servant of Anglo-German reconciliation. He had been among the first to come to Germany in 1919 and was now returning with his wife and four children to begin an extended involvement in the spiritual, as well as the political, life of the host country and in the work of international reconciliation, work that continued until the outbreak of World War II.

Both Cary and Catchpool joined the German Yearly Meeting. They undertook extended speaking tours and arranged similar expeditions for visiting Friends from Britain and the United States. In this manner they hoped to strengthen the Quaker movement on the Continent and build bridges of understanding between their countries and Germans in all walks of life. Sharing German objections to the peace settlement, they had no difficulty in attaining a respectful hearing wherever they went.[64]

Center activity was supplemented in the provinces, though once again in the material rather than the spiritual sphere. In Nuremberg, for instance, Leonhard and Mary Friedrich started a Friends' center for worship but also rented a warehouse where seven hundred families received food and clothing. In contrast to other German Quaker cells, the Friedrichs' group seems to have included a large admixture of workers, many of whom lost their employment as the depression hit their industrial hometown with particular force. In response, the Friedrichs organized a "group parcel scheme," with British help, a rare example of a relief effort for fellow Quakers.[65]

In Frankfurt, Dorothy Henkel used AFSC funds to assist thirty-seven poor families and to arrange "summers in the country" in Alsace for workers' children. In December 1932 the French *Entr'aide Europeéne* sent volunteers to Berlin, among them Gilbert Lesage, clerk of the Paris meeting, and began a weekly feeding of workers' children in the Prenzlauer Berg section.[66]

One may derogate these small alleviations of growing difficulties as being no more than fingers in the dike. Here, as before, Friends could not prevent catastrophes; they could merely intervene, wherever possible, to mitigate their impact. Succeeding to that modest extent kept the commitment alive, maintained the flow of benefactors and volunteers, and nurtured hope. In Philadelphia, Clarence Pickett believed that the Quaker presence in Germany contributed to German-American friendship. "Germany is our natural friend," he assured a correspondent from New Hampshire in 1930, "and they quite frankly feel . . . that they ever got into a war with us was a great mistake." The following year he expressed the conviction that "the day is not far distant" when "a small society of German Friends, standing for those things that are dear to all Friends," and "ready to raise its voice against wrong," would "become firmly entrenched in the life of the country." Acts, like the protest against anti-Semitism, had aroused new interest in the Society, and Pickett expected membership to rise significantly in the years ahead.[67]

Friends in Germany, indigenous or foreign, clung to their mission. Even as members pleaded with Chancellor Brüning for an active policy of disarmament, Berlin Friends held monthly meetings with the local chapter of the Fellowship for Reconciliation.[68] A conspicuous bridging mission was the Berlin Quaker Gerhard Halle's visit to the battlefields of northern France. In Halle we meet another Friend in the powerful grip of an unrelenting conscience that, awakened by his war experiences, grew into a stoic expectation of martyrdom. According to his own testimony, "only voluntary sacrifice, untouched by the postulates of any [confessional] discipline has moral value." Raised in an environment in which "decent people" *(anständige Menschen)* eschewed all contact with the peace movement, he had shared his generation's exaltation when war in 1914 offered what everyday life had hitherto failed to provide: "Experiences that shook the soul to its foundations." In his case these experiences were to have unexpected consequences. As an officer in the trenches he recognized the incompatibility between Christianity and war. He discovered that the enemy were risking their lives for the same cause as he: love of country. Nonetheless, he and his engineers carried out the scorched-earth policy ordered during the German retreat to the Hindenburg line in 1917. They leveled "handsome, well preserved villages" and mined the city hall of Bapaume, which blew up two weeks after their departure, causing great loss of life.

In three meetings, held between May 20 and 22, 1932, near these battle sites, Halle asked his victims for forgiveness. Before an audience of seven hundred in Douai, he acknowledged his country's part in unleashing World War I and accepted a "moral duty" to make reparation for the destruction. At the same time he pleaded for a remission of this obligation, which Germany at this point had no way of fulfilling. Two travel companions shared the rostrum with Halle: Corder Catchpool, who gave an account of his experiences as a conscientious objector, and the German Quaker Gertrude Pulwer, a representative of the International Women's League for Peace and Freedom, who urged the women in the audience to educate their children so that they would strive to bring about a peaceful world. Several members of the audience supported Franco-German reconciliation, while a Protestant pastor, André Trocmé, reminded Halle's listeners that participation in the postwar blockade of Germany had also saddled the French people with a measure of guilt. Trocmé's observations, the only remarks to elicit objections from the audience, drew protests from partisans of the conservative *Action Française*. However, there seems to have been no dissent from the favorable reaction to Halle's decency and courage.[69]

Halle subsequently delivered the same talk to a Berlin gathering of six hundred, organized by the League of Human Rights, and the following day to an open meeting of the Society of Friends, attended by half that number. Here he added impressions from visits to the battlefields of Arras and Vimy Ridge, whose cemeteries included thirty-six thousand German and French graves. These meetings appear to have been the last significant pacifist manifestations before the Nazi takeover. Halle's own reward followed with lightning dispatch: his employer fired him.[70]

Another Quaker mission, undertaken in 1932, illustrates that their work for peace was recognized in a broader context. In 1923, Memel, a city of German population surrounded by a Lithuanian countryside, had been ceded to Lithuania for its use as an outlet to the sea, comparable to the relationship between Danzig and Poland. On February 6, 1932, the Lithuanian government arrested the territory's German executive and replaced him with a Lithuanian. The local legislature, twenty-seven of whose twenty-nine seats were held by German-speaking representatives, denied its confidence to the new governor and was promptly dissolved. New elections were scheduled for May 4, and, fearing trouble, the Minority Department of the League of Nations called on the

Berlin Center to send a British or American Quaker to observe the balloting. This request was seconded by German authorities in neighboring East Prussia, who well remembered the Quaker efforts on behalf of political prisoners in the Ruhr that had created "an atmosphere of justice and love between parties that were quarreling." In response to both appeals, Richard Cary left Berlin on April 29, 1932. He stopped in Königsberg to discuss his mission with the governor of East Prussia, then proceeded to Memel and thence to Kaunas, the capital, for a meeting with the Lithuanian government. Cary pointed out to these officials that tensions in Memel were not just a local problem but were symptomatic of increased political violence throughout Europe. In Memel he found the electoral campaign marred by both Lithuanian and German acts of rowdyism, though he considered them less threatening than comparable clashes in Berlin and other German cities.

Election day saw Cary closeted with the Lithuanian directorate in Memel and a representative of the Lithuanian foreign office, and he undoubtedly shared their feelings of relief when the voting turned out to be "quite orderly." Whether his appeal to his hosts—that a fair contest would demonstrate their country's decent treatment of minorities—contributed to that outcome, cannot be documented. Cary certainly thought so. The vote had not changed the German preponderance in Memel's city parliament. The next day the government withdrew the Lithuanian governor and restored his predecessor. No doubt Lithuania's dependence on German markets for its agricultural surplus, and Germany's interests in Lithuania as a barrier to Polish expansionist ambitions, played a part in the peaceful resolution of this crisis. The fact remains, however, that Quakers had been asked to mediate and had found a hearing for their message of conciliation.[71]

ON THE EVE OF THE NAZI TAKEOVER

German Friends, together with their foreign auxiliaries and benefactors, celebrated the beginning of the restoration of the old meetinghouse in Pyrmont at the end of a busy and committed year. Was this event to be a symbol of a time when they would play a major role in the spiritual and political life of their homeland? The near silence that had greeted their appeal to the major denominations on behalf of Berlin Jews was not a propitious indication. Certainly, in retrospect, one has no difficulty recognizing that the distinctiveness of the Quaker presence in Germany lay in their dogged support for the lost causes of religious tolerance and international conciliation. One cannot begrudge Friends the delight they felt when the roof was raised at the end of the first phase of the Pyrmont restoration, for being a Quaker in Germany was certainly not becoming easier. What Hubben had said in his book, that Quaker's "path of pure Christianity" must pass "through suffering and persecution," and echoed in Hans Albrecht's address to the 1929 Yearly Meeting that "anyone seriously following Christ must be prepared to lose office and property" turned out to be a more accurate expectation.[72] A visiting American coreligionist reported in 1931 that all meetings she attended were permeated by a sense of isolation. The image "of the lonely Quaker" was always present.[73] After the fall of the Brüning government in 1932, Hans Albrecht was bracing for a military dictatorship. Less than three weeks before Hitler's investiture Dorothy Henkel visited Albrecht in Hamburg and found him "tired and depressed."[74]

Less than fifteen years after the arrival of Joan Fry and her small band of British Friends at Berlin's Anhalt Station, the sisyphian labors that Quakerism had volunteered to initiate in the defeated country had filled many stomachs but had failed to change many minds. As our close-ups of the most prominent among German converts revealed, it was possible in Weimar Germany to stay the course of nonconformity and, at the same time, pursue a career that satisfied professional ambitions and moral commitments. That fact alone, however, did not gain a mass following for unpopular causes. Would another revolution, therefore, strengthen Quakerism, or would such an upheaval drive them once more into exile?

2.

The Trials of Revolution

GERMANY AND GERMAN CHRISTIANITY FROM HITLER'S INVESTITURE TO THE NUREMBERG LAWS

The appointment of Adolf Hitler as chancellor of Germany, on January 30, 1933, led to a host of startling, sometimes violent events. Four weeks later the Reichstag building went up in flames, probably set afire by agents of the new government that quickly used the catastrophe as a pretext for outlawing the Communist Party. How Nazis would reinforce legally acquired political power at the expense of other rivals was revealed when authorities announced the opening of Dachau concentration camp. This type of penal institution, new to Germany, became the place where suspected opponents of the government could be held indefinitely and without trial. Suspension of civil rights by the Enabling Act, adopted three days later on March 23, initiated government control of public opinion through censorship and telephone surveillance. The boycott of Jewish business establishments on April 1, although called off quickly because of its negative impact on public opinion abroad, spread panic among another set of victims and triggered a brief wave of emigration.

Popular support of these measures only increased feelings of isolation and despair among assorted outsiders. After the October 14 withdrawal of Germany's representatives from the Geneva Disarmament Conference and the League of Nations, 93 percent of German voters expressed approval of that step and, since all competing political parties had been outlawed by the end of July, elected a parliament exclusively composed of Nazi yes-men. A simultaneous campaign by a new Ministry of Enlightenment and Propaganda discredited news of political oppression as "atrocity tales" and constituted another effective means of curbing critics of the government.

Hitler's purge of opponents within his party on June 30, 1934, led to wholesale executions without judicial proceedings of any kind and left no doubt that a new authoritarian anarchy was putting countless additional lives at risk. Despite the Saar plebiscite of 1935, decreed by the Treaty of Versailles, which returned the coal-rich region to German jurisdiction, Hitler denounced that same treaty's disarmament clauses and introduced universal military service. Finally, the proclamation of the so-called Nuremberg Laws at the 1935 party congress, depriving Jews of their German citizenship, convinced many thousands to seek a new life in any foreign country that would admit them.

Secular Germany readily accepted these impositions for several reasons: because of distrust of Communists and dislike of Jews, because the new tyranny inaugurated public works projects that reduced unemployment, and because it initiated a foreign policy that "broke the shackles" of Versailles. Other European governments seemed disinclined to defend an international status quo that had become discredited not only in German eyes. Britain's Conservative leaders even convinced themselves that Hitler's anticommunism was saving their world from an even more dangerous challenge.[1]

Hitler's demonstrative hostility to communism and socialism, as well as democratic governance, elicited almost universal approval among Germany's Christians, from the large bodies of Protestant and Catholic worshipers to smaller sects such as Baptists, Methodists, Mennonites, Mormons, and Seventh Day Adventists. These members placed their faith in the preamble of the Nazi Party's program that pledged support to an undefined "positive Christianity."[2]

Up to a point this was understandable. Most representatives of the political left had been indifferent, if not hostile, to established and nonconformist religion, the possible exceptions being a few Socialist Christians, such as Emil Fuchs. But when it came to one of Nazism's favorite scapegoats, the Jews, the new order placed major Christian denominations in a quandary. More than seventy-two thousand former Jews and individuals with Jewish ancestors were Protestants, while almost forty-five thousand belonged to the Catholic Church.[3]

The hierarchy of Germany's 20 million Catholics enjoyed the greatest amount of leverage among the country's religious bodies. Organized politically through the Center Party, they were initially courted because their votes were needed to obtain the requisite two-thirds majority in the Reichstag to pass the Enabling Act. The regime's anticommunist poses, furthermore, persuaded Catholic bishops to rescind earlier edicts prohibiting Catholic membership in the Nazi Party. In return for this support, Hitler sent Vice Chancellor Franz von Papen to the Vatican to negotiate a concordat, which was signed on July 20, 1933. The treaty barred clergy from political activity and mandated government consultation before episcopal appointments. It did permit, however, continued operation of Catholic schools, as well as youth and other auxiliary organizations, so long as they did not "meddle" in public affairs, at a time when such groups in the Protestant sector were dissolved and absorbed into the Hitler Youth.

The concordat appeared to embody Hitler's respect for religion, while at the same time ensuring the disappearance of political Catholicism. The Vatican was gratified that earlier accords of this type with individual German states, such as Prussia and Bavaria, were at last replaced by a German settlement, and this only four years after the Lateran accords with Mussolini had ended more than half a century of church-state conflict in Italy. German bishops, in turn, hoped that the treaty would protect their clergy, as well as Catholic civil servants, from dismissal and persecution.

In line with these expectations, the Catholic Church became more willing to defend its members from government strictures, including those of Jewish antecedents. Objections to anti-Semitism, to be sure, were muted, and a rumor that the archbishop of Munich had warned that God always punished the persecutors of Jews was publicly branded as a "malicious invention." But in September when it was learned that Nazi purges of the civil service included both Gentile and formerly Jewish Catholics, the bishops asked the papal nuncio in Berlin, Eugenio Pacelli, to appeal to the government for redress. The German government rejected his request on the grounds that cleansing the civil service of unreliables and solving the "Jewish problem" were not issues covered by the July accord. Only then did it become clear to spiritual and secular Catholic leaders that they had prematurely surrendered their ability to exert a moderating pressure on Hitler. Now the Saint Raphael's Association for the Protection of Catholic German Emigrants, founded in 1871, jumped into the breach with a special project to assist a new wave of Catholics leaving Germany because of political or racial persecution. While the leaders of this effort were determined to protect themselves from any overt philo-Semitic taint, they assisted Jewish converts in a variety of material ways.[4] Protestants, though they outnumbered Catholics two to one, saw no reason to oppose a coalition in which conservatives initially outnumbered National Socialists. Given their hostility to the Weimar Republic and their sympathy for monarchical and authoritarian government, the inauguration of a "national" government on January 30, 1933, initially delighted clergy and laity alike. They expected the conservative leaders to keep the antireligious elements of Nazism in check and were wont to minimize the first excesses of the new regime as trivial when compared "to the ghastly and shameful" events of the 1918 revolution in Germany. Some Protestant pastors and theologians went so far as to see in "Jewry the embodiment of the spiritual poisoning of [their] race" and, therefore, agreed to exclude Jewish converts from the pastorate. Even political moderates, such as Bishop Otto Dibelius, favored the reduction of "disproportionate" Jewish influence, while the martyred Dietrich Bonhoeffer initially believed in the existence of a Jewish problem for which a solution of "new methods" might be needed.[5]

The event that divided Protestants into supporters and opponents of Nazi policy was not persecution of social revolutionaries, democrats, or Jews but the attempt to establish a national Protestant church. This process began with the appointment of a Reichsbishop on July 11, 1933, and was climaxed by the appointment of a German minister for church affairs, two weeks after the promulgation of the Nuremberg Laws. Opponents of this policy of religious nationalization founded the "Confessional Church" *(Bekenntniskirche)*, whose agenda pointed in the opposite direction: a Protestant community freed from German Protestantism's traditional ties to the state.

In 1934 the Barmen Synod of the Confessional Church opposition actually accepted measures for the support of formerly Jewish Christians but took no steps to implement them. A former president of the Bavarian Protestant Synod, finding that his coreligionists were indifferent to the sufferings of non-Aryan Protestants, left "a church that had ceased to be a church." A surprisingly outspoken polemic, published in 1934, castigated German anti-Semitic policy as a measure of German de-Christianization. None of these manifestations, however, changed the fact that no official Protestant agency roused itself to protect the victims. Even though the role of Judaism in the shaping of Christianity continued to elicit lively discussions, and the exclusion of non-Aryans from Protestant parishes might even be recognized as resting on dubious theological foundations, still, the ostracisms continued in all areas of German Protestant church life. A detailed and grim account of the desperate plight of these outcasts, which was submitted by Marga Meusel, a Berlin social worker, to the 1935 Synod of the Prussian Evangelical Church, fell into a void of silence. On this issue, one of the few visible dissidents, the Heidelberg pastor Hermann Maas, concluded in October 1935 that even the Confessional Church, otherwise so vocal in its opposition to state control of conscience, "had simply failed."[6] The two factions of German Protestantism remained all but indistinguishable in their treatment of Jewish converts: both decided to throw them to the wolves. This renders instances of individual dissent among their clergy all the more memorable.

Smaller sects faced a simple quandary: what must they do to survive? Baptists endorsed legislation excluding Jews from national society; Mormons posted "Jews not wanted" signs at their church doors; Methodists agreed that Jews were a threat to German society; and Adventists shunned members encumbered by Jewish ancestry.[7] Apart from the Quakers, only one among the small religious communities known as "Free Churches" seems to have defied the government. The Jehovah's Witnesses, whose membership came from the poorer classes, rejoiced in the privations their pursuit of the kingdom of God brought down on them. In July 1933 they were proscribed for refusing to join the party and, after 1935, for refusing to report for military duty. For the latter failure their men were consigned to concentration camps, where five thousand, more than one-third of the membership, perished.[8]

But the death-defying fanaticism of Jehovah's Witnesses did not change the fact that the overwhelming majority of German Protestants deserted Jewish converts. As a formerly Jewish physician, who had converted to Protestantism in 1916, put it in 1933: "[My children] have lost the protection that Jewry had always and everywhere provided to its members. They have [received] no protection from the Christian [sic] church, and, I imagine, cannot expect any. They are outlaws as Christians; they are outlawed as Germans. Can one imagine a more cruel fate visited upon the innocent?"[9]

A full understanding of the plight of these abandoned Christians quickened Quaker concern for the persecuted in Nazi Germany, a concern pursued without reservation and applied to all victims, regardless of their political or religious beliefs or their ethnic and cultural origins.

GERMAN QUAKER LIFE, 1933–1935

One of the first Quaker reactions to the events of January 30, 1933, was set forth by Hertha Kraus in a letter to an American Friend, dated February 1, 1933: "We have just had a new government. Hitler and the other reactionary groups have joined forces at last. They have the courage of the blind—do not see the abyss. . . . *We have all got to carry on.*"[10] And carry on they did. The time of suffering, foreseen by Hans Albrecht, had arrived. Living by Quaker principles became increasingly difficult under the succession of blows struck by the new tyranny. As was true of other Christian sects, Friends' subsequent conduct was guided by the determination to survive as a religious community. Yet none of the carefully worded periodic restatements of their goals and intentions ever retreated from what they considered to be Christian fundamentals or from the Society's loyalty to its entire membership. In that sense, Michael Seadle's sweeping pronouncement that "the history of the pacifist response to Hitler is the story of Quakers in Germany" does justice to the facts. But when that same observer goes on to claim that Hans Albrecht, as clerk, "made [the German Yearly Meeting] a purely social and religious gathering," he overlooks much of the subsequent German Quaker record.[11]

At the outset, the most obvious indicator of any group's ability to survive is the level of membership. Based on this criterion the survival of German Friends had always been precarious. On October 1932 the German Yearly Meeting had only 199 members. By September 1, 1934, 44 of its members had withdrawn. Of these, 7 lived abroad, including Wilhelm Hubben and his wife, who had both emigrated to the United States, and Bernhard Leyh, who had moved to what was then Palestine. But the membership list of 1934 also lists 63 persons who had joined during the interim, notable among them Pastor Emil Fuchs; the pacifist activist Gerhard Halle; Margarethe Lachmund, the wife of a Mecklenburg judge; the physician Gerhard Ockel, leader of a small but active group in Guben near Frankfurt/Oder; and Heinrich Otto, who after World War II would become the historian of German Quakerism. Throughout the Nazi era, the Society would maintain this steady growth. The increase in membership was kept within modest bounds by the mandatory careful examination of each new applicant. This process was guided by the need to eliminate the infiltration of police spies and to keep out those who merely sought relief from personal and material burdens and who lacked both understanding of and commitment to Quaker principles. This latter consideration guided admissions procedures in all Quaker meetings.[12]

These practices established within German Quaker ranks a degree of stability and trust without which they would have eroded in the Nazi environment. However, when the Executive Committee, the *Arbeitsausschuss*, met in Frankfurt on March 31, 1933, to map the Society's future course, these attributes, so obvious to a historian some sixty years later, could not be taken for granted by a membership facing a government whose ruthlessness, reminiscent of Germany's religious wars of the seventeenth century, placed on them burdens for which they, no matter how ready to suffer for their beliefs, were entirely unprepared.

Hans Albrecht proved a fit leader in this extremity. The precepts he submitted to the committee's membership were neither dogmatic nor defeatist. At the opening session he reminded those assembled that Quakers had never viewed the state with a rigidly positive or negative attitude, adding that "as a religious society they have nothing to do with politics." Such a pronouncement sounded like the synodal verdicts of German Protestantism. But one must read on. Politics, Albrecht believed, do not engender moral renewal. He insisted: "Our task is not to judge, but to help so that justice may break through and the dignity of man be preserved." The dignity of man was indeed in jeopardy, but this writer knows of no leader of any religious or secular organization in Germany at this time who offered to throw it a lifeline. The clerk concluded: "I therefore believe that the time demands of us that we continue our work as if nothing had changed; but we must be more conscious of our responsibilities than has heretofore been the case." In plain language that last phrase demanded that no one should lightly provoke the authorities and thereby endanger individual members or the Society as a whole.[13]

Several foreign Friends have left us their impression of this first serious Quaker self-evaluation after the "national revolution." Bertha Bracey from London, the eventual savior of countless refugees, was especially struck by the appeal to members' individual responsibility. After her return home she assured Hans Albrecht that she would attribute no statement about the German situation to German Quaker sources. Gilbert MacMaster, who was about to exchange his Swiss retirement for another term of service at the Berlin Center, recalls that no one minimized the seriousness of the situation and that he believed the support by foreign meetings would be the strongest weapon in the arsenal of Albrecht's flock. He also took comfort from the presumable fact that "Germany was not Russia" and would not expel Quaker relief teams, as Stalin had in 1931. Mahlon Harvey, from the staff of the Paris Center, seconded this view by recalling that Nuremberg Friends who patronized Jewish stores during the April boycott had not been molested. Few had left the Society, and "most . . . seem willing to bear witness to their conviction."[14]

The subsequent Yearly Meeting at the end of July provided Hans Albrecht with another opportunity to define the German Quaker position as it related to the tasks that lay ahead. First and foremost members were enjoined to treat all "enemies" as "friends." This, the most difficult of all Christian postulates, embodied a reality more transcendent than National Socialist gratification of race and nation or Marxist denigration of religion. Nor, he avowed, would Friends get involved in debates concerning Jewish sources of Christian theology. "Our only task [is] to let the Eternal Light penetrate the darkness . . . that surrounds us." Friends must, he maintained, remain faithful to their principles, "be it on the use of force, be it on questions of race, be it on matters of class."

This gathering, the first in the completed meetinghouse, also reminded Friends that a high level of financial sacrifice would have to be maintained. Restoring the house had so far cost 43,300 reichsmarks, of which 37,600 came from England and Ireland, 3,000 from the United States, 400 from other countries, while 2,300 had been raised in Germany. A residual balance of 3,000 marks would have to be provided by German Friends. Members were also told they might soon have to provide a larger share of the costs of current operations, since depressed financial conditions in the United States and Britain presaged less aid from former providers.[15]

After the Yearly Meeting, the Society requested from the Reich government "that the members of the religious Society of Friends . . . [be] uniformly treated . . . as subjects of a [recognized] religious community." No record of an answer seems to have survived, but the ink on this communication was barely dry when Hans Albrecht received a visit from the Hamburg police. True to his proclaimed commitment to act as if nothing had changed, the clerk described the event in a circular sent to all members. He reported that he had explained Quaker principles and objectives to his visitors and had provided them with a list of members. He had also emphasized that Quakers had no secrets. This explanation seems to have satisfied the police, who voiced no objections to Friends' meetings and activities.[16]

Government toleration of the Society, however, did not ease the burdens the Nazi revolution imposed on individual members. Reports revealed Quaker parents bitterly—and dangerously—at odds with children who ardently embraced the new faith. Such conflicts erupted in households already shaken by the equally tragic consequences of the abrogation of civil rights and the new civil service regulations enacted in March and April 1933, which were designed to eliminate opponents of the regime from public employment.[17] To appreciate their effect on German Friends let us take a look at the socioeconomic profile of the German Yearly Meeting. This profile rests on a list of 92 out of 216 members of the 1934 German Yearly Meeting, whose occupations are known, supplemented by a register of individuals who joined between 1935 and 1945.

At a glance, it becomes apparent that German Quakers belonged to the bourgeoisie, that inchoate entity, maligned and ridiculed by so many social analysts. The "workers" listed here were employed either in bookstores or as artisans in craft shops, not wage earners in industry. This record also confirms a hypothesis by the German Quaker historian Anna S. Halle that one-fourth of the membership were teachers. Of the forty-one in this table, twenty-two lost their positions, indicating that this particular segment of Quaker professionals was hit particularly hard by the purely political criteria that characterized implementation of Nazi civil service laws. There is no indication that any of the victims sought to save their jobs by leaving the Society. This conclusion is reinforced by the near disappearance of government employees from the membership after 1935. Quakers also suffered politically in less exposed categories. At least two members, both bank directors, lost their positions in 1933, one because he was half-Jewish, the other—head of a savings bank in Leonberg near Stuttgart—because of his "political unreliability."[18]

Besides the membership lists, other sources describe the tribulations of German Friends. Hertha Kraus in Cologne received a curt phone call the day after the Nazi takeover, telling her not to return to her office. Fearing arrest, she found refuge with a friend, Gertrude Schulz, in the resort town of Lindenfels in

Occupation	1934 Members	Members who joined between 1934 and 1945	Total
Teachers and librarians	25	16	41
Social workers	4	3	7
Civil servants and other government employees	12	2	14
Business and banking	12	9	21
Physicians and pharmacists	6	5	11
Other professions	11	8	19
Farmers	1	—	1
Clerks	3	1	4
Pensioners	2	2	4
Workers	2	3	5
Family members, widows and single females without profession or occupation	14	17	31
Total	92	66	158

the Odenwald region of Hesse. Shortly thereafter both she and Schulz emigrated to the United States.[19] Dismissal reached Emil Fuchs with similar promptness at the Kiel College of Education. He moved to Berlin, where he was soon arrested, allegedly for spreading "atrocity tales." Thanks to the efforts of friends, both within and without the German Society, he was released but remained under surveillance and was tried in 1935 for insulting the Reich government. He was sentenced to one month in prison and then released. His children's membership in the Communist Party earned the family more persecution. One son escaped to Switzerland, a daughter and her husband, the Communist functionary Gustav Wittkowski, were freed, thanks to the efforts of Gilbert MacMaster, while Fuchs's second son, Klaus, fled to France and eventually settled in Great Britain.[20] Rudolf Schlosser lost his position as head of the Bräunsdorf reformatory and moved to Frankfurt where he was briefly taken into "protective custody." He continued his Quaker mission on behalf of the persecuted, especially Jews, for "he bore in his heart the guilt of the German nation towards the Jews in all its immeasurable weight."[21] During the Easter holiday of 1933 Wilhelm Hubben was visited by the Gestapo, but he was not arrested. But as the new school year began, the local board of education dismissed him from his post as elementary school principal, citing also his "political unreliability." He was invited to the Quaker adult education center at Woodbrooke, and then to Pendle Hill near Philadelphia, where he and his family were to settle for good.[22] Two Dresden teachers, Lilli and Manfred Pollatz, lost their positions. Manfred was briefly arrested then released and—thanks to his standing in the community—given a pension. They sold their house, packed their belongings, and moved to Haarlem in the Netherlands. There they opened a shelter and a school for Jewish refugee children.[23] Elisabeth Rotten, a Swiss citizen of Jewish parentage, who had welcomed the first British Quakers to Berlin in 1919, returned to the land of her citizenship after losing her position in Germany.[24] Alfons Paquet's works were among the books burned at various German universities in May 1933, but he kept his job at the *Frankfurter Zeitung*. Arrested in September 1935 as he was about to depart on a business trip to Sweden, he was taken to the notorious Gestapo prison on Prinz Albrecht Strasse in Berlin but released at the request of the German Foreign Office.[25]

These examples of individual fates, reflecting desperate uncertainties of everyday existence, also strained cohesion within the Society. How extensive the resulting clashes were, how long they lasted, and how many individuals they involved is impossible to reconstruct. Most of this history has died with the participants. But there has survived in British and American archives some record of at least two such episodes that shed light on these tensions. They demonstrate that Quakers were human, that they could be quarrelsome, yet they could keep such divergences within their ranks from becoming destructive.

The first of these incidents I will simply call the Paul Helbeck affair. It involved a founding member of the Society who was also head of the German Democratic Party in the Wuppertal District. His son recalls "as responsible politician [my father] could not watch inactively how the violent took over power." For this reason Paul Helbeck found himself increasingly at odds with Quaker pacifism and withdrew from the Society. His daughter has confirmed these facts. She also recalls, however, that her father wrote an open letter to the Nazi newspaper *Völkischer Beobachter* in which he outlined areas of agreement and disagreement with the party ideologist Alfred Rosenberg's magnum opus: *The Myth of the Twentieth Century.*[26]

Helbeck may have left the German Yearly Meeting on his own accord, but the reasons for that step were more complex than his children remember. A note from their father's hand, dated March 4, 1933, reveals that "the National Socialists pursue an economic route with which [he] substantially agree[d]." He cited particularly the appeals for social cohesion in, and decentralization of, the economy. For this reason he hoped "that in the end the present wild times will yet bring forth something valuable."[27] It is this stance that presumably moved Helbeck to write his "open letter," apparently around Christmas 1933, providing copies to the working committee of the German Yearly Meeting.

This letter, of which I have not been able to find a copy, became the object of a spirited discussion at an Executive Committee session on March 31 and April 1, 1934. Its contents apparently challenged German Friends to consider "how far they can cooperate in supporting the acts of the new government here." For that reason, therefore, some Friends applauded Helbeck's action as a provocation for constructive debate. That debate, however, not only often pitted quietists against activists but also appears to have awakened dormant personality clashes.[28] These emerge more clearly from a set of detailed notes taken at the same meeting by a British Friend. They record a host of indignant reactions to Helbeck's letter. Emil Fuchs, who waxed "rather violent at times," could not understand how a Quaker could find any area of agreement with a Nazi luminary who had accused pacifists of being simply cowards, "at a time when some of them sat in concentration camps." Elisabeth Rotten read Rosenberg's book after receiving Helbeck's missive and professed to be deeply shaken by "the thought that any Quaker could have anything to do with it." For Alfons Paquet, Rosenberg's acceptance of the *Protocol of the Wise Men of Zion*, anti-Semitism's favorite witness for the existence of a Jewish conspiracy to rule the world,[29] was reason enough to reject anything he wrote. "The book," he averred, "is a chemist's shop of poison administered . . . to the poor German people." Even Hans Albrecht, committed as he was to avoiding unnecessary provocation of the regime, scored Helbeck's action. He saw it as an implicit abandonment of the Society's Jewish converts, and as an official of Hamburg's shipping inspection he was totally out of sympathy with the Nazi drive toward economic self-sufficiency, a policy for which Helbeck seems to have expressed particular approval.

Still, Helbeck does not appear to have been without defenders. When Hans Albrecht remarked that Helbeck was free to write to the *Völkischer Beobachter*, but should not have done so as a Quaker, the notes record interruptions from the floor: "Can one do anything else?" Schulze-Gävernitz, the retired Freiburg political scientist, rose to remind his audience that peace in Europe depended on accord among all powers, not on ostracizing Germany. He told his coreligionists: "If we cannot see our task within the new Germany, emigration [is] the only alternative." Still, in the end an Austrian Friend, Rudi Boeck, who was to meet Nazism more than halfway after 1938, rose to demand that Helbeck should resign his membership. The gathering was also informed that Dutch and British Friends, whose forthcoming Yearly Meetings Helbeck had been scheduled to attend as the German representative, would not welcome his visit. At this point Helbeck was still a member of the German Yearly Meeting, and it would seem, therefore, more likely that these outbursts of disapproval, rather than disagreement with Quaker pacifism, account for his subsequent resignation from the German Society.[30]

Differences also arose in respect to the governance of the Yearly Meeting, based on principles as well as personal likes and dislikes. The progression of events on this issue is, however, less clear. In November 1934 the *Arbeitsausschuss* presented members with a proposal to change certain Yearly Meeting procedures. It provided that both clerk and committee members hold their appointments for one year and called for a nominating committee that would prepare a list of candidates before each Yearly Meeting. The Executive Committee, in turn, would each year propose to the Yearly Meeting a candidate for the clerkship. In addition, two adjuncts to the clerk were to be proposed "so as not to impose the responsibility of the meeting's business" on one individual and "to make possible a change in the leadership of the Yearly Meeting." This decision points to complaints that Hans Albrecht conducted German Quaker affairs in too autocratic a fashion, but its effect was his annual reconfirmation until he resigned in 1947. Nor is it clear from the record just how the two adjuncts functioned. Still, their appointment seems to have smoothed the waves of conflict.[31] This return to harmony may also have been promoted by the presence of a "policeman" at the 1934 Yearly Meeting, who does not appear, however, to have reported anything that prompted subsequent government intervention in the Society's affairs. Members nevertheless concluded after this government intrusion that their mission was "to carry their cross, no matter how heavy," and to help each other sustain that burden.[32]

The year 1935 seems, therefore, to have been less strife ridden. Friends became accustomed to dealing with the burdens imposed by the authoritarian order. Chief among these was the quandary facing younger male members after the introduction of compulsory military service on March 16, 1935. As early as 1933 MacMaster had written in his diary that the small Quaker communities on the Continent, especially the German, would be tested most severely "when the question of military service arises."[33] Now that time had come, and the Executive Committee was not slow to set forth the Society's position. It recalled, as was its practice whenever a question of state policy or a state agency was addressed, that ever since Friends' arrival in Germany in 1919 they had opposed acts of violence and rejected "participation in war or its preparation." They also substituted the term *heroic nonviolence,* coined by Alfons Paquet, to avoid the discredited word *pacifism,* and to make clear that their purpose was not an avoidance of physical danger, but rather to demonstrate readiness, tested in Britain during World War I, to undergo any suffering this attitude might impose on them. At the same time, the statement reminded all members that Quakers never forced one another to violate the dictates of the individual conscience. Like the founders of the American Friends Service Committee in 1917, they insisted that "all [Friends] are naturally ready to serve their people without reservation and without consideration of personal safety." Whether that meant donning the uniform, or rejecting any kind of support for the military with its attendant sanctions, remained a personal decision. Nevertheless, the accepted guide to Quaker conduct remained the commandment "Thou shalt not kill," and its implementation in the Gospel according to Matthew 5:44, exhorting Christians to "love your enemy and pray for those that persecute you."[34]

The committee also communicated its testimony to the Minister of War with the request to exempt members from military service on religious grounds. They were promptly informed that a total exemption was out of the question, but that assignment to medical service "and the like" would be considered.[35] One is not surprised to learn that the Gestapo was also aware of the contents of this statement. It chose to identify Emil Fuchs as the chief author. His communist children and the secret police's ignorance of Quaker history no doubt accounted for this choice of a scapegoat. One agent also reminded his superiors, in a report written in June 1935, of earlier Quaker criticism of Nazi activities and concluded: "Considering that the same individuals still lead the society and its publishing ventures, the members of the Society are in no wise urged verbally or in writing to assist in the building of the Third Reich." For good measure the informer enclosed a copy of an article in *Der Quäker* of May 1935, criticizing Alfred Rosenberg's attack on the apostle Paul. He also claimed that Quakers were distributing the German translation of a 1932 French pamphlet called "On the Suppression of the Crime of War."[36]

Quakers unanimously supported the promulgation of their beliefs in print. The chief agent of this resistance was the Quaker publishing house, whose direction was in 1933 entrusted to Leonhard Friedrich. *Der Quäker*, the Society's monthly, still had between four and five hundred subscribers, more than double the membership of the Yearly Meeting. The enterprise also published the addresses of Hans Albrecht, writings of Alfons Paquet, and translations of British and American Quaker tracts, as well as the writings of the pacifist Protestant pastor Wilhelm Mensching. These included a series of brief "biblical lives," provocatively chosen exclusively from the Old Testament.[37]

In 1935 Mensching applied the format of these "lives" to a new series of "Pamphlets of Our Cultural Heritage" *(Erbguthefte)*. Running a dozen pages, each pamphlet provided a one-page summary of the individual author's life, followed by an anthology of excerpts from his or her writings. True to the Quaker practice of openness, each publication included the name of the compiler. Each pamphlet sold for ten pfennig and fitted into an ordinary letter envelope for easy distribution and maximal immunity from censorship. The first nine titles sold fifteen thousand copies in 1936 alone, the booklet on Albert Schweitzer outselling the rest. Additions to the series were advertised in *Der Quäker* every month until March 1942.[38]

While reports indicate that care was taken not to arouse the ire of the Gestapo, which was known to inspect the displays of Quaker publishing, contents certainly expressed sentiments diametrically opposed to authoritarian government and chauvinism. For instance, a pamphlet on the Black Forest–genre painter Hans Thoma (1839–1924) put him on record as the advocate of a German civilization based on fidelity, honesty, and kindliness, to which Nazis professed adherence. At the same time Thoma is quoted as believing "that God never demands that we swear an oath in his name, while it is well known that the devil has often required it." In 1935 another writing spoke of Beethoven's disillusionment with Napoleon, who "will trample all human rights and only serve his ambition," clearly a judgment of a different tyrant. Martin Luther (1483–1546), whose imprecations against Jews endeared him to Nazi propagandists, was also quoted with relative safety as an opponent of tyranny: "The more rigidly the rulers of this world command us by their laws, thus it must and will be, the less we progress." A popular nineteenth-century German writer, Wilhelm Busch (1832–1908), the author and illustrator of popular ballads, including the children's epic *Max and Moritz* (known to every German child before and after 1933), emerges in a pamphlet dedicated to his "less well-known works" as the designer of this authoritarian portrait: "His opinion is the right one! When he speaks you must be silent, lest he proclaim you wicked or even stupid. Such hooligans *[Strolche]*, alas, are not a rare phenomenon."

Other publications in the series concentrated on more controversial individuals. Albert Schweitzer (1875–1965) was quoted as extolling the commandment "Thou shalt not kill": "Next to it everything else pales." And the novelist

Wilhelm Raabe (1831–1910), already an object of official suspicion in his own time, asked: "Was there ever a human being entitled to condemn another to lose his life?" Two pamphlets from the "English patrimony" quoted the assertions of David Livingstone (1813–1873), "that it pains the Father of us all when his children are being . . . killed," and the Quaker Elizabeth Fry (1780–1845), who considered it an honor "to stand on the side of the oppressed."

A similar treasury of humanitarian sentiments was provided by a German Quaker hymnal, brought out by the Quaker publishing company in 1935. Much of its content was taken from traditional hymn books of German Protestantism. They included songs by Paul Gerhardt (1607–1676), who demanded that "God should extirpate all that teach us wrong," and Karl Heinrich Progatzky (1690–1774), pleading that God "take his people out of prison and come down to help make us free." It also included contributions by Philip Spitta (1801–1859), whose God did not distinguish men according to "boundaries, power and blood" but knew only one "holy people that does his will." The Quaker hymn book closed with the old Lutheran hymn "Sleepers Awake," including the exhortation "little band, show thy strength," peculiarly appropriate for German Friends.[39]

Scattered and scarce though they are, some records also indicate that local Quaker groups courageously fought their own battles. We know most about the Berlin group, whose clerk in 1933, Paula Hans, was confirmed in this position, her Jewish descendance notwithstanding. The group's Sunday meetings regularly gathered some forty Friends, while as many as seventy attended on weekday nights. Among its most active members was Emil Fuchs, who started a study group on the Old Testament, as well as Gerhard and Olga Halle. Many members went to risky lengths to assist the endangered, whether Socialists or non-Aryans. As Jews were increasingly excluded from public places, they were invited to Friends' homes and gatherings. In 1934 the Berlin group also began sending books to inmates of the concentration camp at Lichtenburg, after assuring authorities that none of the volumes would contain written messages of any kind. This pledge required that every page of every volume be examined before mailing.

Berlin Friends also organized in 1935 a youth group, serving a twofold purpose: first, to provide a "spiritual home" for the children of Friends who suffered isolation and ostracism as a result of their parents' convictions, and second, to afford peer association for youngsters outside their community who were becoming similarly isolated for political and racial reasons. At the time of maximum membership the group included thirteen children of Social Democrats, twenty-five "racially persecuted"—ranging from Orthodox Jews to offspring of mixed marriages—and only eight Quaker children. Their activities consisted of relief work among Berlin's poor, trips into the surroundings of the capital, joint reading of books that were "lights in the darkness," and an introduction to the frugality of Quaker life. Members neither drank nor smoked and were held to a code of self-discipline, mandating tidiness, cleanliness, punctuality, and prudence. Above all they shared the satisfaction that the company of like-minded peers provided, and together they achieved intermittent escape from their dismal present.[40]

The Gestapo continually scrutinized these activities of Berlin Friends. They noted the preponderance of "illegals" among the membership, observed with disapproval Quaker ties to the Fellowship of Reconciliation, and suspected the group of being the center of a network of a political conspiracy that extended all over Germany and even beyond, including the exiled Social Democratic Party (SPD) in Prague. The fact that these claims resulted in nothing more than periodic interrogations, notably of members of the Halle family, indicates, however, that they were taken *cum grano salis* at higher levels of the Nazi hierarchy.[41]

Teas for Jewish women were held in Nuremberg. Anxiety was a constant Quaker companion in the city where the annual party congress convened. But this did not keep Mary Friedrich from paying demonstrative visits to Jewish stores on April 1, 1933, and from joining the British Friend Elsie Fox Howard on a call on Ernst Röhm, chief of staff of the storm troopers, early in June 1933. But their plea for leniency toward real and imaginary foes of Nazism encountered no sympathy. Röhm was an adamant supporter of the elimination of Jews from public life and expressed the conviction, furthermore, that all political parties had in some way betrayed the fatherland and "could no longer be allowed to endanger its safety." Much of the steam went out of the Nuremberg group, of course, when the Friedrichs moved the operation of the Quaker publishing house, and themselves, to Bad Pyrmont in the early summer of 1934.[42]

In Guben a small group of Friends was headed by Gerhard Ockel (1894–1975), a pediatrician who not only pursued a general practice but also founded a Montessori kindergarten and wrote a number of books on marital problems. In 1934 the group spent two hundred marks to purchase an abandoned railway car where they could assemble to worship. Ockel, like his coreligionists, was greatly troubled by the implications of the Jewish boycott since his congregation comprised a number of Jewish members.[43]

Other groups in Cologne, Königsberg, and Breslau appear to have left no records. The same applies to the Frankfurt meeting that included Rudolf Schlosser and Alfons Paquet. Despite Hans Albrecht's presence, the Hamburg chapter never seems to have been large or active, as is indicated by the fact that the local police seem to have been interested only in Albrecht's activities as clerk of the German Yearly Meeting. In Dresden, Elisabeth Rotten sought, without apparent success, to catalyze the soon-to-be-outlawed Fellowship of Reconciliation to protest the Jewish boycott of April 1 and the government's practice of labeling all reports on violations of civil rights as "atrocity propaganda."[44] In a word, Quakers continued to profess their beliefs in an isolation that was becoming more difficult to endure after Hitler's advent to power. That such activism could, however, be effective is demonstrated by the example of Margarethe Lachmund. Her husband, Hans, a combat veteran wounded in World War I, who had become a judge in Schwerin (Mecklenburg), had as early as 1926 joined a group of young members of the German Democratic Party, "indignant over the weak and timid leadership of democratic parties." Not only did he join the Social Democrats in 1931 but he also became an active member of the local Masonic lodge (the head of which committed suicide in 1933) and the German Peace Society. Surprisingly, Hans Lachmund survived this variety of mistrusted affiliations, largely as a result of the courageous acts of his Quaker wife. Initially, he was suspended from his office and accused of embezzling funds of the Peace Society. While he defended himself against these charges, his wife, Margarethe, welcomed to her home members of a dissolved socialist youth group, with whom she read the German classics so as to help these teenagers to gather their wits and keep from committing "acts of political folly." During one such meeting, SS surrounded the house and took the participants to the local police station. After this intrusion, Margarethe took the bull by the horns and called on the deputy chief of the party in Mecklenburg, Gerd von Körber. That dignitary questioned her about her many socialist and foreign contacts while, at the same time, identifying himself with the anticapitalist wing of the party. In a second meeting she explained that she and her family would have to emigrate now that her husband had lost his livelihood, expressing also the hope that they might still be allowed to visit her mother and mother-in-law who intended to stay in Germany. Körber's response surprised her: "To be honest with you," he reportedly said, "I do not like it that we are left in this country [only] with people who are afraid." He professed to be weary of the sudden influx of Nazi supporters, who denied their past, and he appeared to be impressed by the Quaker woman's forthrightness. A few months later Körber had Hans reinstated, albeit in a smaller jurisdiction, and confided to him: "I know that people like you and your wife will not be converted in a day, but since I believe in National Socialism, I hope that one day our deeds will convince you."[45]

By and large, German Quakers did not allow the German revolution of 1933 to affect their beliefs in the peaceful resolution of conflict or in the equality of all human beings in the sight of God. What this meant to persecuted individuals who came into contact with them was expressed in a letter that a German of Jewish descent, Julius Ursell, who belonged to no church, addressed to the German Yearly Meeting in 1935: "Are you surprised [to hear] that a businessman looks forward, like a little child, to your gatherings and the Yearly Meeting? Worn out by psychological pinpricks and economic uncertainties, it was a respite and uplift to submit to the powerful force the meeting of worship among dear friends provided."[46] What remains unexplained, however, is the uncharacteristic leniency of Nazi authorities in their dealings with the Society as a whole, and on occasion with individual members, at a time when they often dealt harshly with religious groups that were far more pliable. Was Quaker humanitarianism contagious, or was tolerance driven by considerations of self-interest? One explanation may have been that some Gestapo officials had themselves benefited from the child feeding of the 1920s, a fact that would continue to surface in a variety of encounters throughout the Nazi era. Another may have been that while peace advocacy among Germans clashed with government policy, similar efforts among potential enemies were often seen in a different light. An editorial comment in the *Frankfurter Zeitung* of August 29, 1933, pointed in that direction when the writer singled out Quakers as the only sincere advocates of Anglo-German understanding.[47] No less an authority than J. Roger Carter, the last Berlin representative before World War II at the Berlin Center, speculated whether it was recognition of past services, a desire to avoid bad publicity abroad, or because Quakers were so few in number. However, he, too, reached no firm conclusion.[48]

THE BERLIN CENTER, 1933–1935

During the third phase of the Berlin Center's history, beginning in 1933, the tripartite Anglo-German-American consortium reached out to individuals and groups whom the government had ostracized either for political or for racial reasons. This implied disapproval of such policies, an attitude that strained the credibility of Quaker insistence that they had nothing to do with politics. This contradiction, coupled with the police's awareness of it, placed the Quaker presence in Berlin in constant jeopardy. One Gestapo agent expressed it perfectly, at least from the Nazi point of view, in one of his reports: "The Quaker sect is the only foreign organization which does illegal work in Germany in a legal manner."[49]

Operations in Berlin at this time, at cross-purposes with Nazism, might therefore expect to be closed at any moment, the foreign staff expelled in short order, while the center's German workers might disappear into the nearest concentration camp. But until the ax fell, it seemed to be tacitly agreed that everybody stay at their post and lend a hand wherever and whenever they were needed. During the initial years of Nazi ascendancy, the Berlin Center was the only place where "the countless men and women who are now misfits . . . in Germany" could receive aid and advice openly. Friends themselves credited this achievement to their reputation "for honest dealing," not so much above politics as "above political intrigue," and to the record of their friendship for the German people.[50]

Naturally, the center required more than governmental tolerance to stay open. Its operating funds came from Britain and the United States, and that dependence added another element of uncertainty. In 1933 both countries were as deeply gripped by the vise of economic depression as Germany. This reduced charitable contributions destined to aid foreigners; it also limited the extent to which democratic governments could interest themselves in the assaults on liberty outside their borders and provide victims with opportunities to escape.

The resulting hesitant and piecemeal fashion in which Washington and London responded to the suffering inflicted by National Socialism has been sharply criticized by historians, particularly in the United States. Since this criticism has been expressed in work resting on careful research, and demonstrating respect for facts, it has carried weight with the reading public. Few have examined the underlying assumptions of such censorious approaches, which seem to be that the opening of the first concentration camp, or the casting of the first stone through a Jewish shop window, obligated other, freer, nations to come to the rescue of the victims. Yet one must remember that Germany was governed by authorities who satisfied international criteria of legitimacy and with whom both Britain and the United States were at peace. At the outset at least, when the "misfits" of Nazi Germany were still German citizens, the British government, for instance, was restrained by the perfectly proper consideration that gestures on behalf of these outcasts was an "unfriendly act." Britain also hesitated to support a League of Nations mandate for refugees on the practical grounds that such a concession might empower an international organization to decide how many Jews Britain must admit to strife-torn Palestine.[51] In the United States, Europe was a week's sea voyage away. The country did not feel the German upheaval with the same intensity as Germany's European neighbors. Under existing immigration laws German and Austrian quotas, totaling about twenty-eight thousand, had remained unfilled for years, leaving room for the admission of many thousands of qualified immigrants. At the same time elements of American society that had carried Roosevelt into the White House, notably labor unions, had their own urgent reasons for opposing any increase in immigration.[52] The fact that persons of Jewish descent constituted the majority of people fleeing from Germany undoubtedly added to British and American reservations, but here one must go a step farther and remember that the concern of Jewish communities in both countries for their German coreligionists was likewise tempered by fears of the contagion of Nazi Judeo-phobia, especially if abetted by an unprecedented influx of Jewish foreigners. It is impossible to judge whether a lowering of barriers to immigration would indeed have increased anti-Semitism. The fact remains that no persecution of Jews occurred in either the United States or

Britain. Eventually even the admission of seventy thousand persons of Jewish descent to Great Britain between 1933 and 1939 gave no significant boost to British fascism nor did the well-known anti-Jewish dispositions of a Henry Ford turn it into a major organized political force in the United States.[53]

Whatever the limitations and shortcomings of British and American responses may have been, they were formulated by democratic governments, whose constituencies pressed them to admit fewer, rather than more, immigrants. Helping the persecuted of Germany in any form, furthermore, required the preservation of traditional diplomatic contacts. The closing of American consulates in Germany would have been a far greater disaster for potential refugees than were the restrictive policies their officials pursued. Finally, Gilbert MacMaster's observation that "Germany was not Russia" indicates all too clearly that contemporaries did not, and could not, view the Nazi regime in the light in which we see it today. Few foresaw in 1933 that denying a German emigrant access to any country could become a death sentence. Critical judgments, formulated half a century later, merely reflect the omniscience that accumulates with the passage of time and should be tempered accordingly. Neither Britain nor the United States had lapsed into apathy, as the title of one such study of American immigration policy would have it. Their governments were anything but apathetic to the sufferings that these troubled times visited on countless populations. But charity began at home, then as now.[54]

The relief effort, therefore, originated among a variety of nongovernmental bodies, many of them religious, whose tenets imposed on their members a moral duty to help. The most massive effort was launched by the Jewish Refugee Committee and the Central British Fund for German Jewry, founded in March 1933, after the facilities of the Jews' Temporary Shelter in Britain could no longer cope with the tide of newcomers. Speakers for Britain's Jewish community guaranteed that they "would bear all expenses in respect of a temporary or permanent sanctuary for refugees, *so that they would never become a charge on the public purse.*" British Jews sustained that burden until after the outbreak of war, thereby giving rise to the preoccupation of other aid agencies with refugees, both Jewish and Gentile, who were not members of the Jewish religious community and who were primarily the objects of political persecution. In that context, the indifference of international Christianity to the German refugee problem paralleled that of German Christians. Here Quakers clearly deviated from a depressing norm. In France it was the *Foyer d'entr'aide aux émigrés allemands,* headed by a French Quaker, Germaine Mellon, and financed with British Quaker monies; in Amsterdam a more modest hospitality center was established by Dutch Friends;[55] in Britain, Friends' House led the way, and the early pleas for Christian charity by George Bell, the bishop of Chichester, long remained a solo performance among Anglicans. As Bishop Bell himself testified: "Of the Christian bodies, the Friends alone have made a continuous and sustained effort in England, France, and other countries."[56]

British Quakers also went to work far more energetically than did their American counterparts. Efforts in London went into high gear as early as March 1933, only days after the passage of the Enabling Law when an "emergency gathering of Friends on the situation in Germany" decided to instruct the British representative at the Berlin Center, Corder Catchpool, "that he should get what help was necessary to carry on the work that he is doing and *that Friends at home would make themselves responsible for expenses involved in meeting this emergency situation.*"[57] This decision was quickly implemented. A Joint Committee on the German Situation, including Joan Fry and Carl Heath, met on April 17, 1933, supplanted by a more permanent German Emergency Committee, whose secretary was Bertha Bracey, a veteran of German relief work in the 1920s. The committee met weekly in 1933 and biweekly thereafter. The secretary organized the work in the London office and traveled the length and breadth of the country mobilizing local meetings to welcome refugees to Quaker homes and to arrange free places for refugee children in Friends' boarding schools. Gradually, a number of projects crystallized, including the dispatch of an independently functioning operative who was to take funds to Germany for the families of breadwinners who had been imprisoned. In October 1933, Wilhelm Hughes was sent to Germany on the first of several such trips, with instructions "to work independently of the Berlin Secretariat and German Yearly Meeting, being responsible only to British Friends through this Committee." At the same time, Friends were sent to Paris to help finance shelters for refugees there.[58] By the end of November, Hughes returned to report on these activities and was speedily sent back, while Helen Dixon left England on November 24 to open on German soil a rest home "to distressed Germans."[59]

As soon as the German Emergency Committee was organized, donations came in and continued to accumulate at a pace that did not slacken with the passage of time, rising to seven thousand pounds in both 1934 and 1935. Not all of it went abroad. A special-case committee, for instance, financed the emigration of individual German families who had found temporary asylum in Britain and France. Efforts were increasingly focused on Christian non-Aryans and political opponents of the regime.[60] Bertha Bracey suffered a physical collapse from overwork in 1935, forcing her to take several months' leave, but a growing staff kept her office open and continued her work with undiminished energy and efficiency.[61]

The lagging pace of American commitment did, however, darken the prospects for continued involvement at this vigorous level. The 1934 budget of the Berlin Center indicated that while both groups shared equally in office expenses, 62.5 percent of its total finances came from London and only 37.5 percent from

Philadelphia. Moreover, American Friends announced at the beginning of 1935 that their contribution to "Germany work" would have to be reduced by 25 percent, to three thousand dollars.[62] No actual reductions seem to have been made, but even their discussion, as well as the budget proportions themselves, shed additional light on apparent differences in outlook between the two major centers of Quaker life and inspiration.

One standard monograph has, therefore, concluded: "[W]hile the Quakers in Europe, especially the British Friends, organized and maintained refugee shelters and relief work in Berlin, Paris, Vienna and Prague, the American Quakers were unenthusiastic. Only after 1938 did the American Friends Service Committee become a major refugee organization in America."[63] Without going into a word-for-word analysis of this statement, except to note that the Vienna office, for instance, was headed by Emma Cadbury, an American Quaker, we must consider the geographic radius of American Friends' benefactions before depreciating the AFSC's relatively modest involvement in Germany. Such a review must include American Friends' interracial work, also involving Japanese student exchanges, as well as the work of the Interracial Peace Committee. Added to that was an increasingly hard-pressed Home Service Section that in 1933 sent relief to hard-hit areas in Kentucky, West Virginia, and Pennsylvania. The AFSC's coal committee initiated child feedings in all depressed areas, financed to a significant degree by funds remaining in the coffers of Herbert Hoover's American Relief Administration and administered by a staff of fifty-five volunteers. American Friends displayed anything but apathy in the face of contemporary suffering.[64] In light of these needs so close to home, it may be regrettable, but understandable, that the AFSC saw at first no urgent need for a "massive relief program" for victims of National Socialism, taking comfort instead from the fact that "the main sufferers, the Communists, Socialists, and Jews, seemed then to have strong organizations of their own to watch over the welfare of their members."[65]

This view may have been reinforced by a report from the AFSC's man in Berlin, Richard Cary, in July 1933. Regretting that Hitler and Mussolini lacked Roosevelt's ability "to engage in radical action without suppressing his opponents," this observer found treatment of Jews at this point to be similar to "the treatment of German civilians in the United States and England during the war." He also believed that "the status of Jews will improve slowly," while conceding that "they will never obtain justice, just as Germans who suffered in 1914–1918 have never obtained justice." In the same breath Cary warned that Hertha Kraus, a major Quaker source of information about conditions in Germany, "has a streak of intolerance which warps her judgment of the Nazi movement." Jews, furthermore, shared these blind spots and "are helping perpetuate the hostility from which they suffer." Nazis, he had found, were a diverse lot "and deserve as much sympathy as the rest." Friends must continue their traditional friendliness to Germany.[66]

By the time this assessment reached Philadelphia, the AFSC had, however, asked Gilbert MacMaster to return to Berlin as a token of concern, if nothing more. MacMaster shortly thereafter became the full-time American representative, after the overworked Richard Cary suffered a heart attack from which he died on October 16, 1933, at the age of forty-seven.[67] In retrospect, it is beyond question that American Friends always intended to participate in the aid effort in behalf of Germany's victims. The rate and tempo of their involvement simply increased at a slower and more hesitant pace. In February 1934 they appointed a committee to keep abreast of the German troubles, and AFSC secretary Clarence Pickett represented them on the American Christian Committee for German Refugees. In July, Elizabeth Shipley came to Europe to study the German refugee situation. After her return, Pickett's right-hand assistant at the office, Grace E. Rhoads, hoped "something more concrete" might "be worked out as a project of the German Committee here."[68] The distant perspective, however, restricted involvement primarily to the religious sphere. "Giving comfort and a little relief" and "travelling among Friends and others" in search of "closer spiritual fellowship" were initially considered sufficient. The American side clearly still believed that the time to judge the German revolution had not yet come and that sending American businessmen to Germany to build bridges of common interest, and to welcome German exchange students to American universities, would constitute important contributions.[69]

Only in 1935 does the record in Philadelphia reveal a more practical turn. Pickett now urged American Friends to sign affidavits of support for German refugees "who are considered particularly likely to make good in this country." The secretary of the AFSC was on friendly terms with Eleanor Roosevelt, who supported some Friends' programs in West Virginia. During several visits to Hyde Park he drew the president's attention to Quaker efforts in behalf of refugees, both in Britain and in the United States. In Philadelphia the 1934–1935 foreign-service budget of $17,635 was actually overspent, and efforts were set in motion to increase the following year's appropriation by $5,000. American Quakers were increasingly troubled to see how much more their British counterparts were contributing to German relief. In November 1934, Pickett expressed to Bertha Bracey "the embarrassment which we feel over this German refugee situation. You have done far more than we." He explained that American Friends "have not felt the pressure of the problem, due largely . . . to the urgency of the situation here." His discomfort emerged even more starkly in a letter to Gilbert MacMaster. He had no doubt that his side could do more "if we really were under the weight of the world's suffering as we ought to be." This sense of inadequacy was deepened by a visit from Norman Bentwich, who led

Jewish fund-raising efforts in Britain and who expressed deep disappointment over the indifference of "the different Christian bodies" to the sufferings inflicted by National Socialism.[70]

Differences of outlook and commitment at the two main sources of support may have reduced the funds of the Berlin Center, but they created no uncertainty about the center's mission. The work continued to be done by dedicated men and women, performing what they considered to be their Christian duty. Some of them survive only as names, while others have left a more substantial record.

In 1933 the American representative, it will be recalled, was the correspondent of the *Baltimore Sun*, Richard L. Cary, who had resided in the German capital since 1930. We have already quoted his reactions to the Nazi revolution, a mixture of hope and revulsion that gripped many decent people who were forced to witness it. As a journalist Cary saw the Nazi rise to power in the context of an age of revolution, initiated by violent excess but then gradually supplanted by an era of constructive progress. His Quaker beliefs in the goodness of man, combined with his sect's compassion for Germany's harsh fate after 1918, led Cary to hope that all would turn out for the best, as revolutions in "civilized countries" generally did. Such reflections nevertheless drove Cary into a frenzy of activity. He looked after individual families who had been dispossessed, tried to gain access to jails and prison camps, and maintained contact with Jews, liberals, and Nazis in a heroic attempt to nourish a spirit of conciliation in all quarters. He also served on the board of the local American Chamber of Commerce, while his wife, Mary, was president of the American Women's Club. Ravaged by overwork, he died suddenly, on October 16, 1933, and was interred in the Quaker cemetery at Bad Pyrmont. German Friends endowed a Richard Cary Lecture, which was delivered during the Yearly Meeting. His wife carried on his work in Berlin for another year before returning to the United States.[71]

Cary's place was taken by Gilbert MacMaster, who had a capacity for getting on with people of all stripes. One of his valuable contacts was Ernst Hanfstaengl, Harvard alumnus and son of a Munich art publisher, who had become part of Hitler's bohemian entourage in the 1920s. Such connections helped MacMaster's efforts to effect the release of some political prisoners, but his success even on that score declined as the Nazis became more firmly entrenched. The record also indicates that MacMaster had difficulty accepting what he considered to be the disproportionate reemphasis on material, as opposed to spiritual, charity.[72]

Hans Albrecht represented German Friends at the Berlin Center throughout the Nazi years, and much of the work in the office was done for a while by Gerhard Halle, who had lost his regular job; after he found work again, it was assumed by his courageous and energetic spouse, Olga. A student club at the center, not to be confused with the Berlin meeting's youth group, was in the hands of Rose Vickery-Neuse (1902–1993), another British veteran of the *Kinderspeisung*, who had stayed in Germany and married a German teacher of classical languages, Kurt Neuse. Theirs had been the first Quaker marriage to be celebrated in Berlin, but now the husband had been suspended from his job and was waiting to learn whether he would receive another appointment. Rose found her work more worthwhile than she had anticipated. She claimed that the lectures and discussions at her club, open to any young person wishing to attend, demonstrated that even at this point in history strangers could meet and discuss differences "without . . . being too vague" or "stirring up dissension."[73] When she and her husband left Germany in the spring of 1934, her work was first taken over by Mary Cary, then by Brian Price-Heywood, a young British Friend "Esperantist, vegetarian," and "a keen member of the League of Nations Union" with "good German" language skills and a German mother, who was, alas, soon considered to be not "up to the mark."[74] At this point the student club seems to have quietly expired.

The most visible and active figure in the Berlin Center for the first years of the Nazi era was Corder Catchpool. Although he, too, had come to the German capital two years before Hitler's rise to power, his own political involvement in the British peace movement during the First World War prepared him to make an effortless transition from spiritual messenger to activist defender of a new generation of victims. Pursuit of his mission brought him, however, new trials. Humble as well as fervent, Catchpool constantly reexamined his performance and became a center of controversy both inside and outside the Quaker community.

Catchpool was an active member of the Quaker group in Berlin, and both he and his wife were members of the German Yearly Meeting, where they "took care not to influence either group," being both "reserved and tactful."[75] He had always been particularly outspoken in his condemnation of the peace of Versailles. To his abiding sorrow Allied policy had punished a democratic Germany that, in his opinion, deserved and needed every conceivable political and economic encouragement. His report of the events of January 30, 1933, however, attempted to stick to observable facts, allowing readers to draw their own conclusions. He described the multitudes gathering for the torchlight parade, the joy of the news vendor from whom he bought his daily copy of Josef Goebbels's *Angriff* (attack). (Catchpool could be counted on to keep tabs on what the Nazis were thinking.) Eventually, he went home where he could follow the events of the rest of the evening at his radio, later relating how "Berlin has no ear for dance music on *the* night. All Germany wants to take in is this mighty demonstration. The [ether] waves carry the news of the uprising of the German nation throughout the world, at least, so said the announcer."

The next morning the world "awaited events," and Catchpool wondered what had become of two hundred thousand demonstrators in the center of the capital who, two days earlier, had been "shouting *Freiheit* and [singing] the Internationale" as well as "the considerable middle section [of the population] which looks on more quietly and shakes its head in doubt and misgiving at one extreme and the other." Catchpool recalled the 1920 Kapp putsch, aborted by massive protest strikes. In a postscript, added three days later, he hinted that the new seizure of power by the right would this time not be contested. Both Socialist and Communist newspaper offices had been closed, and another Socialist demonstration had been forbidden by the police.[76]

In the weeks that followed, Catchpool counseled the many frightened individuals who visited the center and called for additional staff to "help political victims and visit German Friends." He also collected information about cases of persecution, "which he could bring out of the country by an absolutely safe route," presumably with the help of the British embassy.[77]

The day after the anti-Jewish boycott of April 1, 1933, the Berlin Center office was inundated with letters describing what had happened in a variety of German venues and begging Quakers to exercise a moderating influence wherever they could. Catchpool forwarded much of this mail, often through foreign visitors who were returning to Britain or the United States. But before deciding what else to do, Catchpool consulted the first secretary at the British embassy, Ivone Kirkpatrick, who asked him to return the following day, after Kirkpatrick had discussed events with the ambassador. But the next morning, April 3, the Catchpools' daily matutinal reading of Scriptures was interrupted by the arrival of no less than five Gestapo plainclothesmen. The intruders took husband and wife to separate rooms and grilled them for five hours. The husband was then taken to Gestapo headquarters. As his wife straightened up the chaos of scattered books and papers in Corder's study, she found, to her surprise, the document that explained the reason for this interruption of their devotional routine. It contained the text of the denunciation of the Catchpools by a neighbor who belonged to the SS. He claimed to have learned from an acquaintance of the Catchpools' charwoman that Corder was a Communist, a Quaker leader, and a pacifist; that he frequently entertained visiting foreigners; and that he kept on his desk reports of the mistreatment of opponents of the government. Gwen Catchpool realized what terrible consequences could ensue from such charges and was, therefore, greatly relieved when her husband returned late in the evening of April 4. He was on a kind of probation, having promised not to leave the country or destroy his papers. Meanwhile, questions about his arrest had been raised in the House of Commons, and the British embassy had protested his arbitrary confinement. To what extent these reactions contributed to a subsequent decision by the German government to avoid the arrest of foreigners in the future is a question this writer is unable to answer.[78]

As he was recovering from the shock of this encounter, Catchpool reappraised his role and considered his future conduct. He "realized that he had been avoiding contact with Nazi circles, out of dislike for their doctrines and actions" and thus failed in his duty as an ambassador of goodwill. He resolved, therefore, to make a greater effort "to understand how good men and women came to join the movement, to make real friendships among them, looking for something good as well as seeing what was bad."[79] From that moment on Corder set as his goal the prevention of progressive German isolation that could lead only to war, "whereas contact with democratic countries might eventually alter the nature of the regime, and put an end to its brutalities."[80]

But such resolutions did not restore Catchpool's peace of mind. His arrest caused him sleepless nights for months to come. Successive bouts with measles among his children undoubtedly added to the strain of everyday existence. In June the German police returned Catchpool's passport, enabling him to visit London and seek further emotional relief by putting on paper his "Reflections upon our Attitude towards the National-Socialist Revolution in Germany." He speculated that the return of his passport revealed that Nazi authorities saw in him "a man of goodwill," dedicated to the promotion of "mutual understanding between the English and German peoples," an attitude he assumed to be "a more important qualification [to them] than subscription to Nazi doctrines." As a result he was determined to find ways of rescuing in Germany values now being "trampled underfoot and lost." "In view of our own heavy responsibility for much that has come about," he considered "unmitigated indignation" a useless response to the German revolution.

Catchpool's "Reflections" represented another example of Quaker determination to assume responsibility, not for what they had done but for what they had failed to prevent. He recalled, furthermore, that racism was alive and well in Great Britain and throughout its empire. He restated the conviction that the Treaty of Versailles "and its consequences" rendered miraculous the fact that Germany's revolution had "not come earlier." He urged his countrymen to ponder what new catastrophes might follow an overthrow of the Hitler government. Catchpool thought that he knew the Germans and insisted that they and their leaders sought peace as earnestly as did his own nation.

What then was to be done? German political grievances had to be redressed through the League of Nations. "We must spike Hitler's heavy guns before they are forged." Allies must cooperate with Germany "in disarmament and the removal of injustice." Even if such a policy should in the end fail to prevent conflict, "we shall at least then be in a state of mind which can apply the full pacifist attitude of meeting enemies with love."[81]

Catchpool's new conception of his mission may have put his mental and moral house in order, but it elicited vigorous disapproval at Friends House in London. Bertha Bracey was concerned that this new "pro-Nazi" stance might taint Quakers as a whole.[82] Carl Heath, the father of the Quaker centers, who had refused to attend the German Yearly Meeting in 1933 in protest against the constraints of free expression imposed by the Hitler regime, was even more outspoken. After receiving Catchpool's report he accused him of having accepted the suppression of freedom. He charged his emissary in Berlin with having abandoned his concern for "the multitude of Germans who are not Nazis." The cause of foreign hostility to Nazism, in Heath's opinion, was not prejudice but derived from concrete causes: Germany's new laws, the treatment of Jews and political opponents—including pacifists—and the existence of concentration camps. He, therefore, did not want Catchpool's latest insights to be published. The world needed no Quaker apology on behalf of Hitler. The German Emergency Committee agreed.[83] A more public attack followed when the Berlin correspondent of the *Manchester Guardian*, Robert Dell, claimed that Catchpool "was converted to Nazism, after being arrested and imprisoned [*sic*] by the Nazis."[84]

Such criticism tested the British Quaker: it did not shake his convictions. Catchpool was certain that his modus operandi might soften the rigors of Nazi rule and facilitate necessary access to German officials. At the same time, the hostility that greeted his conciliatory approach also prompted him to do his work with a minimum of consultation with other Friends. Before long that practice produced complaints that "the conduct of the Center is far from satisfactory." Pickett urged that the Berlin operation be placed on a more businesslike basis and become more of a focal point, "instead of simply [providing] quarters . . . as bases for various groups."[85] Rufus Jones, who had arrived in Berlin in November 1934 and found both Catchpool and MacMaster away at the same time, likewise concluded in regard to both men that "puttering along won't do, especially by two men who don't make a team."[86] It was Carl Heath who reversed himself at this point and tried to pacify the disgruntled. He reminded complainers that Catchpool's accessibility was treasured by German Friends and pleaded with his American counterpart to let him "complete his work before coming away." His moderation prevailed in this instance, in part, no doubt, because it was easier to criticize center incumbents than replace them. Rufus Jones contributed little to such a search, other than to specify that Catchpool's replacement should be an "important person."[87]

The difficulties of running the center under these circumstances were, of course, compounded by the fact that the German member of the governing triumvirate, Hans Albrecht, lived in Hamburg and was only intermittently available for consultation. That fact alone relegated to the world of dreams an increased German presence at the center. Prior to Catchpool's arrest it had already been recognized that German Friends were in far greater danger than their foreign colleagues. It was highlighted by Albrecht's second encounter with the Hamburg Gestapo in January 1934. This time the authorities inquired into his connection with Quaker relief for political prisoners, finally instructing him that such work would be permitted only if undertaken on a person-to-person basis, rather than as a group activity. It therefore became advisable to minimize all actions that identified the Yearly Meeting with the work of the Berlin Center. In fact, at one point Gilbert MacMaster proposed that Berlin Quakers rent separate quarters. Lack of funds doomed that idea, and a cautious and uneasy cohabitation continued.[88]

Although personal cohesion remained for the time being beyond the grasp of the three center luminaries, and complaints continued that the British member did not seem to work well with either MacMaster or Albrecht, Catchpool never let up in his efforts to help as well as conciliate.[89] He negotiated a substantial reduction of the center's rent with the building's landlord, the state government of Prussia, and continued to arrange German student exchanges.[90] When other housekeeping tasks accumulated at his desk, due to MacMaster's frequent absence, Catchpool's wife, Gwen, while raising four children, was forced to help out. Olga Halle also assumed a larger workload, and money was set aside to pay for extra help in both households. Catchpool complained about the loss of his typewriter, which the Gestapo had not returned after the search of his home. The finances of the center were forever disrupted by the unpredictable fluctuations of the rate of exchange of a German currency no longer freely circulating. "I have during the last four weeks sometimes felt [that my burden has almost become] more than I could stand," he confessed to Bertha Bracey in February 1934, adding that he would feel less depressed if he could do more for the countless petitioners crowding his office.[91]

In jottings set down during a train ride to Bad Pyrmont in August of the same year, Catchpool has left us a vivid picture of "a day at the office." "An old Jewish actor turns up," who had been told to write but feels that after six months' waiting he is entitled to an interview. A poor, atheist widow, whose son is in a concentration camp, comes to pick up a translating chore for *Der Quäker*. By the way of a change of pace, a functionary of the Nationalist Socialist Student Association ventilates concerns about his country's growing moral isolation. Another man, whose wife has disappeared, visits the center day after day to make sure that she had not miraculously reappeared on the premises. An unemployed teacher, father of three children, the last born while he was in a concentration camp, seeks any help he can get. The divorced wife of a concentration camp inmate needs funds for her child, which her incarcerated former husband can obviously no longer support, and a Jewish Irishwoman who had been teaching

English, faces destitution. Finally, the leader of a youth group wants contact with British Boy Scouts. He is the only member of this disheartening procession whose request Catchpool can satisfy. So goes 1 of 315 workdays in 1934.[92]

At the same time, Corder refused to change his personal policy of Nazi appeasement. Early in 1935, for instance, the German Foreign Office asked him to transmit an invitation to the British Legion, his country's veterans' organization, to visit their German counterparts. That proposal reached the desk of Anthony Eden, Britain's foreign secretary, who warned the British group not to allow themselves to become exploited by Nazi propaganda but raised no objections to such a trip. The Legion's royal patron, the Prince of Wales, expressed warm approval, earning a reproof from George V. The veterans came, and the itinerary of the first of several such expeditions included a meeting with Hitler and a visit to Dachau, followed by a "quiet family supper" at the home of Gestapo inspector Heinrich Himmler. Germany's premier policeman seems to have left a more favorable impression than the führer. The Legionnaires were impressed by his unassuming ways and, so the record claims, by his sense of humor.[93] To Catchpool this visit constituted another piece of bridge-building. In his opinion, propaganda could be made to work two ways. British veterans got to know Himmler as a charming family man, while German veterans learned that their British counterparts valued friendship with former enemies. Germans, he insisted once again, after living among them for many years, were "as decent, friendly, cultured, and reasonable as any other," and their present condition could be improved only with patience. Such an attitude, he assured his fellow conscientious objector Clifford Allen, did not call into question either his love of liberty or any of his other lifetime commitments.[94]

Clearly, neither the center, nor its sponsors, had a master plan for dealing with the Nazi seizure of power. Friends reacted willy-nilly to events and improvised from day to day. In that haphazard context, care first focused on political victims and their families and was channeled through three avenues: the center; William R. Hughes, who was not a Friend at the time but who distributed funds from London; and, finally, a rest home for persons released from prisons and concentration camps.[95] This first concern was shaped by the governmental crackdown on pacifists, not all of them Quakers, and nurtured a determination to continue work for peace no matter how difficult.[96] Yet, causes as such were quickly submerged by the need to comfort large numbers of individuals who crowded the center office, as well as the Catchpool home, which became not only an extension of the office but also a temporary hiding place, at least before the Gestapo raid on April 3, 1933. As of March 13 Corder and his wife harbored one student "and three children, whose father has had to flee abroad." News of arrested acquaintances began to accumulate. At this juncture Corder Catchpool was still groping for the formulation of "some positive, unprovocative pronouncement" in behalf of the growing multitude of outcasts. Gilbert MacMaster at the same time went forth to locate, and possibly free, arrestees—certainly one reason for his frequent absences from Berlin—and he has left us a fairly detailed account of his efforts. Without going through Catchpool's prolonged soul-searching, MacMaster also cultivated contact with Nazi officials, and the new revolutionary tone of "virile rudeness," affected by police and ministerial officials, failed to intimidate him. While he hoped that American and British Friends would put pressure on German diplomats, MacMaster concentrated on individual cases, requesting release, testifying in behalf of defendants, or accompanying intimidated relatives to trials. He hoped that this would induce his Nazi opposites to listen to what "decent people" had to say about some of their victims. His own predisposition, like Catchpool's, to see Germans as eminently civilized ("They do not want to be balkanized or Russianized by any government") imbued him with an optimism that fortified his resolve. Since relatives of prisoners were often afraid to come during visiting hours, he often became the only link between the incarcerated and the outside world.[97]

MacMaster's first success came with the release of retired Major General Paul von Schönaich (1866–1954), head of the Cavalry Section of the Prussian Ministry of War in 1918 and president of the German Peace Society from 1929 to 1933. His arrest had followed hard on the heels of the Nazi seizure of power. During a visit to the police official responsible for this prisoner, MacMaster was at first treated to a furious harangue about the pacifist general's share in spreading "atrocity tales." The American Friend countered that the aged officer had always defended Germany to foreigners and pleaded that he be released under dignified conditions. When MacMaster returned a few days later, he discovered that Schönaich had been discharged the day of his earlier visit, "and under conditions that I could honestly accept."[98]

The American pinch hitter at the center was no less solicitous to Emil Fuchs during his detention. Not only was Fuchs released in short order, but so was his daughter, who had languished in a prison in Kiel. Here MacMaster apprised her jailers of the father's Christian commitment, and the work of Quakers during Germany's darkest hours, and so achieved his humanitarian end. Two of MacMaster's clients escaped before his efforts could bear fruit. Emil Fuchs's oldest son, Gerhard, not yet in prison garb, simply walked away from a prison detail at Brandenburg penitentiary. The Social Democrat Gerhart Seger escaped from Oranienburg concentration camp where MacMaster had visited him and where he had been held for nine months without charge. The two Gestapo men, who informed the American Friend of his disappearance, actually assumed at the time that Seger had drowned himself in the nearby Havel River. They took the occasion to assure MacMaster that he was well thought of "upstairs." Seger subsequently published an account of his imprisonment, thus revealing how alive he was.[99]

Some of MacMaster's protégés required an even more prolonged effort. In January 1934 another old Social Democrat, the carpenter Georg Peter (1872–1944), who had represented Augsburg in the Reichstag from 1919 to 1932, had been taken to Dachau. The two men had become acquainted while MacMaster supervised child feeding in Bavaria, and upon hearing of the old friend's misfortune MacMaster went to Munich to see *Ministerialdirektor* Geiger in the Bavarian Ministry of the Interior, another acquaintance from those days. Geiger sent him to "Herr [Reinhard] Heydrich of the political police." Heydrich, in turn, provided a pass to Dachau, where the American visitor talked with Peter about the old days of their common effort, not only to lift the prisoner's spirits but also for the benefit of the SS officer attending their reunion. On MacMaster's return to Munich, Heydrich promised that Peter would be released shortly, adding that Nazis "would welcome the day when [the concentration camps] could be done away with." But a year later Peter was still being held in Dachau, and it took until January 1935 to get him out.[100] At this point MacMaster's optimism seems to have diminished. He realized that he could help only a very few individuals and began to have doubts about the usefulness of his efforts, reasoning that "one never knows whether the visit of a foreigner helps them or not."[101]

The truth was that these efforts sometimes worked and sometimes failed. Peter's much delayed release was not MacMaster's last success but was followed by the well-known case of the SPD mayor of Magdeburg, Ernst Reuter (1889–1953), later known to the world at large as the post–World War II mayor of West Berlin. Reuter had been taken to Lichtenburg concentration camp in August 1933 and released on January 7, 1934. But he continued to associate with a circle of party friends and was returned to Lichtenburg in June. This time he was charged with the daily cleaning of the camp cesspool. At this point the British Friend Elizabeth Fox Howard also went to work on his behalf. She mobilized Charles Roden Buxton, a Friend and Labour M.P. who had visited Berlin in the spring of 1933, talked to Catchpool (not long after the latter's arrest), and then made the rounds of the new potentates, "even Hitler." Buxton wrote German Ambassador Leopold von Hoesch on Reuter's behalf, and Hoesch, in turn, urged the German Foreign Office to respond to the request of a member of Parliament "whose friendship for Germany is beyond all question." The Wilhelmstrasse brought the case to Hermann Göring's attention. Meanwhile, Howard, unaware of this activity, went herself to Berlin and dragged Catchpool around to see Hitler's favorite pianist and Harvard graduate Ernst Hanfstaengl, then to the Ministry of Propaganda, and finally to the Gestapo. The upshot of it was that Reuter was let out and allowed to emigrate. But other objects of similar solicitations were less fortunate. The Communist Theodor Neubauer, Carlo Mierendorff (a Social

Democratic former member of the Reichstag from Hesse), as well as Schönaich's predecessor as president of the German Peace Society, Fritz Küster, had to wait until 1938 or 1939 for their releases. The lawyer Hans Litten, who had defended Communists in Nazi courts, was murdered at Dachau in 1938, despite Quaker and British Labour efforts on his behalf. Finally, MacMaster's tenacious efforts on behalf of another SPD Reichstag veteran, Ernst Heilmann, did not save him from a violent death at Buchenwald in 1940. Pleas to free Kurt Schumacher were likewise unsuccessful, but he survived to lead the SPD after 1945.[102]

It would appear, then, that by 1935 Quaker efforts on behalf of the politically persecuted had been reduced to a kind of traffic control, finding the proper place to lodge an appeal without providing much concrete assistance of their own.[103] To get a more accurate idea of Quaker persistence in the effort to mitigate suffering in Germany, one must consider another important constraint the situation imposed on them. It resulted from the fact that German Friends constituted part of the Berlin Center's management. Since they were far more vulnerable to Nazi retaliation than their foreign colleagues, Corder Catchpool's arrest notwithstanding, the center had to find ways of operating without endangering Hans Albrecht and the German Yearly Meeting. That did not preclude efforts on behalf of German Friends. Richard Cary traveled to Dresden, only weeks before his death, to effect Manfred Pollatz's release from prison, a success credited in large measure to Pollatz's "obvious sincerity and decency of character." Finding German Friends employment was another endeavor that offered the additional advantage of not consuming scarce foreign resources. Thus, Gilbert MacMaster found Gerhard Halle a position with the Quaker Oats Company, even after that company's German office had taken pains to disclaim any connection with the Society of Friends. Invitations to Woodbrooke became a means by which Hertha Kraus, Wilhelm Hubben, and a Catholic social worker from Cologne, Katherina Radke, were moved out of danger.[104]

Still, the effort to minimize overt German Quaker involvement could not be carried to the point where it might halt the entire relief effort. One way of staying a straight but increasingly narrow course was to send center funds to Corder Catchpool personally, so that they would not appear on center books and would not be credited to the center's bank account. At the same time, however, British Friends continued to insist that they had nothing to hide and were not breaking any law since their work was not driven by political motives. If it benefited political opponents of the regime, it was because they were the ones who were suffering. Despite the criticism to which Catchpool had been subjected, he was left free to do whatever his conscience dictated and was trusted to protect German Friends without jeopardizing the existence of the Berlin Center.[105] This regimen of improvisation did, however, not spare Hans Albrecht another Gestapo inquiry in 1935, nor did it save Catchpool from another interrogation at the Prinz Albrecht Strasse on April 21, 1935, where he again displayed the kind of fortitude that justified the confidence placed in his judgment and where his claim that he had never compromised Quaker principles in his dealings with the Nazi regime was again confirmed. He parried the accusation of empathy with "enemies of the state" and earlier Quaker indifference to the persecution of Nazis with the retort that Nazis had never sought Quaker assistance. With equal firmness he insisted that his office never sought to influence German citizens' attitudes toward Nazi legislation. Finally, he reminded his questioners that the Quaker presence in Germany had invariably been dedicated to the promotion of Anglo-German friendship.[106]

These statements may not have convinced Catchpool's interrogators, but the inquiries themselves remained without consequences. The German Yearly Meeting was not affected; the Berlin Center remained open; and William Hughes continued to commute between London and various German destinations, "responsible only to British Friends."[107]

In the autumn of 1934 the London office, furthermore, had written to Göring "that a wise and humane treatment of prisoners was a necessity for a Christian state" and coupled this contention with an appeal to close the concentration camps. Hughes was also charged with pressing this effort. The steps he took provide us with another interesting example of the Quaker modus operandi. While we know that his request for a meeting with this powerful official was politely declined, we can also document that his concern was discussed at the highest level of the Nazi hierarchy. Göring brought it to the attention of Himmler, who was at that time Göring's subordinate as "Inspector of concentration camps," who counseled that Quaker intentions must not be allowed to endanger Germany's welfare. Concentration camps, in Himmler's opinion, remained indispensable as the most effective tool against enemies of the state.[108]

Hughes, nevertheless, continued to maintain contact with Göring's staff. Before returning to London he wrote to the Prussian minister-president's personal secretary, Fräulein Grundtmann. He thanked her for trying to get him an appointment with her employer and concluded: "May I say, personally, how much I have appreciated the reception I have met with from *all sorts of people* in your country, how sincerely I wish for you all happiness and success in the future, and how anxious I am to help to remove the 'stumbling blocks' which are in some cases still keeping us apart."[109] It was obviously the continued expectation of Friends that their example would in time persuade Nazis to moderate their stance on a host of local and international issues.

Before Hughes returned to Germany early in 1935, Catchpool feared that "the police will want to see him." It appeared at first that he was unduly pessimistic. Hughes had in 1934 been allowed to visit the Lichtenburg concentration camp; in February 1935 he and Catchpool were also admitted to Dachau. They asked to see three Socialists on whose release they were working, with mixed success as we have seen, and to be allowed a look at punishment cells. Their wishes were granted, and all in all they found the camp to look better than they had anticipated. Hughes was quite aware that this was the impression their guides were instructed to convey but also concluded that such facilities as a camp library could not have been set up for their visit alone. It was his impression, furthermore, confirmed by some inmates' families, that physical abuse was now the exception, rather than the rule. At the same time, however, the number of arrests did not decline. Returning emigrants were particularly likely to be detained. Hughes's subsequent request, directed to the Berlin Gestapo, to give inmates furloughs was summarily refused.[110]

MacMaster also discussed the closure of concentration camps with Hans Thomsen of the chancellery staff, who gave him no cause for optimism either. According to Thomsen, Nazis had faced prison under the Weimar Republic. They were, he claimed, still prepared "to take their punishment, if tables turn against them." He, therefore, concluded correctly, "that [the Nazis] are not ready yet to dispense with concentration camps."[111]

Even as Hughes and Catchpool were admitted to Dachau, Nazi patience with Quaker activity was no doubt further strained by the knowledge that many of Hughes's clients often came first to the Berlin Center to find an ear for their troubles. Catchpool appears to have kept some personal record of these appeals, which he turned over to Hughes whenever the itinerant benefactor returned to England to draw more money for his work.[112] Another source of Nazi distrust was MacMaster's departure for Saarbrücken after the Saar plebiscite but before the German takeover of the territory. In a temporary office he helped stranded German refugees escape to France. The Gestapo claimed that he was in contact with Max Braun, who had led the unsuccessful campaign for the "status quo," that is, continued League of Nations governance. MacMaster, of course, finding himself in the center of another human catastrophe, which Quakers—as he saw it—were the only ones to address, was not interested in Braun's politics but was merely attempting to help individuals escape Nazi retribution.[113]

It is therefore not surprising that the relatively copious remnants of Gestapo reports on Friends for 1935 abound with speculations on Quaker conspiracies, though never explaining what the objects of such conspiratorial activities might be.[114] These reports also reflect an undercurrent of frustration as they warn that Quakers tried to give to their "political work for the peace movement a maximally harmless character in the form of charitable undertakings." This, according to Gestapo agents, was the Quaker way of averting sanctions against activities hostile to the state.[115] The political police in Bavaria likewise claimed that members of Socialist organizations were receiving money, food, and shelter from the "Quaker sect." In this manner Friends spread their pacifist views through "stragglers from all political camps who have contacts with illegal circles."[116]

Hughes himself was finally detained in Berlin, on May 16, 1935. Like Catchpool on such occasions, he did not panic. He explained his presence to have two purposes: to assist suffering members of the lower classes and to study the cultural institutions of the Third Reich firsthand. He did not reveal his contacts, and, although he carried on his person reports the Nazis characterized as "atrocity stories," he was then let go because, according to one report, there was no evidence that he was disseminating them. This interrogation did, however, end Hughes's work in Germany. After his return to England he received word, we cannot tell from what source, not to visit Germany again, advice he heeded until after the infamous Kristallnacht. A subsequent report from a Gestapo agent, identified only as "S 4," concluded that the time had come to rein in the Quakers. To facilitate their surveillance, this source recommended, they should be allowed to maintain only one office in Germany, with staff recruited exclusively from German members.[117]

There is no indication that this proposal was seriously considered at higher levels of the bureaucracy, and the work of Friends continued, including the rest home opened in 1933—first in Falkenstein near Frankfurt, then in Bad Pyrmont—for persons who had been imprisoned or undergone other hardships. It was first managed by Helen Dixon, but subsequently other hostesses succeeded her for three- or four-month intervals. The daily maintenance cost of five marks per person was met by the German Emergency Committee, which also defrayed the cost of guests' travel to and from their homes. The house was able to accommodate six to eight persons at a time, and the average stay was two weeks. A flexible daily schedule helped the inhabitants to relax safely and to quietly regain a measure of psychological equilibrium, at the same time, as several former guests testified, "having their faith in human goodness restored." Another beneficiary, invited after a long illness while her husband was in a concentration camp, recalls that "we practically forgot what dreadful things we had left behind us." Because it softened the bitterness that many occupants of the home felt toward their tormentors, Friends also believed that the home constituted "no disservice to the government." Here, too, the German Yearly Meeting was not overtly involved, though German Friends tacitly supported a project from whose benefits, in this case, their own members were not excluded. Altogether the refuge welcomed about eight hundred victims during the more than five years of its existence, including Ernst Reuter and other Social Democratic victims of governmental vengeance: benevolence that was again disapprovingly recorded by the ever watchful secret police.[118]

This view of the home as another Quaker-sponsored gathering place for "enemies of the state" may account for the decision to make an example of at least one of the hostesses, Elizabeth Fox Howard. On August 13, 1935, she left Berlin for London. Corder Catchpool saw her off and handed her several letters to be delivered personally at Friends House. One was from a father to a son who had escaped to England. She also had in her possession several pamphlets of the Confessional Church, which she was planning to read on the train. At the Belgian border she was removed from the train with her luggage. After a strip search carried out by a policewoman, she was taken to the Gestapo office in Aix-la-Chapelle and then sent back to Berlin where she underwent the usual questioning about contacts with enemies of the state. She was released the next evening on condition that she leave the German capital without further contact with anyone in the city. But she did not take the train the following morning. Instead, she went back to the Prinz Albrecht Strasse to ask that no one identified through information gathered from her effects should suffer as a result. From Howard's account one gets the impression that in her case, as in that of Catchpool and Hughes, and in the conversations Margarethe Lachmund had with Nazi officials in Mecklenburg in 1933, party agencies manifested a certain grudging respect for individuals who faced them without apparent fear. In this instance, Howard retrieved her papers from the Gestapo and then took the next train back to England. The Gestapo report of her arrest reflects once again a degree of frustration because the letters found on her had been "so cautiously written that they did not suffice to make a case in court." Howard, the report went on, furthermore "claimed to be unaware of their contents and was unable to provide information either about their authors or their addresses."[119]

Howard's misadventure was not an isolated event. There followed Gestapo interrogations of Catchpool and Albrecht, mentioned earlier in different contexts. These gave Catchpool the opportunity not only to restate Quaker positions but also to assure Nazism that the work for political prisoners was the exclusive responsibility of British and American Friends and did not involve the German Yearly Meeting. His assertions seem to have been believed; in fact, Catchpool's questioners in Berlin assured him once again that there was no objection to inquiries about individual prisoners and that such inquiries would not redound to the disadvantage of such individuals.

British Friends nevertheless worried about the future of their work in Germany. Paul Sturge, general secretary of the Friends Service Council, speculated that an order to close the Berlin Center might come next, unless the authorities preferred to "let us go on in the hope that every now and again," as in the case of Elizabeth Howard, the Quakers themselves "will provide them with a source of useful information." Meanwhile, just as Howard herself learned from her experience to exercise greater caution on future trips, so Friends in general saw themselves constrained to examine constantly how to do their work in this restless and violent German universe. How quickly they learned may be indicated by the fact that they did not publicize Howard's detention. They simply carried on as if nothing had happened. Howard shortly thereafter returned to Frankfurt, where she continued to work until a few days before the outbreak of World War II. Throughout her subsequent service in Germany she remained unresponsive to the Gestapo's advice, proffered during her detention, that Quakers should do their charitable work through the National Socialist Welfare League.[120]

By 1935 both German and foreign Friends had not yet been forced to reduce their activities. However, they could not make long-range plans; they made the best of opportunities as they arose. They took care not to go underground but did make occasional attempts to circumvent the law. At the same time, they had, at this point, not lost hope that their example of charitable openness might yet modify Nazi behavior. They also sought to demonstrate that they would give help wherever it was needed, regardless of the ideology of the petitioner. It must be remembered that Quakers as such had no built-in sympathies either for the masters of Germany or for many of their victims or for atheists who were as likely to knock on their doors as were Christians and Jews.

This indiscriminate receptivity to petitioners of all shades of belief and unbelief also resulted in the Berlin Center's involvement beyond the political boundaries of Germany and may provide another reason that the Nazi authorities let them continue their work. In some instances these activities provided benefits to German interests more substantial than the information gleaned from Elizabeth Fox Howard's handbag.

3.

Quakers and Nazis beyond Germany's Borders

When the Nuremberg Laws were enacted, Quaker concerns for the persecuted in German-speaking Central Europe were no longer confined to Germany. By then the Berlin Center had been instrumental in establishing the first Quaker boarding school on the Continent, Quakers had been succoring victims of political violence in Austria, and were once more being called upon to moderate the conflicts between the Lithuanian government and that country's German minority. All three projects cast additional light on the way in which the fragile relationship between Quakers and Nazis persisted.

THE QUAKER SCHOOL IN THE NETHERLANDS

Since the beginning of their history Quakers had founded successful schools that invariably deviated from the pedagogic norms of their environment. Howard Brinton described this variant Quaker role in the history of education in these words: "The Quaker schools were pioneers in at least three fields [*sic*]: They endorsed equal education of boys and girls, the use of non-violent methods, and the introduction of scientific and practical subjects into the curriculum." As a result of their bold pedagogy, Quaker schools, in the nineteenth and twentieth centuries at least, were attended by many children who came from homes holding different religious convictions.[1]

Quaker schooling established an early, if tentative, foothold in Germany when Ludwig Seebohm began instructing twenty-five children at his home near Bad Pyrmont in 1796. In 1804 Friends established a boarding school for girls in the same area. But Quaker emigration, in protest against compulsory military service, decimated the constituency of these schools and led to their closure in 1818. All that remained was a Quaker school in Minden in Westphalia. A chronicle of that community tells us that it taught the three Rs, sought to inculcate respect for God and his "holy commandments," and sought to help children understand the physical world around them so that they would become "sensibly thoughtful human beings." The teachers "maintained friendly intercourse with the children, thus developing an instructive dialog with them." This was a far cry from the compulsory Prussian system, initiated by Frederick the Great and largely run by retired or disabled army sergeants.[2]

By the middle of the nineteenth century the Minden community had faced the same difficulties that had earlier extinguished the Pyrmont meeting, and Quaker education in Germany had become a memory. At this point a new educational reform effort arose in Germany: the rural school home movement *(Landschulheimbewegung)*. Initiated by Hermann Lietz (1868–1919), it advocated pedagogic practices that resembled to a remarkable degree the goals and methods of Quaker schools (although I have nowhere found any trace of conscious contact between the two strands).

Between the turn of the century and 1914, Lietz founded several schools that sought to raise "strong, cheerful, enterprising, and liberty-loving" boys and girls, who were "unconditionally truthful" and prepared to contribute to the school community all of their intellectual and moral resources. Their teachers, in turn, saw themselves as friends, not as masters.[3] Lietz's associates included Gustav Wyneken and Paul Geheeb, who eventually founded their own schools after their mentor decided to admit only "Germanic" students to his model community.[4] Despite irreconcilable political differences that separated their founders, all of these boarding schools retained fundamental similarities: academic training that prepared some pupils for entrance to German universities and instruction in crafts, trades, farming, and household management that provided alternative curricula for children with different gifts and goals.

These boarding schools also placed marked emphasis on the development of the creative faculties (music, fine arts, and the theater) and insisted not only that teachers "maintain friendly intercourse" with their charges but also that each school constitute a self-contained entity where students and teachers assumed joint responsibility for service as well as governance. In a word, these schools exemplified the same trinity that inspired Quaker education: competence, good sense, and commitment to service.

After World War I these characteristics of the German-reform boarding school flourished nowhere more uncompromisingly than in Salem, a school founded by Kurt Hahn—in subsequent exile the founder of Gordonstoun in Scotland—and at the Odenwald school of Paul Geheeb who also was driven from Germany in 1933. At Salem students were taught "to choose the good" and to embrace truth, so that their education would nurture empathy for mankind inside and outside the campus. Geheeb's pupils called teachers by their first names, received no grades, operated an innovative system of self-government, and did well in state-administered final examinations. The experience prompted one of its exiled alumni to exclaim many years later: "To think that such a school could once upon a time exist in Germany!"[5]

After the founding of the German Yearly Meeting in 1925 it was not long before members wanted to make their own contribution to the perpetuation of Quaker educational goals and the movement for educational reform in their country.

They saw the divergence between the autocratic spirit of German public education and their own principles as a constant threat to their children's spiritual and moral well-being. Neither brotherhood nor truthfulness loomed large in German classrooms. Everywhere authority took precedence over "friendly intercourse." History texts, in particular, glorified military exploits and Germany's prewar political order. Accordingly, Quaker publications provided a running critical commentary on differences between German schools and Quaker education.[6] Some of these observations illuminated parallels corresponding to the practices of German boarding schools, thus documenting that two kindred but historically unrelated educational movements might indeed be properly joined.[7]

An American Friend, Anna J. Branson, visiting German Friends in 1931, reported that "the problem of bringing up Quaker children in a world not Quaker came up at almost every session" she attended.[8] That same year the German Yearly Meeting appointed a special committee to consider the establishment of a Quaker school that would provide elementary and secondary instruction, including academic as well as artisan training. Religious teaching was to be nonsectarian but was to include Bible study and the history of other religions. The goal was an educational community that constituted a "social unit down to the lowest kitchen worker." The seriousness of educational planning was reflected in the membership of the committee that included the triumvirate of the Berlin Center—Hans Albrecht, Richard Cary, and Corder Catchpool—as well as the most active educational reformers among German Friends, Wilhelm Hubben, Manfred Pollatz, and Elisabeth Rotten.[9]

It soon became clear, however, that the German Quaker community lacked the resources to found a school. The membership of the Yearly Meeting was small and was scattered from the Alps to the Baltic Sea. There was no location equally accessible to all Quaker children. By October 1932 the committee was still looking at sites and recognized that a school could survive only if it was able to recruit a substantial portion of its enrollment outside Quaker circles, as well as outside Germany, and only if it could count on a major capital infusion from London and Philadelphia; the latter requisite unlikely to materialize, given the world depression and Richard Cary's opinion that the German school project was completely unrealistic.[10] Friends, unaware of the American member's skepticism, meanwhile awaited responses to their appeals abroad before they would decide whether or not "to risk the experiment in September 1933."[11]

But by that time a new Germany was no longer disposed to tolerate a Quaker school within its borders. Therefore, the need for such a school elsewhere on the Continent was now greater than ever. Considering the hard blows the Nazi revolution delivered to Quaker households, the resumption of school planning in the spring of 1933 was initially driven by the need to find employment for the teachers among Friends who had lost their livelihood. But as the numbers of such victims grew, it became clear no one school could absorb the burgeoning ranks of the distressed. At the end of 1933, therefore, the focus shifted. A Continental Quaker school, regardless of location, would be designed as a refuge for children whom the new political order deprived of access to a good education. Teachers in such a school would be recruited on the basis of talent, not personal need.[12]

Other anomalies remained. A school for the persecuted might well be a "a Quaker school with neither Quaker teachers nor Quaker children" and "a German school not in Germany." The original purpose to rescue Quaker children from a hostile educational environment had given way to needs both broader and more complex.[13] In the final analysis Quakers were never primarily concerned with helping one another but rather with pursuing a course that conformed to their traditions of helping the distressed. Accordingly, the new school on the Continent was to become a haven for gifted children whose families faced political ostracism in Germany or were in the course of building new careers abroad.[14]

At this juncture the search for a site shifted to the Netherlands where Piet Ariëns Kappers, a prosperous coffee importer and clerk of the Dutch Yearly Meeting, founded in 1931, took a number of practical steps. He sought out G. Bolkestein, section chief for secondary education in the Dutch Ministry of Education, to learn under what conditions a school for foreign children could be established in his country and what requirements had to be satisfied to allow also Dutch students to attend such a school. Kappers also wrote to ninety property owners about a suitable site. His efforts quickly led him to Eerde Castle (near Ommen in the province of Overijssel), an eighteenth-century manor house surrounded by seven and a half acres of grounds, owned by Baron Philip D. van Pallandt. In 1922 this owner had placed manor and grounds at the disposal of the self-styled Theosophic "world leader" Krishnamurti and his ephemeral Order of the Star. After the dissolution of the order in 1929, the *Kasteel* was briefly a resort hotel, but when Kappers's quest began it stood empty. Thanks to its recent uses, the plant included a dormitory and other outbuildings that could accommodate 100 to 110 persons. Given the ethnic composition of the anticipated enrollment, Eerde's suitability was enhanced by its proximity to Germany.[15] The owner's sympathy with the enterprise was also important. Pallandt had worked with Quaker relief workers after World War I, notably in Austria; his friend Krishnamurti was no stranger to Friends House, where he had spoken in 1928; and, finally, Pallandt's wife was an alumna of the Odenwald school.[16]

Kappers knew of the earlier German school project and its intellectual indebtedness to the German reform-school movement. This knowledge helped give shape and purpose to the fledgling enterprise. He was likewise acquainted with British Quaker schools. Kappers also looked beyond the current emergency created by National Socialism and viewed the school in Eerde as a permanent part of a yet to be constructed network of Continental Quaker schools, reflecting the best and newest in European educational reform.[17]

However, the precise nature of this pedagogic synthesis remained the subject of some discussion. German Friends still hoped, above all, that the school would build permanent links between the young exiles and the native culture they had been forced to leave behind and would perpetuate in a more congenial environment the achievements of the German educational reform movement. The Dutch obviously preferred the more balanced prospect of an international Quaker school, while Bertha Bracey in London, who became the major fund-raiser for the enterprise, reminded her Continental partners that British financial support would soon falter unless British Friends could actively contribute their extensive boarding school experience to shaping the school. Her views were reinforced by the fact that of the roughly twelve hundred pounds raised by the time the school opened in April 1934, more than 80 percent represented British donations.

Nevertheless, an undated budget, based on the conservative expectation of forty paying pupils for the first year, anticipated that receipts would cover only 90 percent of the operating expenses.[18] When the school opened, therefore, its financial base remained precarious. The recruitment of a faculty was likewise far from complete when the first students arrived. By March 1934 four candidates for the headship had either declined or—in one instance—made it clear that acceptance hinged on the candidate's failure to obtain another, more desirable, appointment. The apparent front-runner for the position had withdrawn after suffering a heart attack. After these setbacks, the German and Dutch members of the founding committee discovered Katharina Petersen, a school administratrix in Frankfurt/Oder, and a former colleague of Emil Fuchs's in Kiel, who had also been suspended for refusing to commit herself to the "new Germany." She agreed to assume the task in an acting capacity and was chosen before English board members knew anything about her past or her qualifications.[19] Second, Kurt Neuse, whose extraordinary pedagogical gifts quickly turned Eerde into a school of remarkable quality, was accepted by the board "to say it quite honestly, only because his wife is a member of the English [*sic*] Yearly Meeting." Neuse had been teaching Latin and Greek before his suspension from the Prussian school system but was to teach English at Eerde. The school's founders had only his wife's assurance that he was qualified for that task. Rose Neuse, who became the comptroller and secretary of the school, was the only British citizen, and the couple were the only Friends on the staff.[20]

These circumstances raised these nagging questions: How could a school with a predominantly non-Quaker staff be a Quaker school? How could it accommodate students of varying religious backgrounds? The first part of this conundrum solved itself as five teachers gradually joined the Dutch Yearly Meeting.[21] One of two teachers from Great Britain, Evelyn Green, arriving in the autumn of 1934, was also a Friend. But what about the children? During the planning stage Piet Kappers had insisted that each child was entitled access to parental modes of worship. However, the dietary laws of Orthodox Judaism imposed limitations, assuming that Orthodox parents would entrust their offspring to a Quaker school.[22] Eerde consequently became a haven for children not Jewish by religion but affected by Nazi assumptions of Jewish racial identity, raised in homes either no longer Orthodox or converted to Christianity or without any organized religious affiliation. It was, of course, equally accessible to Gentile youngsters whose parents suffered persecution on exclusively political grounds. The resulting population showed no disposition toward religious dogmatism. Although Katharina Petersen, during her first visit to Britain after assuming the headship, felt constrained to assure British Friends that religion was "an important subject," it was not a visible part of the curriculum. Without pressure of any kind, however, Quaker tolerance triumphed as the Sunday morning silent meetings of worship became "a significant component, *perhaps the very center of community life.*" Attendance was voluntary but nearly unanimous, while some teachers and students worshiped at Catholic or Protestant churches in Ommen.[23]

The history of the school commenced April 4, 1934, with the arrival of the first two students, Bruno and Johannes Lüdecke. These two siblings were archetypal of the kind of student that would populate Eerde. Their half-Jewish father, dismissed from his position as director of the Brunswick State Bank's Holzminden branch, had been forced to move his family into the guest room of his wife's parents in Berlin. When the Lüdecke brothers first arrived at Eerde they found no school, only a collection of empty buildings. Johannes later recalled: "Beds, chairs, and tables had not yet arrived, so that we slept the first night on the floor." The next day Katharina Petersen joined them, accompanied by the housemother, Josepha Einstein—at that time the wife of a Hamburg physician—and the head of the kitchen staff, Marie Kuck, a former associate of Rudolf Schlosser's at the Saxon state reformatory in Bräunsdorf. Einstein's two children doubled the size of the student body. The first task of this mixed contingent was to clean house, set up beds, unload furniture, and begin work in a garden whose harvest of vegetables would become an important part of the school economy. Piet Kappers and Hans Albrecht also assisted in the sometimes grimy task of setting up shop. On Sunday, April 8, the weary band held the first Quaker meeting in the castle's great hall, where, surrounded by impressive Gobelin tapestries and portraits of wigged Pallandt ancestors, Piet Kappers invoked a God who knew no nations and no races, a fitting introit to a new life.[24]

By the end of the year more than forty newcomers swelled this charter team, and by the end of 1935, the student body reached one hundred, including thirteen Dutch and three British students.[25] These figures document that the school was filling a pressing need and, despite its improvised beginnings, was a flourishing institution. The unsystematic recruitment of administration and faculty seems to have worked out better than a more orderly process might have. Another faculty recruit, a young German history teacher named Werner Hermans (1905–1994), whom the chauvinistic tenor of German instruction had already driven into Dutch exile in 1931, was brought to Eerde's attention by the Pallandts. Initially the only Dutch speaker on the faculty, he became at once a key figure in the growing school along with his wife, Thera, a potter, who became the most popular crafts teacher. Another appointment that aroused initial uneasiness, occasioned by its seeming irrelevance to the school's needs, was that of the art historian Max Adolph Warburg, the "starry-eyed, gentle and sensitive" son of the world-famous luminary in that subject, Aby Warburg. The founders' correspondence leaves no doubt that this hire was tied to the expectation that Max Adolph's uncle and namesake, head of the still-powerful Hamburg banking firm, would assist the school financially. That expectation was disappointed, but young Warburg turned into a more than competent teacher of German literature, and his evening slide lectures on medieval art became an attraction for aristocratic and patrician first families of the region, providing them an impressive insight into the school's quality and the distinction of its growing faculty. Even more important than any of these fortuitous coincidences was the harmonious development of the human equation, expressed best in a report by the housemother Josepha Einstein: "There is here no barbed wire between grownups and children."[26]

Only once between 1934 and the German invasion of the Netherlands in 1940, when Nazi fiscal policy stepped between the school and its proliferating German clientele, was the enterprise in serious jeopardy. On Thursday, September 23, 1934, Katharina Petersen recorded in the school diary: "Today, as I write, I face the alarming question: How much longer shall I be maintaining this diary? The new German currency law has been published which outlaws all transfer of funds for the purpose of study in foreign countries. . . . No one can resist the paralysis emanating from this fact. . . ." On that day the school had forty students, thirty-seven of whom came from Germany. This was the end if the problem could not be resolved.[27]

The crisis resulted from a German trade deficit of 215 million marks and a gold reserve that had declined to one-third that amount, thus prompting the German government to prohibit all payments to creditors abroad and issuing exemptions only on the basis of the demonstrated "economic essentiality" of a given transaction. Travelers were allowed to take no more than ten marks per person out of the country. Many weeks of uncertainty ensued. Comptroller Rose Neuse traveled to Berlin to negotiate an agreement that would grant German parents permission to pay school fees. After an inconclusive session at the German Ministry of Finance she hurried to London to consult British Friends. The search for *Devisenkinder* (children whose fees were paid by relatives or other benefactors outside of Germany) took on particular urgency. An agreement was not reached until March 19, 1935. It provided that parents in Germany could send fees up to a monthly total of three thousand marks to the Berlin Center, while an equivalent amount in pound sterling was transmitted to Eerde from Friends House. The accord was renewable at six-month intervals and therefore continued to cast a perpetual shadow over the school's existence. No one could ever be sure of the renewals that actually followed each other regularly, the last to come after the German occupation of the Netherlands in 1940. Rose Neuse recalled that the arrangements gave her a maintenance budget of .60 guldens per school inhabitant per day; a staff payroll allowing room, board, and 25 guldens per month per person; and 37.50 guldens per couple, if both husband and wife were in the school's employment. To the end of her days she remained proud of the fact that she was not only able to avoid deficits but also able to accumulate a special reserve for unexpected needs. It should be added that this spartan salary scale applied equally to every employee from the headmistress to the Dutch kitchen staff.[28]

Meanwhile the school continued to grow. In the summer of 1934, Otto Reckendorf joined to provide instruction in mathematics and general science. His wife, Edith, a professional weaver and textile designer, added significantly to the crafts repertory. In October the first full-time teacher for Dutch children, Jan Boost, joined the faculty, and the following year four students, under the supervision of Kurt Neuse, sat for the Oxford School Certificate. All passed at high level; Bruno Lüdecke—who knew no English when he arrived at Eerde on April 4, 1934—achieved distinction. As the number of students preparing for the British diploma grew, the English staff increased with the arrival of Evelyn Green and the mathematics teacher Betty Shepherd. Dutch students, most often youngsters who had difficulty adjusting to life in Dutch public schools, generally prepared for eventual transfer to trade and business schools.[29]

In the summer of 1936, Katharina Petersen observed with satisfaction that the "founders of the school have achieved what they contemplated, a homestead-in-being for many adolescents that need it." That was demonstrated not merely by academic achievements but by the entire community life. Eerde was a happy place. Even as its existence hung in the balance, in the fall and winter of 1934–1935, faculty and students developed an irrepressible capacity for celebration of important traditional holidays: the Dutch prelude to Christmas (St. Nicholas's Day), Advent, and after these holidays—Carnival. Such festivities involved more than the dismissal of classes. At the school's first Carnival all seventy-five students and teachers appeared in a variety of homemade costumes. Neuse and Warburg put on a Punch-and-Judy show, while elementary pupils performed a play by the Nuremberg Meistersinger Hans Sachs. The birthday of the school's founding became another imaginatively observed occasion. It featured a variety of theatrical and musical performances and the display and sale of crafts produced in the school workshops. Early in Eerde's third year, on June 6, 1936, a swimming pool opened, built by students under the supervision of the history teacher, Werner Hermans.[30]

A word must here be added about the school's rich musical life. This was largely the work of William Hilsley. Born in London in 1911 to German parents who separated after his birth, he returned to Germany with his mother shortly before the outbreak of World War I. After graduating in 1930 from Kurt Hahn's school at Salem, he enrolled in the Academy for Church and School Music, but the events of 1933 forced the son of a Jewish father to cut short his studies. Eerde thus became the beginning both of his teaching life as well as of his exile. When he arrived on January 28, 1935, he was offered "no salary, but pocket money, a room of his own, food and laundry." "We have a piano and a grand piano," Katharina Peterson told him. "How the school will survive financially is quite uncertain, but if you have the courage to join us, please do." The twenty-three-year-old music student had no other prospects, and so he stayed. Two weeks later he put on a concert in observance of Handel's 250th birthday, using both faculty and student soloists. "How he got it all together in this short time one hardly knows," Petersen wondered in her diary, adding: "At last we have in prospect a musician, who knows something, electrifies the children, who is young, but critical, and possesses pedagogic talent." Later that year he presented an open-air performance of Christoph Willibald Gluck's one-act opera *The Queen of May*, the first of several such ventures at whose apex stands the presentation of the same composer's *Orfeo e Euridice* in the fall of 1937. Billy Hilsley's magical talents accounted for the fact that sooner or later everybody in Eerde stood on some homemade stage, playing, singing, or declaiming.[31]

Another feature of German boarding school life found a place in Eerde: student government. Periodic assemblies of the entire community made decisions about rules of conduct. The advice of teachers naturally carried uncommon weight, but teachers did not run this institution. The chair was always occupied by a student, almost invariably of the age group closest to graduation, elected for one term. Early in 1935 students also elected a committee of ten that applied and implemented school rules and had jurisdiction over all areas of community life, except instruction. The most visible aspect of their work was the sharing of responsibility with faculty for the supervision of the school after the evening meal, including the "lights out" ritual for the different age groups.[32]

This bare chronicle leaves much unsaid that would carry the narrative beyond the scope of this book. A future author of a history of the school will have to deal with many aspects transcending its ties to the Society of Friends. A community of different generations, most of them transplanted suddenly and unexpectedly into a foreign country, was troubled by many centrifugal forces. Katharina Petersen's energetic determination to make the place work at all costs stepped on toes both old and young. The growing collection of children, whose broadest common denominator was homesickness, made unusually heavy demands on a faculty whose members had themselves been uprooted from established homes and careers. They had to teach as well as console, sometimes literally day and night. The two housemothers, for instance, both came to Eerde in part to enable their own children to leave Germany, and in both instances this personal rescue mission involved separation from their husbands.[33]

Nor do the records, ample though they are on so many aspects of school life, contribute to the solution of the continuing mystery of Nazi cooperation with yet another Quaker venture, designed to succor what they considered to be enemies of their paranoid state. To come closer to an explanation of this uncharacteristic tolerance, we must next turn to Quaker operations in Austria and Lithuania.

VIENNESE TUMULT

Anyone who has read Franz Werfel's novel *Barbara* knows that Vienna in 1918 was a hungry, desolate city. The oversized metropolis contained one-third of the population of the Republic of German Austria. Its districts teemed with unemployed bureaucrats of a vanished supremacy and the operators of an economy suddenly cut off from established markets and sources of supply. These denizens of a haggard reality were straddling two incompatible spheres, described by Werfel as "one that was not yet quite dead, and the world of its heirs who took over the property like goods after a sale." The scene reminded Werfel of the time when Rome fell and new states proliferated within the dying empire's precincts, "a time of disintegration that did not point to any persuasive alternative."[34]

Quaker relief in the former imperial capital concentrated on children below school age, and at the peak of its operation fed an estimated sixty-four thousand. As the recovery of Austria's truncated economy faltered again and again, the Vienna Center continued this work well into the 1930s. In contrast to Germany, it received no reinforcement from local Friends. Much of the work was being directed by an American stalwart, Emma Cadbury (1875–1965) from Moorestown, New Jersey. After graduation from Bryn Mawr in 1897, she was active in local and regional Quaker projects, but after the death of her parents, in 1924, she decided to go to Vienna for a six-month term of service. Her stay was to last fourteen years, most of them spent as joint representative of the AFSC and the FSC.[35]

No amount of personal sacrifice by this American Friend could, however, relieve the frustrations of Viennese life that turned up the volume of ethnic hatreds, including anti-Semitism. University and society "stank of Jew hatred," according to the testimony of a political refugee from Germany who arrived there in the summer of 1933. At that time the catalyst of anti-Jewish prejudice was not necessarily National Socialism but rather Catholic fears that Orthodox Judaism constituted a threat to Austrian society and its traditional values. A large literature of Austrian Catholic thought purveyed the conclusion that Jews were not entitled to civic and social equality in a Christian state. On the contrary, such a state was obligated to put an end to what Catholic propagandists considered to be the deplorable effects of Jewish emancipation instituted by the French Revolution and Napoleon.[36]

Despite this rising militancy against Jews, extending from the Austrian primate, Cardinal Theodor Innitzer, who lived "in a world deeply colored by prejudice and bias," to the average parish priest, it was political persecution that ushered in a new phase of Quaker relief work in Vienna. Following Hitler's accession to power in Germany, Austrian conservatives, who had supported the aborted Austro-German customs union in 1931, were seized by fears that the new Germany would invade their country and effect a union by force. Chancellor Engelbert Dollfuss turned to Italy for help and found that the price for Mussolini's support was the destruction of Austria's Socialist movement. Socialists in "red Vienna," realizing that their government would gladly throw them to the Fascist wolves, took to arms on February 12, 1934. But their paramilitary *Schutzbund* was no match for the army and the Catholic *Heimwehr*, and after four days their uprising collapsed, followed by a dictatorship headed by Dollfuss, who led the only remaining legal party, the Fatherland Front. Apart from the outlawed Socialist Party, the new regime was also opposed by Austrian Nazis, bent on political union with Germany, and the Protestant minority that feared that the militant Catholicism of the new regime would trigger another Counter Reformation.[37]

Emma Cadbury, who, according to Rufus Jones, was "terribly overworked" but did a better job running the Vienna Center than did her counterparts in Berlin, sought immediate help for the victims of yet another wave of political persecution. Although an aid fund, established under the patronage of the chancellor's wife, was ostensibly nonpartisan, Quakers discovered at once that Socialist housewives in various municipal housing complexes did not plan to appeal to the government for succor, no matter how dire their plight. These women feared that their children would be taken from them and sent to Catholic orphanages. Some claimed to have asked for help and had been told that they would have to join the Fatherland Front first. Meanwhile, Socialist men had been cut off from the dole, and municipal employees feared losing their jobs. Some

Socialist families had actually been evicted from their apartments and not even been allowed to take their belongings with them. Cadbury concluded, therefore, that a foreign, neutral organization would have to supplement government attempts to dress the wounds of civil conflict.[38]

The International Trade Union Council quickly provided the means required to make Cadbury's plans a reality. Friends in Vienna were asked to administer funds, mostly contributed by the council's British and French member organizations. The donors agreed "that [Friends] could not be bound by any political considerations in administering relief," and, in view of the splendid Quaker record of assistance to an impoverished Austria during the past fifteen years, the government raised no objections to the resulting enterprise, also agreeing not to interfere with Quaker relief activities. Within six weeks, more than seven thousand families received help of various kinds. All in all, an estimated fifty thousand pounds was expended, an amount far in excess of what Friends' strained resources could have provided at that time.[39]

Soon, however, another call on Vienna's Quaker Center involved a cause that would not elicit similar international sympathies. On July 25 a band of Austrian Nazis seized the chancellor's office on Ballhausplatz and murdered Dollfuss. Their attempt to take over the government failed, however. Mussolini massed his troops at the Brenner Pass, and, in Berlin, Hitler was constrained to disavow the Vienna putsch. Since the fighting in Vienna had been accompanied by other equally unsuccessful uprisings—notably in Styria—and had inflicted death and injury in high places, the government response was even more draconic than it had been in February. Nazis everywhere were seized and committed to internment camps. Once again thousands of families found themselves without breadwinners, and this time the authorities were "quite prepared to let them suffer."[40]

At this point a prominent Mennonite in Germany, Benjamin Heinrich Unruh (1881–1959), came to the Berlin Center to discuss a relief scheme for the victims of this second Austrian civil clash. Unruh, a native of the Ukraine, had fled to Germany during the Russian Revolution, settled in Karlsruhe, and led in the founding of an organization, called *Brüder in Not* (Brothers in Distress), whose purpose was to finance Mennonite emigration from the Soviet Union. Since this community consisted exclusively of ethnic Germans, Unruh's organization was generously subsidized by the Weimar Republic, to the tune of six million marks in 1929 alone, and claimed to have rescued 120,000 individuals. When the Soviet government halted all emigration to Germany in 1933, however, *Brüder in Not* was left with a considerable balance on its books but no place to spend it.

As indicated earlier, Mennonites were among German free churches that supported the Nazi regime, and in July 1934 both the German Foreign Office and the Propaganda Ministry had actually considered sending Unruh to the

United States on an "ostensibly spontaneous and private mission" to "refute the grossest American misconceptions concerning [Germany's] political and religious situation."[41] While that trip did not take place, there can be no doubt that Unruh's visit to the Quaker office in Berlin was expressly sanctioned by officials in the Wilhelmstrasse.

Friends in Berlin may have been unaware of these ramifications, though not of Unruh's central role in Soviet Mennonite resettlement. Certainly he did nothing to expose his government connections when he came to the Prinz Louis Ferdinand Strasse, offering a down payment of fifty thousand marks and even much larger sums during the coming winter if Friends would undertake their distribution among suffering Nazi families in Austria. He also suggested that Quakers attempt to raise additional monies from their coreligionists in Germany and other countries. Unruh himself promised to seek assistance from Mennonites in Canada and the United States. In a subsequent letter to Gilbert MacMaster, he recapitulated a sanitized version of his latest mission. He asked the "Society of Friends to undertake a piece of Christian relief service" in behalf of victims of "the recent and devastating fighting in Austria." Since Friends had been able to help other victims "with the concurrence of the Austrian government," he claimed to have been delegated "by our relief committee" to ask them to include in their charity also the prey of more recent "disasters." He concluded with the hope "that this work of Christian neighborliness may bring much blessing, especially in furthering the cause of reconciliation."[42]

Quaker reception of Unruh's proposal was mixed, but Friends spent much time and thought during the remainder of the year considering how it might be carried out. MacMaster reported Unruh's visit to a meeting of Quaker relief workers in Prague. Next, the German Yearly Meeting provided American and German Friends another opportunity to consider the project and its implications. The difficulties were obvious. Austrian sanctions against the perpetrators of the July coup were not eliciting on their behalf the kind of international response that had followed the February battles. It was also clear to all concerned that Unruh's "relief committee" was operating with German government money. That fact alone would rule out Quaker distribution, because the Austrian government was not expected to permit aid to Austrian Nazis financed from Berlin. The question was also asked whether German Friends could get involved in such a scheme without being compromised. Hans Albrecht wanted no part of the whole business. While his own flock was suffering from Nazi depredations, he could not support the distribution of sums, many times the size of the annual budget of the German Yearly Meeting, to Hitler's partisans in another country. He castigated Unruh's mission as a Nazi attempt to use the Society of Friends for their own ends. Knowledgeable foreign Friends also warned that volunteer staff at the Vienna Center might balk at assisting the families of Nazi assassins.[43]

But Friends in Britain and the United States remained reluctant to turn their backs on any aggregation of political victims. While Friends House wanted it understood that their Society was "not just a relief organization which can be used by any group of people for helping those with whom they share political sympathies," Emma Cadbury was instructed, nevertheless, to ascertain under what conditions authorities in Vienna would permit distribution of Nazi aid.[44] American Friends in Vienna, as well as in Philadelphia, furthermore, saw here an opportunity for a "useful demonstration that [they] were not particularly interested in one political party," to which was added the hope that aid to Austrian Nazi families "might possibly have helpful repercussions for the German Friends."[45] Rufus Jones went even further when he warned that it "would seem like discrimination to continue to help Socialists and not Nazis." He also doubted that the distribution of food to Nazi families could serve National Socialist propagandistic ends. Clarence Pickett, in fact, believed that Friends "should be profoundly grateful for the opportunity offered" and urged the AFSC's Foreign Service Section "to use [their] facilities in an expression of the spirit of reconciliation," thus echoing Unruh's plea to Gilbert MacMaster.[46]

In September 1934, Rufus Jones journeyed to Vienna, where he gained the impression that if aid for Nazi families could be financed by an international fund, administered by the Quaker Center, of which German contributions constituted merely one element, "there should be no [Austrian] objection to receiving it." This notion was confirmed after Jones had discussed the matter with the new Austrian chancellor, Kurt von Schuschnigg, in the presence of the American minister, George Messersmith. Jones consequently wrote to Herbert Hoover, asking for a contribution from the dormant American Relief Administration (ARA). His goal was an international resource "perhaps [to] be called a Quaker Relief Fund, which would be handled through the Quaker Centre." Jones added a number of wide-ranging observations that placed the Austrian problem in a European context. He was quite aware of the difficulties adhering to an internationalization of Nazi aid. Yet, there was "probably no place in the world where help is more desperately needed" than Austria. Stabilizing that country was an important political objective, and he suggested that Hoover consider his request in that light.[47]

Even after Hoover had advised Friends that the residual funds of the ARA had long been spent for relief in depressed areas of the United States, American Friends kept looking for other sources of financing. Pickett appealed to Oswald Garrison Villard, editor and owner of *The Nation* and an officer of the International Relief Association, this time "on [his] own authority," for he felt "deeply concerned in the matter and [was] hoping for help and light." Minutes of the December and January 1935 meetings of the Foreign Service Section in Philadelphia record a suggestion that Jewish contributions might be solicited "as a gesture of goodwill" for a fund whose purpose would be expanded to assist both Austrian Nazis and German refugees. But in February "there was nothing further to report," and with Corder Catchpool's suggestion from Berlin that the Quaker appeal for an amnesty for political prisoners in Germany might be strengthened if accompanied by a similar petition to the Austrian government, the documentary trail ends in failure.

The fact remains that the logic of Quaker commitment precluded the exclusion of any group from the benefit of their humanitarian concerns, even if it risked turning the Vienna Center into a perceived agent of the German government.[48] Rufus Jones was wise to emphasize the importance of Austrian pacification to all of Europe. Hans Albrecht was undoubtedly correct when he warned his British and American colleagues that Unruh's visit to the Berlin Center constituted an attempt by Nazi officials to use Friends to advance their political interests in Austria. Sixty years later it is also possible to see why both Nazis and Quakers might not have mourned the failure of this enterprise for long. From the Nazi point of view, the desire to use Quakers to maintain contact with Hitler's supporters in Austria, after the führer had disavowed their putsch, was soon superseded by a policy of transforming Austro-German relations into an "internal problem between the Reich and Austria."[49] The creation of an international Quaker relief fund for Austrian National Socialists would have impeded that new course. It is today no less clear that any aid to Austrian Nazis would have obstructed subsequent Quaker efforts to assist German refugees. Both in Britain and in the United States any organization ready to distribute German money to Austrian Nazi families would have lost credibility among all groups disposed to support such efforts. In the long run, therefore, both parties had reason to be relieved at their failure to establish a modus operandi.

For the record, of course, the Society of Friends had once more demonstrated its willingness to help people whose welfare concerned the German government. Before long this indiscriminate humanitarianism would be put to the test again, this time with more encouraging results.

RETURN TO MEMEL

A year later Corder Catchpool was on his way to Lithuania on a mission similar to the one in Austria: he was trying to get a group of ethnic Germans out of the prisons of that country. And just as in the case of the Viennese episode, Clarence Pickett in Philadelphia considered it "gratifying to be able to render assistance to Nazi prisoners, because we have a good deal to do with the prisoners who are held in Germany by the Nazi government" and because the Gestapo detention of Elizabeth Fox Howard, as well as the interrogations of William Hughes and Corder Catchpool earlier that year, had demonstrated how potentially dangerous the efforts on behalf of German political prisoners could be.[50]

This second Quaker involvement in the affairs of Lithuania and Memel was another consequence of the German 1933 revolution. Since an aggressively revisionist Germany might someday reclaim the German port city, Lithuanian authorities kept a particularly close watch on the political organization of the minority community there. In the summer of 1934 growing Nazi penetration of local politics prompted the authorities to arrest prominent German politicos and to put Memel under martial law. On December 14, 1934, 126 German activists went on trial for high treason under a new law "for the protection of people and state," a flexible device for oppression that must have sounded uncomfortably familiar to many observers on both sides of the controversy. Four months later 4 defendants received death sentences that were quickly commuted, while 85 were given a variety of prison terms, ranging from one and a half years to life. Nevertheless, subsequent elections to the Memel legislature, which had been dissolved during the imposition of martial law, left Germans with a majority of twenty-five to four.[51]

At this juncture an unnamed acquaintance of Gilbert MacMaster's asked the Berlin Center to intervene on behalf of the German prisoners, one of whom had just died, while another suffered from a serious lung disease. At the time the request arrived there was no American representative "who in the past has assumed such roving ambassadorial tasks" in the German capital, so that it fell to Corder Catchpool to respond. Encouraged by the British embassy, he arranged for his wife and Olga Halle to spell him at the office.[52]

Upon receipt of his Lithuanian visa, the British Friend, frugally traveling by third-class railway carriage, followed the trail blazed by Richard Cary in 1932. Upon his arrival in Lithuania he was given free access to the prisoners but was also required to make a report to the Memel governor's office after each visit. In a further memorandum, requested by the Ministry of Justice, he candidly explained that Lithuanian prisons were "both dirty and primitive," a condition he diplomatically ascribed to the area's Russian past. In communications addressed to other Friends, however, he explained that conditions were actually not as "terrible" as reported in the German press. The prisoners themselves, he discovered, were less concerned about their living conditions than about what they considered to be the injustice of their sentences. In typical Quaker fashion Catchpool saw both sides of the inevitable conflict between jailers and prisoners. He doubted that the victims had serious subversive intentions, but he believed that Lithuania's government was genuinely alarmed by the political activities of the German minority. He also saw to it that his contact at the chancellery, Hans Thomsen, knew of his trip. His report to the German official was clearly designed to point out that Friends were as concerned by the plight of German "enemies of the state" in Lithuania as they were with victims of Nazi suspicions in the Reich. As a result he also forwarded a copy of his letter of

November 1935 to President Smetona, which ended with a plea that his country "be generous enough to grant a general amnesty to the Memelland prisoners" at Christmas.[53]

The fact remains, however, that the Lithuanian authorities were almost as deaf to humanitarian appeals as their German counterparts. Catchpool's first trip seems to have contributed more to the cleaning of Lithuanian prisons than to the release of the prisoners. His report to the minister of justice likewise reached President Smetona, but the release of the condemned proceeded only by a trickle, even after Christmas. In May 1936, therefore, Catchpool requested permission for a second visit and after completing a lengthy questionnaire was kept waiting for three months before permission was granted. This time he visited both the prisoners and their families and pleaded their cause once again at the Foreign Office in Kaunas.[54] And just as Rufus Jones had not confined his report from Vienna to specifically local conditions, so Catchpool used this second trip as an opportunity to learn more about the Baltic region. He interrupted his stay in the Lithuanian capital long enough for a flying visit to Riga, the capital of Latvia, which left him with a set of contradictory impressions. He found cleaner prisons and learned, furthermore, that whereas the cultural face of Lithuania had been marked by Russian and Polish ascendancy, in Latvia a similar domination had been exercised by an ethnically German nobility. To the Germanophile British Friend, that somehow meant that Latvia was better able to stand as an independent nation. This did not, however, blind him to the fact that the country's leader, Karlis Ulmanis (1877–1940), was as much a dictator as Germany's führer, because everywhere in Riga "you see pictures of him, looking fierce." In one respect, of course, Latvia did not differ from its neighbor to the south: it, too, feared Germany more than the Soviet Union.[55]

Yet, Catchpool was puzzled to discover that in 1936 Germany had renewed a commercial treaty with Lithuania without exerting any pressure on behalf of the Memelland prisoners. He speculated that this leniency might still be a component of Germany's *Drang nach Osten.* "I think that Germany needs Lithuania in the anti-Bolshevist front it is trying to raise," he mused, "which situation Lithuania knows how to exploit." Such exploitation of German interests had, however, limits. What the Quaker observer could not know was that Lithuania had tried to inject the prisoner issue into the treaty talks, hoping to get Germany to provide asylum for Memelland leaders after Lithuania had pardoned them. But German negotiators refused to include Memel in the agenda, a stance that the prisoners unknowingly abetted when they agreed to ask for a pardon but not to leave Lithuania after their release. What it all added up to was that when Catchpool arrived in Kaunas on his second visit, only sixteen Germans had been released, while seventy remained behind bars. Finally, what none of the parties in this Quaker mission knew was that Germany was keeping

Lithuania in reserve as a possible prize to offer Poland in return for an eventual cession of the Polish Corridor.[56]

After the British Friend's second visit, however, the tempo of release quickened, but a few still remained in their cells at the end of 1937. This prompted a third visit late in March 1938, after Germany had annexed Austria. This time Catchpool did not have to wait long for his visa, and he was astonished by the unaccustomed courtesy of Lithuanian officials at the border. By Easter the last German had been amnestied, ostensibly in observance of the twentieth anniversary of Lithuanian independence from Russia. Catchpool could, therefore, believe that two years of work had contributed to the solution that had been his goal. There can be no doubt that his visits had helped the morale of prisoners and their families to whom he demonstrated that the world had not forgotten them. But whether the ultimate success of his efforts was due to his persuasiveness or to Lithuania's precarious position between the Soviet Union, Germany, and Poland is another matter. The German minority was one enemy the Lithuanian state could control, and it is doubtful that Quaker pleas alone could have lightened that group's lot. Still, Friends had stepped in to help when no one else would. As it turned out, Memel was returned to Germany in March 1939, but not before Quakers had once again demonstrated that their willingness to alleviate suffering could be mobilized on behalf of any oppressed group, regardless of its political and ideological coloration.[57]

4.

From Nuremberg to Danzig

NAZI GERMANY: CONSOLIDATION, EXPANSION, PERSECUTION

Any truthful chronicle of the four years that followed the promulgation of the Nuremberg Laws makes ugly reading. The German dictatorship succeeded step-by-step in consolidating its position in the face of dwindling opposition at home and abroad. In the summer of 1934, the Röhm revolt and the assassination of Austrian Chancellor Engelbert Dollfuss had substantially reduced the international credit of the "new Germany." But the seamless transition from President Hindenburg's death on August 2, 1934, to the formal assumption of dictatorial powers by Hitler, followed by the German victory in the Saar plebiscite and that territory's return to German control in January 1935, demonstrated how easily the regime could survive such public-relations setbacks.

Italy's invasion of Ethiopia shattered what was left of the common front against Nazi Germany and paved the way in March 1936 for the German denunciation of the Locarno Pact and the dispatch of a token force into the hitherto demilitarized Rhineland. Ensuing foreign protests remained purely verbal and elicited from the German dictator merely another protestation of his peaceful intentions, coupled with an offer to sign a nonaggression pact with France. In November, Hitler took the lead in recognizing the insurgent government of General Franco in Spain and joined Italy, now Germany's ally, in supporting the Spanish rebellion. German foreign policy had left behind the grievances against Versailles and was unashamedly rocking the status quo wherever it saw an opportunity.

Hitler began to expand the borders of the Reich in 1938. On March 12, Austria was occupied. No shot was fired on the Austrian side, and the following day a cheering multitude gathered on Vienna's Heldenplatz to witness the martial homecoming of its native son. At the end of a restless summer Hitler demanded the cession of the northern and western fringes of Czechoslovakia, generally, if inaccurately, referred to as the Sudetenland, with its 3 million German-speaking inhabitants. His concomitant assurance that he would make no further territorial demands convinced many men and women of goodwill that this absorption of Germans, though involving territory that had never been part of a German state, did not justify another European war. Neville Chamberlain, Hitler's major partner at the Munich conference where this transfer was agreed upon, also knew very well that the few British divisions back home were all that his country could initially contribute to such a conflict.

Chamberlain also concluded a personal bargain with Hitler, stipulating that any future change of the European status quo would be preceded by negotiations. As a result, the prime minister claimed that he had secured "peace in our time," a prospect that earned him a triumphal reception by his relieved countrymen when he returned from the Bavarian capital.

That "time" turned out to be woefully short. On March 15, 1939, Germany annexed the remainder of the Czech portion of Czechoslovakia, after the government of Slovakia had proclaimed its own independence from Prague. Chamberlain was not consulted, either before or after these breaches of the peace. Six days later, the führer also paid a flying visit to Memel, now at last ceded by Lithuania: a minor prize in his growing collection of territorial trophies.

This succession of triumphs had convinced Hitler that his rivals in Europe were "worms" and that the distant United States was too effete to bar his progress. In April 1939 he continued his reckless course by denouncing the 1934 nonaggression pact with Poland and the Anglo-German naval accord of 1935, on the grounds that the two countries had become partners in an attempt to encircle Germany. Simultaneously he pressed for the cession of the Polish Corridor and Danzig, and on August 23 his foreign minister, Joachim von Ribbentrop, signed in Moscow yet another nonaggression pact, this time with the Soviet Union. Despite British and French pledges of support to Poland, the coast was now clear for a settling of accounts with this German neighbor; the invasion began on September 1, 1939. It was to change more than Germany's eastern borders.

Germans, meanwhile, found it increasingly difficult to resist the blandishments of success. Even as fear of Germany soared abroad, the dictatorial edifice was reinforced in a variety of ways at home. Not the least of these was the perfection of governmental record keeping. Early in the history of the regime, the president of the German Statistical Society, Friedrich Zahn, declared that "by its very nature statistics are an ally of the National Socialist movement." He promised to bring about the "complete recording and classification of the entire population." The resulting system gradually gathered a complete record of every German's work history (1935), health profile (1936), military service chronicle (1938), and, finally, in 1939, a comprehensive file recording each person's familial and ethnic antecedents. This demographic omnibus was the work of five thousand "scientific soldiers of National Socialism," the giant workforce Zahn had enlisted by the time World War II broke out.[1]

More visibly, the regime imitated Lenin's New Economic Policy of the 1920s by tightening its control of the strategic heights of the Germany economy. This goal was more difficult to reach in a country more integrated into the international economy and Western Europe's pluralistic culture than had been the case in the remote Russian empire. Just as in the case of Russia, however, the absence of economic and military expertise in party ranks slowed its implementation. Without the willingness of old-time bureaucrats to support Hitler's design of German regeneration it might well have foundered. Thus, German diplomatic representatives in foreign capitals, predominantly career men whose service had begun under the kaiser, loyally defended every broken promise of their leader. In the economic sphere, regimentation until 1937 was overseen by Germany's former commissioner of currency, Hjalmar Schacht, who had ended the disastrous postwar inflation in 1923. Schacht's seminal role in the shaping of economic policy continued after the enactment of the first Four-Year Plan in 1936. Even after Nazi stalwart Walter Funk supplanted him in the cabinet in November 1937, Schacht remained president of the Reichsbank until 1939.

The army's hierarchy, whose leaders likewise had first donned their uniforms before World War I, proved on the whole no less pliable than the diplomatic service. In 1938, when Hitler took over the Ministry of War, two docile senior generals, Wilhelm Keitel and Walter von Brauchitsch, became the obedient executors of his orders to a growing defense establishment whose members had sworn a personal oath of loyalty to him.

By 1936, furthermore, party men exercised complete control of public opinion and of social services. The Ministry of Propaganda under Josef Goebbels not only saw to it that every German newspaper reflected party views but also established compulsory membership in state corporations comprising writers, artists, and musicians, thus helping eliminate from creative life anyone who resisted the party line or failed the test of Aryan purity. The National Socialist Welfare Organization (NSV), headed by Erich Hilgenfeldt, grew from a modest section of the party hierarchy into a bureaucracy that controlled most social services. Much of its work was financed not by the state budget but by a variety of "voluntary" contributions individuals found it difficult to evade.[2]

Under these circumstances the ongoing civil war against opponents grew ever more merciless. Germany became increasingly an "occupied country." In 1936 Heinrich Himmler, the founder of Dachau, left Munich to become head of the German police. His concentration camps evolved from improvised to permanent places of torture: Dachau, Sachsenhausen, and Buchenwald for men, Ravensbrück for women. In May 1938 alone, more than five years after the takeover, Gestapo files recorded 1,036 political arrests: 33 Catholics, 14 Protestants, 194 members of other religious groups, 198 Jews, 410 Communists, 29 Social Democrats, and 158 other "enemies of the state."[3]

In 1938 an Aryan Social Democratic welfare worker in Hamburg attempted to explain to British Friends why he had left Germany after undergoing his share of torture and deprivation. He depicted his nation as a community where teachers were forced to impress on children "the very opposite of what is true and right" and, "more terrible still," where children learned to despise the God "whose altars still stand." To spare himself and his offspring "a life of lies for the sake of simple survival," he had chosen to leave his native land to wait for the day when he might contribute to the founding of a freer, truly "new Germany."[4]

This description of a merciless tyranny fitted the country's religious life. Even the Confessional Church was silent on the Nuremberg Laws, and a prominent Tübingen theologian told a gathering of Nazi historians in 1937 that Christianity had always been anti-Jewish, in part, he claimed, because Jews themselves had abandoned the Old Testament for the Talmud.[5] German Methodists thanked the "Lord of Hosts" for the annexation of Austria and the Sudetenland and, after the march into Prague, praised Hitler as "the blessed savior of the nation sent by God."[6] Christians who refused to compromise their religious beliefs suffered increasingly draconic sanctions. At the beginning of 1936 the Swedish Lutheran chaplain in Berlin, Birger Forell, reported that 250 Protestant pastors were in prison, 39 had been suspended from their parishes, another 30 had been forbidden to preach, and 38 ministry students had been expelled from their seminaries. "My friends in prison," he added, "have informed me that the treatment is now much worse than it was a year ago."[7] The Catholic dean of Berlin Cathedral, Bernhard Lichtenberg, continued to pray for Jews and eventually paid for his boldness with his life.[8] In July 1937, Martin Niemöller, once troubled by the Judaization of the German pastorate, was arrested for opposing state incursions into traditional church autonomy. Some of his brethren, nevertheless, continued to preside over burials of non-Aryan Christians without suffering for this act, but Confessional Church pastors—who prayed for peace during the Munich crisis—incurred the wrath of Alfred Rosenberg, the Nazi party ideologist, who declared: "He who so assaults the nation's soul in an hour of great emergency has lost the right to be a shepherd of souls." Another wave of arrests followed in the wake of that attack.[9]

A Württemberg pastor had the courage to tell his flock on November 16, 1938, one week after the Kristallnacht: "A crime has occurred in Paris [the murder of a German diplomat by a Polish Jew whose parents had been expelled from Germany.] The murderer will receive his just punishment because he transgressed God's law. We mourn with our people the victim of this criminal act. But who would have thought that this single crime in Paris would elicit so many crimes here in Germany?" The pastor was arrested and imprisoned without trial.[10]

The most visible of Nazi victims, Germans with Jewish ancestors, suffered ever more cruelly in the years just before the outbreak of World War II. Their fate was sealed by another accomplishment of Friedrich Zahn's "scientific soldiers": a card catalog of "all non-Aryans in Germany."[11] Whoever they were, wherever they might reside, they were in a card file in the hands of the nearest Gestapo office. Enterprises they still owned and positions they still occupied had to be surrendered. Exemptions of World War I combat veterans from these strictures were no longer granted, and an ungrateful nation also consigned them to dismissal without pensions. Though they knew no home and no allegiance other than Germany, they and their families were forced to seek asylum outside the borders of their native land.[12] Clarence Pickett's prognosis, formulated in 1934, that "most Jews will remain in Germany, will be driven in on themselves, but will suffer through," was like a voice from another age.[13] A grim by-product of the latest tightening of the screw was that the German Jewish community, as long as it had a choice in the matter, would not assume responsibility for victims who did not worship in the synagogue. This left "legal," as opposed to religious, Jews "hanging in the air." Their existence in limbo was shared by their children who were excluded from public elementary schools at the end of 1938.[14]

Between 1933 and 1939, to put it in cold statistical terms, the percentage of gainfully employed men in the Jewish population declined from 48.1 to 15.6. Of Germany's 286,000 Jews remaining in 1939, more than 70,000 were on the relief rolls of Jewish organizations; a statistic in part attributable to the fact that one-fourth of those left behind were older than sixty-five.[15]

These data bespeak Nazi determination to break the spirit that still bound many German Jews to their country of birth. In November 1938 the assassination of a German diplomat in Paris by a Polish Jew led to the burning of Jewish shops and places of worship and was rightly seen by Howard Elkinton, the American representative at the Berlin Center from 1938 to 1940, as a "happy excuse" to set in motion a process "which I expect will not stop *till all the Jews are out or dead.*"[16] Though an accurate prediction in the long run, Elkinton actually saw farther into the future than did the Gestapo. Himmler's men, for the moment, appeared satisfied merely to get as many Jews as possible out of the country, and they sanctioned the release from concentration camps of every Jew "intending to emigrate."[17] When the war began, the Nazis had destroyed all "pre-conditions for a continued Jewish existence in Germany." How they would implement their omnipotence in the future was theirs to determine.[18]

Mischlinge, persons of mixed Jewish and Gentile parentage, continued to live in a purgatory of their own. Professions, farming, all trades and crafts requiring membership in the German Labor Front—the monopolistic successor of German labor unions—were closed to them. Their own "growing proletarianization" was exacerbated by their children's inability to attend universities and trade schools. After the Kristallnacht, they were also excluded from welfare benefits and barred from places of public entertainment.[19]

Life in Germany, then, had become unbearable for many Germans. Emigration was the only solution but became more difficult with every tightening of the screw, and not only for German Jews over the age of sixty-five. Where could one go?

A CHRONICLE OF CLOSING DOORS

The story of German emigration during the prewar Nazi years has been difficult to chronicle because so little evidence exists to reconstruct it. German statistics are unreliable, except for so-called non-Aryan adults, a category that does not appear in the record until 1937.[20] What published figures there are on Gentile emigration to other European countries and the United States grossly understate reality. Furthermore, the distinctions made between Germans and Jews lack cultural and legal validity. Until 1935, Jews born and living in Germany were Germans, legally, culturally, and psychically, as evidenced by the country's largest Jewish civil organization, the *Central-Verein deutscher Staatsbürger jüdischen Glaubens* (Central Association of German Citizens of the Jewish Faith), which demanded from its members "fidelity to the fatherland."[21] Even after Nuremberg, leaving one's native habitat for foreign places and people, coupled, as it was, with dependence on the unpredictable benevolence of strangers, remained in the eyes of German Jews a bad bargain. Accordingly, many who left in panic in the spring of 1933 returned within a year.[22] In the years that followed, material considerations increased the reluctance to leave. Emigration not only offered an uncertain future in an unknown world but also, after the enactment of currency controls in 1934, meant that the emigrant left home with little more than the clothes on his back. "On the one hand, Germany [wanted] to get rid of her Jews, on the other hand, she [wanted] to keep their money."[23]

After the annexation of Austria—which created a "Greater Germany"—more Jews swelled the non-Aryan population than had hitherto left (about 200,000). New brutally rigorous measures, applying only to the new territory and offering the choices of concentration camp or emigration, reduced the number of Jews in Germany to about 320,000 when the war began.[24] The comings and goings of these hapless individuals were controlled by the Reich Association of Jews in Germany, whose masters at Gestapo headquarters no longer allowed them to distinguish between religious and lapsed members of the hunted minority.[25]

Those who had left by September 1939 tended at the outset to favor host countries whose national culture resembled Germany's: Austria, Switzerland, and Czechoslovakia, where German was exclusively, or at least widely, spoken, as well as countries in Germany's geographic proximity. Among the latter, France, the Netherlands, as well as Italy—before the enactment of Jewish disabilities in 1938—exerted a more powerful attraction than either Great Britain or the United States.

Poverty-stricken Austria was the primary magnet for individuals living by the pen: a visible group but not substantial in numbers. That country provided scant employment opportunities for professionals or other white-collar workers. Czechoslovakia attracted several hundred thousand political refugees, particularly Social Democrats who established their party-in-exile in Prague, but the German incursions of 1938 and 1939 put them to flight once more. Between 1933 and 1939 Switzerland accepted eight thousand refugees, including five thousand Jews, but by the spring of the latter year would admit no more. Until 1944 it explicitly denied Jews the status of political refugees. In the canton of Schaffhausen, a largely communist network helped an unknown number of political and ethnic illegals across a peculiarly convoluted stretch of frontier, and on the eve of the war the Swiss Aid for Emigrant Children received permission to bring another three hundred into the country.[26]

Among Germany's other neighbors France remained the mother of exiles, as it had been in the preceding century. In 1933 twenty-five thousand sought refuge there, an estimated 40 percent of the entire German exodus for that year, joining countless White Russians, East Europeans, and refugees from Fascist Italy who arrived in the homeland of freedom, equality, and brotherhood after 1917. Although the influx from Germany prompted the government to institute new visa requirements, five thousand fleeing the Saar after the plebiscite of January 13, 1935, and between six and eight thousand additional escapees from Austria received asylum on French soil. By 1938, however, the number of illegal immigrants coming to France exceeded the number of those legally admitted, and unless they escaped the vigilance of police they wound up in prisons or internment camps. The Popular Front government, installed after the 1936 elections, eased the enforcement of restrictions and was in the process of developing a humane statute on refugees when it fell two years later. Fear of a resurgent Germany fueled suspicions that many of the German newcomers could become a potential fifth column, while other concerns among groups basically in sympathy with large German immigrant groups likewise contributed to a rejection of large-scale admissions. Communists believed that German comrades should stay at home and fight fascism at the source. The Jewish community, many of whose elders remembered the Dreyfus affair, were torn between compassion and fear of resurgent anti-Semitism in their own country. Catholics were especially divided. In the hierarchy only Cardinal Verdier, the archbishop of Paris, and the bishops of Nice and Toulouse supported a more generous accommodation of refugees. Some laymen went into action after the annexation of Catholic Austria. An *Accueil français aux Autrichiens,* headed by the well-known poet and novelist François Mauriac, and supported by the cardinal as well as the prominent convert and neo-Thomist Jacques Maritain, aided both Catholics and Jews. The Protestant *Comité d'entre'aide Europeéne des églises* seems to have shared this ecumenical disposition, but archives are largely silent on the results of Protestant efforts.[27]

It must not be forgotten, furthermore, that France had additional problems on its hands. The outbreak of civil war in Spain in 1936 brought another four hundred thousand exiles across the country's southern borders.[28] On September 1, 1939, the French refuge, so hospitable at the outset in 1933, was closed, particularly to Germans who on that day became enemy aliens. In another year France would produce refugees of her own.

By 1938 the Netherlands, a territory of fourteen thousand square miles with 8 million inhabitants, and an unemployment rate that amounted to 5 percent of the total population, harbored an estimated twenty-four thousand German refugees, 70 percent of whom were Jews. Another eight thousand had, between 1933 and 1938, arrived and departed for other destinations. After the annexation of Austria, refugees were stopped at the border, but following the Kristallnacht an additional two thousand entry permits were issued, a figure that was soon increased to seven thousand, thanks in large measure to the Dutch Jewish Refugee Committee's promise to provide support for these coreligionists. Subsequent refugees from Czechoslovakia, however, found closed doors, and in October 1939 the Dutch government opened a camp for refugees at Westerbork: an installation that would serve more sinister purposes during the war years.[29]

A neighbor like Poland, anxious to get rid of a Jewish population exceeding 3 million, offered no hope to political or racial outcasts either. During the summer of 1939 even refugees awaiting British or U.S. visas were mercilessly driven back to Germany. Among the Scandinavian countries, Denmark, whose entire population was less than that of the German capital, was understandably intent on avoiding actions that might offend Germany. Norway, whose population of 3 million included thirteen hundred Jews, admitted no one. In Sweden compassion, especially among the clergy, tended to be confined to Protestants. An aid committee for German refugees favored well-educated, solvent immigrants. German visitors to the country needed no visa as late as 1937, and immigration laws permitted entry of political refugees. But in September 1938 all borders were closed to Jews, a step enthusiastically supported by a wide spectrum of groups, ranging from the professions to labor unions.[30]

The League of Nation's appointment of a "High Commissioner for Refugees from Germany" did not improve the lot of that country's outcasts. That official was obviously unable to dictate to member countries how many refugees they should absorb. An ineffective international conference on refugees, convened at Evian in July 1938 at the initiative of President Roosevelt, merely demonstrated the scope and the intractability of the problem. Poland and Romania, with a combined total of nearly 5 million Jews, callously expected the international community to help them get rid of their Hebrew minorities, too. Governments of overseas areas that figured in many rescue plans as prime prospects for resettlement made it clear they would not welcome these dispossessed multitudes. The Philippines agreed to make room for a mere ten thousand, and vast Australia set a limit of fifteen thousand. Canada's closed-door policy, which has been harshly, but not unfairly, identified with the slogan: "None is too many,"[31] confirmed Chaim Weizmann's bitter aphorism: "The world seems to be divided into two parts: Places where Jews may not live and those which they may not enter."[32] Unless Great Britain and the United States, the homelands of most Quaker missionaries on the distraught European Continent, took the lead in formulating significant alternatives, Jews in Central and Eastern Europe faced annihilation.

Britain's willingness to absorb refugees was enhanced by the continued commitment of the Council for German Jewry, which assumed financial responsibility for Jews fleeing Germany. After the invasion of Austria, some refugees were turned back at Croydon airport, but the resulting press criticism led to a quick easing of restrictions. According to one count in 1938, Britain at that point harbored between eleven and thirteen thousand German exiles. During the last nine months before the outbreak of war another forty thousand were added to that number.[33]

Not all of these unfortunates came to the British Isles. The migration of Jews from East, as well as Central, Europe to the British mandate of Palestine had skyrocketed from around ninety-five hundred in 1932 to more than sixty thousand in 1935. At that point the rapidly growing Jewish presence triggered an Arab general strike. In response the government fixed twenty thousand as the immigration quota for 1938. Although this population movement had produced an economic boom in the Holy Land, Neville Chamberlain wrote his sister in April 1939, "If we must offend one side, let us offend the Jews rather than the Arabs," and he closed Palestine to any more Jewish entrants.[34]

In the wake of the Kristallnacht, however, Parliament passed special legislation to admit an additional 10,000 children from Germany and Austria. The first transport of 320 youngsters arrived at Harwich on December 2, 1938, and by September 1, 1939, 9,354 had traveled that route, 7,482 of them Jews, the rest consisting of various denominations and mixtures of Jewish and Gentile ancestry. Another 3,500 found asylum in the Low Countries and France—only temporary escapes, as it turned out.[35]

The United States, a "nation of immigrants," made no special provision for victims of Nazi persecution. Political and cultural pluralism meant then, as now, that free expression was legally inviolate. Certain policies, such as the sterilization of individuals considered biologically inferior—now associated with Nazi governance—had long been accepted by members of the scientific estate and the population at large. In 1937, for instance, a survey by the magazine

Fortune found that two-thirds of the polling sample favored the sterilization of habitual criminals. American eugenicists generally refused "to recognize the inseparable connection between eugenic and ethnic racism in Germany."[36] Stereotypical prejudices against a variety of ethnic groups were also well established, and between 1933 and 1941 more than one hundred anti-Semitic organizations proliferated throughout the country. A Quaker pamphlet, *Refugee Facts,* published in 1938 and intended to make the case for more admissions on the grounds that immigrants would enrich American life "both commercially and culturally," also emphasized that 31 percent of German refugees were Christians and added that this percentage could be expected to rise "if the Christians of the United States increase their assistance to their coreligionists." Regardless of such pleas, xenophobic voices reverberated throughout the country. The Catholic hierarchy's hostility to diplomatic recognition of the Soviet Union, republican Spain, and Mexico's anticlerical government, along with the agitation of a popular radio priest, Detroit's Father Charles E. Coughlin, impeded actions on behalf of refugees. Some Protestant churches with historic German ties tended to interpret the news from Germany as malevolent exaggerations, although the Protestant press as a whole reported Jewish persecution in Germany more fully than did its Catholic counterparts. There also remains the paradox represented by another component of the New Deal coalition, the "solid South," which practiced policies of racial segregation, yet remained remarkably hostile to Nazi Germany. But the powerful southern bloc in Congress also exhibited no disposition to support the admission of more refugees.[37]

Increasing American immigration quotas remained a political impossibility. This fact was demonstrated when the Wagner-Rogers Bill, providing admission for an additional twenty thousand children, never reached the floor of the House of Representatives, while the nonsectarian Foundation for Refugee Children succeeded in bringing only ten victims into the country before the war brought about its dissolution.[38]

Despite these obstacles, the fact remains that more than one hundred thousand Germans and Austrians entered the United States between 1933 and 1941, 98 percent of them refugees from Nazism. Together with Great Britain's effort, including the unpredictable levels of admissions to Palestine, the United States made a considerable contribution to the solution of Germany's self-inflicted "Jewish problem." If one adds to that the numbers finding asylum in France, the Low Countries, and Switzerland, as well as a number of reluctant overseas territories, one is forced to conclude that the vast majority of persons who wished to leave Germany between January 1933 and September 1939 were able to do so.[39]

That more could have been saved, then and later, is equally and tragically true. But a civilization that had long been accustomed to combining the primacy of the national interest with the legitimacy of representative government proved incapable of executing a 180-degree turn on short notice and placing the welfare of strangers, no matter how harrowed, above that interest. The governments involved went as far as they thought their constituents would accept and, as in the case of Britain, sometimes even relaxed their immigration laws. At the heart of the tragedy was neither the xenophobic Swiss police, Neville Chamberlain's confused dislike of Jews, nor the pettiness of the United States Congress. The root cause of the problem was the dialectic of the nation-state: an ideology representing a utopia, where all men were equals as the members of the national community. When the formal attainment of an ethnically coherent state did not resolve the social and economic problems of the emergent national society, the search for scapegoats ensued. This search produced a new hierarchic distinction between those who belonged and those who were excluded, largely on the basis of irrational criteria. In the course of this process many nation-states experienced variations of the kind of internal conflict that divided Germany after 1933.[40]

As one American expert on refugee questions saw it on the eve of World War II: "If Eastern Jews [in Lithuania, Poland, Romania, and Hungary] begin to move on any large scale, Europe will be faced with a refugee catastrophe greater than any that has confronted it in modern history."[41]

QUAKER FINGERS IN THE DIKE

The above pessimistic conclusions did not discourage the Society of Friends, whose members, convinced that there is good in all of us, continued to search out and mobilize virtue wherever and whenever they could.

In London, Quakers continued to be the most visible and effective Christian friends of the German refugees. Among other Christian leaders no one outdid Bishop Bell—whose sister-in-law Laura Livingstone went to Berlin in 1937 where she became a faithful ally of the Berlin Center's work—in his efforts on behalf of non-Aryan Christians. Repeated, if unsuccessful, visits to Germany to stir Protestant compassion there, and energetic fund-raising efforts in his own diocese, testify to that.[42] At Friends House, Bertha Bracey continued to be the most steadfast philanthropist on the scene. After a physical collapse at the end of 1934,[43] she resumed her work with undiminished energy. Her commitment sprang "from the same faith and the same deep concern for the liberty of the human spirit and the sacredness of human personality, which led [us] to protest against the injustices of Versailles, to intervene on behalf of German prisoners in the Ruhr, to feed German children, students, professors and other members of the impoverished middle classes."[44] Forever goaded by the knowledge that limited means would continue to prevent her from helping everyone everywhere, she labored at her station to increase what means she could. No refugee conferences, no demonstrations, nor support of angry proclamations—even the World Conference of Friends at Swarthmore in 1937—could pry her from her desk. "I have to husband my strength for my particular job at this time," she wrote Clarence Pickett.[45] That job included talking to individuals who came to her office—one such a Jewish girl who had spent three years in German prisons—pressing her government, as well as the League of Nations, for more substantial aid measures, and traveling up and down the British Isles raising money. Although Bracey was convinced that salvation of the persecuted lay not at the doors of Friends House, but in Germany, where only the "enlightenment of German conscience" would end the war in which she had enlisted, she was not idly awaiting such a miracle. By the end of 1938 a staff of fifty-nine, many of them volunteers, were working with her in crowded rooms whose access was "blocked with refugees waiting for interviews which had to be held in corridors, because no more office space was available." That same year she also assumed the secretaryship of the Inter-Church Council on German Refugees, and when the Center for Refugee Aid opened at Bloomsbury House in 1939, she, with an even larger entourage, moved to this new venue with an accumulation of fourteen thousand case files. Even under the crushing load of these multiple duties, her vision rose above individual tragedies and proliferating case histories. As the prospect of collective German conversion became an ever more distant mirage, she pleaded with the league commissioner for refugees, Sir Herbert Emerson, to place "the whole emigration problem . . . on a broader and more constructive footing." She urged that countries of low population density, such as Brazil, Canada, Mexico, and Rhodesia, be offered development loans on condition that they admit additional refugees. But such letters remained unanswered, and Bracey had to be content to generate her own small-scale miracles at Bloomsbury House. In the first six months of 1939, the German Emergency Committee, which she still chaired, obtained 1,195 immigration permits. More than 200 of the committee's charges were being trained at nine agricultural training centers. Almost 500 were settled in the reluctant dominions of Australia and New Zealand. It goes without saying that she was part of the committee that persuaded Sir Samuel Hoare to support the bill admitting an additional 10,000 children to Britain.[46]

Bracey's work merely reflected the spirit of commitment that had pervaded Britain's Quaker community since 1933. After the Kristallnacht the Council for German Jewry asked Friends to go to Berlin to survey the damage. That dreadful year, 1938, also saw the establishment of a domestic bureau for refugees in Edinburgh—staffed, though not financed, by Friends—which soon faced as many as one hundred job seekers per day, "often wives without husbands and vice versa, children without parents," all people "who had no place to go and needed immediate employment." Many were among the twenty thousand middle-class refugee women who entered domestic service between 1933 and

1939. A few cracked under the unaccustomed conditions of helplessness. Others committed suicide, including an eighteen-year-old girl who did so in the Edinburgh office.[47]

Quaker aid to refugees in two other European countries deserves at least a brief mention. One modest, but tenacious, effort was the *Service Internationale d'Aide aux Réfugiés de la Société des Amis,* in Paris. For three years it was headed by Paula Kurgass (1892–1937), another German veteran of Quaker child feeding in the 1920s. Kurgass had been a social worker and a Socialist member of the Berlin City Council. Arrested on July 23, 1933, she is said to have been freed after the British Friend Edith Pye wrote to Hitler on her behalf. Following her arrival in Paris she took charge of Quaker relief for refugees. Until May 1938 her office assisted and subsidized 2,085 persons stranded in the French capital. Kurgass gave her life to that effort. Exhausted and vacationing in Switzerland, she collapsed and died at the cantonal hospital in Zurich on September 28, 1937.[48]

In the Netherlands a substantial financial effort was naturally devoted to the support of the Quaker school Eerde. Nonetheless, a lounge and meeting place for refugees in Amsterdam was opened but soon closed after evidence showed it was being penetrated by Gestapo informers. In 1938 a new committee for refugee work, including the Quakers Luise Lieftinck and Manfred Pollatz, was organized with the financial support of the American Friends Service Committee. Some of its members, such as Pollatz, included among their duties regular visits to Friends in Germany. A Dutch historian, chronicling his country's Protestant response to Germany's Nazi revolution, concluded that "in many respects the [degree of] the Quakers involvement in refugee work set a shaming example *(beschamend voorbeeld)* for the larger units of Netherlands Protestantism."[49]

These activities, though morally exemplary, especially when one considers the small Quaker meetings that maintained them, were steadily being overshadowed by the growing commitment of American Friends who stepped into the breach with increasingly massive and visible efforts, particularly after the German annexation of Austria. If that contribution grew more slowly than comparable British involvement, it was not due to "apathy" but to the unexceptionable tendency to see the refugee in European, rather than exclusively German, terms. There were the "dreadful possibilities contained in the Italo-Abyssinian war," which detracted attention from the "hopeless and despairing people" seeking to flee Germany.[50] In February 1937 the AFSC decided to initiate nonpartisan relief in Spain, a plan that received the State Department's seal of approval in April. Before long, a team of workers, headed by Alfred Jacob, organized another vast feeding of children on both sides of the battlefront, an estimated 250,000 by the end of 1938.[51]

Not every plan bore fruit; not every concern could be implemented. In November 1935 the formation of the American Christian Committee for German

Refugees had raised hopes that substantial funds would be collected and entrusted to the AFSC for distribution to the Berlin Center. Optimistic estimates promised massive assistance to that third of the German refugee population not of the Jewish faith.[52] To meet their needs the committee hoped to raise four hundred thousand dollars to be entrusted to various Friends centers in Central Europe as well as Paris. The AFSC was quick to accept such a mandate, stipulating only that appeals for money avoid attacks on any government. Clarence Pickett, furthermore, pointed out to the committee's secretary, Frank Ritchie, that Friends abroad were in the habit of keeping host governments fully informed of their activities and being the sole judge of who should be helped.[53] Unfortunately, the sums that the American Christian Committee for German Refugees actually collected never approached Ritchie's projections and played a negligible part in financing the work of the Berlin Center, to say nothing of other projected recipients. Records indicate that the committee actually sent $215 per month to Berlin, increased by $10 in February 1938. Even those sums arrived irregularly and could not be counted on.[54]

So far as direct American Quaker contributions to the Berlin Center were concerned, the tide really had begun to turn in the spring of 1936 when Albert Martin, an assistant professor of German at Brown University, and his wife, Anne, child of prosperous Philadelphia Quakers, arrived in Germany to take the place of Corder and Gwen Catchpool. In January 1937, Gilbert MacMaster likewise put himself, once again, at the disposal of Philadelphia's Foreign Service Section "to visit Berlin Center whenever possible."[55] Two months later Hertha Kraus, former municipal director of welfare in Konrad Adenauer's Cologne and now associate professor of social economy and research at Bryn Mawr College, joined the Philadelphia committee as counselor for refugees and consultant to the refugee section. As Clarence Pickett reported to Albert Martin, she had "on her own initiative" carried on such an advisory role for some time and now the AFSC "decided to give some assistance to her." Thenceforth the Berlin Center was to correspond with her directly about prospective immigrants.[56]

Concurrently, American Friends increased their share in the costs of the Berlin operation to one-half of all expenses. In May 1937, Clarence Pickett also asked Alfred Scattergood, another bearer of an illustrious Quaker name, to spend six weeks in Germany to help the AFSC discharge its responsibilities arising from "the plight of non-Aryan Christians." Shortly thereafter Pickett met with the departing German ambassador, Hans Luther, to apprise him of the widening Quaker effort on behalf of German exiles. The German representative invited him to have tea at the embassy, where he met Luther's successor, Hans Dieckhoff, and the new consul, none other than Hans Thomsen, Corder Catchpool's contact at Hitler's chancellery. Pickett found both men "well disposed towards Friends" and hoped that their acquaintance would help improve cooperation between Philadelphia and Berlin.[57]

By the end of 1937 the American Friends Service Committee had spent forty-seven thousand dollars on its relief activities in Europe, an effort far more substantial than that of any other Christian agency in the United States. But the year was 1938, with its multiple tragedies, which finally resulted in a clear, desperate commitment to "make a new and fruitful start." A new Refugee Service Committee was formed, chaired by Robert Yarnall, and its membership included such seasoned and knowledgeable workers as Anne Martin and Gaby Derenberg, a German social worker. Hertha Kraus's counseling office was moved to Philadelphia and staffed by an assistant to keep the work going on days when she was meeting her classes at Bryn Mawr.[58]

The events of the Night of Broken Glass prompted Friends to issue their own appeal to Christians in the United States. Once again they stressed the large number of Christian victims. The situation, they pleaded, concerned "every Christian in America." "We urge you," the circular added, "to tell the story of this suffering to the members of your congregation, and ask their help. We urge you to set aside one Sunday, or Thanksgiving Day, for an offering in [the victims'] behalf."[59] It is impossible to gauge the effect of this appeal. No one had time to tabulate returns. Instead, Clarence Pickett journeyed to Washington to speak to German Ambassador Dieckhoff before his return to Berlin, a retaliation occasioned by the recall of the American ambassador from the German capital. Pickett discussed Quaker plans for increased relief activity in Germany, and Dieckhoff promised to urge his government not to put any obstacle in their way.[60] Finally, the American Friends Service Committee decided to send members on a fact-finding mission to survey conditions in Germany and determine in the greatest detail possible what could and should be done.

What followed was an episode long on drama, if short on results. On December 2, three Friends, Rufus Jones, George Walton, and Robert Yarnall, left New York on the *Queen Mary*. They reached Berlin on the 8th and immediately counseled with Howard Elkinton, the American representative at the center, Paul Sturge from Friends House, the Dutch Friend Jim Lieftinck, and with Hans Albrecht. Once aware of actual conditions, the group decided on the spot to get as many people as possible out of the country. That was, of course, easier said than done. A visit to the chief of the German Foreign Office's American Affairs Section merely earned them a reprimand for failing to secure an introduction from the American embassy and the suggestion that they should work through the section on Jewish Affairs in the Ministry of the Interior. Robert Yarnall next visited the central Jewish organization in Berlin where Cora Berliner pleaded for the establishment in the United States of "large, concentration camps where we can hold [Jews] until they can come in under the 27,000 per year quota." Since December 11 was a Sunday, the American group attended worship at the Berlin Center and in the afternoon paid a rather incongruous visit to the grave of Frederick the Great in Potsdam. On Monday they finally made an effective contact with their own embassy and received help and encouragement from Consul Raymond Geist, whose forebears had fled Germany after the unsuccessful revolution of 1848 and who had done relief work in Vienna in 1919. He also offered practical advice, recommending that his visitors draft a plan of what it was they wanted to do and abandon the idea of seeing Hitler. He suggested instead that they negotiate with the Gestapo. Geist quickly arranged an appointment at the Prinz Albrecht Strasse where the delegation was told to present themselves on the 19th. Meanwhile, they were also properly introduced at the Foreign Office, where they garnered, however, no more than the advice that "wealthy Jews in America raise their own money" to assist the impending wave of emigrants. On the afternoon of the 15th they met Erich Hilgenfeldt, the head of National Socialist social services, who assured them that his office treated "everyone alike . . . Jew, Christian, Aryan, non-Aryan." He shrugged off the outrages of the Kristallnacht with these words: "When an incident sets off the people . . . nothing can be done to stop them." Robert Yarnall added in his diary: "He did not say that it might not happen again."

On Monday the 19th Geist took Rufus Jones and his associates to Gestapo headquarters, where they dealt with two "hard-faced" men in Reinhard Heydrich's office. The three Friends presented them with a carefully crafted message emphasizing, once again, Friends' traditionally close and friendly relations with the German people and their equally persistent opposition to the peace settlement of 1919: "We represent no governments, no international organizations, no parties, no sects, and we have no interest in propaganda of any form." The statement even asserted that at the time of the *Anschluss,* Quakers "were distributing food to a large number of Nazi families." Now they had come once again to help, not to blame, and "to inquire in the most friendly manner whether there is anything we can do to promote life . . . and to relieve suffering." Rufus Jones thought their statement softened the expressions on the faces of their German opposites, and, after some discussion, the SS officers called for a recess during which they promised to present the Quaker plans to their chief. While they were waiting, the Americans bowed their heads "and entered upon a time of deep, quiet meditation and prayer—the only Quaker meeting ever held in the Gestapo!" When the two men in uniform returned it was to tell them that they could proceed with their work of Jewish evacuation and that other Quaker representatives would be permitted to travel unhindered throughout Germany and Austria to implement their purpose. Jones asked what tangible evidence of this accord the three emissaries could take from this meeting. The answer was that nothing had to be put in writing, because every word "spoken in this room has been recorded." The three Americans were glad that their reflections and prayers during the absence of the German negotiators had been silent, and the two parties parted in a friendly atmosphere. The SS officers solicitously helped their visitors into their coats and saw them to the door, while the Friends left convinced that "a miracle [had been] wrought by the way of love."[61]

Clearly, Quakers were hard to discourage. Frigid receptions at the German Foreign Office, Hilgenfeldt's cynical dishonesty at NSV headquarters, even a viewing of the widely heralded, prurient exhibit at the old Reichstag building, "The Eternal Jew," which made them feel "like taking a shower, after coming out," nothing could temper their exhilaration after emerging from the grim precincts of the Prinz Albrecht Strasse.[62]

The days that followed impressed on the three Friends the urgency of their task but did not diminish their determination or, one suspects, their optimism. A meeting on December 20, with the chief rabbi of Berlin, Leo Baeck, and Cora Berliner convinced them that speedy evacuation of Jews ("before April 1939") was the highest priority. Hjalmar Schacht's advice, proffered that afternoon at the Reichsbank, that the United States "and other countries" make a start by taking in fifty thousand refugees, was likewise underlined by a statement emphasizing the need for immediate action: "Be quick, for nobody knows what will happen in this country tomorrow."[63]

In the United States, meanwhile, the entire mission continued to be seen as a breakthrough. *The Friend* anticipated "that our governments will not only send notes of protest, but will make a practical gesture of welcome to those for whom America with all its faults must seem a land of hope." The *Christian Century* credited Rufus Jones and his companions with awakening Germans to "the judgment of the Christian conscience" and bringing to German Jews a message of goodwill from American Christians, "an assurance that they were not without friends in their hour of distress." It also advocated the admission of children on the scale welcomed by Britain and the Netherlands, identifying the AFSC as "the promoter and clearing house for that enterprise."[64]

At 20 South Twelfth Street, the AFSC's main office in Philadelphia, plans proceeded as if the promise of Nazi cooperation had indeed removed the chief obstacle to a massive rescue effort. Pickett sought and received an immediate grant of one hundred thousand dollars from the American Jewish Joint Distribution Committee to finance the work of a new team of Quaker commissioners to be sent to Germany. Plans were drafted for a camp to house refugees who were expecting to receive visas to the United States within the next three years. In the same spirit of unquenchable sanguinity Rufus Jones told his hometown meeting of South China, Maine, about transit camps-in-being, and the admission of twenty thousand children to the United States, there to be settled "while they are waiting for their parents to emigrate," as if all of these plans were about to become reality.[65]

But plans remained plans, and the miracle of the Prinz Albrecht Strasse turned out to be spurious. The rest of America embraced other priorities and saw in the large-scale admission of refugees an invitation to social upheaval of daunting magnitude. As he was working to get the bill to admit the twenty thousand children through Congress, Clarence Pickett was the first to suffer the dousing of his enthusiasm. From Louis Taber, the master of the National Grange, he learned that this major representative of American agriculture "would rather give $10.00 to find places for those children in some other land, than to give 10 cents to bring them here." Taber also feared that the children's "terrible suffering" was certain to have produced "many distorted minds and warped economic viewpoints which may be serious in the future development of our democracy." Republican Senator Robert A. Taft of Ohio believed that the twenty-seven thousand Germans and Austrians, entitled to admission under current quotas, constituted a more than adequate American contribution to the German problem. He, like many of his contemporaries, believed that the settlement of others in what we would today call the Third World was the perfect solution, and he also had his doubts about the wisdom of separating children from parents. Vainly, Pickett sought to discredit these arguments by pointing to the fact that the most developed regions of the globe were also often the most densely populated, and he quoted Sir Samuel Hoare to the effect that eleven thousand refugees in Britain had created fifteen thousand new jobs. Closer to home he drew attention to the opening of a shoe factory in Baltimore, by the exiled Czech magnate Tomáš Bat'a, that was expected to provide work for five thousand individuals.[66] But none of these arguments converted the unbelieving.

Pickett gradually began to lose heart as his correspondence with the Dutch Friend Luise Lieftinck indicates. As Quaker member of the Dutch Aid Committee for Racial and Religious Refugees she had asked him why the United States did not assume a share of the refugee burden commensurate with the three thousand children she claimed her own small country had admitted between March 1938 and June 1939, and she echoed the pleas of German Jews for the establishment of holding camps for visa applicants. Pickett had to explain to her that any admissions that limited the immigrants' freedom of movement conflicted with the U.S. Constitution, and he reluctantly went on to prognosticate that "we shall do well if we succeed in preventing a reduction of . . . [immigration quotas]."[67]

While returning from Berlin in December 1938, Rufus Jones and his companions met a representative of the Jewish Joint Distribution Committee in Paris who asked them where the victims of German pogroms could actually hope to find asylum. Jones had no answer to that question, but the *Christian Century* editorialist of January 18, 1939, did: "The mass migration of the Jews of central and eastern Europe," he warned, "[is] beyond the reach of human agency. We might as well talk of evacuating the Chinese to save them from the Japanese."[68] As in the case of the aborted mission to aid Nazi families in 1934 Vienna, the

Quaker mission to Berlin can be appreciated only as a determined effort to stem a burgeoning disaster. The American Friends Service Committee could raise money and support its representatives to the Berlin Center. Beyond that, it was powerless.

REFUGEE AID IN THE TRENCHES:
THE BERLIN CENTER AND ITS GERMAN CHRISTIAN ALLIES

Amid the setbacks and failures of relief and evacuation projects hatched abroad, the leadership exercised by American and British representatives in Berlin during this period remains all the more worthy of remembrance, as does the brave and self-effacing work of a growing center staff of Germans, and a circle of German Christian allies, some of whom would pay a heavy price for their valiant commitment to the moral maxims of their faith.

The impending departure of Corder and Gwen Catchpool undoubtedly hastened the decision by the AFSC and the FSC to support three "Anglo-Americans" for the German capital posts: Albert and Anne Martin from the United States and Margaret B. Collyer from Great Britain.

Just how and why Albert and Anne Martin—who were to spend two years, from 1936 to 1938, in Berlin—were chosen, remains a mystery. It has been claimed that the Oxford Quaker Henry Gillett had met Martin at Pendle Hill in the summer of 1935 and suggested him to the AFSC. Minutes of meetings at which the Martins' appointment was approved provide no details concerning the origins of their candidacy.[69] The question is of more than antiquarian interest, however, because Albert Martin was as different from Corder Catchpool as it was possible for a Quaker to be. A native of Rhode Island, he attended Brown University and then, in 1917, received a Ph.D. in Germanic languages at the University of Wisconsin. After the completion of his studies, he enlisted in the United States Army and was commissioned a second lieutenant in October 1918. His discharge in February 1919 was followed by his marriage to a fellow graduate student: the Quaker Anne Haines, a member of the Swarthmore, Pennsylvania, monthly meeting. The years following World War I saw a decline in the number of students of German, and the young husband spent the next eight years in business and farming until he secured an nontenured appointment at his alma mater.[70]

Albert Martin was no birthright Quaker, but the son of sincere, undogmatic Christians in whose home there was "no grace at table" and a marked indifference to religious ritual. By the time he reached adulthood he agreed with Spinoza that the persuasiveness of Judeo-Christian beliefs derived from their pragmatic morality. He was also convinced that the beliefs enunciated in their Scriptures were "appropriate to their times, not universally significant." His own evolving moral code was nurtured by readings from a long list of thinkers:

from Plato to the first five volumes of Arnold Toynbee's *A Study of History.* This heritage led Martin to conclude that "one's religion is . . . too important to be left to others, [such as] theologians and religionists." He joined the Society of Friends four years after his marriage because it presented to him "the most intelligent group of Christians [he] had ever met." Somewhat inconsistently, he also agreed with William James that Quaker beliefs constituted a religion of veracity, rooted in inwardness, and a return to a way of life in harmony with the original Gospels.[71]

When Rufus Jones discussed the Berlin appointment with the Martins, the couple readily embraced "the opportunity to support the German Quakers, who were having a hard time under Hitler." Brown University granted Albert leave for the second semester of 1935–1936, and, after that interim, he did not hesitate to resign his post. The family "parked" their oldest son, Joseph, at Westtown, a well-known Quaker boarding school, and then proceeded with their youngest offspring, Richard, to settle in an apartment in the Witzleben section of Berlin.[72]

At the time of the Martins' arrival, Corder Catchpool was still very much in charge of many Berlin activities, although his family had returned to England, chiefly to spare his children enrollment in Nazi schools. For reasons no longer clear, he was disturbed to learn that the American couple was to succeed him,[73] but this did not slow for a moment his ongoing public relations campaign with Nazi officials. He had for some time complained to Hans Thomsen, the Foreign Office liaison at the chancellery, that a maladroit Gestapo informer, who attended Berlin meetings of worship and frequently dozed off before they were concluded, constituted a degrading and annoying presence. In January 1936 his protests were successful when Thomsen finally told him: "We thought it was about time that [this surveillance] stopped." In the same expansive vein, the German diplomat also secured Catchpool an appointment with the head of the Nazi welfare organization, Erich Hilgenfeldt, who received him cordially and showed him snapshots of his children "who benefitted by the *Quäkerspeisung,* in Berlin many years ago." After the Martins arrived, Corder, in response to Hilgenfeldt's invitation, introduced the American Friends to him, and the four then made a tour of the organization's new headquarters, followed by luncheon in a "charming canteen."[74] Nor did Catchpool forget, shortly before his departure, to address another urgent plea to Frank Ritchie to increase his committee's slight and irregular $215 contribution to the Berlin Center. "It is heartbreaking work," he wrote, "to turn away unhelped people."[75]

Catchpool remained in the country for the German Yearly Meeting, as well as the Olympic Games, but then decided that "we had probably better get off as quickly as possible without hanging about unnecessarily. . . ." He did not hide the fact that he departed reluctantly and would have remained in Germany, had it not been for his family.[76] Even after his connection with the Berlin Center ended, he continued to be involved in a variety of Quaker projects on the Continent and to pop in and out of the German capital until war actually broke out.

Catchpool's British replacement, Margaret B. Collyer (1889–1966), whose stay in Berlin coincided with that of the Martins, has left fewer traces in the record. She seems to have stayed close to the center, where the daily traffic of petitioners kept her busy enough, and she revived its English Club, where she enjoyed teaching English literature to the membership.[77]

Albert Martin, on the other hand, had come to make "a fresh start." He wanted to bring order into the center's administration and improve the quality of the office. To gain these ends he depended on the support of the German Friend Olga Halle, whose energy and knowledge of the German scene quickly made her indispensable to the American newcomer. It took this partnership only one month to convince Martin "that things [were] shaping up more and more, so that we are every day clearer as to how we can best spend our energies here."[78]

Whether Martin's no-nonsense, roll-up-your-sleeves spirit was the best way to deal with the constant difficulties facing the center remains difficult to ascertain. His determination to face adversity head-on did not necessarily overcome it, and there can be no doubt that he made few friends outside the center office. Nor did he take to Hans Albrecht, no doubt in large measure because his own pragmatic religious attitude—in contrast to MacMaster's—favored less concern for the "inner light" and more for the concrete troubles of Germany's persecuted. Unlike Corder Catchpool, Martin exhibited no disposition to see the Nazi side of things. "There is no compromise possible between the NS philosophy and our own," he wrote to Philadelphia from Copenhagen, whither he escaped periodically to write his often angry reports.[79] Petty quarrels with officialdom over confiscated Quaker pamphlets, and the ongoing debate with tax authorities over the center's exemptions, quickly convinced him that "life is almost unbearable for every decent person in Germany."[80] He prophesied that Germany was "going to be an unhappy place in which to live for the next fifty years, like Spain," adding bitterly, "unfortunately the Germans have more to suffer than other people in order to learn." In contrast to his British predecessor, he found himself incapable of assuming a neutral position between friend and foe. He wished that his government would end all financial dealings with Germany and even go so far as to discourage tourist visits, adding: "We shall never have any influence as mediators if we have ever compromised . . . [with] these ruffians." At the same time he tacitly admitted that this hostility might lead to the dead end of complete failure. As the end of his stay approached, the exasperated professor feared that it was only a matter of time before the German "radicals" ("Hitler, Göring, etc.") would close the center.[81]

In view of his confrontational stance, it is not surprising that Albert Martin remained no less intent on helping political prisoners than had Catchpool and, in the process, took greater personal risks. His younger son's admittedly imprecise recollections of the two years in Berlin dwell particularly on his parents' help to people who sought to escape from the country, implying that their actions may have included violations of currency laws.[82] Certainly, Albert and Anne Martin belong on a roll of honor of foreign Quakers—including Catchpool, Hughes, and MacMaster—who tried to ease the lot of concentration camp inmates.[83]

The most conspicuous case the new American representative inherited was that of Carl von Ossietzky, the pacifist editor of the well-known political weekly *Die Weltbühne*. Ossietzky was a German peace activist who had already run afoul of the law under the Weimar Republic when his magazine published an article exposing German rearmament violations of the peace treaty. His eighteen-month prison sentence was shortened by an amnesty in December 1932, but under the Nazis his days at liberty were numbered, and from 1933 to 1936 he was shunted from concentration camp to concentration camp. As news of his declining health reached the outside world, German refugee groups in Britain and France mounted a determined campaign for his release, the only effective intervention by exiles on behalf of a prisoner inside Nazi Germany. In England this effort also received Quaker backing. Funds were channeled to support Ossietzky's alcoholic English wife, and in the summer of 1933 his daughter, Rosalind, was brought to England and sent to school. When Ossietzky was finally freed in 1936, "no less a personage than Gen. Göring" handed his release papers to Albert Martin. Since Ossietzky had no home to call his own, and was suffering from tuberculosis, Martin took him to a private hospital and assured the receiving nurse "that [he] would be responsible for all expenses."[84]

To the Nazis' vocal consternation Ossietzky received the Nobel Peace Prize after his release: an act of international defiance that prompted a furious Hitler to forbid Germans to accept all such awards in the future. Worse, it hardened German resistance to other efforts on behalf of German political prisoners. Lord Allen of Hurtwood, Catchpool's fellow conscientious objector of World War I, sought to appease Nazi ire with a letter to the *Times* (London) in December 1936 in which he praised the German "exercise of mercy and forbearance." This was followed by a message from the Germany and Holland Committee to the Propaganda Ministry and the Gestapo, giving "sincere thanks for the recent release of Carl von Ossietzky." But these gestures availed little. Months later Hurtwood concluded that "as long as the German government is able to say that every time it shows consideration for any of these prisoners, we'll turn them into political storm centers of agitation, they will never respond to our appeals." No Quaker was allowed to visit the dying man after the award had been made, and he passed away in a sanatorium on May 4, 1938.[85]

But efforts on behalf of other victims continued. Friends undoubtedly had a hand in the 1938 freeing of the Social Democratic journalist Carlo Mierendorff.

Others, such as the party's former Reichstag member from Cologne, Wilhelm Sollmann, and the Hamburg social worker Rudolf Schubert, found refuge at the Quaker adult education centers Woodbrooke and Pendle Hill. Such activities are evidenced in Gestapo reports and, in another particular instance, in the memoirs of Hilda Koch, published anonymously in 1940. Her husband, who had spent 1933 in a concentration camp, received upon his release a three-year sentence for high treason. Hilda and her son escaped to Zurich in 1938, while her husband was turned back at the Swiss frontier. She credits the Martins with engineering her husband's second successful crossing of the border and the family's eventual emigration to the United States. Koch also recalled the Martins' visit to the Quaker rest home and praised their "tireless efforts on behalf of many unhappy people." But the fact remains that the continuing efforts for two Social Democrats, Heilmann and Schumacher, and one Communist, Neubauer (which are discussed in Chapter 2), failed. Equally unsuccessful were efforts to negotiate the release of Pastor Martin Niemöller—the most widely known leader of the Confessional Church—who had been offered refuge in Sweden. Quakers were even barred from attending his trial.[86]

In 1938 a deeply depressed Martin prepared to leave Berlin. He was not even sure it was worthwhile spending much time for farewells in London, because "we have nothing very cheerful or helpful to say." But he did call at Friends House one last time, in part because Henry Gillett, his original sponsor, had arranged an appointment with the British foreign secretary, Lord Halifax. True to his convictions, and at the request of Carl Gördeler—the former mayor of Leipzig and prominent German resistance leader who visited him twice in the summer of 1938—Martin counseled the head of Britain's foreign service to make no further concessions to Nazi fanaticism: a piece of advice his host was no more disposed to follow than would be Neville Chamberlain later that year at Munich.[87]

However, after returning to the United States, Martin went on a lecture tour in the course of which he expressed surprisingly ambivalent judgments about Germany. Like Corder Catchpool in 1933, he declared that its people were no keener on war than the British and French and "that the German majority would not support a war for long." Only later, as an octogenarian writing his memoirs, would he revert to the views that characterized his earlier reports from Berlin. Toward the end of his life, Albert Martin concluded that Germans must "expect to pay the price for the awful barbarism unleashed by the maniac Adolf Hitler and his associates." Since Britain and France had ceased to be great powers, he confessed to sleeping more easily because Germany had been divided after 1945.[88]

The Martins' successors were Howard and Catherine Elkinton, who in 1918 were the first married couple to be sent abroad as Quaker volunteers. Howard, a member of a well-known Philadelphia Quaker clan, was a Haverford graduate and served as a purchasing agent for the Philadelphia Quartz Company. Some

of their expenses were to be defrayed "from other sources," presumably the
Elkinton family, while the AFSC undertook to pay the tuition of their two children
at the Quaker school Eerde in the Netherlands.[89] The Elkintons arrived before
the departure of their predecessors and gave them an opportunity to become
acquainted with Howard's "kind heart and level head."[90]

Elkinton would obviously need both. He emerges from his letters as an unusually resilient and cheerful individual. Though living more in the mainstream of
American Quaker society, he was a man after Martin's heart, ready to lift burdens
and not unduly encumbered with theological baggage or idealistic assumptions
about the ubiquity of human virtue. Like Bertha Bracey, he saw the "Jewish
problem" as a wound Germans had inflicted on themselves. "We can as Quakers
help a few lame dogs over the fence, but we should be constant in our efforts
to bring the problem back to Germans" was a typical Elkintonian assessment
of the tumult that followed the Night of Broken Glass. Patiently, he soldiered
through the "heavy days" in November and December 1938, while his wit and
his calm kept up spirits at the center. Under his guidance, the lackadaisical
spirit of earlier years did not return, and Friends in London, in particular, were
impressed by his organizational skills and the promptness with which current
business was dispatched.[91]

As war approached in 1939, Elkinton channeled most of the refugee work to a
second office and reduced traffic at the Louis Ferdinand Strasse to a manageable
level. Here the office staff, increased by two capable German ladies, Eva Schaal
and Grete Sumpf, continued to provide space for the activities of the Berlin
meeting and to receive and answer correspondence from other Quakers. The staff
retained charge of finances, maintained contact with embassies and consulates,
and received visitors who were not primarily concerned with refugee cases. They
also continued to schedule visits to Friends throughout Germany, an important
activity during these demoralizing years.[92]

This division of labor would have been difficult to implement had it not been
for the arrival, in the summer of 1938, of Roger Carter, a twenty-six-year-old
graduate of Rugby and St. John's College, Cambridge, who provided an invalu-
able adjunct to Elkinton's managerial talents. Though twenty years younger than
his American counterpart, Carter quickly assumed a full share of the center's
burdens. Most important in the short run was his readiness to share with Elkinton
the work in what the older man called the "daily clinic of despair."[93]

Since Catchpool's tenure, the victims closest to the center's concern had
been Christian non-Aryans. After the passage of the Nuremberg Laws, Corder
focused on persons "generally speaking not eligible for assistance from Jewish
organizations." Catchpool was particularly troubled by the fact that the younger
generations of *Mischlinge* and Jewish Christians were "leaving school without
any prospects before them." One Quaker school in the Netherlands could not

rescue all of them, even if, as he hoped, those with three out of eight, or one out of four, Jewish forebears might yet be accepted into the national community. Nor was he unmindful of the plight of young mixed couples who could no longer get married unless they could emigrate together.[94]

Albert Martin also addressed the same worry with his characteristic fervor when he insisted in one of his periodic missives from Copenhagen: "It is certainly high time that the united Christian church showed the German government that we stand by our fellow Christians in Germany, come what may." He further stressed that unless Christians mobilized for that purpose, they deserved "the contempt of the Fascists and the Nazis." In the spring of 1937 the government's dissolution of the Paulus Union of non-Aryan Christians aroused Martin's particular ire: He begged Pickett and Bracey to consult with all Protestant bodies within their purview and urge their representatives to meet in Berlin. If nothing drastic was done, he warned, Friends would soon have to provide for hundreds of thousands, rather than merely thousands, of refugees. At this point, fourteen months before the Kristallnacht, Martin's vision of the future differed only by degrees from what eventually happened. He foresaw that Jews would slowly disappear from Germany "into Palestine, etc." Non-Aryan Christians would likewise become extinct "if the attitude of the German government continued for 25 years." "The older ones will gradually die off and the younger ones will seldom marry or have children."[95]

After the pogrom of November 1938, the focus on non-Aryan Christians was temporarily blurred as an avalanche of reports from many parts of Germany described the frightful plight of all racially proscribed persons. Despite the threatening circumstances attending his earlier departure from Germany in 1935, William Hughes returned and went to visit victims in many towns. Wherever he went he "seemed always to be meeting people who were just off to attend a funeral," either of a victim of assault or of a suicide. In Chemnitz he met four Jewish wives who had just received the official query: "Where do you wish the ashes of your husband to be delivered?" In nearby Erfurt he learned that all Jewish men had had to sign a pledge to be out of Germany within three weeks. In the old arch-episcopal city of Mainz, at the confluence of the Main and the Rhine, Hughes discovered that the Jewish suicide rate reached a point where "town authorities have turned off the gas in every Jewish home." In Frankfurt and Heidelberg he found that Rudolf Schlosser and Pastor Hermann Maas carried on their "risky and heroic work," and Hughes begged British Friends to visit both. Occasionally the roving ambassador saw a pathetic ray of light: in Eisenach all food stores refused to serve Jews, but every member of that ostracized group appears to have had Gentile friends who did their shopping for them. His travels also confirmed on a larger scale that the most pressing need was not food, but assistance to emigrate.[96]

Nazi sanctions were not confined to Jews residing in Germany. A teacher of the Quaker school Eerde, Max Adolph Warburg—after a visit to Hamburg for the burial of his mother—was stopped at the border and thrown "into the jug at Bentheim" because he carried an expensive camera. Accused of currency smuggling, he was allowed to continue his trip only after his banker uncle and namesake had paid a bribe of twenty thousand marks. Elkinton also learned while sojourning in Holland that German customers of local firms inquired whether Jews were employed, hinting that they would take their business elsewhere unless the offending individuals were dismissed.[97]

If there was any good news to report at the end of 1938 it was the fact that the work of the Berlin Center proceeded unabated in conjunction with a coalition of courageous German Christians—both Gentile and non-Aryan—whose efforts during the last year of relative peace stands in heroic contrast to the cowardly silence of most German faithful. Notable among the Protestants was Heinrich Grüber who broke with the anti-Semitic party line of Germany's Evangelical Church. Born in the Rhineland of a Dutch mother, he sported impeccably conservative credentials, as befitted a German Protestant of his calling. Since 1918 he had been a member of the conservative veteran's organization, the Stahlhelm, and during the 1920s he also ran a voluntary labor service. In 1933 the new minister of labor and national leader of the Stahlhelm, Franz Seldte, chose Grüber to head Germany's new compulsory labor service, but the appointment was overruled in favor of Konstantin Hierl, a retired army officer and Nazi Party stalwart. Three years later Grüber became chaplain of the Dutch community in Berlin and in 1938 took the civil servant's oath of allegiance to Hitler—now also demanded of the clergy—but added the reservation "as long as it does not conflict with the evident will of God." Gradually, he was drawn into scattered and uncoordinated German efforts to help non-Aryan Christians, but after the Kristallnacht he committed himself fully to this service. Eventually, the *Büro Grüber* contained a staff of thirty-five (including numerous non-Aryans) who dealt with the Gestapo and foreign aid organizations—especially in Britain and the Netherlands—and developed a network of trustees throughout Germany.[98] Grüber's clerical collaborators included Birger Forell, the Swedish community chaplain in Berlin from 1929 to 1942; Bishop Bell's sister-in-law Laura Livingstone; such uncompromising Christian shepherds across Germany as Walter Böhme at Leipzig's *Thomaskirche;* retired pastor Carl Mensing in Chemnitz, pilloried by Nazis as "pastor of the Jews"; Martin Richter in Dresden; two non-Aryan clergymen in Nuremberg, Hans-Werner Jordan and Johann Zwanziger; as well as Hermann Maas in Heidelberg, who warned a gathering of Confessional Church divines in 1938 that Christianity in Germany had become quite as much an alien as were the Jews.[99]

Friends at the Berlin Center trusted and depended on Grüber sufficiently to prompt Roger Carter in February 1939 to move his counseling activities to the pastor's office. Elkinton even considered sending the center's Grete Sumpf to the United States to visit Protestant groups and attempt to galvanize them into emulating "the work done by Germans" for the outcasts from Nazi society.[100]

At the same time, work on behalf of Catholics of Jewish ancestry was continued by the St. Raphael's Association, which had originally been supported by Caritas, the general Catholic welfare organization. But in 1938 the government threatened Caritas with the loss of its tax exemption, and sponsorship of the association's aid committee was assumed by the diocese of Berlin, using funds derived from church collections that were not subject to state control. The dean of Berlin Cathedral, Bernhard Lichtenberg, a man cut from the same cloth as Pastor Grüber, headed this activity. The work was rendered difficult inasmuch as ordinary Catholic parishioners did not, as a rule, contribute to these endeavors. Nevertheless, the St. Raphael's Association claimed that it had secured foreign refuges for 1,390 emigrants between 1933 and 1938.[101]

A fourth party in this brave welfare coalition was the so-called *Büro Spiero*, headed by Heinrich Spiero, a prominent *Judenchrist* and a well-known and prolific historian of German literature. Spiero had founded the Paulus Union, an association of non-Aryan Christians whose platform proclaimed loyalty to Germany and its government and insisted that its members were true, rather than mere "baptismal certificate," Christians. But the Nazi government was not accepting affirmations of loyalty from a group it had decided to exclude from national life and dissolved the union. Spiero subsequently suffered a stroke but recovered and devoted himself to "the mitigation of spiritual and material suffering" among his fellow victims. Most of his staff were gradually absorbed into the Grüber organization.[102]

By June 1939 these groups and Friends, chiefly represented by Roger Carter, agreed to divide their growing workload. Grüber and Spiero would look after Protestants, the St. Raphael's Association would continue its work on behalf of Catholics, and the Berlin Center would concentrate its resources on behalf of "the racially persecuted without confessional ties."[103]

Friends nevertheless continued to look for additional solutions. Another emissary from Philadelphia, James Vail, discussed with civilian and Gestapo officials the establishment of a transit camp in Hamburg's free-harbor region. But it soon became clear that such a site could accommodate no more than four thousand, and representatives of the Jewish community pointed out to him that any such installation on German soil would simply become another concentration camp.[104] In the end, the Berlin Center had to return to doing the best it could for unchurched non-Aryans and any other individuals who "for some reason cannot be helped by confessional organizations."[105] They and their confederates of mercy were, however, able to execute one major venture that lifted the gloom pervading their world in the last year before the war: the dispatch of ten thousand children to England, fifteen hundred to the Netherlands, and a sprinkling to Switzerland. A look at the surviving evidence reveals a succession of fits and starts, interlaced with bureaucratic snarls and complications, but whose cumulative result was an unqualified success. Everyone on both sides of this odyssey kept pushing and got this multitude out of the country before the war began. Roger Carter looms large in the correspondence between agencies on both sides of the Channel, as well as in the minutes of the coordinating committee that mobilized the quota of children from Christian Jewish families. All members of that committee—Protestant, Catholic, and Quaker—were approved by the Gestapo, whose representatives attended its deliberations but, from all appearances, were content simply to rubber-stamp its decisions.[106]

Little of that record reflects, however, the heartbreak that accompanied this departure of thousands. The transports, usually numbering between one and two hundred children, were led by non-Aryan adults—the Gestapo did not permit Aryans to supervise them—who took their charges to the country of refuge and then returned to their native land from which many of them would never escape. A Berlin mother remembers her last walk with her fourteen-year-old boy through the familiar streets of the city. The next day she saw him depart under the supervision of a police official "for whose sake we must suffer homelessly and hopelessly." Another day passed, and then she received a telegram from England: "Arrived safely." That was all she was to hear or know about her child for years to come. A girl, who departed two days after her sixteenth birthday, also went to the station with her mother. She "gave me a kiss and the train moved. . . . I would never see her again." A ten-year-old boy said good-bye to his mother at the station entrance and watched her walking backward "to prolong her last look at me." Before his train crossed the border, Germans took nine of the ten marks he carried and rummaged through his pathetic baggage. None of these lucky victims knew, of course, what the alternative to their traumatic separation from their personal, social, and cultural roots might have been. But here, too, history records exceptions to routine cruelty. Erna Philipp, in charge of the migration office in Rhineland-Westphalia, took eleven trains back and forth across the border to England and remembers "her" Gestapo man, always helpful and kind, doing everything in his power to have all papers in place and on time. On the eleventh trip, shortly before the outbreak of the war, she broke her word to return and stayed in England.[107]

The last transport left Germany on August 30, 1939, and arrived in Britain after the invasion of Poland had begun. The rescue had continued until one minute after midnight. What else had the center and its Christian allies accomplished by September 1, 1939? The Catholic aid effort placed 2,270 refugees abroad, nearly a quarter of the more than 10,000 potential emigrants the Association of St. Raphael counseled. The estimate that Grüber and his associates throughout Germany accounted for between 1,700 and 2,000 successful departures is, at least in part, guesswork. As to the Quakers, several sources credit the Berlin Center with effecting 1,135 emigrations. That this figure is far too low is confirmed by the records of the German Emergency Committee, which account for 6,000 refugees from Hitler's domain reaching Britain before the outbreak of World War II. We also know of another 39 individuals whom Mary Friedrich in Bad Pyrmont helped leave Germany. But no precise total can be established, as Roger Carter's own modest assessment of the Berlin Center's accomplishments illustrates: "It is difficult to say," he has concluded, "and probably beyond real determination what success Quaker efforts have had. To what extent intervention with authorities, support of families, or the spiritual and physical resuscitation in the Rest Home yielded tangible results, belongs to those human secrets which very likely will never be revealed." Anna Halle agreed with him in 1988 to end an ongoing controversy over precise numbers, while rightly asserting that the figure 1,135 fails to tell the whole story.[108]

Nor do we know all we would like to know about the psychological condition of Quaker helpers, other than what they occasionally revealed in their reports. Corder Catchpool was heartbroken because he could not do more. The Martins became so obsessed with suspicions of ubiquitous police surveillance that they would disconnect their phone whenever they were not using it. Many have remained silent. The committee records at Friends House reveal a continuous awareness of the depression that was the constant companion of Friends working in Germany, without going into details.[109]

All too soon some of them would be relieved of their tasks, if not their anxieties, for clients and friends left behind. As German and Soviet diplomats were putting the finishing touches on their nonaggression pact in the last week of August 1939, Roger Carter became convinced that "an acute danger of conflict existed." British journalists had been leaving Berlin, and the French government advised its citizens to depart. He wrote to Vienna and Frankfurt advising British Friends to go home. On the evening of August 22 a counselor at the British embassy warned him that "a juicy young man" such as he "would be the first to be interned in the event of war." On August 23, American and German members of the Berlin Center decided that he should leave, not merely because internment would keep him from working elsewhere but also because his confinement would give the Nazis a hostage through whom they could control the center's continuing work. After turning over the center bank account to his associates, he took the night train out of the country. Howard Elkinton was now in sole charge.[110]

Elkinton realized that emigration had reached its limit and that helping and comforting the hopeless would thenceforth be his chief task. He remained his stoic self: "We are not anticipating other difficulties until they arise. When they come we shall try to deal with them as best as we can." A one-thousand-dollar draft from Philadelphia assured him that the material means to carry out this sensible plan would remain at his disposal.[111]

THE GERMAN YEARLY MEETING, 1935–1939

Few German Friends benefited from the herculean effort to clear Germany of political and racial victims. Most of them exhibited no consistent interest in leaving their country. The survivor Anne Halle has likened their attitude to that of the Social Democrat Carlo Mierendorff, when he asked: "What will our workers think, if we abandon them?"[112] They, too, regarded emigration as an abandonment of their mission. Halle's own parents considered this choice but in the end could not tear themselves away. Alfons Paquet likewise weighed, and then rejected, the search for a new life abroad. Gerhart von Schulze-Gävernitz, the Freiburg professor whose son was well established in the United States, never seems to have considered joining him. The same applies to Leonhard Friedrich, whose brother had settled in Pennsylvania before World War I. Margarethe Lachmund believed that Aryans should not compete with Jews for scarce places on consular waiting lists. Elisabeth Heims, a Munich Friend, received a visa and then tore it up. "Emigration makes no sense," she reasoned. "There is nothing I can do for mankind in the United States that I cannot accomplish here."[113]

Foreign Friends tended to agree. Hertha Kraus and Clarence Pickett repeatedly discussed a few cases of German Quaker families looking for a way out but were reluctant to support them in the name of the AFSC. They did not underestimate the strain under which German Friends lived but never abandoned the fundamental view that Friends' "first obligation [was] to encourage as many . . . as possible to remain in Germany and continue to participate in the life of the country, at least as long as they possibly can without jeopardizing conscience." Even Gilbert MacMaster's suggestion to get some of them "away for a short time" was rejected, because funds were needed for purposes considered more urgent. Only Albert Martin dissented. Given his pessimistic estimates of the Berlin Center's future, he did not wish to see foreign Friends fold their tents before the largest possible number of German members had been rescued. He viewed them as potentially desirable additions to the American Quaker community; he also disagreed with Pickett's views on religious grounds, pointing out that Nazi Germany was not Cromwellian England (where a George Fox could witness among his fellow prisoners). He likewise denied that it was possible to stay in Nazi Germany "without jeopardizing conscience." But his remained a minority opinion. As late as 1939, Bertha Bracey advised Roger Carter that Friends should not be encouraged to leave, but to remain and keep up the fight for religious liberty. Only with the approach of war was this spartan discipline sufficiently relaxed to exempt Jewish Friends, several of whom were extricated at the last moment.[114]

Tangled up in this dilemma was also this question: to what extent should foreign subsidies of the German Yearly Meeting, or the GYM, be used to relieve material distress among German Friends? In November 1936, London's Germany and Holland Committee—successor to the German Emergency Committee—agreed to "consider with sympathy any suggestion which German Friends cared to make as to using [such subsidies] temporarily . . . for relief purposes," provided such needs resulted from "the political situation." German Friends were no less cautious about making relief payments to their members. At the end of 1936 the GYM's Executive Committee urged them to meet material needs in their own circle as best they could, reminding everyone that the Society was not a charity.[115]

Related to these discussions were the continuing difficulties attending the maintenance of foreign subsidies during the depression. A reduction was perpetually on the table, and a 10 percent cut, apparently suggested by Hans Albrecht, was accepted by all sides in 1936. Nonetheless, one still heard complaints in Philadelphia, London, and Berlin that some German Friends tended to ask for help before making a good-faith attempt to solve their own problems.[116] No foreign Friends could forget that the original purpose of American and British contributions had been the dissemination of the Quaker message, a goal rendered ever more difficult after 1933. They also wanted to avoid any course that could be misconstrued as interference in the autonomy of the GYM.

Occasionally Hans Albrecht would rise to defend the German Society against foreign imputations of improvidence. "Rice Christians," he reminded Paul Sturge, had certainly flocked to meetings in the 1920s, more interested in feeding their bodies than their souls. But the threats of the 1930s, coupled with the careful selection of new members, had eliminated that element from the ranks of his congregation. Albrecht also pointed out that one item from the agenda of financial controversy—travel expenses—could not be substantially reduced if satisfactory contact was to be maintained among the isolated members of Germany's scattered Quaker community. In the end, no major budget changes were adopted, and Clarence Pickett's renewed assurance to the German Yearly Meeting that foreign Friends continued to be ready to help without exercising authority seems to have closed this potentially divisive debate.[117] But it did leave a degree of resentment in Hans Albrecht's heart and caused him to consider other ways of reinforcing the GYM's independence. Signs of this umbrage surfaced in an anonymous report from Berlin in 1936 as well as in later observations from Anne Martin, recorded shortly after the German annexation of Austria. She believed that Albrecht wanted to strengthen the GYM in step with German expansion in Central Europe, and reported that he "dreams constantly of the German Yearly Meeting drawing the Swiss and Dutch and Scandinavian and Czech Friends away from England and America and taking them under his wing, not realizing that these groups haven't his political allegiance and would rather give up than succumb to German domination."[118]

The absence of other evidence—confirming or denying widespread interest in such a Quaker *Mitteleuropa*—leaves one free to wonder to what extent Martin's was not an excessively politicized interpretation of the ongoing German Quaker dilemma. Certainly, the gross of the German membership had more urgent concerns than the formation of a Central European yearly meeting, living, as they did, under increasingly difficult circumstances. They turned out to be particularly loath to make any concessions to the Nuremberg Laws, and their fidelity to their Jewish members remained unqualified.[119] Albrecht himself continued to resist government harassment and intrusions, especially the continuing surveillance of his mail. Quakers, he reminded the authorities, had never engaged in partisan politics, but demanded of the state, as of themselves, a level of conduct conforming to the "religious and moral postulates of the gospels."[120]

That was audacious language indeed, and one has to wonder, once again, why such pronouncements were not followed by the clerk's arrest. One can only postulate that "international Quakerism" was possibly more potent than the favorite Nazi chimera of "international Jewry." German missions in the English-speaking world certainly commended Friends to their superiors in Berlin. In September 1935, for instance, Hans Luther, the German ambassador to Washington, emphasized the "humane and amicable attitude" American Quakers had always displayed toward Germany. A year later, the German embassy in London explained the important role Quaker-owned enterprises and banks played in Britain's economic life and, at the same time, reminded the German Foreign Office that "numerous British Quakers remained friendly" toward Germany. This dispatch concluded, therefore, that sanctions against the sect in Germany could have a most unfortunate impact on Anglo-German relations. In 1937 Hans Albrecht took time off from the Swarthmore World Conference to visit Luther in Washington and was told that Friends everywhere constituted a vital link between his country and the outside world.[121]

Accepting these straws in the wind at face value does not denigrate Albrecht's courage. He was not privy to two of these three exchanges, but lived in a world where government behavior in general, and police responses in particular, remained wholly unpredictable. Sanctions against other less visible Friends certainly continued. Rudolf Wieding (1889–1970) from Hanover spent two years in prison for failing to deliver to the police some pamphlets he had received in the mail, which were adjudged to be subversive. Otto Weis was arrested in Mannheim, after criticizing the government, and survived his release in 1940 only by a few months.

But a certain aggressive disregard for Nazi authority continued to succeed along with that of Hans Albrecht. In 1936 Gerhard Halle completed a biography of Otto Lilienthal, Germany's first aviation pioneer and uncle of his wife, Olga. Before publication was possible, the work required the imprimatur of Hermann Göring's Air Ministry, which was, however, not granted because contents of several chapters were considered objectionable. Upon being informed that ministry officials would rewrite the offending sections, Halle withdrew the manuscript. In the meantime, it appears, aeronauts outside of Germany began to wonder aloud why Lilienthal, who was as important to his country's aviation as the Wright brothers were to that of the United States, was not being glorified by Germany's Nazi masters. Göring had his staff look into Lilienthal's antecedents, and, after it was established that they were impeccably Aryan, lifted the veil of silence. Hitler's second-in-command assumed the patronage of a suddenly emergent Lilienthal Society, and Gerhard Halle's book was put back on the table. In return for accepting a brief, bland preface by Göring, the manuscript was published unchanged. That, however, did not end Quaker Halle's intransigence. When the Lilienthal Society invited him to attend its 1938 plenary meeting, he declined on the grounds that he did not "share the National Socialist world view." Less than a year later, he also refused to participate in air-raid drills, claiming such an exercise would burden his conscience because it undermined confidence between nations. All of this passed without so much as a policeman's knock on the door of his home.

Margarethe Lachmund was another Quaker who stoutly resisted pressures to conform, despite the fact her husband had been reinstated as a judge. When questioned by the Gestapo after her return from the Swarthmore conference in 1937—particularly about her continued loyalty to Jewish friends—she answered: "Make your laws more humane and not a single Jew will henceforth know my name." In August 1938 she once again approached the deputy party chief of Mecklenburg on behalf of a Jewish physician who continued to be harassed although he was a disabled veteran of World War I. She inquired of this official, a participant in the same war, whether he had forgotten that Jews as Germans had fought in the trenches and that the skills of Jewish physicians had saved many German lives. She claims to have asked whether he could be sure of the purity of his own cause if it required the humiliation of men "who once fought in the forefront of our country." We do not know whether Lachmund's questions were answered, but her protégé was not touched during the Kristallnacht and was subsequently allowed to escape to the relative safety of Hamburg, where he survived World War II.[122]

Gestapo surveillance of Quaker activities was also kept within certain officially sanctioned bounds. Prior to the 1936 Yearly Meeting, instructions to the Bad Pyrmont police stressed that the "greatest care" should be exercised and that surveillance should be confined to securing a list of those attending, together with an indication whether or not compulsory military service had been discussed. Here, too, one may wonder whether the presence of fifty-one foreigners, including twenty-six Britons and twelve Americans, accounts for such atypical moderation. In 1937 instructions emphasized that the Gestapo presence at the yearly conclave be inconspicuous.[123]

Even the surveillance of local meetings continued to proceed cautiously, as is evident in the copious reports on the small Quaker group in Guben, an assemblage that appears to have been astonishingly outspoken. Agents reported "derogatory remarks about General Göring" and a speech by Joan Fry in which she explained that she hated Hitler because he did not respect every human being as a child of God. As late as November 1938, a member of the Guben congregation was reported to have distributed literature of the Fellowship of Reconciliation, and the visiting Emil Fuchs told a meeting that mistreatment of concentration camp inmates continued unabated, while still another visitor from Berlin spoke out about the German people's fear of another war. None of these accounts affected the Gestapo policy of deferring reprisals, a practice deemed necessary to protect the identity of the informant. For like reasons authorities did not detain members for individual interrogation.[124]

Amazing as these episodes appear in retrospect, at the time they did little to boost Quaker morale. All that German Friends could be certain of was constant surveillance. This meant, as Hans Albrecht reiterated before the last two prewar Yearly Meetings, that they always trod a "narrow ridge between danger and wrongdoing," between following their conscience and, in the process, endangering their physical safety, or granting concessions to the state that might mean abandonment of their faith.[125] This condition circumscribed the simple truth that concluded the report of an anonymous foreign visitor to the 1936 Yearly Meeting: "It is not easy to be a Quaker in Germany today."[126]

The travails of the Nazi era also did not keep German Friends from continuing to reach beyond their own small community. Their publishing company, now camouflaged as the Leonhard Friedrich Verlag—in conformity with a law prohibiting religious publishing enterprises—continued its work. Their monthly, *Der Quäker*, once again counted almost six hundred subscribers, more than twice the GYM membership. By 1937 the sale of brochures, books, and calendars was sufficiently brisk to retire all debts. At this point German Friends decided the time had come to enter the universe of international relief work and asked the German Foreign Office to allow them to join other Quaker teams feeding children on the Nationalist side of Spain's civil war. This request was, however, vetoed by the Gestapo.[127]

While the Yearly Meeting was for many isolated German Friends the only regular contact with greater numbers of their coreligionists, some larger local meetings still managed to maintain a life of their own. In Berlin, Friends continued their social activities for individuals barred by law from places of public entertainment. Olga Halle, along with Willy Wohlrabe—another member of the large Quaker contingent of former schoolteachers—guided the growing youth group. As one former member recalls these last years before the war, its ranks continued to include " 'mongrels,' like me, . . . or children of parents in concentration camps or otherwise politically persecuted." Six members were among the ten thousand children transported to England, and eventually all its Jews, except one whose parents would not allow the family to be separated, were able to leave Germany.[128] The plight of the desperate was likewise a constant concern of the group in Frankfurt, where many members of that city's large Jewish community found their way to Rudolf Schlosser's office, and where, therefore, the pressure of fear and frustration constituted an unusually heavy burden on the small band of local Friends.[129]

One must also not forget that such good works were carried out by persons who had to endure torments of their own. In Breslau, Fritz Legatis continued in the employ of the legal department of German Railways, but in a more subaltern position than the one he had occupied in Königsberg. Dresden Friends represent a particularly poignant array of personal afflictions. Agnes Martens-Edelmann, because of her membership in the Fellowship of Reconciliation, lost her license to practice law and worked as a legal aid; Johanna Hans spent time at the rest home to recover from a nervous breakdown; and Herbert Weinert suffered the blow of a son joining the Nazi Party and telling his parents "that the personal injustices that have occurred were necessary at the moment." In Leipzig a tormented Otto Pabst was living with a staunchly Lutheran wife and two sons who were preparing to become Lutheran pastors, all of them lacking, he was convinced, "any conception . . . of the possibilities [offered] by a religion as simple as Quakerism." In Halle "a congenial group of friends of Friends," sharing the sect's pacifist convictions, had been dismissed from their positions: two clergymen and several teachers, including Edwin Bernhardt, a former gymnasium principal. One teacher's wife went "completely to pieces" and found admittance at the rest home, while her mother took charge of the family's three children. In Freiburg, Schulze-Gävernitz's non-Aryan wife suffered a similar breakdown.[130] The courageous Guben meeting also contained its share of political casualties. The physician Gerhard Ockel, its resourceful leader for several years, was excluded from the local medical society, whose secretary he had been. Shortly after that expulsion, he attended a regional medical conference where Jewish participants were physically separated, and, because he sat with that group, was ostracized a second time. In 1937 Ockel was offered the directorship of a sanatorium in the Harz mountains and left the town where he, his wife, and son had become outcasts. Other Guben victims of the new order included the former SPD city councilor, Erna Peter; the former director of the municipal theater, "the Jew Julius Glass"; and the former gymnasium teacher Erich Mohr, dismissed "for his pacifist attitude" and "kept under surveillance."[131]

By 1937 it had also become clear that an earlier government promise to allow Friends to confine their services to noncombatant branches of the military was not going to be kept. "Requests of this kind," the minister of war explained to an inquiry from the secret police, "can only be decided on the basis of written requests. There is little likelihood of a special regulation of this matter, since this could not be reconciled with the nature of military services."[132] As a result, the question of how the GYM should conduct itself when younger members appeared in uniform came before the Executive Committee during the 1937 Yearly Meeting, a gathering the police obviously did not penetrate. Friends had come to understand that refusal to serve could mean a death sentence. Such a dilemma faced one young man who was mustered for officer training. He refused this distinction twice and also declined to join any party organization. Finally, after a third order, he entered basic training, a concession that caused him much anxiety about his standing among Friends. He was reassured, however, when older members once again refused to expect him and his generation to take risks from which age protected them. Manfred Pollatz, still editor of *Der Quäker*, though living in Holland, appears to have been the only committee member who insisted on the "absolutist position" that Quaker rejection of violence be followed by the refusal to enter any army. His rigid stance earned him a reminder that his residence in a relatively safe haven did not entitle him to be so unbending. He did not prevail, and the consensus remained that membership in the Yearly Meeting would not be denied to young members of the German armed forces. During a meeting of worship that followed this wrenching exchange, peace descended once more on the gathering as individuals rose and asked forgiveness for any intemperate statements they might have made in the heat of controversy.[133]

An equally intractable issue for the GYM surfaced after the Kristallnacht when Grete Sumpf of the center office and Margarethe Lachmund demanded that Friends issue a public protest against the Nuremberg Laws and their increasingly violent application. Emil Fuchs supported them, while Hans Albrecht and a majority of the membership rejected any demonstrative act that would jeopardize the existence of the German Society.[134] At the beginning of 1939 the clerk himself was reinstated as inspector of ships in the port of Stettin and thus went to work for a government plainly preparing for war.[135]

The conclusion, therefore, is inescapable: German Friends were never wholly united when it came to responding to Nazi actions. Individually and in groups they expressed their opposition to the regime through a variety of defiant acts, some of them involving individuals on both sides of the military-service and public-demonstration controversy. One of the few remaining survivors of this time of struggle insists that history has vindicated Hans Albrecht, both as leader and as guide of the German Yearly Meeting. By American and British standards of deliberative assembly he may have appeared an autocrat, but he operated in a time and place that "did not favor open consultation. The survival of the Society depended on leadership . . . both strong and discreet and [he] exhibited both of these qualities."[136] Even after he returned to his profession, a network of twenty-five Quaker trustees, stretching from Königsberg to Munich, remained on duty, alert to any opportunity to aid the persecuted, be they Christians, Jews, or unbelievers.[137] Everyone did his best to serve God and to survive.

THE BATTLE BEYOND GERMANY'S OLD BORDERS

The Quaker School in the Netherlands

After the enactment of the Nuremberg Laws, non-Aryan boys and girls not only suffered the humiliating rejection by German society but also had to endure the breakup of their families, tormented by the loss of careers, by unemployment, and by the growing need to search for a foreign refuge. For the lucky victims among these hapless youngsters, the Quaker school Eerde would become their only home for some time to come, and the school would afford them their only protection from a hostile world. Even pupils whose families remained intact experienced in Eerde a sense of belonging that most ordinary boarding schools did not provide. In 1938 one such pupil revealed to a recent graduate that no matter how happy a holiday in the bosom of her family had been, she was shocked by the surge of relief that accompanied her return to the dormitory room she shared with three other girls.[138]

This growing importance of the school to so many uprooted young people strengthened the newborn community to such a degree that it could now survive, without major ill effects, the departure of Katharina Petersen in 1938. Prematurely retired for political reasons from the educational system five years earlier, the continued payment of her pension was in 1937 suddenly made contingent on her return to Germany. Since she had no other income, she was forced to comply. The Germany and Holland Committee in London even sent, on her behalf, a plea to "the German authorities" that she be permitted to remain as director of the school without forfeiting her benefits, but the appeal went unanswered. When the taxi carrying Petersen to Ommen station disappeared from the view of the crowd that had gathered in the castle yard to bid her farewell, a sudden silence descended, which expressed "more profoundly the depth of [everyone's] pain than any resounding words of farewell."

Petersen had no plans and no prospects, and in her new and unaccustomed solitude steeled herself for the catastrophe that was about to engulf the world. After the Kristallnacht she was so paralyzed by sadness and shame that for weeks she could not even open a book. Visitors from the school kept knocking at her door, but they cheered her only briefly. Surrounded by moral chaos, her separation from Eerde remained a greater loss for her than it did for the community she had left behind.[139]

Following Petersen's departure, the board appointed Kurt Neuse as acting headmaster, a step the faculty warmly supported. However, it was obvious that the governors of the school would have preferred someone else, one reason being the new director's tolerance of individuals whom William Hilsley attracted to Eerde: a group that included acolytes of the German poet Stefan George (1868–1933), whose circle was noted for its intellectual and social elitism and its homoerotic preferences. Initially courted by the Nazis, George had disdained their advances and had chosen exile in Switzerland. As a result, some of his disciples were subjected to constant police scrutiny, usually on the grounds that their intellectual snobbery clashed with the professed egalitarianism of the Nazi revolution. Consequently, some of them left Germany soon after their master. One of these exiles from the George *Kreis* was the poet and critic Wolfgang Frommel (1902–1986), who settled in Amsterdam in 1937 and became a frequent visitor to Eerde, where his lectures on art and literature dazzled many of the older students.

Frommel's visits troubled Piet Kappers in particular. He seems to have feared that the school might turn into a hangout for homosexual intellectuals and, to forestall such a disaster, asked the new headmaster to bar Frommel from the premises. Neuse refused, arguing that an individual's sexual preferences—at that time still viewed exclusively as a matter of personal choice—were his own affair, so long as they did not involve students.[140]

To be sure, this embroilment never became public and did not affect the school as it continued to flourish. When the third academic year began in the autumn of 1936, 103 students were in attendance: 96 boarders and 7 day-students. The number of Dutch children had risen to 17. Shortage of space necessitated the opening of another dormitory, at the villa "De Esch," where 18 students lived under the supervision of Werner Hermans and his wife, Thera. The search for additional space continued but was hampered by a lack of appropriate facilities.[141]

By the end of 1938 the student body reached its prewar maximum, approximately 150, including 21 Dutch pupils and 15 offspring of faculty. Staff had risen to 16. By September 1939, 300 children attended or had passed through the castle's classrooms and, in many cases, completed an education from which German racial decrees would otherwise have excluded them.[142] As indicated before, the semiannual concern about a possible cancellation of the currency clearing turned out to be groundless, and German parents continued to transmit monthly fees to the Berlin Center.[143]

This blossoming of the only accredited Quaker school on the European Continent also induced the AFSC in 1938 to urge American Friends to consider sending their children to this educational oasis "where children from different countries might study together, according to liberal and progressive methods of education, and the Quaker ideal of giving young people an all-round training for a full life."[144]

Growth and the regular extension of the clearing accord also improved the school's finances from year to year, so that Rose Neuse was able to propose in 1939 a pension fund for the faculty.[145] Earlier fears that the idyllic life inside the castle moat would incapacitate students' ability to make their way independently in foreign parts likewise proved to be unfounded. During the last two years before the war, success stories, confirming a far more heartening result, proliferated. Some holders of the Oxford School Certificate continued their education at St. Andrews University in Scotland, while five Eerde graduates residing in the United States attended colleges and universities extending from Swarthmore and Haverford to the University of California in Berkeley. Others successfully pursued vocational training. Gerda LeRoy was to become a kindergarten teacher in Amsterdam; Carl Jacoby, a particularly promising intern of Thera Hermans's pottery studio, was continuing to perfect his craft in New York; Peter Liebermann, after finishing an agricultural course in England, was working on a farm in Australia; and younger alumni of Heinz Wild's elementary school, who had rejoined their families abroad, were excelling in schools as far apart as Portugal and California. Some, whom circumstances forced to move back to Germany, remained particularly determined to maintain their contact with the school and wrote regularly to friends and teachers. Scholastically, they too made their mark in this inhospitable climate to which they had been constrained to return.[146]

Creative pursuits continued to be an integral part of school existence. A presentation of Hugo von Hofmannsthal's Salzburg version of *Everyman* followed the exciting performance of Gluck's *Orfeo e Euridice* in 1937, and Christmas 1938 was observed with a full-fledged orchestral performance of Bach's Cantata no. 161, *"Nun kommt der Heiden Heiland,"* while Evelyn Green drove her charges in the spring of 1939 to essay nothing less than an abridged version of *Hamlet*.

With an ever greater number of pupils unable to join families in Germany for vacations, the school became a year-round institution, where holidays had to be planned with the same care as lessons. At Christmas a tree in the forest was decorated and illuminated, with students and teachers gathered around it in the deep snow, breaking the sylvan silence with prayers and carols. Everyone felt "brought together by a divine power."[147]

Such experiences and emotions also deepened the sense of Eerde as a community of equals: a collegial entity of teachers, housemothers, and kitchen staff, "all sitting genially together, talking about everything and then some." One Dutch teacher, accustomed to the class divisions and the formality *(deftigheid)* of her nation's society, found this experience both new and invigorating. Such egalitarianism also permeated instruction. Faculty were not enthroned in lonely eminence at elevated desks in front of their classes, but sat, flanked by their charges, at large oval tables, creating a more informal setting. Perhaps for the first time in their lives, children came to class filled with eager anticipation and enjoyed their work. After hours, teachers began to attend meetings of the elected student committee of ten, and members of the committee, in turn, were invited to join faculty meetings.[148]

But even in such a participatory democracy there was still need for spiritual guidance, and Kurt Neuse, who spoke at most Sunday meetings, filled that requisite. His were not pious ruminations on scriptural or secular texts, but rather carefully reasoned lessons for survival. One such, delivered in the spring of 1939, illustrates this particularly well as the former Prussian schoolmaster admonished his audience, as he often did, to brace for a hard and exacting future and to shoulder burdens cheerfully. He extolled the necessity of work, which he defined as acts that had to be performed whether one enjoyed them or not. No society, he explained, could function without its members carrying out tasks they would gladly have left to others, adding: "If a brief human existence has been sweet, it was due to the toil that accompanied it."[149]

This sermon accorded with a practical measure that brought such a reality closer to Eerde's carefree atmosphere: the establishment of an agricultural annex. It began modestly with the rental of one hundred more acres of land from Philip van Pallandt, along with a request to the Dutch government—increasingly determined to stem the influx of German refugees—to permit enrollment of fifteen young exiles who would receive two years' worth of training before moving to other countries. One of the AFSC's roving commissioners in Europe, Robert Balderston, offered funds to the school that would finance construction of a dormitory for twenty students, and at the same time promised to find graduates places on Australian, New Zealand, and North American farms. A certified

Dutch teacher of agriculture took charge of this operation, and when Eerde celebrated the fifth anniversary of its founding, this expansion had become an accomplished fact, adding to the Quaker school's catalog of achievements.[150]

Suddenly, however, these successes were threatened by events beyond the control of ordinary humans. As the summer progressed, war seemed increasingly inevitable, and when the last prewar board meeting convened at the castle on August 27, 1939, members faced an unexpected exodus of students. Parents, in Britain and the Netherlands in particular, notified Neuse that their children would not return at the end of the vacations. Others made their offsprings' continued attendance dependent on whether the school—only twenty miles from the German border—had made provisions for an orderly evacuation should Germany invade the Netherlands. Finally, there arose the question: what would happen to the clearing if Britain and Germany went to war?[151]

Such understandable concerns turned out, once again, to be premature, since it was to be a while before the war and its consequences reached Eerde. There was no invasion and no need for new financial arrangements. Two weeks after the outbreak of hostilities, an American Friend reported that school life continued normally. At the request of Howard Elkinton in Berlin, the AFSC agreed to a one-time subsidy of three thousand dollars to replace funds usually received from Britain. At the end of 1939, eleven children departed without panic, including four for the Americas and three for New Zealand. Kurt Neuse's persuasiveness had apparently prevented more departures; in some instances children seem to have talked parents into letting them stay. Eight new students—including five Dutch, two Americans whose father worked at the consulate in Rotterdam, and one German—steadied enrollment at eighty-five. The composition of the student body was gradually changing as Dutch numbers at all levels increased, and Eerde's survival was not yet in danger.[152]

The Feeding of Sudeten German Children in Czechoslovakia

The failed attempt to use ostensibly Mennonite monies for Nazi family relief in Austria after the July 1934 putsch did not end contact between this sect and the Berlin Center. In a sense, this strange relationship grew out of their differing compromises with the German military-service laws enacted in 1935. Friends saw these laws as yet another cross for their young members to bear, while Mennonites—also leaving response up to individual members—generally bore their impositions more cheerfully. Benjamin Unruh, their most visible contact with authorities, explained to his benefactors in the Nazi bureaucracy that his brethren's opposition to military service had grown out of their earlier resistance to persecution by the state, but now that the new Germany tolerated their beliefs—even as it closed other free churches—all reasons for such protestant

behavior had disappeared. Mennonites, therefore, whether in military service
or not, were unreservedly allegiant to Hitler.[153]

Unruh's attestations served him well, and he continued to act as liaison with
the Berlin Center whenever the German government wished to enlist Friends
in the furtherance of the country's interests. The case for relief of Nazi victims
had, therefore, hardly been closed when the Mennonite worthy was dispatched
to broach another project outside Germany's borders: food relief for regions
of the Sudetenland, where shrinking markets had created high unemployment
among mostly German workers in glass, porcelain, and textile manufacture. The
problem was the same as in Vienna: how to channel German resources across the
border, with Quaker help and the approval this time of the Czech government.

Mention of the project first appeared in Corder Catchpool's correspondence
with Friends House in 1934, but it was not until 1936 that Friends decided
to accept financing from the Mennonite *Brüder in Not* agency.[154] At that time
Bertha Bracey asked Catchpool, whose term of service was about to expire,
to represent British Friends on a Czech committee reviewing the proposal.
Corder was not only willing but his genuine enthusiasm for the mitigation of
suffering, wherever it might occur and whomever it might strike, turned him
once again into an effective conciliator among conflicting interests, including
Czechs who distrusted Germans bearing gifts and Germans unwilling to help
Czechs, who, Friends insisted, must not be excluded from the benefits of such
a program. Initially, he also found the small community of Friends in Prague
so bitterly divided over the question of whether they should participate at all
that "they almost ceased to function as a group."[155] In the end, *Brüder in Not*
largesse was accepted but its governmental origins camouflaged with the Quaker
name, and another attempt was made to find donations elsewhere so as to give
the venture a genuine international profile. In the end the Czech government
contributed a substantial 3 million crowns and became the major benefactor
of the program. On May 15, 1936, an agreement on how to allocate the funds
was reached among the Czech Ministries of Welfare and Foreign Affairs, the
Czech National Bank, various Czech and German welfare organizations, Czech
Friends, and their British and American counterparts. The money was to be used
in districts bordering Germany, and relief was to be confined to localities with an
unemployment rate of 9 percent or higher. Food purchased was to be distributed
by local welfare offices. Based on the ethnic composition of the population
involved, 80 percent of all aid would go to the German children, the remainder
to Czechs. How Catchpool contrived this consensus, while still involved in
the resuscitation of German prisoners in Lithuania, remains a mystery. The
record shows that he was outraged by Prague's treatment of Czechoslovakia's
Germans, calling it a shocking example of a democratic state playing "directly
into the hands of Hitler." If he expressed these feelings at the negotiating

table, he may well have shamed the Czech side into compliance. He also enlisted the support of German Social Democratic refugees, who had no reason to bolster Nazi support for Sudeten Germans, but who, in keeping with their socialist principles, recognized the need to assist victims of the depression. The German Ministry of Finance, meanwhile, raised no objection to large transfers of currency, and the first installment of fifty thousand marks, one-sixth of the total Czech commitment, arrived at Christmas of 1936. Catchpool continued to make periodic trips to Czechoslovakia during which he distributed funds in conformity with Quaker guidelines. His extemporaneous methods of management raised the ire only of Albert Martin, who found himself at the receiving end of German communications about a project of which he had been completely unaware. That fence was, however, quickly mended, and in 1937 Martin accompanied his British predecessor in Berlin on one of the trips to various relief centers in the afflicted region.

During this operation, too, Catchpool's sense of achievement was diminished by the realization that the work reduced, but did not end, Sudeten misery. As he watched "terribly pale, thin and undersized" children greedily devour their meals, he occasionally felt "that further sight of such misery was more than [he] could bear." Some of the youthful recipients were chosen by local physicians, some merely by lot, and he "witnessed the heart-rending spectacle of emaciated youngsters watching their more fortunate peers troop off for a good dinner." Corder ruefully compared these wan specters to the sturdier offspring of miners in Britain's most depressed areas, whose weekly assistance was, he claimed, ten times the amount received by their Czech counterparts. Altogether he dispensed 150,000 marks from German sources to this child feeding, receiving the last installment in November 1937. His reports do not explain how the equivalent of 300,000 marks, contributed by the Prague government, achieved its purpose.[156]

After the German takeover, following the Munich conference, the Sudeten German Party assumed these responsibilities, and so Friends withdrew. A 1939 report of the enterprise, prepared by the German Foreign Office, credited its success to the German Red Cross and Unruh, without once mentioning the Society of Friends or the Czech contribution.[157]

This cavalier disregard for the Quaker role did not, however, keep the German government from sending Unruh to the Berlin Center one last time in the middle of August 1939. This time Friends were asked whether they would "consider undertaking some kind of relief work for the German minority in Poland." Corder Catchpool, in Germany at the time—on a mission that will be discussed in the next chapter—visited Unruh at his home in Karlsruhe, but there is no evidence that the German Mennonite discussed this last initiative with him. Roger Carter doubted whether Germans in Poland required humanitarian relief and suggested that German and Polish-speaking Friends might first be sent to assess conditions on the ground.[158] But nothing concrete seems to have been undertaken, and, on August 24, Fred Tritton concluded that "there is no evidence at all to show that the Polish minority [sic] are in a bad way and that their condition needs an independent inquiry."[159]

That was to be the last word on the issue. Three days later Tritton urged Carter to leave Berlin, and six years would elapse before British Friends would return to help Germans, whose need this time would require no extensive prior investigation.

Vienna and Prague, 1938–1939

After the emergencies of 1934, the Vienna Center concentrated support on a relatively small contingent of four hundred Christian, non-Aryan refugees from Germany. This work elicited contributions from the Swedish Society for Israel, and irregular one-hundred-dollar gifts sent by the American Christian Committee for German Refugees, which also helped settle some families in Colombia. Friends were able to make regular monthly payments to some half dozen particularly deserving cases and to provide "emergency doles to more or less vagrant petitioners (some 15 weekly), often in the form of food tickets." The number of persons in need, was, however, expected to increase by as much as 50 percent in 1938, as hardships in Germany and the influx of individuals who had been unable to find refuge in other countries grew.[160]

The German invasion in March 1938 changed all that and put the Vienna Center into a state of permanent emergency. All of Austria's 200,000 Jews were now being hunted. More than 175,000 of them lived in Vienna, belonged to the middle and upper-middle class, and many occupied substantial positions in commerce, banking, the professions, and cultural life. Geographic concentration added to their vulnerability. At first, self-appointed avengers carried out "many small and large-scale thefts of Jewish property." After two months these vigilantes were curbed by the party and occasionally deported to Dachau along with their victims. But as depredations became less random they became more efficient. The Nazi regime eventually stripped Austrian Jews of an estimated 2.25 billion marks of capital and property.[161]

Mistreatment of Jews exceeded anything witnessed in Germany up to that point and precipitated a far more panicky exodus than that following the Jewish boycott of April 1, 1933. By the end of 1938 the number of non-Aryan emigrants from Austria was about five times the German total for that year.[162]

It was not long before the staff of the Quaker office in Vienna mounted a heroic campaign of rescue. In 1938, as in 1934, they did so without the cooperation of the small meeting in the Austrian capital. As early as May, Anne Martin had taxed Vienna Quakers with a lack of courage, contending: "They will probably take on protective coloring and keep quiet." When Robert Yarnall visited Vienna in the aftermath of the Kristallnacht, he was surprised to discover that Rudolf Boeck, Vienna's representative on the Executive Committee of the German Yearly Meeting, was "a real, honest, enthusiastic Nazi." For Boeck, as for other Nazis, the November pogrom "was a spontaneous uprising of the people." When Yarnall pointed out that this "spontaneity" occurred at the same time throughout Germany, his Austrian vis-à-vis replied, without thinking, blinking, or blushing: "Yes, you see, these things must be planned or else they get out of hand." Boeck and local Quakers also insisted that Quakerism was "a faith and a way of life which should not be confused with charity." As a result, the Quaker office at Singerstrasse 16 became less a "center" of the Society of Friends in Austria, but more an outpost for British and American welfare workers.[163]

However, these foreign Friends soon found other allies. The most surprising among them was Austria's Catholic primate, Cardinal Theodor Innitzer, who had earlier assured Hitler that he admired the achievements of National Socialism, along with his bishops, who also rejoiced that the annexation of their country had "fulfilled thousand-year-old yearnings of the [Austrian] people." These encomiums notwithstanding, the cardinal contributed three thousand marks to the Jesuit Georg Bichlmair's work on behalf of formerly Jewish Catholics. Nor did he in any way obstruct similar activities by a prominent laywoman, Countess Emanuela Kielmannsegg, who privately organized and maintained a staff of ten persons for that purpose.[164]

Other benefactors included a mysterious Dutchman, Frank van Gheel-Gildemeester, whom some contemporaries identified as a philanthropist while others viewed him as a racketeer who primarily protected Jews who could pay for his services. The new power brokers, including Göring's Austrian brother-in-law, Hans Fischböck, remembered assistance Gheel-Gildemeester had provided to Nazi families in 1934, and they permitted him to open a new office that unquestionably assisted many prospective emigrants. Surviving correspondence confirms that the Dutchman had access to influential individuals and possessed the ability to single out cases for which a persuasive argument could be made to Nazi potentates.[165]

Another Quaker ally, in every respect above suspicion, was the Swedish Lutheran pastor Sobe Hedenquist, whose mission in Vienna has been credited with helping nearly half of Vienna's seven to eight thousand formerly Jewish Protestants to escape.[166]

A special role in the Vienna aid effort was played by various roving representatives of child-rescue organizations, including Truus Wijsmuller-Meyer of the Dutch Committee for Aid to Children. Since 1933 she had been working with her country's Committee for Special Jewish Interests and had often proved herself a virtuoso improviser; for example, she once smuggled six Jewish children from Hamburg across the Dutch border. Upon learning that Princess Juliana was on the train, she managed to place her charges in a compartment next to that of the royal lady. In spite of having no papers, the children were allowed by guards to pass over the border, rather than cause a commotion within hearing of the princess. When Wijsmuller-Meyer first arrived in Vienna on December 3, 1938, she straightway bearded the ruthless Adolf Eichmann in his den. Boorish, arrogant, and contemptuous of all "do-gooders," the omnipotent local master over Jewish life and death first insisted, before he would hear her out, that she document her own Aryan descent: only afterward did he agree to give her the remainder of the week to assemble a transport of six hundred Jewish children. With the help of Lola Hahn, a Warburg married to an Aryan German, she met that goal and went on to lead several similar expeditions, from both Austria and Germany, the last one on December 31, 1939.[167]

Still, after the entire rescue-mission terrain has been surveyed, one finds that Emma Cadbury's small but growing band remained the major mediator between hunters and hunted. Though Emma herself collapsed late in 1938 from overwork, aggravated by arthritis, the work went on, helped by a diverse influx of observers and volunteers. The visiting Clarence Pickett found the office coping with an uncontrollable flood of petitioners, including a sudden irruption of Social Democratic refugees from Czechoslovakia. Robert Yarnall and his wife, Elizabeth, joined the force, determined to disregard fears about growing American anti-Semitism, to do their "clear duty to help [Austrian Jews] in their extremity." Aged Gilbert MacMaster once again relinquished his retirement in Basel to assist with the rescue efforts. This veteran of every Quaker campaign in Central Europe since 1919 visited old friends, among them a woman stripped of her pension even though she was the widow of the 1911 recipient of the Nobel Peace Prize, Alfred Fried (1864–1921). The wife of Ludwig Quidde (1858–1941), another German peace pioneer, was found living with her sister from the proceeds of the sale of her cello. "When that [money] is gone," she told MacMaster, "we can sit down quietly in the kitchen and turn on the gas." He also tried to comfort families of Austrian pacifists, and used his acquaintance with the new *Gauleiter*, Josef Bürckel, whom he had met during his sojourn in the Saar after the 1935 plebiscite, to free the leader of the Czech colony in Vienna.[168]

Another samaritan, Irish journalist Hubert T. Butler, came to the Vienna Center on his own initiative and recalls his days there as "the happiest time of my life." As an old man he pondered the paradox of being "happy when others were miserable" and attributed it to the sense of fulfillment engendered by work that was saving lives. Butler had found a kindly official at the Mexican legation who would issue visas for the asking. These documents might not get the recipient into Mexico, he consoled himself, but they could get him or her out of Vienna.

Butler also remembers that this sense of satisfaction permeated the daily lives of all British and American workers at the Vienna Center, where he claims to have been the only non-Quaker; but a letter to his wife written in November or December 1938 tells a less buoyant story: it describes days when endless, and often fruitless, interviews left "one utterly drained of sympathy and ideas and resourcefulness."[169]

Uncertainty about the nature and effect of Quaker work also interspersed MacMaster's reports from the Austrian metropolis. As he watched the procession of tens of thousands of applicants at the United States Consulate, he calculated that it would take fifty years to evacuate every individual wanting to cross the Atlantic. At the same time, he remained the last "old-timer" on record who could never quite accept that Quaker volunteers in Vienna had become welfare workers instead of apostles of a unique kind of spirituality. Nor could MacMaster divest himself of the traditional Quaker assumption that it took two parties to generate conflict, and that support of one party alone did not address the origins of any confrontation. He prayed "that the Jews be given the fortitude to bear the load of suffering that was being put upon them and live it down, and [thereby] prove themselves to be the stronger." Unaware of what still impended, he added: "Many of them will have to do this in any case. They cannot all get away."[170]

Such philosophic detachment eluded most of the younger staff. Working months on end, seven days a week, they snatched irregular meals at their desks between tearful interviews. After closing hours they stayed for long stretches dictating to exhausted secretaries. Tessa Rowntree—then in her early twenties—the last survivor of the group, was visiting a cousin in Germany when Austria fell. She immediately rushed to Vienna where she had "a rather nerve-racking time of it." She, too, now admits that the work often left her out of sorts, even with victims, but she remained at her post.[171]

Amid the chaotic desperation that held both benefactors and petitioners in its pitiless grip was one person who seems to have kept her composure: Käte Neumayer, another non-Quaker, whom Hubert Butler had forgotten. An Aryan Austrian Catholic and the only full-time paid worker besides Emma Cadbury, she appeared "a tall, dignified, thin woman with reddish hair," who "seemed to have definite command of all office detail." How it was possible for her to do this work, not only after the Nazi invasion but also after war gradually stripped the office of its foreign occupants, remains a mystery I have not been able to unravel.[172]

Against a backdrop of more than 100,000 Jews leaving Vienna between the German invasion and the outbreak of World War II, Käte Neumayer's "command" of the business at hand is documented in surviving records that provide a far more detailed account of the achievements of the Vienna office than do the records of the Berlin Center. According to the meticulous statistics that survive, 6,000 cases, representing 13,745 persons, were registered between March 15, 1938, and August 28, 1939, and 2,408 of this total were ultimately able to leave. They included 1,588 men, 509 women, and 311 dependents, the largest number, 1,264, going to England, 165 to the United States, and 107 to Australia. Major occupational categories included 241 white-collar workers, 119 physicians (the majority of 179 registrants), and 101 students. At the same time, Vienna Center Quakers succeeded in transporting 882 children who left Austria without their families; there were 665 still awaiting transport when war broke out.

Not all the work was done in Vienna. A branch office in Graz seems to have operated at least during part of 1938, confining its work to paying subsidies to sixty persons in the city and an additional ninety throughout the province of Styria.[173]

Three days before the outbreak of World War II, Neumayer reported that "the foreign workers [had] left . . . for a holiday in Switzerland," from where they wired that they had gone to England "for the time being." Armed with a power of attorney, left by her departed colleagues, she "hoped to carry on as long as possible." She expressed gratitude for the confidence reposed in her but added that she looked forward to "a time . . . when we can all work together as before."[174]

However, not all foreign workers left for home right away. Tessa Rowntree joined "the loosely assembled group of people representing several international organizations in getting as many people out of Czechoslovakia as possible." Their work was plagued by periodic warnings from "some of the official representatives of the allied countries," to the effect that they should be "very much aware" of "evidence that Hitler and the Nazi regime" were using the exodus as a way "of pushing their own subversives." Once their suspicions had been aroused, they did indeed discover that the tales of woe told by some of their clients "were completely fabricated." On another occasion when Rowntree was escorting German political refugees from Prague through Poland, officials there seem to have been doing their best to obstruct escape from the Czech capital. This time they took her off the train, claiming irregularities in her papers, and forced the transport to proceed to port in Gdynia, and thence to England, without her. It should be noted here that as late as March 13, 1939, relief workers had received no indication that Prague would shortly fall to the Nazi conquerors; but now, two days later, many individuals possessing all necessary papers and tickets were left stranded. A week later Tessa accompanied a group of seventy-one—fifty-two women, fifteen children, and four men—on a last desperate sally, this time across Germany. This last exit proceeded without a hitch, for, as she subsequently related, German "officials [at the frontier] were fortunately not very interested in us." A last group of thirty left the occupied Czech capital by the same route on March 24, this time shepherded by Martha Sharp, an American Unitarian. Sharp's last act of mercy was a donation of money to a group of eighteen Jews left stranded at the Dutch border in Bentheim. Their papers, too, were not in order, and they could neither go on to Holland nor return to Germany. One can only guess at their ultimate fate.[175]

Rowntree finally repaired to her homeland, angry and frustrated that the outside world had allowed her and her associates to be surprised by this third Nazi invasion in one year. "It seems criminal that those of us working for refugees in Prague were not given a little notice, as we might have packed off hundreds of refugees, whose emigration plans were almost or quite completed," she wrote to the editor of the American *Friend*. "Now they are in concentration camps, or have committed suicide or have gone illegally to Poland." What she did not reveal was that she and her companions had spent much time after March 15 stuffing papers and passports down toilets in their hotel. "We felt that had the Nazis found the passports and the owners that would have been the end for many of the latter." Still, she wanted to return even now, and desisted only upon the urgent advice of British diplomats, who also took pains to clear all other foreign relief workers from what was now the Protectorate of Bohemia-Moravia. When she returned to Prague in 1945, during Czechoslovakia's short-lived liberation from tyranny, she discovered to her sorrow that some of the Czech Quakers she had come to know in 1939 had also perished in German concentration camps.[176]

Thenceforth, Quaker relief work in Central Europe would conform to the changing map of the area and be centered in Berlin. Britons had gone home to avoid internment, and American Friends carried on alone until their country entered the war. But before I turn to tell of the war years, I shall have to digress briefly to consider another, separate, aspect of the Quaker relationship with National Socialism: the involvement of British Friends in the effort to prevent war through appeasement of the Nazi regime.

George Grosz's "Christ with the Gas Mask." (courtesy Archiv der Akademie der Künste, Berlin)

Clarence Pickett, secretary of the American Friends Service Committee. (courtesy AFSCA)

Gilbert MacMaster, an American representative at the Berlin Center. (courtesy AFSCA)

Rufus Jones, the spiritual leader of American Friends between the two world wars. (courtesy Quaker Collection, Haverford College Library)

Berlin Center staff in 1925. Thomas Kelly is in the middle. (courtesy Quaker Collection, Haverford College Library)

Berlin Center staff in 1940. Howard Elkinton is on the far left. Leonard Kenworthy is on the far right. (courtesy AFSCA)

J. Roger Carter, the British representative at the Berlin Center from 1938 to 1939. (courtesy Friends House, London)

Bertha Bracey, the backbone of the British Quaker effort on behalf of German refugees.
(courtesy Friends House, London)

Elizabeth Fox Howard, a British Quaker worker in Frankfurt and the first hostess at the rest home for Nazi victims. (courtesy Friends House, London)

Corder and Gwen Catchpool and their children and nanny in Berlin in 1933.
(courtesy Friends House, London)

Alfons Paquet, German Quaker writer and
journalist. (courtesy German Yearly Meeting)

Emil Fuchs, German Christian Socialist, Lutheran pastor, and Quaker luminary. (courtesy German Yearly Meeting)

Ko.. ...uonslager Dachau
Kommandantur

Am 6.Oktober 1944

Entlassungsschein.

Der Schutzhaftgefangene   Erwin P o l l t z ,

geb. 21.1o.86   zu Dresden

war bis zum heutigen Tage im Konzentrationslager Dachu vegmahrt.

Laut Verfügung der Baäphssicherheitauptamt BerFlH 21.9.44 IV 1 A 6b-H.Nr.
21263
wurde die Schutzhaft aufgehoben. Er wurde angewesen, sich sofort bei der Ortspolizei-
behörde seines Wohnortes zu melden.

Lagerkommandant

N/0073 4.43. 3000

Manfred Erwin Pollatz's release from Dachau. (courtesy Inge Pollatz)

Manfred Pollatz and his daughters in 1964. (courtesy Miep Lieftinck)

Margarethe Lachmund. (courtesy Peter Lachmund)

Olga, Gerhard, and Anna Halle in Pyrmont in 1932. (courtesy Anna Halle)

Mary and Leonhard Friedrich. (courtesy German Yearly Meeting)

Hans Albrecht in 1939. (courtesy Etta Mekeel)

Katharina Petersen, headmistress of Eerde from 1934 to 1938. (Hans A. Schmitt)

Billy Hilsley, Eerde's master of music. (courtesy Billy Hilsley)

Orfeo and Euridice, *performed at Eerde in the autumn of 1937. (courtesy Kurt Weingarten)*

Eerde castle. (courtesy Roger Carter)

Kurt Neuse, Eerde's master teacher and the 1938 group of candidates for the Oxford School Certificate. (courtesy Charlotte Shalmon-Warburg)

On the left: Heinz Wild, who taught the elementary school. On the right: Werner Hermans, history teacher and headmaster from 1940 to 1943. (courtesy Werner Hermans)

Max Adolf Warburg and his daughter Maria in 1941. (courtesy Maria Warburg-Mills)

Josi Warburg, Eerde's first housemother. (courtesy Maria Warburg-Mills)

The controversial Jan Boost, Eerde's first Dutch teacher. (Hans A. Schmitt)

Elisabeth Schmitt, a housemother and teacher, was eventually placed in charge of the Jewish children at "De Esch." (Hans A. Schmitt)

Hermann Isaac, who was deported to Auschwitz. (courtesy Richard Schmitt)

*Klaus Seckel, the youngest deportee. His parents survived the Holocaust.
(courtesy Richard Schmitt)*

5.

British Friends and the Appeasement
of Nazi Germany

Up to this point we have observed how Quakers brought aid and comfort to ethnic and political victims of persecution in Central Europe. We have seen how they stood ready to help individuals and groups without prior inquiry into their beliefs or origins. Now we must focus on their role among political peacemakers in Britain, dedicated to sparing Europe another multinational conflict.

For several years the German government's response to overtures by British appeasers was sufficiently cordial to encourage their continuation. While despising the peace loving as deeply as they did the Jews, Nazis recognized that some of these pacifists occupied prominent positions in British political life, notably in the ranks of the loyal opposition in Parliament. German officials were equally delighted to discover that these advocates of peaceful conflict resolution also demanded revisions of the peace settlement following World War I that their country had sought ever since the Treaty of Versailles was signed. The resulting meetings of men and minds represented a strange contradiction: Nazi officials welcoming pacifists to Germany—most of them also Socialists— even taking them to see Hitler, feting them at banquets, both in Nuremberg (at party congresses) and in Berlin, while their German counterparts languished in concentration camps. In Nazi eyes these Britons were bona fide friends of Germany and considered worthy of a warm welcome at the highest level.[1]

On the British side these comings and goings also involved at times "strategically placed members of certain minority Christian sects" who sought to practice in the field of international politics "the virtue their faith had . . . enjoined upon them." Included among such practicing Christians were George Lansbury (1859–1940), leader of the opposition from 1931 to 1935; Clifford Allen, Lord Hurtwood, former head of the Independent Labor Party; as well as three Quakers: Lord Noël-Buxton (1869–1948), minister of agriculture in two Labour governments; his brother, Charles Roden Buxton (1875–1942), member of Parliament from Accrington and chairman of the Labour Party's Advisory Committee on Foreign Affairs; and Corder Catchpool, the peripatetic, long-term pillar of the Berlin Quaker Center, "a man whose goodness approached the saintly." All of them believed that the Nazi revolution was the product of the iniquities of the peace settlement following World War I and were confident that by lending an ear to German grievances they were performing a major service for the cause of peace and justice.

These men belonged to an Anglo-German group that represented a left-of-center coalition of pacifists, several of whom, as conscientious objectors, had served prison sentences in World War I. Among their most important German contacts were Margarete Gärtner, head of the government-sponsored Society of Political Economics (founded in 1922) who claimed friends in both major political parties in Britain, and Ribbentrop's adviser, Fritz Berber, head of the German Academy for Politics and a former pacifist and alumnus of Woodbrooke: after 1933 he became an ardent spokesman for the German campaign to recover the nation's "sovereignty, honor, and freedom."[2]

Several members of the Anglo-German group were admitted into Hitler's presence and took at face value the führer's periodic assertions of his peaceful aims. Noël-Buxton visited him in 1934, after which he joined Catchpool on a guided tour of some concentration camps, an experience that did not diminish his faith in continued collaboration with "reasonable Germans." Hurtwood's two meetings with Germany's dictator were highlighted by Hitler's assurance that he sought no arms race with Britain, nor with the rest of Europe for that matter, and that he was willing to sign an accord that would limit Germany's naval rearmament to 35 percent of Britain's tonnage: a suggestion that was all too speedily implemented by the London government.[3] However, the Labour peer's efforts to free political prisoners—such as the lawyer Hans Litten, courageous defender of Communists in Nazi courts—were in vain, as were his pleas for an end to anti-Semitic depredations. Still, he came away from these meetings with the conviction that Hitler was a man of peace.[4] Hurtwood even persuaded himself that the conduct of German domestic policy was moderating. On June 28, 1935, he wrote the *Times* (London): "And now that we in Britain are so genuinely anxious to heal the wounds of inequity which we ought never to have inflicted upon our German neighbors, I am convinced [that appeasement] would go far to making this new reconciliation [that is, the naval agreement] wholehearted and spontaneous." Germany's aggressive posturing in international affairs, he had already assured the *Daily Telegraph* after his return from Berlin in January, did not represent belligerent intentions "but her sense of grievance. She wants peace both because she knows that she would be crushed in war" and because her postwar generation was more interested in domestic reform "than external aggression."[5] Hurtwood's obsessive concern with conciliating a former enemy may have been induced by the knowledge that he was dying of tuberculosis. It should be added that his efforts to bring about a better world never lessened his concern for German political prisoners and never silenced his condemnation of anti-Semitism. As an invited guest to the 1936 Nuremberg party rally, he was appalled by Goebbels's diatribes against the Soviet Union, which, to him, implied that "Germany wishes to exclude Russia from the European family—a monstrous proposition." He nevertheless continued to cling to every shred of hope, particularly after Hitler's renewed peace campaign following the remilitarization of the Rhineland. He wondered whether the king himself could not meet Hitler and explain to him "the British Mind." His most sweeping proposition, however, was for a general conference, predicated on Germany's return to the League of Nations: a step Hitler had cynically hinted at being willing to take. As one prominent historian and critic of appeasement has put it: Hurtwood "was prepared . . . to temper his moral concerns with an apparently more practical commitment to the overriding need for peace, and for justice *on issues in which Germany appeared the wronged party.*"[6]

The same motives that drove Hurtwood also actuated his friend Corder Catchpool, who saw Hitler's pacific pronouncements after the Rhineland occupation as a "last chance" for peace. In his view, Nazis had "their own way" of offering friendship, and "that makes things difficult," but their sometimes incongruent behavior must not diminish efforts to save their country from isolation. Charles Roden Buxton, too, agreed with Hurtwood's concept of a comprehensive settlement whose parties would not dwell on one another's past offenses, but concentrate, instead, on "their present needs and aspirations." In line with the expectations of the moment, Buxton placed more emphasis on understanding Germany's grievances than on France's fears of a resurgent neighbor. The league, he added, should facilitate the process of negotiation by placing Article 19 of the covenant—which authorized the assembly to propose changes in existing agreements—ahead of Article 14, which called for joint action against its violators.[7]

The last member of this circle of British humanitarians to visit Hitler was George Lansbury, patriarch of the British Labour Movement, who arrived in Berlin on April 1, 1937. Lansbury first attended a Quaker meeting of worship at the Berlin Center, which was to be a more satisfying experience than was his conversation with the führer the following day. At this meeting, Corder Catchpool, who was to interpret for him, was rudely pushed aside in favor of Paul Schmidt, the resident *Dolmetscher* of the German Foreign Office. By this time Hitler had become less accessible, less obliging, and less communicative. On this occasion he agreed to attend a conference devoted to the discussion of international problems only if some other country took the initiative to convene it. How little that concession signified became evident when Lansbury and Catchpool's version of the encounter was not included in a subsequent communiqué to the press. Lansbury came away feeling sorry for, and superior to, his German host, whom he described as "a very lonely man [who] has no spiritual background to fall back on." He also remained convinced that the

German dictator would "not go to war unless pushed into it by others. He knows how a European war will end."[8]

For Catchpool, however, this latest fiasco justified no relaxation of his own pursuit of peace. A few weeks later he was back in Germany with Henry Gillett and Rufus Jones's young Haverford protégé, Douglas Steere, to examine the "arbitrary Polish boundary" in Upper Silesia. He also suggested to Clarence Pickett, of whose friendship with Eleanor Roosevelt he may have been aware, that a meeting between Roosevelt and Hitler should be arranged. Throughout 1937 the Memel issue and the child-feeding scheme in Czechoslovakia gave him additional opportunities to visit Germany. In October he met Konrad Henlein, the leader of the Sudeten German Party, who "gave him the impression of a straightforward, moderate and able man." He also filled dozens of speaking engagements in Britain, where audiences were eager to profit from the wisdom born of his intensive and extensive German experience. He warned that a fear of impending economic catastrophe filled that country with a sense of doom that might lead to other incalculable disasters. Noël-Buxton was an equally tireless traveler to Berlin at this time and worried that conflict over the Sudetenland might drag Britain into war. To him, concessions to Germany, no matter what their result, would at least leave Britons with a clearer conscience than the events of 1914 had provided.[9]

The crisis years of 1938 and 1939 required increasingly daring leaps of faith on the part of British pacifists. Some of them were beginning to lose heart. So unqualified an advocate of appeasement as the journalist Sir Philip Gibbs launched his latest polemic for peace—much of it based on information provided by Corder Catchpool—with a catalog of chilling reservations elicited by the invasion of Austria. Germany, he admitted, had manifested "a ruthlessness of will bound to be regarded as a threat to other states." Recent events, indeed, had "dimmed one's hope" for peace.[10]

Catchpool, however, remained impervious to this defeatist spirit. He seems to have expected particularly salutary results from his contacts with Fritz Berber. He was in the process of arranging a meeting with the German will-o'-the-wisp, which was also to include Hurtwood and Noël-Buxton, when the Austro-German crisis moved toward its climax.[11] Though it is not clear whether that particular engagement was kept, the following summer saw the itinerant Quaker hard at work setting in motion a Hurtwood mission to Prague and Berlin as the next claim on Germany's agenda, cession of the Sudetenland, moved to the center of the international stage. Quaker appeasers agreed that this issue justified no call to arms. Noël-Buxton considered the territorial integrity of Czechoslovakia an "untenable cause," and Catchpool wondered how any Briton who had supported war in defense of Belgium in 1914 could countenance a confrontation to prevent, as he saw it, Sudeten German self-determination. He proposed, instead, to save Czechoslovakia by appealing to "better elements" in Germany.[12]

While Catchpool may have believed that such a faction existed, and that it wielded sufficient influence to determine German policy, his dying friend Hurtwood, on the other hand, was approaching the deeply painful conclusion that Berlin had hoodwinked British friends of peace. "On several occasions I have realized," he wrote Lord Halifax on March 14, 1938, "that to become a public protagonist of goodwill with Germany without saying something on the other side of the question has led the Germans to exploit us and our advocacy." The disappointment rife in these lines was no doubt deepened by the news of the death of Hans Litten, his protégé, at the hand of his jailers. But even as Hurtwood successfully petitioned the home secretary, Sir Samuel Hoare, to grant asylum to Litten's widow and family, and even as his confidence in German tractability was dimmed, he was able to separate specific humanitarian tasks from a wider duty. "If we are to knock down Hitler and Mussolini we must first put them as much in the wrong as possible" was one explanation for his simultaneous decision to support the transfer of the Sudeten Germans to Germany. When Corder Catchpool visited him on June 6, 1938, it was decided that the two would shortly depart for Germany and Czechoslovakia. Visits to Ribbentrop and Czech President Beneš were put on the itinerary. Then Hurtwood's physical condition took a turn for the worse, and he considered asking the Friend to select another companion. Finally, Catchpool went alone to prepare the ground in both capitals, using Fritz Berber as his liaison with the German Foreign Office. By late July, Hurtwood was well enough to deliver what turned out to be his valedictory to the House of Lords. He admitted that continuing oppression in Germany was impeding the peace "which we all desire established." Just when a realization of past errors had created unprecedented goodwill among the British people, Germany had seen fit to halt its growth with new barriers of misunderstanding. "I have myself known what it is to be the [prisoner] of His Majesty's Government . . . for quite a considerable period of time," he reminded his audience, and he knew, therefore, firsthand, that any government was on occasion capable of proscribing unpopular opinions. "But the persecution which is being carried on in Germany is not that of persecuting opinion, but of persecuting blood." He went on to clarify that he had long favored colonial concessions to the Reich, but now, he asked: "when we see the tragic evils which are being perpetrated in Germany," what would a transfer of these territories signify for native populations? He concluded with an earnest plea, not for more understanding for Nazi Germany, but for more concern for suffering Jewry. "We should gain in the end by restoring the Jew to the dignity which he ought to possess by liberating his spirit with some measure of happiness after the centuries of persecution."[13]

Early in August, Hurtwood and Catchpool boarded a plane on their way to essay the impossible—vaulting the latest German obstacles to peace. The altitude of air travel and an unusual heat wave in Berlin aggravated the former's physical suffering. "Some day," he told his companion between coughing fits and lung hemorrhages, "a bout will come and carry me off." From the edge of the grave he warned Ribbentrop that if Germany launched a sudden attack, Britain would be bound to take military reprisals. Then he proceeded to Czechoslovakia, pleading with the Sudeten Germans—who mistook his private mission for an official one—to agree to a four-power conference and spending two days in Prague with Milan Hodža, the Czech minister president, as well as with the leader of Sudeten German Social Democrats, Wenzel Jaksch. On August 15, Hurtwood and Catchpool, who "was taking loving care of [him]," were back in Berlin before returning to London to report to Lord Halifax what they had seen and heard. The dying peer's recommendations comprehended a more qualified accession to German demands than the Munich conference was to produce. He favored Sudeten German self-determination but hedged by international controls that would include a four-power guarantee of the territorial integrity of the remainder of Czechoslovakia. Nazi treatment of ethnic, political, and religious minorities ruled out, in Hurtwood's opinion, an unconditional cession of the contested territory. A helpless spectator, he could only watch as subsequent events confirmed these misgivings. After a prolonged confinement in a Swiss sanatorium, he died on March 3, 1939, mercifully spared the events of March 15 when all the hopes to which he had dedicated his life collapsed. He was cremated at Lausanne on March 6, and his widow scattered his ashes on Lake Geneva "to float past the building of the League."[14]

Meanwhile, Catchpool's British coreligionists continued to oppose war. One of them, Horace Alexander, an expert on India and a great admirer of Mahatma Gandhi, insisted that these setbacks called for no Quaker retreat from the religious and moral principles they had embraced since the days of George Fox. "The worship of national strength is perhaps the supreme blasphemy of our age," Alexander had told a meeting at Friends House on November 18, 1938. Friends must, therefore, "stand firm in [their] refusal to participate in war or in preparation for war."[15] These Quaker pacifists may have derived additional comfort from Roger Carter's report that many Germans thanked Neville Chamberlain for saving the peace, not, however, if they heeded Carter's ominous addendum: "But no one seriously believes that this was [Hitler's] last territorial demand."[16]

The German occupation of Prague validated this assumption, while the subsequent campaign for the return to Germany of Danzig, and the Corridor separating East Prussia from the remainder of the country, proved that Hitler was pursuing an agenda of expansion completely at variance with earlier gestures of pacific moderation. It is difficult under these circumstances to explain what expectations attended continued Quaker efforts to find a common ground, unless it was a stubborn determination to do one's moral duty as long as war between Germany and Great Britain had not actually been declared.

Much of this activity involved periodic meetings with Fritz Berber, but it cannot be claimed, on the basis of available evidence, that his views carried any weight with Hitler. He provided anxious Friends with someone official to talk to, but some of his responses must have convinced many of them of the utter futility of this ongoing verbal intercourse. Berber visited London in March 1939, and in June he gave Catchpool another extended interview. At that time the Quaker "saint," while frankly shaken by the German march into Prague, could still understand Germany's professed fear of encirclement, which he considered "not completely without foundation." Under these circumstances Berber's continued willingness to meet remained a source of hope. His last and most elaborate proposition to Catchpool—unaccompanied by any claim that he was speaking for his superiors—was cold comfort indeed, for he demanded that Britain accept the status quo of March 15, the transfer of Danzig and the Corridor to Germany, and recognize German colonial claims, while promoting his country's secure access to such raw materials as Swedish ore and Romanian oil. Once Germany's territorial demands had been met and her quest for economic security had been satisfied, Berber implied, she would become a peaceful member of the international community. At the same time he made it clear to Catchpool that he did not seriously expect these conditions to be met and that he had given up all hope for peace. The British Friend, however, would not accept that conclusion and proposed that they meet again in October.[17]

Meanwhile, Roger Carter, from his own busy perch at the Berlin Center and Grüber's office, was seconding Catchpool's effort to arrange other missions of understanding, possibly including a visit of P. H. B. Lyon, headmaster of Carter's alma mater, Rugby, and a conspicuous peace activist, as well as goodwill exchanges of Boy Scout troops and choirs. In June and July he accompanied both Charles Roden Buxton and Catchpool on fact-finding visits to Danzig, during which the visitors called on members of the city's senate and League Commissioner Carl Burckhardt. The dogged steadfastness of his more experienced companions, who refused to shed the conviction that the just cause of peace would prevail provided that sufficient energy was committed to its service, seems to have strengthened his own fragile faith in the immediate future. As he confessed more than half a century later: "It was, of course, pretentious of us to think that any action on our part could make one iota of difference, but 'leaving no stone unturned' was the dominant thought in our minds."[18]

Roger Carter also had another conversation with Fritz Berber, on a three-hour flight from Salzburg to Berlin, on July 28, 1939, during which the German official warned him that "we might very likely expect a surprise one of these days," a statement Carter interpreted as meaning that some kind of agreement with the Soviet Union was in the offing. Berber also repeated what he had told Catchpool in June, that a diplomatic settlement of the Polish boundary was unlikely, and he was no less firm in rejecting Carter's suggestion that German expansion should undergo "a pause to allow the present heat of feeling to die down." The führer, he explained, "was a priori against unnecessary delay." Political liberalization of the German regime in Bohemia-Moravia was equally out of the question, but he thought that a German guarantee of the remainder of Polish territory, combined with Polish docking rights in Danzig, might be considered. In other words, Berber offered a reprise of the Munich fiasco, and again we have no way of knowing whether he did so officially or whether he was freelancing.[19] Carter simply passed on the information to Charles Roden Buxton and returned to his other work.

The last stones appear to have been turned in the middle of August. In London both Chamberlain's adviser, Sir Horace Wilson, and Charles Roden Buxton, in his capacity as foreign-policy counselor to the Labour Party, drafted comprehensive proposals for a settlement of Anglo-German differences, especially in the economic sphere. The German ambassador, Herbert von Dirksen, forwarded both to the Wilhelmstrasse. When they remained without response, Dirksen decided to come to Berlin, probably on August 13, where he found that these appeals "had simply been tossed into the wastepaper basket by Hitler and Ribbentrop." The die was cast.[20]

Neither Buxton nor Catchpool knew that, however. The latter now turned to another German contact from past campaigns, the Mennonite Benjamin Heinrich Unruh. While on his way to some mountain climbing in Switzerland— his favorite hobby—Catchpool stopped in Karlsruhe to inform Unruh of the continued search for a way to prevent war. The Mennonite had the mistaken impression that his Quaker visitor was on an official mission and promised to inform his control officer, Councillor of Legation Kundt, in the cultural section of the Foreign Office. An appointment was arranged, and Catchpool and Buxton arrived in Berlin on August 15. Whatever proposals they presented do not seem to have survived but may have been nothing more than a rehash of suggestions Berber had earlier rejected in his plane conversation with Carter: liberalization of Czech governance and an ironclad guarantee of Polish territory once Danzig and the Corridor had been ceded. Clearly, the visit produced no results.[21]

The onset of war convinced Noël-Buxton that destruction of Nazi Germany was now Britain's most urgent task. His brother, on the other hand, resigned his chairmanship of the Advisory Committee on Foreign Affairs when the Labour Party threw its unqualified support behind the war effort. Charles Roden Buxton still held that an accommodation with Germany was possible, even after the end of the Polish campaign. Horace Alexander met Berber in Switzerland at Christmas. What he hoped to accomplish and what they talked about seems likewise unknown. Catchpool spent the remainder of 1939 vainly trying to persuade Dutch and Belgian leaders to organize an international group of mediators. He continued to plead with Lord Halifax to search for ways of ending the war. In Germany, Berber—the lapsed pacifist—trumpeted the Western powers' responsibility "for the frivolous war into which they had dragged Germany on September 3, 1939."[22]

Why recapitulate these comings and goings that no one who counted seems to have taken seriously even at the time? It is to show that opportunities were lost, not by the illusion of appeasement but by the illusion that violence could produce a viable order in Europe. All these kindly, Christian, pacifist men of goodwill were to be justified a thousand times over by the terrible years that followed. War could have been avoided, but—to quote Catchpool once more—"there were too few working for peace" and "too many acting in an exactly opposite spirit."[23] Certainly, too few on Germany's side. The peacemakers failed, but they did what they should have done. Their hopeless quest has not transformed the world, and their cause remains as lost as ever. Yet, we cannot but admire and respect them for their "Inner Light" that radiated so much hope for so long during the darkest times. They continue to set a moral if not pragmatic example for the rest of us.

6.
Quaker Work in Time of War

A GRIMMER CONTEXT

War and early victory failed to soften Nazi hearts. Their victims, German Jews, in particular, continued to feel the full force of their fanatical hatred. On September 1, 1939, a curfew was imposed on Jews in the Reich, followed by the order to turn in their telephones and radios. In October the first deportees left Vienna for Poland, and in February 1940 the first transport from Germany left Stettin for the same destination. On September 1, 1941, compulsory wearing of the yellow star added another infliction to the steady succession of inhumanities. Departure for safer havens, all but impossible as Hitler's empire expanded to the Pyrenees and the gates of Moscow, was outlawed by a decree dated October 23, 1941. One month later another law mandated the confiscation of all properties that deportees had left behind, and the Wannsee Conference on January 20, 1942, completed plans for cleansing Europe of Jews. Thenceforth the gas ovens would work relentlessly until Auschwitz was abandoned by retreating German armies to advancing Soviet troops on January 27, 1945.[1]

Offspring of mixed marriages continued to be yanked to and fro. At the start of the Polish campaign they were called to active duty, but, because mistreatment of their Jewish relatives might undermine their devotion to the German war effort, Hitler—who considered them a military liability—authorized a directive on the eve of the 1940 campaign in the west that returned them, as well as spouses of Jewish and half-Jewish wives, to civilian life. Some exceptions were, however, made, especially of men decorated for bravery in past campaigns, but the führer also put a stop to that in 1942. Yet, when defeat loomed in 1944, he was forced to abandon this exclusionary policy, and many *Mischlinge* were called up again to serve in construction battalions mobilized to build defensive installations. Even so, the long-term future of these "mongrels" was extensively debated at the Wannsee Conference, where representatives of the SS wanted them exterminated, unless married to Aryans, and then only on condition that they submit to sterilization. Debate about the demoralizing effect such measures would have on Aryan relatives of these victims led to an impasse. Even Goebbels agreed to postpone any decision until the end of the war. Nevertheless, extermination ultimately became the lot of half-Jews who were deported along

with Jewish inmates of concentration camps and of half-Jewish children in
welfare institutions who were euthanized during the last two years of the war.
Clearly, the fate of German half-Jews could range from the distinction of an Iron
Cross to oblivion from a lethal puff of gas.[2]

That any non-Aryan should have wanted to wear a German uniform in World
War II will only surprise members of later generations who encounter Nazi
Germany in history books. They must once more be reminded that before
1933 German law recognized no legal distinction between Jew and Gentile
and that during the next twelve years many German descendants of Jewish
forebears decided that their expulsion from the ranks of the German nation
was so misguided an act that they were obliged to disregard it. In their hearts
they remained German, and love for the country of their birth, and its heritage,
continued unchanged. A few such stubborn loyalists were saved by miracles, but
most of them shared the fate of 150,000 Jewish Germans who perished during
the Holocaust, some taking their lives by eating poisoned mushrooms—after
sleeping pills had become too expensive for them.[3]

All but a few exceptional Christians in Germany remained indifferent to
the Jewish tragedy. Some chaplains in the armed forces even distributed anti-
Semitic literature, and the Confessional Church's protests on behalf of religious
freedom did not, as a rule, include Jews.[4] The German Mennonite Benjamin
Heinrich Unruh, who had enlisted Quakers in various Central European relief
projects, believed until his death that the near extermination of European
Jewry could have been prevented if Allied governments had supported what
he considered "the only possible and realisable plan": deporting 4 million of
them to the French colony of Madagascar, a project Hitler briefly considered
after the fall of France. Unruh may not have known that this scheme was not
conceived as a refuge but as a ghetto to be headed by an SS police chief,
the same arrangement under which the killing grounds in Eastern Europe
operated. Needless to say, no advocate of this enterprise ever explained how
4 million human beings, in time of war, were to be transported and settled
on this remote island. How deep widespread unconcern for Jewish destiny
went may also be judged from the fact that it was shared by the German
resistance, many of whose participants embraced Nazi assumptions of Semitic
inferiority.

This cumulative, staggering callousness makes the relatively few digressions
from the depressing norm all the more unforgettable: one was a public protest
staged on February 27, 1943, by Aryan wives of arrested Jewish husbands. On
orders from Goebbels, these women gained the release of their spouses one
week later. What they did not know was that the propaganda minister told his
staff, "We'll get them [back] after Stalingrad [where the German Sixth Army had
surrendered to the Russians on February 2] has blown over."[5]

Goebbels had no difficulty keeping that promise. Since October 18 of the previous year, the German Ministry of Justice had received Hitler's permission to relinquish to Himmler jurisdiction over "Poles, Russians, Jews, and Gypsies," because, as Minister Otto Thierack asserted, "Justice can contribute only little to the extermination of these ethnic categories." In other words, Jews in Germany no longer existed under the law, except as objects of extinction.[6]

THE BERLIN AND VIENNA CENTERS: TRANSFORMATION AND LIQUIDATION

Six weeks after the outbreak of World War II, Reinhard Heydrich, head of the German Security Police, issued his periodic report on the "political attitude of churches and sects." He lumped Quakers with a small group of free churches "whose international connections and pacifist attitudes [turned] them into valuable auxiliaries of Germany's opponents abroad."[7] In spite of this pronouncement Quakers were able to continue their work, but the range of their activities was steadily shrinking. The Berlin Center—ready for the worst but committed to staying the course to the finish—continued its work as the seemingly imperturbable Howard Elkinton had promised; his overriding goal remained to "keep open" and "stand by German Friends." He welcomed American visitors, who came to help out, but warned them that blacked-out Berlin was not a pleasant place for women and that food shortages ruled out service by individuals with delicate constitutions.

The daily routine chores were largely performed by a staff of German Quaker women, among whom Olga Halle, Martha Röhn, Eva Schaal, and Grete Sumpf are names that crop up again and again in Elkinton's reports, invariably followed by warm accolades. These ladies spoke to the unending stream of increasingly demoralized visitors, besides answering the phone and typing the correspondence. The material reward for this taxing, and often dangerous, work never exceeded barest subsistence.[8]

At the same time, AFSC commissioners were roaming Europe in support of enterprises sponsored by a variety of international aid organizations. After the rapid German advance into Poland—ending with that country's surrender on September 27, 1939—Herbert Hoover organized a Commission for Polish Relief, which provided food and clothing for 150,000 Polish refugees in Lithuania, Hungary, and Romania. When the fighting ended, Hoover dispatched a longtime associate, William C. MacDonald, to the defeated country to work along with Homer L. Morris, former director of child-feeding services in Berlin and now a professor at Earlham College, and Howard Elkinton. Their mission was to seek permission, from both British and German authorities, to send supplies through the blockade and supervise their distribution. The British were reluctant to cooperate, insisting that feeding the distressed was the responsibility of the invader who had caused the problem. For the duration of this aid effort, they confiscated supply ships and intermittently released them only after the London government was satisfied that the cargoes would actually go to the American committee rather than to the Germans. On the German side, no clear policy emerged at any time. At first they rejected any foreign involvement in Poland. In November that policy was moderated but quickly reversed once more. In February 1940 the occupier relented again and allowed Hoover's emissaries and the American Red Cross to distribute what supplies had meanwhile been pried from British hands at Gibraltar: mostly condensed milk and food supplements. When war began in the west, the effort came to an end, but not before half a million dollars' worth of provisions had been dispensed.[9]

The Berlin Center also played a significant part in this episode. Quaker commissioner Homer Morris arrived in the German capital as the Polish campaign was drawing to a close. He, too, was troubled by the usual uncertainties as to whether Nazis would allow assistance to their enemies by representatives of democratic countries and whether Quakers could agree to support a relief effort controlled by a government that was "making war on the world." At the German Foreign Office it was suggested that matters might be helped if these American humanitarians would, at the same time, inform the world how German occupiers tried to alleviate suffering in Czechoslovakia and Poland.[10] The American embassy was likewise skeptical and far from cordial when Morris called upon Chargé d'Affaires Alexander Kirk and Consul Raymond Geist. The atmosphere on these premises changed markedly, however, when the visitor from home offered two thousand dollars to assist in the repatriation of Polish Americans stranded in Berlin. "This may be a good way to start Polish work, even though it is a way that we had not thought of," Morris confided to his diary.

At one point in October 1939, German relief to Poles was temporarily in the hands of the National Socialist welfare monopoly headed by Erich Hilgenfeldt, who was willing to accept Quaker participation but who soon developed second thoughts when Friends insisted on the inclusion of Jews as well as their own control of distribution. Still, the three representatives of the Hoover committee received, on October 9, clearance to join a caravan of German NSV officials and finally, on October 17, departed—along with this entourage—for Warsaw. About ninety kilometers east of Berlin, the car in which Howard Elkinton was riding skidded off the road. Elkinton was thrown clear, suffering a broken shoulder and right leg. By evening he had been returned to the Charité, Berlin's prestigious public hospital, where his concerned Nazi hosts called the famous surgeon Ferdinand Sauerbruch to attend him. Three days later the expedition departed a second time, without Elkinton. After an overnight stop in Lodz, the group arrived in Warsaw where they met with Polish, Jewish, and German representatives and where the German civil commissioner in the Polish capital "stood ready to cooperate in any way possible." But a Hilgenfeldt crony, Karl Janasky, thrilled by the power he wielded, showed little concern for suffering mankind around him, refused to relinquish control of distribution, and categorically opposed assistance to Jews, thus seemingly ruling out Quaker involvement.[11] However, as in the case of the action on behalf of Nazi families in Vienna, Friends did not immediately withdraw. They reasoned that even a discriminatory relief program could give aid to people in need. Jews in Poland, they concluded, would be without resources anyway as long as the German presence continued and, therefore, Quaker efforts in behalf of other groups would not take anything from them. But events on the battlefield soon resolved the Quaker dilemma. As Germans celebrated victory after victory, the need to impress the world with humanitarian pretensions disappeared, and so did German sponsorship of all Polish relief.

Meanwhile, Elkinton was receiving excellent care but remained hospitalized until November when he was sent home to recuperate. The Berlin Center continued its business with the help of two replacements: Alice Shaffer and Elizabeth Shipley. At the end of 1939, emigration cases were still being tended to, and a total of 22 adults and 5 children were ready to depart; 10 more cases with North and South American destinations were in the process of completion. Of the 173 cases under active consideration, 50 percent involved non-Aryans without religious affiliation who received not only counseling but also financial assistance.[12]

At the beginning of 1940, Rufus Jones averred that all was well with Quaker activities in Germany. He maintained "that the Quakers [were] the only religious people who have been undisturbed during the entire Hitler regime," an assessment some German Friends would have found difficult to accept. His rosy views rested on no specific evidence of recent vintage but may have constituted the afterglow of his own December 1938 trip when he "got everything he asked for" and received "every indication that the Quakers were not only appreciated but held a favored position in Germany." "Nothing since has happened," the Haverford sage concluded, "to change this attitude."[13] Such glowing delusions were echoed by *The Friend,* which reported, shortly after the beginning of the German offensive in the Low Countries, that the Berlin Center was in full throttle and once again under Howard Elkinton's steady leadership.[14] But even while the dissemination of material and psychological solace continued, Elkinton himself, closer to the scene, understood that an era was ending. He comprehended that deportations would soon clear Germany of its Jewish population and that most of the constituency of the center's work, both ethnic and political, was rapidly disappearing. Nor could he doubt, especially after his convalescent stay in the United States, that his country's neutrality was not forever and that the American presence at the Berlin Center might soon come to an end. He discussed the future with Hans Albrecht, and they agreed that the German work of the AFSC would soon have to be taken over by the German Yearly Meeting.[15]

Still, when Elkinton's term in Berlin ended in July 1940, he was succeeded by yet another American, Leonard S. Kenworthy. It was during Kenworthy's one-year stewardship that the transfer of the center into German hands would take place.

Leonard Kenworthy, born in 1912, was the son of Midwestern Quakers. His father, a graduate of Harvard Divinity School, taught at Earlham College, from which the son received his B.A. in 1933. Leonard next completed an M.A. in history at Columbia University, where he wrote his thesis under the direction of Allen Nevins, whose biographies of Grover Cleveland and Hamilton Fish had earned Pulitzer Prizes. He spent the following decade as a social-science teacher at various Quaker schools and was on the faculty of Friends Central School in Overbrook when Clarence Pickett asked him, in the late spring of 1940, to head the Berlin Center. As in the case of Albert Martin, the record does not explain why he was chosen, only that he accepted and left for Germany in June.[16] His memoirs include a helpful précis of his activities. The intention had initially been to have him oversee the office, while an older Friend, Henry Cadbury, the Harvard Bible scholar, would be delegated to visit German Quakers. When Cadbury was unable to accept that call, because he was about to spell the exhausted Clarence Pickett at the Philadelphia office, this task was added to Kenworthy's duties, and during the ensuing year he saw every member of the German Yearly Meeting at least once.[17]

Kenworthy arrived in a Berlin of cheering multitudes, lining the streets to watch a victory parade that celebrated the fall of Narvik and Allied withdrawal from Norway. This martial first impression increased his eagerness to seek out kindred spirits, and so he began to circulate among Berlin Friends and visited Pastor Grüber's establishment. On his first Sunday in the capital, he attended a lively monthly meeting, and during the following week he knocked on various official doors: the U.S. embassy, the Foreign Office, and the local American Chamber of Commerce. He also met with M. C. Lehmann, an American Mennonite missionary who was in the midst of another attempt to organize Polish relief, a project that turned out to be as unsuccessful as the earlier Quaker effort. Soon Kenworthy faced the same harassment by the Gestapo that had marred the sojourns of his predecessors. During a visit to Chemnitz he was questioned but quickly released after reminders of the *Kinderspeisungen* reassured his questioners of his good intentions. When he received a summons to headquarters in Berlin, he gratefully accepted Olga Halle's brave offer to accompany him. There he was asked to explain the nature of Quaker silent meetings, a request his German companion countered with an invitation to attend Sunday worship and find out firsthand. "The officer seemed satisfied" but did not respond to the invitation.

Kenworthy's attendance at the only wartime conclave of the GYM likewise failed to ease the young Midwestern Friend's discomfort in his unaccustomed surroundings. Admiration for his courageous German coreligionists was tempered by the unexpected discovery that a Quaker gathering could be so different from any he had grown up with: "Long lectures, strange people, strange language . . . wonderful spirit," but "too many old people . . . nevertheless, memorable days," he jotted in his diary. He was also gripped by the same consciousness of cultural inferiority that afflicted many Americans of his generation when visiting Europe and, therefore, took advantage of the many cultural offerings of his surroundings: the Philharmonic and the opera as well as performances of religious music. He labored tenaciously to improve his German by working his way through a long reading list of German classic and contemporary authors and, as he did so, pondered the inexplicable contradiction between an established civilized order and the country's current exaltation of violence. Long workdays continued the "clinic of despair," and, along with his other duties, Kenworthy sedulously kept up the flow of books to POW camps. He estimated that during his time he was able to help another one hundred individuals to escape from Germany's political, cultural, and moral chaos. This full schedule, however, did not spare him "lonely evenings and weekends and times [when he] was homesick." This summa of disappointments, leavened, as it was, by buoying cultural and human discoveries, still left him with a vision of Germany as a strange, sinister, at best enigmatic, land.[18]

There was no escaping the fact that the American Quaker presence in Germany was coming to an end. In March 1941 the committee supervising the Berlin Center, of which Kenworthy was now the only foreign member, decided that all instructions covering relief activities must thenceforth be signed by the clerk of the German Yearly Meeting, adding: "L. S. Kenworthy's name also should not appear, as the American Friends no longer direct Berlin Center." The same committee also reminded everyone that Friends were "a Religious Society and . . . the religious side of the work should appear in any statement of an official nature." Kenworthy himself wrote Philadelphia in his last report: "Our greatest task is providing spiritual nourishment or cultivation of new spiritual growth." The international Quaker mission in Central Europe was now returning to the purpose that had justified the continued Quaker presence in Germany during the decade between the *Kinderspeisungen* and Hitler's accession to power.[19]

On June 5, 1941, Kenworthy left Berlin for the United States. The youthful teacher returned deeply stirred by his admiration for German Friends, who—despite their different ways—remained in his eyes true representatives of another Germany and who were now forced to fight their battle for survival unassisted. As a farewell gift he gave every staff member at the office a copy of Ernst Wiechert's *Von den treuen Begleitern* (Of the faithful companions), written in praise of German poets Matthias Claudius, Goethe, and Eduard Mörike, whose work the author and former inmate of Buchenwald honored for sustaining him in a dark present. These writers, Wiechert explained in his essay, were the angels God sends "to the thirsty wanderers in the desert" during every time of trial.[20] This gift symbolized Kenworthy's sorrow as he left his faithful band of wanderers in the desert surrounding their office on Prinz Louis Ferdinand Strasse. On his way home, via Lisbon, he was jolted by the "disgraceful amounts of food served in [his] hotel" and was consoled only by a visit to a camp near Estoril, where one hundred children from Czechoslovakia, Germany, Austria, and Poland "en route to the U.S." were being sheltered. As he watched a full moon rise over the Tagus, he sighed: "Life was made for sights like this—not blackout." He boarded the *Exeter* for home, reaching Bermuda the day after the Germans invaded the Soviet Union. There a British inspector wanted to know what he had been doing in Berlin for a year and what he could tell him about conditions there. Kenworthy, still so much in the grip of his association with German Friends, refused to divulge anything about his experiences and impressions. He had been on a religious mission was all he would say.[21]

American Friends visiting Germany spoke highly of Leonard Kenworthy's "stunning" service in that country. Such observers also saw the center's work increasingly in spiritual terms. "There is no more wonderful work that Friends are everywhere privileged to do than . . . visiting Quaker families," one of them wrote.[22] Kenworthy's elders in Philadelphia reposed complete confidence in the work of this "thoroughly rounded Quaker" but considered the liquidation of the American presence at the center to be his chief mission. As early as October 1940, Douglas Steere, on a tour that included POW camps in Silesia, reported that the German Yearly Meeting was ready to take over in Berlin and recommended that no American should be sent, unless requested by German Friends.[23] In a later report, Kenworthy likewise urged that foreign Friends should only come to visit their German coreligionists and leave the center's work to them. In a final irony, the Gestapo recommendation of five years earlier—that this course be mandated to facilitate police control of center activities—was now accepted by the Quakers themselves, though certainly not for the same reason.

In the American view, this retreat was tactical, not substantive. Large sums continued to be paid to the Hamburg-Amerika Line "on behalf of individuals, known to [the AFSC]," for emigration from Nazi Germany. Other candidates were also considered for Kenworthy's succession, just in case the German Yearly Meeting should request another American.

In June 1941, Howard Elkinton, back in Europe, also found that the "German Committee can really function better without us." Given the deterioration of German-American relations, he decided that "an American in our [*sic*] office is a liability rather than an asset." In the last months before U.S. entry into the war, the German attitude toward foreign Quakers had undergone a significant shift. The memory of feeding German children in the 1920s was replaced by outrage against Quakers perceived as "servants of the Jews" *(Judenknechte)*. Elkinton, therefore, allowed that a foreign Friend who spoke good German might stay in the country "to look after civilian internees" from Allied nations but must keep his distance from the Berlin Center. Even that, he warned, was "no job for a cub."[24]

Though it is mentioned only once in the American archival evidence, and though it played no visible role in arriving at these decisions, the merciless Nazi crackdown on German allies of the Berlin Center must have preyed on Quaker minds as these changes were implemented. On December 19, 1940, Pastor Grüber was arrested and confined to Sachsenhausen concentration camp for two and one-half years. His deputy, the non-Aryan Pastor Werner Sylten, was taken to Dachau in February of the following year and murdered there in 1942. Seven members of Grüber's staff eventually shared Sylten's fate. Otto Hirsch, head of the government-controlled Reich Association of Jews in Germany—who had accompanied one of the last children's transports to England and withstood the temptation of staying—was taken to Mauthausen on February 26, 1941, where he died five months later. In June of the same year the government dissolved the Catholic Association of St. Raphael, and the organization's representative in Prague ended up in Ravensbrück concentration camp for women, where she died in 1943. The Catholic diocese of Berlin's Emergency Service *(Notwerk)* came to a standstill in October when its head, Father Bernhard Lichtenberg, was arrested after publicly praying for Jews. He died two years later on a transport to Dachau.[25] Amid this succession of draconic retributions, American Friends sought to avoid any act that would give Nazi authorities a pretext to proceed against center staff in Berlin or Vienna. German Friends would have to map their own precarious course and take only those risks that their conscience called on them to take.

And so the Berlin Center approached the end of 1941, operating under what Howard Elkinton called the "stormy weather plan." It stayed open four days a week, the work of alternate days being directed by Olga Halle or Martha Röhn.[26] Both continued a full schedule of interviews: "Although we cannot give any outward help, it is very important to talk to these unfortunate persons and to strengthen them spiritually." After emigration had been stopped, a group of twenty-eight clients remained who were in the process of getting the necessary papers together. Two of these were hidden at the Halle home in Lichterfelde and were then spirited out of the country. The rest were doomed. The memory of these desperate petitioners pursued Halle and Röhn to the end of their lives; a delirious Olga Halle recited their names on her deathbed. What remained was the work on behalf of civilian internees and prisoners of war, including six Quakers in a British ambulance unit taken prisoner in France. Two weeks before Pearl Harbor, the center signed off to American Friends: "We hope that the American Friends Service Committee knows of our good will, even though we can do very little. Please keep up your confidence that we are willing to work in the spirit of Quakerism." Inquiries from Philadelphia as to whether German Friends would welcome two "mature" Americans, whose duties would not include service at the center, arrived too late to require any response. American Friends, too, "could only bide [their] time, when under other circumstances [they] can again restore contact."27

Meanwhile, the Vienna Center had "practically folded up," but it had done so neither quietly nor peacefully. Käte Neumayer continued to search avenues of escape for her charges. She attempted to evacuate some of them via China, after Italy's entry into the war in June 1940 closed another highway to a major port. Her last battle was a futile attempt to help one hundred emigrants stranded in Trieste.

But the correspondence from Vienna in 1940 and 1941 was not so much a record of Neumayer's tenacious rearguard actions on behalf of Austrian Jews as it was an account of her dogged insistence that she be recognized by all Friends as head of the Vienna Center. Her claim to this office rested on the power of attorney left her by departing British volunteers in 1939 and by an AFSC letter recognizing her as "acting director." To her American correspondents this authorization signified only that she could run the shop until they sent a successor; to Neumayer it meant that she was next in line of succession. These divergent interpretations were not resolved even after another American, Margaret Jones, was sent to Vienna to replace the British contingent. Jones decided that as long as the work, about which Neumayer knew far more than she, got done, she would not make an issue of who was in charge. After the American left in July 1940, operation of the Vienna Center was also left to German Quakers, and Berlin sent Grete Sumpf, who promptly organized a Bible study group—distinct from the Vienna meeting—and taught English to a group of Jewish students. She was equally content to leave the office in Neumayer's charge. When Douglas Steere visited Vienna, after Sumpf's arrival, he advised the AFSC to explain the true state of things to the Austrian stalwart but added this astonishing qualification: "It is important that this not give the impression that [Sumpf] is now OVER Frl. Neumayer, for that is not the case." Clearly, American Friends, who still financed the center, could not bring themselves to pronounce a sentence that would deeply hurt the feelings of a woman who had served at great risk and with great devotion and unmatched competence. But when the time of American withdrawal arrived, Neumayer's direct wire to Philadelphia was cut, and her tenderhearted patrons there could no longer protect her. The concomitant financial drought forced German Friends to put the entire Vienna staff on one month's notice. When Neumayer's employment contract expired in July 1941, she was reduced to the same status and finally dismissed on September 30. American Friends' reluctance to clarify her status before withdrawing left that "unpleasant task" to Hans Albrecht.[28]

Käte Neumayer disappeared from the Quaker record, and it has been impossible to find out what became of her. The Jewish staff of the Vienna office did not survive the war, while local Friends to the end maintained their hostile distance from the Vienna Center. Their meeting also continued to restrict attendance to Aryans, indicating their spiritual remoteness from German Quakers. The conduct of Viennese Friends remains unique in Quaker chronicles of the time, except for Fritz Berber, the Woodbrooke alumnus and one-time friend of Friends. Berber continued to speak for Hitler's new order until after the July 20, 1944, attempt on the führer's life, when Ribbentrop allowed him to join the staff of the International Red Cross.[29]

The Quaker presence in Central Europe was now reduced to the membership of the German Yearly Meeting to whose labors we must turn next.

THE GERMAN YEARLY MEETING DURING WORLD WAR II

The tasks at the shrinking centers in Berlin and Vienna fell to a German Quaker community facing an increasingly difficult struggle for physical and spiritual survival. The 1940 Yearly Meeting was the last to be held during the war, and the absence of that recurring focus of Quaker life heightened the loneliness and vulnerability of its membership. At their local meetings they thenceforth confined testimonial speech to readings of Scripture or musical performance. Surrounded by enemies, they were additionally weighted down by their burdened consciences and a deep sense of individual and collective inadequacy; they felt "a sense of shame and responsibility as Germans for what [was] being done in Poland" and "for the continually renewed pressure upon the Jews."[30]

Other vestiges of communal existence—the common search for spiritual certitude, meetings of executive and financial committees, publication of the *Quäker* and the Heritage Pamphlets—continued for another two years, while good works never abated. What little historical record survives testifies, at the same time, to German Quakers' abiding confidence in their inner resources and to the indestructible vigor of their convictions. It also confirms the soundness of the selection process by which they continued to admit new members. The men and women who joined and stayed true to the German Society of Friends during the war years remained, to an exemplary degree, incorruptible.

A visit by Leonard Kenworthy and Emil Fuchs to the Wartburg—where the outlaw Martin Luther translated the Bible—provides a striking illumination of this Quaker firmness. As they stood before this shrine of German Protestantism, Fuchs told his companion that he had turned his back on the assumptions that guided him as a young man. Martin Luther and George Fox, he explained to the American Friend, had been moved by similar visions of the equality of all believers in the sight of God and the individual's direct relationship with the deity, which neither required nor brooked service of priestly mediators. But Luther, in Fuchs's eyes, subsequently defected from the truth when he made his peace with the privileged orders of his time, whereas Fox never retreated from his principles and thus became the true prophet of the Reformation.[31] A more reflective, but equally steadfast, conviction speaks from the surviving wartime correspondence of Hans Albrecht. As he saw it, Friends' beliefs spanned the entire range of Christian practice, from the mysticism of Orthodoxy and Roman Catholicism to the radical rebellion represented by various strands of Protestantism. Christians whose faith embraced such a range of belief could not doubt the validity of their position. But he was as aware as anyone that times of war invariably forced Friends to ask themselves daily where they stood "with their unshakable peace testimony. Do they stand at the end, before the breakdown of all their work and hope for peace, or do they stand at a new period in their history that compels them to face the reality of the world . . . and to think through and attain a much deeper understanding of their task?" Choosing the latter option, the German clerk, not for the first time, believed "what was valid in the seventeenth century has perhaps no application now," except for George Fox's "serious admonition" that Friends owed their existence to "that [divine] power that did away with the cause of all strife." Albrecht's synthesis thus incorporated both the rejection of all violence and the acceptance of military service that the German Yearly Meeting had sanctioned for its younger members.[32] No matter what restrictions the state might place on the Society's joint activities, German Friends, Albrecht remained confident, would persist "as a group of like-minded seekers keeping their contact with one another and striving towards the establishment of a New Spirit in this weary land of Germany." The victory he anticipated did not beckon on the battlefields of Russia but on the arduous course of spiritual fidelity. As the departing Kenworthy subsequently reported to Albrecht's daughter and son-in-law in the United States, he had not lost heart, and his clerkship of the German Yearly Meeting remained "his chief joy in life."[33]

Such hardy confidence also suffused the texts of the Heritage Pamphlets *(Erbguthefte)* that continued to roll off the press and pass through the mails until 1942, when the government outlawed all religious publishing in Germany. The last of these publications affirmed the Quaker message with startling boldness when one of them quoted the Swiss poet and novelist Conrad Ferdinand Meyer's (1825–1898) subversive maxim that decency be placed above patriotism. Friedrich Schiller (1759–1805) spoke to Friends in a similar vein when he reminded them that the state was no end in itself but was merely an agent intended to develop the capacities of its citizens. Even more at odds with Nazi norms was Adalbert Stifter's (1805–1868) contention that each polity was the product of a civic compact for the common good, ruling out a government's right to suppress dissent. The last two pamphlets, published in 1941, purveyed even bolder deviations. In one, Peter Rosegger (1843–1918) insisted: "If we strove more to live for the fatherland, it would perhaps not be so often necessary to die for it." That text, found in the baggage of a dead German soldier on the Russian front, earned the editor of that pamphlet, the retired teacher and Friend Marie Sturm, a two-year prison sentence. The other 1941 pamphlet was equally unequivocal. Devoted to the work of the Protestant pastor and SPD member of the Württemberg state legislature, Christoph Friedrich Blumhardt (1842–1919), its language seemed to anticipate the condition of German Quakerism in World War II. The outbreak of hostilities in 1914 had not diminished Blumhardt's faith in, and commitment to, a good, benevolent society, nor had it reduced his trust in Christ's promise that the meek would inherit the earth. Violence, he avowed, was a dead end, and—even as many died in the trenches for their nation—he exhorted German Christians that they owed devotion to one cause only: "The will of God, the father of all nations."

Faithful to their beliefs, German Friends continued to perform the material tasks that were imposed on them. Hans Albrecht voiced this dedication in a letter to an Irish Friend in 1943: "I feel very strongly that one should not try to escape but that one belongs here, that one must not leave the suffering, but rather suffer with them."[34] True to this principle, the Berlin Center continued to send whatever help it could to prisoners in a variety of camps. In cooperation with the international YMCA and with the approval of German authorities, they dispatched books and other supplies to prisoners of war. The center also asked Friends to contribute musical instruments, sheet music and recordings, art supplies, games, and athletic equipment, as well as costumes for theatrical performances. Even equipment for a playground in a camp for civilian internees figures on a long list of desiderata circulated among members. Such support continued until 1945 even though the center's financial resources barely sufficed to cover shipment of these gifts.[35] The office kept shorter and shorter hours, eventually opening only one day a week. On Saturday, February 3, 1945, an air raid did such heavy damage to the premises—happily when the building was empty—that they had to be closed. In Pyrmont, meanwhile, Mary Friedrich steadfastly tended, and defended, the Meeting House, even after it had been turned over to the local Hitler Youth.[36]

So much for open, legal Quaker work. Other implementations of Quaker principles would, in the days to come, often contravene official policy and entail greater dangers for donors and distributors. The Berlin meeting's youth group continued to function in this hazardous context. Its young members participated in the state-supported work for prisoners of war as well as the clandestine dispatch of packages to Theresienstadt and to French inmates of Dachau. Gradually, however, their numbers dwindled as members emigrated, were drafted, deported, or went into hiding. At some point, around 1942, the remainder appears to have been schismatized when some older Friends objected to their discussion of "general, secular" topics. Unable to agree on a common course of action, the young "secularists" of the membership subsequently met at the home of the Quaker architect Franz Hoffmann in the Berlin suburb of Eichkamp.[37]

Many individual adult Quakers quietly and unobtrusively joined the ranks of other brave Berliners who risked their lives to find hiding places for Jews. Almost all Friends in the capital, unbeknownst to one another, joined this effort, their attitude being: "No one knew what the other one was doing and that was as it should have been."[38] Typical of such individuals was a former gymnasium teacher Elisabeth Abegg (1882–1974), who had been forced into retirement in 1941. For the remainder of the war, her apartment, which she shared with her eighty-year-old mother and an invalid sister, became a refuge for several Jews whom she camouflaged as "bombed out relatives." On these crowded premises she also maintained a day school for non-Aryan children.[39] Gerhard and Olga Halle also hid fugitives in their home. In addition, Olga became the heroine of a terrifying interlude that occurred while traveling in a train compartment she shared with a Jewish woman. Quite unexpectedly, police entered to search their section. Olga pointed to the lady—who fortunately was speechless with fright—and indicated that she was a deaf relative whom she was taking to Berlin. The inquisitors wished her a pleasant journey and moved on.[40] The "half-Jewish" social worker Gerhard Schwersensky and his wife, Ilse, provided another example of such daring: they concealed as many as five Jews at a time in their two-room apartment in the Lankwitz section of Berlin.[41]

Nor were such displays of mettle confined to the capital. In Karlsruhe, Lydia Neubrand stood by her Jewish friends and organized the dispatch of packages to Badenese Jews deported to Gurs in southern France. In Munich, Rudolf and Annemarie Cohen launched a similar enterprise that sent as many as one hundred packages a week to Jews in Poland. The Cohens subsequently determined that Nazi officials, convinced of their omnipotence, "never entertained the thought that we would dare oppose their orders" and never caught on to their postal underground. Gertrud Luckner, who had completed her doctorate at Freiburg in 1931 under the aegis of Schulze-Gävernitz, joined Friends—with approval of the Catholic Church—and became a key player in the rescue of Catholic non-Aryans. During the war she established an extraordinary arrangement with the local chief of police who warned her whenever "transports and other actions" impended. One such transport she was able to stop altogether by securing the hospitalization of a group of aged victims.[42] In Pomerania, Margarethe Lachmund looked after a varied collection of the persecuted: Friends in prison and Jews in Polish ghettos. Surviving letters of deportees acknowledge weekly consignments from her and other "unknown persons," most of them members of Quaker groups in Cologne, Frankfurt, and Munich; toys for the children, tools, and seeds for tiny gardens. As one inmate of the Piaski ghetto wrote to her daughter—married to an Aryan and thus spared her parents' fate—"Quakers are our only ray of hope."[43]

For reasons already discussed, German Friends had not taken a dogmatic stand on members' support of the war effort, and there is no record of any collective refusal to engage in work that implemented official policy in that sphere. The extant lists of men who suffered the death penalty for resisting the call to arms include no members of the German Yearly Meeting.[44]

Quakers were, however, also part of this resistance to a greater degree than has hitherto been chronicled. On the margin of Quaker life stands the case of Hermann Stöhr (1898–1940), a Ph.D. in political science, who has left a remarkable pioneering book on American foreign aid since the early nineteenth century.[45] Reputed to be a member of the Fellowship of Reconciliation, he was probably a friend of Friends and had never joined the German Yearly Meeting. When called to perform military service, Stöhr told authorities that he could work for his fatherland but "that he could not bear arms." Resolute in his beliefs to the end, he was executed at Plötzensee prison in 1940.[46] Two other instances of German Quaker refusal to don the uniform occurred in the Netherlands. One involved Karl-Heinz, the son of Manfred and Lilli Pollatz. Prepared to die for his pacifist convictions, he yielded only after German officials told him that his continued refusal would also cost the lives of his parents. Allowed to complete his medical education, he became an army physician and died on the eastern front in the last months of the war. In his case the Quaker postulate that one's actions must never endanger the life of others supervened. The second called to service was Kurt Neuse, who was until 1940 the acting head of the Quaker school Eerde, a veteran of World War I, and, as such, already registered with the active reserve. His summons came in September 1944, and, after discussing other alternatives with his wife, he reported for duty and then went into hiding. After his disappearance, Rose Neuse called on German authorities to help find the missing father of her four children. The Germans were as baffled as she pretended to be, but they do not appear to have expended much energy in a search for the elusive reservist. What they did not know was that Neuse had found refuge in the attic of his family's residence, where he remained until Canadian troops liberated that section of the Netherlands in April 1945.[47]

Finally, there remains the case of Gerhard Halle, who had already demonstrated his opposition to the Nazi regime and its policies in a variety of ways.

When he was notified by local police in 1937 to report for the purpose of determining his military status, he did not follow that order. Instead, he wrote a letter to the Berlin Army Command, enclosing his World War I record, and declared himself ready to give his life in the service of Germany "unless a higher duty restrains me." But since his conscience also dictated respect for the life of others, he professed his inability to "participate in military service or its preparation." This petition fell, however, into a void of silence. In 1942, when a massive call-up of reserve officers followed heavy losses in Russia, Halle was summoned again and presented himself once more at the headquarters of the Berlin Command. There he reiterated his refusal to return to active duty. He claimed to do so as a Christian and emphasized the personal nature of his decision, reminding his interviewers that the Society of Friends left this issue to be settled in accordance with each member's conscience. The interview ended with his affirmation that before aiming a rifle at another human being he would turn it against himself. Halle was sent home and told to await further orders. Three weeks later he was called back for a health check. The physician suggested that he might claim exemption due to wounds received in World War I, but Halle insisted that his scars were not debilitating and that he was refusing to serve on moral grounds. A final interview with an officer of his own generation ended with the instruction that he should return home and not discuss his visit to headquarters with anyone. Again nothing happened; he received no formal release from service nor was he disciplined for his conduct. But as the war in the East dragged on, and its full barbarity became known, Halle himself began to have second thoughts. He understood the moral dilemmas facing young German officers in that theater and came to the conclusion that it was his duty to put on the uniform once more and go forth to do his part in the prevention of atrocities. Again he wrote to the local command, probably in the autumn of 1944, this time volunteering for active service against the Russians. However, the prompt, brief response expressed regret that his services would not be required.[48]

Why no one reported Halle to the Gestapo remains a mystery. It was certainly not because he had turned into a conformist civilian. His most provocative act after the beginning of the war was a letter to the block leader of the Nazi Party in his Lichterfelde neighborhood, protesting the euthanasia of individuals with incurable afflictions. He reminded the addressee and "his party comrades" of the moral precepts "that have founded our German *Kultur*" and that this policy "seriously violated." "As long as Germans spend a large portion of their income on tobacco and alcohol," he added, "they [could] afford the expense of supporting the chronically ill." He pointed out that the brutalization of individuals who carried out these killings would eventually threaten their fellow citizens and their surroundings. He, therefore, urged the block leader and the party to call the guilty to account "for this stain on the shield of honor of the

German people." The recipient of his appeal did not respond, nor does he seem to have passed it on to any of "his party comrades."[49]

Other surviving letters of Halle's condemned the starvation diet on which foreign workers in Germany were forced to subsist, and also include appeals to German Friends not to be satisfied with just sending packages to prisoners of war but "to work out a clear, positive attitude on *all* aspects of public life."[50]

Other German Friends, engaged in acts of opposition to the government, did not get off as easily as had Halle. A list, recently completed by Käte Tacke, includes twenty-one German Quakers who went to prison or concentration camps for a variety of derelictions against the Nazi state. Fourteen more had to explain themselves to Gestapo interrogators. Two Quaker women, Hermann Stöhr's wife, Ursel, and Inge Aris died in prison. Five Jewish Friends went to the death camps, including Elisabeth Heims, who had refused to use the U.S. visa provided by her brother. Head of a home for Jewish girls in Munich, she perished with her charges in Riga.[51]

Quaker inmates of concentration camps included the teacher Marie Pleissner (1891–1983), a member of the German Democratic Party under the Weimar Republic. She, too, was forced to retire in 1934 and subsequently supplemented her pension by giving private English lessons. In 1939 she expressed indignation about the invasion of Poland to a student who promptly reported her to the police. She was taken to Ravensbrück, where she collapsed on a work detail but survived after her father managed to get her released in 1940.[52] The same fate overtook the Freiburg Quaker and Catholic Gertrud Luckner. Because of her good relations with local police, she was not arrested in her hometown, but taken off a train by the Düsseldorf Gestapo on March 24, 1943, and transported to the dreaded camp for women where she spent the remainder of the war.[53]

Of five Quaker men, three—Franz Doeppner, Ewald Overschelp, and Bruno Tangermann—seem to have left no record of their ordeals. More is known about two Friends incarcerated in Buchenwald. Albert Graf, yet another gymnasium teacher in Quaker ranks and an activist in the German peace movement, was tortured so severely that he emerged permanently disoriented and incapable of "uttering a coherent sentence."[54] The best known and most fully documented instance of the detention of a German Friend in Buchenwald is that of Leonhard Friedrich, for many years treasurer of the German Yearly Meeting and manager of its publishing company. Shortly after the last issue of the *Quäker* had been put "to bed," and after his work had been terminated by the general prohibition of religious publishing, he boarded a train to Stuttgart on May 29, 1942, to attend a meeting of the GYM's finance committee. At the station he was met by two Gestapo agents who took him to the local prison and then to the Hanover penitentiary, where he spent the next four months and where his wife was permitted to pay him brief weekly visits. Mary Friedrich pleaded her husband's case at Gestapo headquarters in Berlin and called on Hans Albrecht to assist in gaining his release. The clerk was quick to respond and once again drew on his diplomatic skills to explain the position of Friends in a way calculated to ensure their toleration by authorities. "The work of Quakers," he wrote in his petition, "is limited to counteract as much as possible the *causes* of war, not to ambush a people struggling for its existence. They see the possibilities through mutual understanding and the effort to remove injustices among peoples." For examples he reviewed recent Quaker history: child feeding, protests against the Allied blockade of Germany, Quaker opposition to the Treaty of Versailles, succor of Germans detained during the French occupation of the Ruhr, the effort on behalf of German prisoners in Memel, and the feeding of hungry children in the Sudetenland. This, he reiterated, was "what Quakers understood as service [in the cause] of peace," adding that "we reject, however, very sharply any political pacifism in a bad sense that betrays its own country." Finally, Albrecht insisted, once again, that German Friends had no international ties, and while their beliefs had originated in England, their faith was spiritually rooted in German mysticism. In a word, he summoned a prodigious repertory of arguments from a rich reservoir of positions he had, on various occasions, taken in the past. Whatever later generations, from their safe perches, may think of these arguments, they must not forget that Albrecht was taking a considerable risk by intervening at all, that he was attempting to save a valued associate's life, and that he was not writing to enhance his reputation with posterity. What makes the entire episode so valuable to students of this chapter of a dark past is the fact that all individuals involved were genuinely terrified by the prospect facing Leonhard and afterward never attempted to conceal their panic. Indeed, extreme fear speaks only too eloquently from Mary Friedrich's last appeal to the same official whom Albrecht had addressed: she insisted that her husband "never refused any service to the state, so it is wrong to assume he would refuse military service if this were required of him." Friedrich himself pleaded in a similar vein, even going so far as to maintain that his kindness to Jews was merely part of his duty to acknowledge "the principle of Christian love." None of these pleas availed. According to the secret police, the prisoner's past conduct revealed "his politically negative attitude toward the National Socialist state" and undermined "the unity of the German people." That he survived was very likely due to the unexpected intervention of an SS officer who transferred the sixty-seven-year-old inmate from deadly work in the prison quarry to clerical duties, after he had learned that Friedrich was one of those Quakers who had fed him as a child.[55]

Other Friends came face-to-face with death in ways familiar to millions of families on both sides of the battle lines. The names of Theodor Baumann, Karl-Heinz Pollatz, Bernhard Paquet, and Harald Bartsch, an Eerde alumnus, figured among Friends killed in action. Heinz Hagen, who had joined the Berlin meeting in 1938, died on the Russian front five years later. Closer to home, the Yearly Meeting lost two of its pillars in 1944. On February 9, Alfons Paquet suffered a fatal heart attack in a public shelter in Frankfurt, and in December, Rudolf Schlosser, while visiting his mother to help celebrate her birthday, was killed in an air raid in Kassel.[56]

The cumulative impact of these numerous tragedies, coupled with ceaseless government chicanery at the German Society's expense, depressed and embittered even Hans Albrecht. Another blow fell in May 1944 when the Yearly Meeting's remaining funds were confiscated. In a letter to its loyal, but ineffective, lawyer he vented his anger over this persistent mistreatment. It outraged him all the more deeply, he explained, because Friends' "internationalism" had consisted of maintaining contact with Germany's friends abroad, while foreign Quakers had since the beginning of the war looked after German internees and prisoners of war and "publicly protested against the [Allied] conduct of the air war." "Is it surprising that one is overcome with bitterness?" he concluded.[57]

As the war drew to a close, and as the section of Berlin in which the clerk resided after the evacuation of his office in Stettin was being taken over by Russian occupiers, he cleared his mind of such anger, however, and rejoiced that he "could once again think ahead." Rumors of impending peace circulated in the neighborhood, while he looked forward to ending this "underground existence and becom[ing] once more a human being." "What tasks lie ahead of us?" he exulted as he moved books and belongings out of the cellar back into his upstairs apartment. In another part of town Olga Halle and her family sought and found quiet comfort in Albert Schweitzer's autobiographical writings, sharing the Alsatian Renaissance man's faith in the impending rebirth of their nation's civilization.[58] To the east in Pomerania, Hans and Margarethe Lachmund were writing their own chapter in the history of that rebirth: they, together with other members of a clandestine cell of the National Committee "Free Germany," negotiated the peaceful surrender of Greifswald, a town of forty thousand with a university founded in the fifteenth century.[59]

Though the Quaker's encounter with National Socialism had ended in Germany, it is not the end of this story. From a conflict with limited objectives on Germany's eastern border, the virus of war had infected all of Europe, and Friends had had to face the common enemy beyond Germany. How some of these subsidiary clashes turned out must now be told.

DUTCH DIKES BREAK

German and Dutch Quakers in the Netherlands faced threats as dire as those faced by their confreres in Germany, but in a less solidly hostile environment: fascism in this more tranquil region made fewer converts than it had in Germany, even before it became tainted by collaboration with a foreign invader. Barely 8 percent of Dutch voters opted for the National Socialist *Bond* (NSB) in 1935: the party's best showing. At the time of the German invasion, Dutch Nazis occupied only four of one hundred seats in the lower house of the country's Estates-General.[60] The majority of voters supported the Protestant Anti-Revolutionary Party or the Roman Catholic State Party, while the secularist vote, less than 40 percent of the total, was three-fourths Socialist and one-fourth Liberal. This constellation resulted in a stable succession of "middle of the road" coalition governments.[61]

There are indications that the Germans initially intended to grant Germanic Netherlanders a considerable amount of autonomy. The appointment of the Viennese lawyer Arthur Seyss-Inquart as Reich Commissioner—who quickly surrounded himself with a staff of fellow Austrians—encouraged expectations of a reasonable modus vivendi. Moreover, after five days of unsuccessful armed resistance, the majority of Dutch citizens were resigned to living in a Europe dominated by Germany. From these cooperative predispositions emerged a political movement, the Netherlands Union, founded in the summer of 1940. Led by a group of high-level civil servants, it sought to preserve a modicum of self-determination. By February 1941 it counted eight hundred thousand members, recruited from all major parties, including the Socialists. But it was not long before some of its members were arrested, in part as retaliation for the internment of Germans in the Dutch East Indies. Dutch Nazis—whose head, Anton Mussert, had been promised leadership of a new government—took these detentions as a signal to commence a campaign of attacks on offices of the Union, as well as on street vendors peddling its paper, *De Unie*. The birthday celebration of Princess Juliana's consort, Prince Bernhard, on June 20, 1940—which was demonstratively observed by the population—provided another opportunity for the Germans to attack the Union's "antiquated political concepts," a euphemism for the party's undisguised loyalty to the House of Orange. In December 1941, realizing that it could not be turned into a servant of German interests, the Nazis finally dissolved the Netherlands Union and declared the NSB the only legal party.[62] While Mussert vainly waited for his inauguration as Holland's führer, the expanding world conflict and the obvious irreconcilability of Dutch and German expectations were producing the same smoldering civil war that characterized occupations elsewhere. German retaliation against acts of defiance became as ruthless as it was in other occupied areas. Between 1940 and 1945, 2,800 Dutch citizens were condemned to death by German courts; another 20,000 died in concentration camps, while a similar number starved during the final year of occupation when the food ration dropped to 500 calories a day.[63]

These figures do not include the far larger number of Jewish victims, both Dutch and foreign. At the beginning of 1941, 140,245 Jews resided in the

Netherlands, of whom roughly 14,500 were German refugees. About 126,000 belonged to synagogues; the rest were Christians or Jews without religious affiliation. Some 20,000 were partners in mixed marriages. Until the invasion, Jews in the Netherlands had the same rights and opportunities as other citizens and residents. Anti-Semitism, organized or individual, played a negligible role in Dutch life. German legislation, which mandated segregation in 1941, including the wearing of the yellow star, changed all that. During the occupation, a country that claimed to be less anti-Semitic than "perhaps any other in the whole Christian world," witnessed the deportation of 107,000 Jews of whom 5,500 survived. Another 14,000 succeeded in leaving the country, while 16,000–20,000 found hiding places. However, of the latter, 8,000 were betrayed and/or ferreted out by the Gestapo and local police and then delivered to one of two collecting camps, Vught or Westerbork, both way stations to the gas chambers.[64]

The number of Jews who survived in hiding indicates that here, as in Germany, some ordinary citizens—goaded by their consciences—bravely defied the policy of extermination and went to dangerous lengths to save lives. However, while doing so, these stalwarts often placed the lives of family and neighbors in jeopardy as well: individuals who were not aware of, or might not have sanctioned, their illegal, clandestine acts.[65] Nevertheless, these saviors assumed these psychological burdens, encouraged very often, tacitly or implicitly, by their churches, which opposed the persecution of Jews far more massively and openly than was the case in Germany.

Dutch Protestants and Catholics reached the point of confrontation with the occupier from different directions. Before the war, no major Protestant denomination had taken a public stand against persecution of the Jews in Germany; several later explained that they had never taken collective political positions but had left decisions in the secular realm to individual members. On the other hand, the Catholic Church, as early as 1934, forbade priests to join the NSB and extended that ban to all church members two years later.[66] This exclusion continued during the occupation and was explicitly extended to banning Nazis from receiving the sacraments. The staffs of Catholic papers and magazines eventually joined the nazified Netherlands Union of Journalists but refused NSB advertising. The Church's official press adviser, Father Titus Brandsma, became one of the hostages taken in retribution for Catholic recalcitrance and died at Dachau.[67]

Protestant prewar neutralism quickly waned as occupation policies hardened. The Protestant Aid Committee for Racial and Religious Refugees was disbanded in the summer of 1940, but not before proclaiming that it was "the duty of every Protestant Christian . . . to practice Christian charity in regard to the hapless exiles who depend on our Committee." Vigorous Protestant protests followed every discriminatory law from October 1940 onward. The Reformed Church asked its clergy to pray for the Jews, and by 1943 it authorized ministers to exclude National Socialists from communion and confirmation. When occupation authorities gave six hundred Jews in mixed marriages, imprisoned at Westerbork, the choice between sterilization or deportation, the Calvinist hierarchy protested this "shameful practice," and, for once, German authorities—anxious to postpone a showdown—revoked the decree. In addition, non-Aryan Protestants at the camp were either released or sent to Theresienstadt, where most of them survived. A 1943 edict sending young Dutchmen between eighteen and twenty years old to labor service in occupied Russia was likewise rescinded.

Other protests against mistreatment of Jews were launched in unison by Catholics and Protestants. But when their texts were read from Catholic pulpits, while Protestant churches merely circulated them among the pastorate, the Germans in angry retribution sent ninety-two Catholic Jews to Auschwitz. Some critics to this day continue to insist that the churches could have saved more lives by using their leverage with an occupier reluctant to take them on in a country where they exercised so much political clout. That may, alas, be true, but no one can accuse Dutch Christianity of remaining silent as Nazi terror took its course.[68]

Quantitatively, the Dutch Society of Friends was but a small drop in this sea of conflict and anguish. According to admittedly incomplete records, the Yearly Meeting claimed only thirty-five members when World War II erupted. That number included ten German refugees: the four Pollatz children, whose parents had continued membership in the GYM, and four German members of the teaching staff at Eerde. (A fifth, Werner Hermans, had become a Dutch citizen in 1939.) Even more exclusively than their German brethren, Dutch Friends represented the professional and entrepreneurial middle classes. Piet Ariëns Kappers remained the *spiritus rector* of this tiny community and, as clerk, exercised the same leadership as Hans Albrecht did in Germany.[69]

Some of the functions of the Berlin Center were, in fact, moved to Amsterdam in 1939, where Mary Champney represented the AFSC until two heart attacks in December 1939 forced her to return to the United States.[70] Raising funds for the school in Eerde was a major, but by no means the only, function of the Amsterdam office. Homer Morris, for instance, used a visit in November 1939 to confer with Dutch cabinet members about means of mediating the war, supplementing similar efforts by British Friends Corder Catchpool and Percy Bartlett. Margaret Collyer, Roger Carter's precursor in Berlin, arrived from London the day after Champney's departure and pursued with equal energy support for refugees in various Dutch internment camps. Eventually, foreign participation in such efforts was cut short by the German invasion. Collyer barely escaped capture; her last report indicated that local Friends, including

Manfred and Lilli Pollatz, had assured her that the work in Amsterdam would continue.[71]

The Yearly Meeting, scheduled for May, was not held until June 1940, and no minutes were kept. In July, Friends began relief work in Rotterdam, which had suffered one of the first massive urban bombardments of World War II. In October they joined other churches in expressing to German authorities their "deep sorrow" occasioned by anti-Jewish measures. As their monthly bulletin, the *Vriendenkring*, explained the following month: "We have never known a Jewish problem in the Netherlands. The close bond that exists between Calvinists and the old Testament accounts for the fact that we understand one another." In the face of impending Jewish suffering, Friends saw it as their task to help them "and teach them their father in heaven wants only what is good, even if we, his human children, cannot see that." Although the Amsterdam Center closed at the end of 1941, the Yearly Meeting's Executive Committee asked Seyss-Inquart in the summer of 1942 to permit Jewish families, scheduled for deportation, to leave their children in the care of the Society of Friends. Kappers requested a meeting to discuss the practical measures necessitated by that commitment. In January 1944 the DYM petitioned for the release of its member Adele Finkelstein, who had been taken to Vught, and in May they sent the text of a prayer for political prisoners to SS Police Chief Hanns Rautter, together with a resolution expressing the Society's unqualified opposition to the death penalty. None of these communications received a reply or affected German conduct.[72]

Friends were, however, recognized as a legitimate religious association both by the occupier and by the Dutch Reformed Church, an acknowledgment that gave them the means of defending the non-Aryan members of their Society. Their bulletin, unlike the German *Quäker*, continued to appear throughout the occupation, and the Yearly Meetings continued until the Low Countries became a battleground. Food and other supplies were sent to inmates at Westerbork and Vught, but requests to visit the recipients were denied. Dutch Friends also assumed "the guardianship over some forty half-Jewish children, for whom no other organization could care." Two members, Laura van Honck and Maria van Everdingen, who occupied a home at 463 Prinsengracht in Amsterdam where they entertained German soldiers and scandalized the neighborhood, were discovered, after liberation, to have harbored twenty Jews. Five other members went to concentration camps, and four spent the last year of the occupation in hiding.[73]

Two centers of Quaker activity in Holland continued to be, exclusively or cooperatively, run by German Friends in exile. After settling in Haarlem, Manfred and Lilli Pollatz from Dresden opened a school for refugee children that housed as many as fourteen, who were generally between the ages of ten and sixteen. Thanks to financial support from British and American Quakers, as well as from such personal acquaintances as the Dutch banker Eduard Vis, they were able to stay open even after Manfred's pension was discontinued in 1936, when he refused a government order to return to Germany. Both husband and wife provided the bulk of the instruction, supplemented by a local teacher of Dutch, and by their son, Karl-Heinz, who provided rudimentary classes in science.[74] While foreign Quaker visitors have left a host of approving reports of a home "where all live together and work together" and where these children, torn from their environment and settled in a household of strangers, were "beginning to blossom out," daily life was grueling and often less than idyllic for the family and their charges.[75] Manfred and Lilli had their hands full providing a home for their own children, as well as for the other occupants. All pupils were chosen for their extraordinary intellectual endowments, but none of them could pay their way. This placed a heavy burden on the young refugees, each of whom had to demonstrate in the classroom—where Manfred, in particular, appears to have been an unrelenting taskmaster—that he or she was worthy of being there. In addition, to save the expense of domestic help, every member of the household rose at six and spent two hours before class doing chores. One of the Pollatz daughters ran the kitchen, while another was a tireless knitter of sweaters, sold to provide some of the home's operating capital. Still, Margaret Collyer reported, shortly before her hasty departure, that the children looked "very well and certainly plain living and high thinking go together. Most have no place to go and no one to support them, except Friends who know of the good work done *in this fine Spartan training ground,* and take pleasure in sharing the work."[76]

Such accomplishments required a colossal inner strength, in addition to a penchant for Christian charity, which Manfred displayed in abundance and may have derived, in part, from a traffic accident he suffered when he was eight years old. He bore the resulting loss of his left leg so stoically that few of his acquaintances were even aware of his handicap. More important was his abiding sense of mission to defend a German civilization whose stewardship he would, under no circumstance, concede to Hitler and his followers. That was a task that had crossed Germany's boundary with him. A no-nonsense Friend like Howard Elkinton might disdain the Pollatz posture of "Deutsch outpost responsibility,"[77] but Manfred paid no attention to such reservations. One can, however, not help but wonder how his uprooted pupils managed to appear so cheerful and contented to outsiders under the uncompromisingly zealous tutelage of this cultural missionary. To be sure, they were permitted a minimum of Dutch instruction—enough to satisfy the Dutch Ministry of Education—but other than in those lessons and Lilli's classes in English, they were allowed to speak only German, even when outside the house. Other house rules must have increased the young refugees' feelings of alienation. Lilli Pollatz, for instance, would admit only Quaker children to her family's Sunday worship.[78] In practice that may have meant that these meetings were a family affair, relegating the children of strangers, on one level at least, to an outsider status. Severe discipline extended to every phase of communal life. Inge Pollatz recalls a day when a group of youngsters, weary of peeling potatoes, no longer took "pleasure in sharing the work" and simply went on strike. As a result of this act of defiance, no one ate that day, and it was never repeated.

Still, the spartan regimen ultimately justified itself. Separation from home and family was a shattering loss no one could overcome by indulging in bouts of self-pity. A merciless fate could be mastered only by an equally merciless battle against one's own weaknesses and shortcomings. Survival was the prize all alumni carried away from the Pollatz home. In spite of the rigor of these years, the memory of rescue has left a heritage of love and respect for Manfred and Lilli Pollatz. Many alumni remained in regular contact with Manfred long after they had reached adulthood and were proud to let him know that their subsequent professional achievements had justified his exertions on their behalf.[79]

If maintaining home and school at Westerhoutpark in Haarlem was a grim struggle in times of peace, it became a desperate one after the invasion, and its tragic course revealed that husband and wife demanded even more of themselves then they had of their children. When, in 1941, all Jews had to be cleared from the Netherlands' coastal provinces, Manfred succeeded in finding hiding places for all children who lived in his home at the time. Nor did the family give up the struggle for the persecuted. They now provided asylum for small children of Dutch Jews and, in collaboration with the Dutch underground, also procured false papers for Jewish adults. But the days of good deeds were interrupted when denunciations by a neighbor led to Manfred's arrest on May 14, 1943. He was kept in an Amsterdam prison under appalling conditions until August and then taken to Vught and thence to Dachau, where he arrived on May 25, 1944. His desperate son went to Gestapo headquarters to plead for his release. What kind of a bargain he struck cannot be reconstructed, but it appears he agreed to become a medical officer in an SS unit, on condition that his father be released. The fact that Manfred was indeed discharged from Dachau on October 6, 1944, makes this plausible, although documentary confirmation has been impossible to come by.

Manfred Pollatz returned to Haarlem to find his wife dying of breast cancer. However, this adversity did not prevent the couple from sustaining their home as a hiding place—subsidized by the National Committee of the Resistance— until the occupier requisitioned the house in the last months of the war, forcing them and their daughters to find refuge with friends. The cup of the family's suffering ran over when early in 1945 Karl-Heinz was reported missing in action, possibly—in the opinion of his surviving family—because he had promised his family never to abandon a patient on the battlefield. Whatever the circumstances, he died faithful to the ideals for which his parents continued to live.[80]

Eerde's wartime history is easier to reconstruct than the sparsely documented Pollatz saga. It is no less tragic, however, and it has left its own heritage of controversy.

Financially, the school managed to survive the invasion, initially thanks to American subsidies, and then by the increase of Dutch students that created new and more reliable sources of income. In addition, after April 1940, some German parents were able to secure individual permits for the transfer of fees. Special summer courses for Dutch children were another means of wiping out deficits that accumulated during the regular school year. As a result, salary cuts instituted in 1940 were revoked the following year. At the end of 1942, the institution's bank account actually registered a surplus of thirty-five hundred guldens. By the following autumn, fees from eighty-two boarding students provided so substantial a cushion that Rose Neuse once again considered the inauguration of a pension fund.[81]

Graduating students continued to prepare for a final examination that preserved form and substance of the Oxford School Certificate. Most remaining German children no longer had homes to which they could return, unless their parents lived in the Netherlands, and during the first Christmas of the occupation found consolation in good skating on the flooded meadows and the parties given by various faculty members. On April 4, 1941, the schools' seventh birthday was celebrated, and while the internment of Billy Hilsley—a British citizen— severely curtailed musical life, no less than three plays were staged that month, all comedies! In May the open-air theater on the castle steps resounded with rehearsals and subsequent performances of *As You Like It*.[82]

But as the summer wore on, impending doom waxed unmistakable. At the beginning of the 1941–1942 school year, Eerde was ordered not to accept new pupils, and Piet Kappers went to The Hague to negotiate an exemption for Dutch children. Then came a heavier blow: on September 1, 1941, the remaining Jewish children were segregated from their peers and sent to the "De Esch" dependency under the charge of a Jewish faculty member, Elisabeth Schmitt. This step, in line with the general application of German racial laws to the Netherlands, was preceded by much soul-searching and constituted the first of two developments that divide to this day Friends, alumni, and their descendants into opposing camps. Refusal to obey would have closed the entire school, and many witnesses remain who believe that this is what should have been done. But Kappers's insistence to save Eerde at all costs carried the day. The Dutch clerk had a promise from Seyss-Inquart's deputy, Friedrich Wimmer—a friend from his university days—that the occupier considered every member of the school community to be a Quaker, and, therefore, Jew and Gentile alike would be safe, so long as German edicts were observed and no one engaged in any illegal acts. As Frits Philipp, a board member of Jewish extraction, in hiding at the time, explained at the end of the war, the course of compromise was chosen "to protect the Jewish tutors and pupils at Ommen."[83]

Interaction between the two Eerde entities continued, however, even after headmaster Hermans—who had replaced Neuse after the invasion—left no doubt in the minds of all concerned that the castle and its immediate surroundings were closed to Jewish children. A former denizen of De Esch claims that after September 1941 no one at the castle consorted with the inhabitants of the Jewish dependency. Actual events reflect a less clear-cut separation. The castle's kitchen staff continued to cook for the Jewish children, and Elisabeth Schmitt's son Richard—son of an Aryan father but continuing to reside at De Esch in clear violation of German instructions—brought food to that compound in a cart hooked to his bicycle. Kurt Neuse visited the house regularly and spoke there during Sunday meetings of worship. It is also known that Hermans himself allowed two new Jewish students into the castle school, in total disregard of the instructions from the board to admit only applicants whose identity papers documented their Aryan descent. These two Jewish children—with forged identity cards—were discovered when their father paid them a surreptitious visit that led to the arrest of all three. It is worth noting that this episode was not followed by any sanctions against the school.[84]

Another controversy that continues to simmer relates to the degree of trust that Eerde's board and faculty placed in German assurances that the Quaker school was inviolate. While there seems to have been no doubt in Kappers's mind that he could count on his friend Wimmer, some dissent was voiced, especially by Wolfgang Frommel, who urged the Dutch clerk to find hiding places for the children at De Esch. Kappers is said to have threatened to report Frommel to the police if he encouraged such disappearances. While this particular episode comes to us secondhand, eyewitnesses survive who tell of similar threats to the children themselves. The teacher in charge at De Esch, Elisabeth Schmitt, believing as unconditionally in Kappers's judgment as Kappers trusted his German contact, impressed on her youngsters that an escape into the underground was risky for the escapee as well as for the rest of both school communities because it would expose everyone to German retribution. Discussions of the issue at the castle produced the same conclusion. The risks of disappearance are confirmed by the eight thousand "divers" *(onderduikers)* who were caught and by the hundreds delivered at irregular intervals to Westerbork. At the same time, the myth that deportees would be consigned to labor rather than extermination camps continued to be believed throughout the country, long after the gas ovens at Auschwitz were going full blast.[85]

In the end, the skeptics were, of course, proved right. Five De Esch children who went into hiding survived. Four of them were hidden in Amsterdam by Wolfgang Frommel; the other was caught, sent to Auschwitz, but lived to tell about it. These escapes were likewise not followed by German sanctions. Four others left openly to rejoin families in Amsterdam and were deported with their parents and siblings. The remaining nine were taken to Vught on April 1, 1943, when the province of Overijssel was "cleansed of Jews." The last days these young martyrs spent at De Esch were marked by "great calm. Everyone [was] kind, cooperative and helpful as in the old days." A despairing Piet Kappers came to the school for a last farewell and rode the train to Arnhem with the deportees, who—convinced that all they faced was hard physical work—seem to have been in good spirits. They wrote regularly from Vught, asking for news from the school, and one of them—Hermann Isaac—acknowledged the receipt of packages with books he had requested: Latin and German classics and a copy of *Le Chanson de Roland*. Another survivor of Auschwitz, enrolled at Eerde after the war, first heard about the school when he met Isaac at Auschwitz III, or Monowitz-Buna, and remembers his ability to overcome "the bitter cold, the lack of food, and all [our] immediate needs by reciting long passages of German classics," a manifestation, he concluded, of " 'inner light in outer darkness' [that] fits Hermann perfectly. Nothing could describe him better." But in the end, all nine Eerde children died, some on westward forced marches after the closing of Auschwitz.[86]

If any additional confirmation of the worthlessness of German promises was needed, it arrived on November 30, 1943, when Eerde was ordered closed by December 15 and its premises transformed into a shelter for Hitler Youth members from Germany. Several teachers moved to De Esch where they huddled for the remainder of the war, including army deserter Kurt Neuse, who hid in the attic. They seem to have subsisted on the remaining surplus in the school coffers, as well as on the produce from the school's agricultural enterprise that staved off the hunger that became the lot of so many urban Netherlanders. Max Warburg, his wife, Josepha, and their children went into hiding, as did Otto Reckendorf. The latter, however, was discovered and sent to join a construction battalion, while his wife continued to support herself and their two children from the sale of goods produced in her studio. Elisabeth Schmitt, who had up to 1944 been protected by her marriage to an Aryan husband, was arrested and taken to Westerbork on March 29 of that year. Although local police had given her ample warning before bringing her in, she, faithful to the instructions given previously to her hapless charges, made no effort to get away. After a week in Westerbork she was released and returned to De Esch. There she continued to give lessons to faculty children. Philip van Pallandt kept up spirits with daily news of the Allied advance, gleaned from BBC broadcasts. The baron continued his own resistance against the invader. In an underground shelter, he concealed a Dutch officer and two American aviators. Finally, a Canadian tank rolled up the gravel road in front of De Esch on April 11, 1945, and it was all over—all except the mourning that would go on forever.[87]

OTHER QUAKER REARGUARD ACTIONS

This war chronicle of involvement cannot close without mentioning the work that American and British Friends continued even after the German and Dutch venues had become inaccessible. In France they ministered to inmates confined to camps in the southern regions and helped other refugees to reach, and then escape from, the unoccupied sector of that defeated country. At Gurs, for instance, they fed as many as twelve hundred persons a day. Much of their work was done in conjunction with twenty-five other Jewish and Christian organizations that met regularly at Nîmes to coordinate their efforts. Yet, when the leader of French Protestantism, Marc Boegner, protested in 1943 to Marshal Pétain against the inhuman conditions under which his government turned over Jews to the Germans, he extolled Quakers alone as the shining example of Christian charity. Boegner's complaints may account for the fact that members of the Nîmes committee gained an audience with both Pétain and Prime Minister Pierre Laval, the latter promising that ten thousand refugees—with visas to enter other countries—would not be delivered to the occupier. During this time Quakers also worked with another old friend, André Trocmé, the pastor who more than a decade earlier had exhorted a French audience—during Gerhard Halle's 1932 journey of atonement—to temper their judgment of Germany with the consciousness of their own failings.

Early in 1941, American Friends negotiated with the German ambassador in Lisbon an agreement under which the Belgian Food Administration would set aside stores for the feeding of children, provided these supplies were matched by equal amounts of food brought in from the United States.[88]

American Quakers also assisted refugees in their Rome office until U.S. entry into the war forced their departure. But they returned in 1944, by which time we also find them working out of Casablanca and railing against the snail's pace at which inmates of North African concentration camps were being returned to freedom.[89]

Friends never left neutral Spain and Portugal, two countries where papal intervention occasionally stopped the delivery of German refugees to the Gestapo. In Madrid, however, the AFSC representative, David Blickenstaff, had to work under the auspices of the International Red Cross because Spain did not recognize the Quakers as a religious community. He and his staff assisted internees at Camp Miranda—whose facilities compared favorably with similar installations in France—and helped repatriate them or move them on to new homelands as quickly as the war and cumbersome consular machinery permitted. Blickenstaff's efficient work seems to have grated on the Germans, who fantasized in a December 1944 issue of the formerly prestigious *Hamburger Fremdenblatt* that his real name was Hirschfeld and that he was playing a leading role in channeling communist agents to North Africa and the United States. He translated the piece and sent it to his colleagues in Lisbon "in order to keep [them] well informed regarding all of the varied activities of [the Madrid] office."[90]

After Pearl Harbor, American Friends also had to transfer the care of refugees stranded in Japan to an indigenous Tokyo-Yokohama Committee for European Refugees, but not before they had made—throughout the preceding summer—desperate efforts to crank up the reluctant visa-granting mechanism of the State Department in behalf of these unfortunates. One American Friend, Edith Forsythe Sharpless (1883–1956), who had taught in Japan since 1910, actually stayed in the Japanese capital until September 1943 because she wanted to do nothing that would give Japanese Friends the impression that their American brethren were "withdrawing from fellowship with them."[91]

Nor did the offices in London and Philadelphia slacken their efforts on behalf of the hunted and homeless, wherever they might have drifted. Bertha Bracey, still tirelessly working in the Bloombury House, was recognized for her prodigious achievements and offered the Order of the British Empire. She agreed to accept this honor only after she had been assured that "her pacifist convictions were understood" in Whitehall. From 1944 onward much of her time was devoted to planning the rescue of survivors after the war, for—as she wrote in the magazine *International Affairs*—"the Anti-Semitic policy of the Axis Powers [will present] one of the most urgent and tragic problems in the postwar world." At the same time, the AFSC reported that dozens of volunteers in America were contributing tens of thousands of hours of service to hundreds of refugees, satisfying their material and medical needs and training many in skills they would need to enter the American labor market.[92]

British Friends also continued to speak publicly to the German people in a spirit of reconciliation. On December 17, 1944, the day after the beginning of the Battle of the Bulge, Elizabeth Fox Howard broadcast this message over the BBC: "If we, the Society of Friends, should ever be able once again to take our small part in bringing the star of hope to your people, we shall rejoice with all our hearts. But this new and better world will not come without your help. We want you to wake up, to cast away apathy and fear, to repudiate the evil deeds done in your name." Until the end of the war, Howard, William Hughes, and Margaret Collyer worked to ease the lot of German internees and prisoners of war, without, at the same time, neglecting Britain's own refugees from cities ravaged by the air war. Meanwhile, the dispatch of books and other supplies to British and French POWs in Germany kept alive a tenuous contact with German Friends engaged in similar work. "Some day," Howard firmly believed, "we shall renew the old fellowship and clasp each other's hands again, forgiven and forgiving."[93]

Throughout this six-year ordeal Quakers never could convince themselves that they were doing enough, and they never wearied of repeating that others were doing more. After accepting her Order of the British Empire, Bertha Bracey even grumbled—and not without reason—that the same honor should also have been given "to a member of the Jewish community, which carries the larger burden." At no point, however, did these Friends take surcease from their labors and wait for better days. Their commitment was as open-ended as human misery itself.[94]

7.
The Year 1945 and All That

PICKING UP THE PIECES

On May 8, 1945, the Nazi regime, long in the crumbling, disappeared from the surface of the earth. With it the German state disintegrated into four zones of occupation and a number of other areas annexed by the Soviet Union, Poland, and Czechoslovakia. Allied troops also restored the Republic of Austria to its former independence.

Anyone traveling through the defeated country during the months following V-E Day could not help but notice that Germans looked better fed and more stylishly attired than the inhabitants of the countries they had recently occupied. That apparent well-being was ephemeral, of course, and did not rest on genuine prosperity. Material goods of all sorts were in short supply, especially food for toddlers and children whose turn it now was to suffer for the misdeeds of their elders.

Restoring normal conditions was not easy. Military administrations in each sector of occupation had orders to remove Nazis from all levels of administrative authority and to turn over the management of every public sector to Germans untainted by previous support of Germany's fallen masters.

It was in the midst of this physical and moral anarchy that Quakers resumed their service to suffering Germans. If any one group knew what the arrival of "year zero" required of the victors, it was the Society of Friends. In Britain, in the spring of 1942, some of its members had established "a special ad hoc Post-War Service Committee" and begun training one thousand volunteers from various denominations, and the following year Friends also joined a newly organized Council of British Societies for Relief. It was not long before teams of relief workers in Cairo were awaiting a green light to work in the Balkans, and some of them crossed over to various Greek islands in the fall of 1944. About the same time, a Friends' Ambulance Unit (FAU) began operations in France, moving into Germany in February 1945, while another group entered the Austrian provinces of Carinthia and Styria from Italy. By May 1945 young British Friends were working in Sandbostel camp near Hamburg—which held both prisoners of war and German political prisoners—and had entered Belsen concentration camp, where "conditions were so terrible that women were [at first] not allowed to work there."[1]

Quakers, however, were not the only civilian relief workers who stood ready to tackle the vast devastation the war had left. In Britain thousands had expressed their readiness to serve in that cause well before victory was ensured; their ranks even included Jews and other immigrants who had earlier been forced to flee Germany. In Hampstead groups of thirty underwent a rigorous two-month course to prepare for these heartbreaking and backbreaking endeavors designed to limit the sufferings of their enemies. Not all went abroad; some stayed in Britain, readying German POWs for a constructive role in their country's future. Among Friends' most popular aids in this educational effort of captured adversaries were fifty thousand reprints of the Heritage Pamphlets originally published by Leonhard Friedrich.

The bulk of these volunteers went to the Continent, and by 1946 there were 160 at work in Germany alone.[2] This time they were not cold-shouldered by military authorities—as their predecessors in 1919 had been—but enjoyed the status of army officers, were outfitted in uniforms modeled on British-army battle dress (colored gray instead of khaki), and shared military accommodations, rations, and transport. Half of their general expenses were assumed by the budget of military government. Living well among the hungry troubled them, of course, but they assuaged these feelings of guilt by defying prevailing regulations that forbade "fraternization" with German civilians.[3] During the first winter of peace, Friends Relief Service took over from the Friends' Ambulance Units, and in the U.S. and French zones representatives of the AFSC assumed similar responsibilities in conjunction with a consortium of relief agencies. Once again they displayed their firm belief that "they knew not 'friends' or 'enemies,' not 'victors' or 'defeated,' but only human beings needing help, regardless of nationality."[4]

The labors of these men and women of goodwill turned out to be a great deal more complicated than any of them had anticipated. Devastated Germany harbored a politically and psychologically diverse population: German victims of Nazi brutality and foreign forced labor, together with other "displaced persons" who might merely be awaiting repatriation or seeking, often with desperate determination, to avoid a return to homelands in communist Eastern Europe, including the Soviet Union. At one time fourteen teams alone worked at that daunting task of what one Quaker participant called with characteristic modesty, "relief work among a few thousand of the half million Displaced Persons in Germany."[5] Before many months of peace had elapsed, their clientele increased again as German prisoners of war began to return, along with the flood of refugees from former German provinces in the east. As in 1919 primary effort went into feeding hungry children whose suffering the unusually harsh winter of 1945–1946 only increased. In support of this endeavor, an appeal was made to families in bankrupt Britain to tighten their belts one more notch and share what little they had with German children.[6]

Work in displaced-person camps placed the greatest stress on volunteers' emotional resources. One of them tells of the terror the visit of a Soviet repatriation commission spread among displaced persons in Goslar. These helpless people, facing victimization by another ruthless enemy, turned on their Quaker benefactors, who, in their eyes, had suddenly emerged as allies of these Russian tormentors. Even a successful effort by Friends that stopped forced repatriation altogether could not wholly mend this tear in the fabric of confidence that had until then united these victims and their protectors. The upshot was that relief workers now also assumed responsibility for finding refuges for these men without countries, and—what was often far more difficult—for their wives and children. Equally distressing was the need to get mutually hostile ethnic groups within camps to work with each other and with postwar German authorities whom inmates understandably resented, no matter how good their intentions.[7]

Among Quakers toiling to overcome these multiple challenges were familiar names: Corder and Gwen Catchpool, Roger Carter, Margaret Collyer, William R. Hughes, and Tessa Rowntree, who all reenlisted, as well as Elizabeth Fox Howard, now seventy, who returned in April 1946 to officiate as the first hostess in the reopened Quaker rest home in Bad Pyrmont. Her charges, once again invited for a two-week respite from conflict and suffering, now included displaced persons as well as Germans.[8]

There is some evidence that the novices among volunteers working under Quaker auspices were no more immune from a certain uncritical benevolence toward suffering Germans—and concomitant hostility toward occupying authorities—than had been their precursors in 1919. Passages in the surviving letters of Joel Carl Welty, an AFSC worker in the French zone, reminiscent of Joan Fry's account of her work in "Downcast Germany" after World War I, reflect this bias. It troubled Welty that a considerable portion of the destruction around his work site in Coblentz had been inflicted by American action, and he bristled at French highhandedness against German civilians, ascribing it to the fact that "French soldiers and officers are adventurers or come from broken homes or [are] escaping from disagreeable situations at home." One wonders what minute study of French society undergirded these hostile assumptions and why Welty failed to take into account what French men and women had for five years suffered at the hands of "German adventurers." Even when a French official treated him courteously, he could not resist the comment that this "was very unusual behavior for French Bureaucracy." His was the reaction of someone well-intentioned who cannot accept, or justify, any motivation of revenge or retribution. In time, however, Welty, too, became more fair-minded. In 1947, when a German criticized the American bombardment of the cathedral and university town of Freiburg, Welty tersely reminded him of the German air attacks on Canterbury and Coventry.[9]

The fundamental Quaker mission, to help the suffering, could not be modified by the fact that its beneficiaries now included former oppressors. On that issue Joel Welty also spoke firmly to some German victims of the vanished tyranny who complained about Quaker kindness to former Nazis. "I told [them] . . . that Quakers made no distinctions politically and any other way," and, he added, "that perhaps Nazis needed our message more than anti-Nazis." William Hughes, ministering to Nazi inmates in internment camps from September 1946 to November 1947, saw this service as a continuation of his crusade, begun in the 1930s, against punishing individuals for their political beliefs. The case may well be made—certainly this writer would make it—that the lot Hughes was now serving deserved their fate because of what they had *done,* whereas former Nazi victims had been mistreated for what they *believed.* But Friends refused to make this distinction, because, in their eyes, all victims were equally deserving of succor. Their principles permitted no deviation from that standard, and who was to decide which beneficiaries of their forbearance were unworthy? Certainly in the Netherlands, where Quaker relief teams arrived in November 1945 to distribute food and clothing among survivors in the ruins of Rotterdam and the devastated countryside around Arnhem, indiscriminate charity served a variety of needy groups, ranging from stateless refugees, whom the Nazis had stripped of German citizenship, to the children of imprisoned Dutch collaborators. In one documented instance, Quakers even employed a "cheerful, hard-working girl, because her father was a Quisling and she found it hard to get a job." This humane position—often controversial and unpopular—was unexpectedly vindicated when, in 1947, the British Friends Service Council and the American Friends Service Committee became joint recipients of the Nobel Peace Prize. While there was no dissent anywhere challenging the justice of the award, its motivation reflected once again that the world at large appreciated Quakers as purveyors of relief for the distressed. The recipients stressed, therefore, that their "humanitarian service is based on religion."[10]

Generosity toward erstwhile tormentors also guided the conduct of some German Friends who had felt the heavy hand of oppression. Peter Karl Krüger, another uprooted German teacher, had run a home for political refugees in La Coûme, France, which became a sanctuary for Spanish orphans and French Jewish children in 1941. Arrested by the Gestapo in 1944, he subsequently fell into the hands of the Russians, who did not free him until 1949. He returned to La Coûme and ran the home as a place for delinquent and orphaned children until 1972. The man who had denounced him to the Germans was executed after liberation, to which Krüger later commented sadly: "[His betrayal] cost me in all 5 years, it cost him his life." Hanna Jordan, daughter of a Gentile father and a Jewish mother, graduated from Eerde in 1939 and returned to her family in Germany, where, eventually, all were forced into hiding. At the end of the war she and her parents emerged from three separate hiding places into a world of utter devastation. After returning to their home in Wuppertal, they went to work— first in a converted air-raid shelter crowded with adults and children, then in a neighborhood center financed by the AFSC—to help rebuild their country. Hanna's years in a Quaker school, followed by her conversion, had taught her well to withstand the temptation of hatred and move on to a constructive life. Katharina Petersen, the former headmistress of Eerde, who spent much of the war as a humble private tutor to the children of affluent parents, followed William Hughes's example and went among SS internees. She stressed to these postwar inhabitants of Sandbostel their duty to forget past commitments to National Socialism, overlook present tribulations, and prepare to become constructive participants in the restoration of their battered homeland.[11] When a former Nazi official professed to having undergone "the deepest religious experience" during his internment, German Friends, to whom he spoke about this conversion, rejoiced that he was " 'returning home' in the deepest sense of the word."[12]

However, such attempts to reconstitute individual lives were only a small part of the communal resuscitation pursued by German Friends, once they had found their bearings in a world unaccustomed to peace. In Pyrmont, Mary Friedrich once again took possession of the Quaker Meeting House and on June 20 welcomed her husband, Leonhard, back from Buchenwald. Soon FAU personnel came for regular visits—twenty-one in August and September alone—and helped the survivors establish contact with the outside world. In Berlin "it dawned upon" young Anna Halle one day in early May that no more bombs would fall and that the Gestapo would not return to interrogate her and her family. As soon as she and her parents had reestablished contact with mainly American Friends, they, too, devoted themselves to aiding a multitude of victims in their metropolis of ruins. In June, Hans Albrecht walked five miles from the city outskirts into town to inspect the battered locale of the Berlin Center. Two months after that dispiriting survey, the premises were sufficiently refurbished to accommodate meetings of worship, and as many as sixty attended the first Sunday in October, huddled in a room without heat and without windows. By the end of the year Albrecht and the Halles, along with other Christian groups, were helping Christian and unchurched "non-Aryans" in Berlin who were not included in relief assistance to Jewish survivors in the former capital. These Friends, once again, took particular responsibility for those who had no ties with any religious community.[13]

By September, Friends in Germany had established offices in each zone, although contact between occupation sectors was confined to meetings in Pyrmont. On July 14, 1945, the first Executive Committee meeting convened— with only Hans Albrecht unable to attend—and reconvened in October, this time augmented by Fred Tritton from London and the American Friend Erroll

Elliot from Indianapolis. Unfortunately, no record of these proceedings seems to have survived, and we do not know whether these gatherings went beyond celebrating the coming of peace and the blessings of survival. In February 1946 a consortium of foreign relief agencies likewise chose the meetinghouse for a major planning session where they decided on a strategy to cope with the complexity of German relief. Meanwhile, Leonhard Friedrich had reopened his publishing house, which became the first such enterprise in the British zone to receive a paper allocation. The first postwar issue of *Der Quäker* appeared in July 1946.

In Bad Pyrmont itself, local German Friends also found plenty of work. The town, used as a hospital city during the closing weeks of the war and thus spared destruction, was so crowded with refugees that its population was three times its normal size. The need for hospital facilities grew as more and more amputees arrived, and a Quaker Volunteer Committee was formed to succor these unfortunates. Several Quaker wives opened a sewing room where people were able to purchase repaired clothing at minimal prices. This workshop was aided by bales of cloth sent by the British Friends Relief Service and the AFSC, while the Pyrmont City Council assumed the cost of maintaining the premises.[14]

Meanwhile, a frustrated Hans Albrecht was attempting to regain control of his scattered and divided flock. His initial efforts were demonstrably ineffective as he learned on a visit to Britain in 1946, during which he discovered that some German Friends were already communicating their views on the future of the German Society to British coreligionists without his knowledge. Many of these correspondents appeared to be reconciled to a Society divided along zonal boundary lines, an arrangement, Albrecht feared, that would convince Friends in the relatively isolated Soviet zone that the rest of German Quakerism had abandoned them. He also sought to set in motion a concerted effort to found a German Quaker school, and he seems to have believed that future committee and yearly meetings should decide whether, and under what circumstances, individuals who had left the Society during the preceding twelve years might be readmitted. On this issue he was apparently less forgiving than most German Friends. In an August 1946 circular, he explained that those who had dropped their membership must remember that the sacrifices of those who had remained faithful ultimately ensured the continued Quaker presence in Germany. However, the October 1946 meeting of the Executive Committee took a more noncommittal stance reminiscent of earlier flexibility on the issue of military service. It expressed understanding of what motivated those who had believed that, "under prevailing conditions," they could serve the cause of peace better outside the Society, and it refused to censure those who acted in a way "that differed from the path prescribed by Quaker witness. *We know that none of us is without blemish.*" As far as I have been able to determine, both parties overrated the importance of this issue. Inquiries have brought to light only two cases of such readmissions, one of a Friend who had dropped out in 1939 for purely personal reasons. The same assembly also considered the question of founding Quaker schools "on German soil," and—as in 1931—appointed a committee to pursue the matter. But now, as then, no concrete results followed these deliberations.[15]

In July 1947 the first postwar Yearly Meeting gathered at the traditional site. At this time Hans Albrecht, past seventy, weary, and no longer representing a united Society or a clear consensus on major concerns, resigned the clerkship he had held for twenty years and was succeeded by Willi Wohlrabe, who lived in the Soviet zone and whose tenure would last only one year. Albrecht remained an active participant and a frequent speaker at subsequent convocations until his death nine years later at the age of eighty-one.[16]

By that time, the German Quaker community had long been divided between two German states. Emil Fuchs became the leader of the DDR's Yearly Meeting, after an extended physical and spiritual odyssey. It began in 1943 when the old Christian Socialist and his grandson, Klaus, disappeared into the mountains of Austria, and it continued in 1945 with his return to Frankfurt, intent on making his contribution to a new Christian and Socialist Germany. For two years Emil vainly sought support. German Socialists did not encourage him, preferring to deal with the established churches, and even German Friends no longer showed a disposition to follow his lead. Late in 1947 the search for a mission led him to Pendle Hill in the United States, where some individual Friends respected and admired Fuchs's unbending character, but where the Quaker community as a whole also did not resonate to his beliefs. On his way back to Europe, in July 1947, he detoured to visit his son Klaus, the well-known physicist at Harwell, and then reached his final destination: the Karl-Marx University of Leipzig, which offered him the chair in religious education. There he spent the rest of his long life, under a tyranny that considered some tolerance of religious activity to be politically expedient. During this relatively quiescent period he wrote three volumes of memoirs, of which only two appeared in print. He no doubt recognized that he did not fit entirely into the German state of workers and peasants when he confessed to a visitor: "I am not altogether popular with the authorities." It was undoubtedly true, but not to a dangerous degree.[17] When his son Klaus was arrested as a Soviet spy, Emil came to his defense. He was certain that this act of betrayal had produced the balance of terror needed to prevent other uses of nuclear weapons after Hiroshima and Nagasaki.[18] Three years later, Emil's ninetieth birthday was marked by the publication of a compendious volume of tributes whose contributors included Albert Schweitzer ("We know each other though we have never met"); Friedrich Siegmund-Schultze; Margarethe Lachmund; and a host of British and American Friends: Corder Catchpool's widow, Gwen, Fred Tritton, Henry Cadbury, Clarence Pickett, and Douglas Steere. Among these, only Pickett expressed uneasiness about the honoree's accommodation to the German dictatorship of the Left.[19]

Other German Friends found East Germany a less hospitable habitat than had Fuchs. Fritz and Martha Legatis, as well as Käte Provinski, became part of the forced exodus from—now Polish—Silesia. In Eichkamp near Berlin, Franz Hoffmann was briefly arrested by the Russians a day or two before the end of the war and returned home so changed physically that his wife at first did not recognize him. The family's tribulations continued when the upper story of their residence was commandeered and turned into a bordello for Russian soldiers, a situation that lasted for more than a month, despite Hans Albrecht's almost daily efforts to put a stop to this appalling imposition.[20] The bourgeois, liberal Lachmunds likewise found themselves victims of past and present excesses. Despite Hans Lachmund's membership in the National Committee "Free Germany" and his part in the bloodless surrender of Greifswald, he now paid for his judicial reinstatement a decade earlier. Arrested by the Russians as a former Nazi official, he wound up before the DDR's Peoples Court, whose proceedings—like its forerunner—constituted a mockery of evidence and law. He received a long prison sentence and was not released from the nefarious Waldheim camp near Chemnitz until 1953.[21]

Other German Friends had to cope with the postwar chaos much like millions of their compatriots. Most of them resumed professional lives from which the Nazis had driven them. Marie Pleissner, a founder of the Liberal Democratic Party in the Soviet zone, returned to the classroom. Katharina Petersen in Hanover became the first German woman to rise to the rank of ministerial councillor in the provincial Ministry of Education and, like Bertha Bracey, earned the Order of the British Empire, in her case for her contribution to educational reform in the British zone. Two alumni of the Guben meeting also returned to their professions: Heinz Mohr became a teacher in Berlin, Gerhard Ockel a physician in Frankfurt. Carl and Eva Hermann, freed after serving two years of their prison sentences, settled in Marburg, where Carl assumed the post of professor of physics. Gertrud Luckner, a survivor of Ravensbrück, returned to Freiburg, and the Cohens in Munich now employed their charitable energies in the service of displaced persons and former concentration camp inmates. Grete Sumpf went to work for Pastor Mensching, the German pillar of the Fellowship of Reconciliation. Though each Quaker family had to fight personal battles of reconstitution, "every single Friend quickly committed in some community effort for the planning of new services and revival of old ones in an expression of common responsibility."[22]

In Vienna, Rudi Boeck never seemed haunted by his Nazi past. At war's end he went back to his work as architect in the municipal administration of the

Austrian capital, and some ten years later, after Hans Albrecht's death, claimed in a letter of condolence to the son of the deceased that the longtime leader of the German Society of Friends had always been his model, "not only as Quaker but as a human being."[23]

In the Netherlands, finally, Friends came to terms with burdens of the past in a variety of ways. In Haarlem, Manfred and Lilli Pollatz, without news from their soldier son since January, gradually gave up hope of ever seeing him again. Lilli, in the grip of her final illness, wondered "if there will be much chance to work for God's Kingdom under our ideals in a time like ours." Death released her from both pain and doubt on March 1, 1946, and the house on Westerhoutpark became a relief center, largely financed by the AFSC. Manfred continued as a member of the German Yearly Meeting and felt especially honored when its members invited him in 1948 to deliver the annual Richard Cary Lecture. In due time, he recovered his German pension and devoted himself to the pursuit of his literary, historical, and pedagogic interests. The most visible result of these preoccupations remains his catalog of the 1962 Frans Hals retrospective, a prelude to the tricentennial of the passing of Haarlem's most famous inhabitant. However, despite his fanatic commitment to his cultural roots, he became a Dutch citizen and never lived in Germany again, returning only occasionally to receive medical treatment for his childhood injury, which had been aggravated during his imprisonment.[24]

The Dutch Yearly Meeting counted forty-three members at the end of the war. Like its German counterpart, it had to wrestle with a troubled conscience. A report, signed by Piet Kappers's wife, Luise, and written about a month after the end of the war, confessed that "it has been no simple matter during these past years to live up to what we profess. We have experienced how difficult it has been to remain honest and sincere under all circumstances, and also to be conscious of our personal responsibility for everything that happened." How to remain "honest and sincere" persisted as a bone of contention among Dutch Friends long after the war and the occupation had ceased to be a subject of daily reflection and stocktaking. The group continued to be divided between those who held that a Quaker must always tell the truth—a position exemplified by Piet Kappers's dealings with occupying authorities—and those who believed, especially when dealing with Nazis, that truth could be compromised whenever veracity might cost lives.[25]

Recriminations and moral dilemmas notwithstanding, Piet Kappers continued his effort to reopen Eerde and keep the promise of making it more than just a refuge for victims of Nazi oppression. Neither the occupation's wake of destruction and hunger nor the inability of British and American Friends to commit any part of their strained resources to his visionary endeavor discouraged him. Once he found a clientele in the children of civil servants of the Dutch government-in-exile, who needed a school where they could finish an education begun in Great Britain, there was no stopping him, and in May 1946 the Quaker school Eerde rose, phoenixlike, from the ashes of occupation.[26] It had even less equipment now than in 1934, and much of its faculty, German by birth, went through an anxious interim when expulsion to Germany threatened. Kurt Neuse, in particular, was most vulnerable for having served—no matter how nominally—in the reserve of the German army.[27] Eerde's last principal, Werner Hermans, escaped this trial, thanks to his naturalization in 1939, and was appointed commandant of an internment camp for Dutch Nazis: as a Quaker, he guaranteed humane treatment of these collaborators, a promise he fully lived up to.[28]

But these uncertainties proved only temporary. The Neuse family and Elisabeth Schmitt emigrated to the United States, while Max and Josepha Warburg settled in Britain. Otto Reckendorf, Heinz Wild, and Billy Hilsley joined the new school's faculty. In 1948 an attempt was even made to bring Katharina Petersen back as head of this postwar enterprise, but she declined because she did not believe that a German could presently head a school in the Netherlands. She was also unwilling to leave her post in Hanover, where competent civil servants, unencumbered by a Nazi past, were in short supply.[29]

In the long run, however, Kappers's dream of Eerde's perpetuity died with him. When the school's lease was not renewed in 1958, Friends relocated the school at Beverweerd Castle, near Utrecht, with Hilsley remaining as the last holdover from the original faculty. Twelve years later, three years after Kappers's death, the Dutch Yearly Meeting decided that the student body had come to represent a degree of affluence that neither deserved nor required their continued support. Like Eerde, Beverweerd ceased being a Quaker school. The need for such an institution had been tied to the Nazi terror after all.[30]

CONCLUSIONS

This book, describing the encounter of Quakers and Nazis, has rested on no conceptual framework, and the events it describes confirm no consoling maxims and point to no comfortable prescriptions ensuring a better future. It may leave us with the hope that sparse columns of the Society of Friends will continue their struggle to temper man's inhumanity to man by mobilizing again and again the nameless to help the nameless, by more "unhistoric acts"—as George Elliot put it—carried out by obscure men and women "who lived faithfully . . . and rest in unvisited tombs." It is a fragile expectation when one considers that the example Quakers have set, though earning them respect and admiration throughout the world, has not converted many to join their ranks. On the contrary, throughout Europe and the United States their numbers since World War II have been declining.[31] Being a Quaker, or acting like a Quaker, remains difficult, with or without Nazis. Difficult because a Friend's lifelong dialogue with God represents a far more stressful mode of submission than the ritual worship of an idol associated with an immutable corpus of commandments. Silent prayer carries the Quaker into unknown regions, whose landmarks no one can interpret for him. To avoid merely hearing echoes of his own inclinations, and merely seeing reflections of his own preoccupations, the communicant in silent worship fortifies himself with the antidote of humility and the unswerving acceptance of responsibility for society's failures. Therefore, Quakers, though their "spirit and work might go on silently from one year's end to the other in every part of the world," have never doubted that all their endeavors have fallen short. In that spirit Hans Albrecht apologized to German Jews for harassment by storm troopers in 1931, while Luise Kappers accepted Dutch Friends' responsibility for everything that happened during the German occupation. In spite of their achievements, a perpetual sense of failure drives Quakers to do better in the future.[32] That nagging conviction of inadequacy remains constant in their dialogue with God and mankind. When Bertha Bracey read the first reports from Belsen, she agonized—"Did we make the wrong decision not to speak out?"—knowing that Friends had failed to reveal much dark knowledge during the preceding decades because such outspokenness would have put an end to their work in Central Europe altogether. Could she, or any Friend, ever be sure that Quaker measures had been not only insufficient but also mistaken?

No historian will ever be able to answer that question, least of all this writer. The subtitle I chose for this project indicates my indecision. "Inner Light in Outer Darkness" expressed one judgment. Quakers, inspired by what they took to be the enlightenment God's will brought to their seeking hearts, descended into dark places they hoped to illuminate with the light of divine mercy. One such bastion of darkness was Germany: first embittered by an inexplicable military defeat that placed the nation at the mercy of its enemies, then, buoyed by newfound strength, turning mercilessly upon real as well as imaginary domestic and foreign foes. But the main title of this book eschews a formula of confrontation. It reads "Quakers *and* Nazis," not "Quakers against Nazis." Describing Quakers attempting to mitigate the sufferings Nazism inflicted, it offers no chronicle of combat. Nazis inflicted suffering on Friends, but Friends did not, could not, reciprocate.

In 1931 Hans Albrecht, the clerk of the German Yearly Meeting, apologized to a Jewish congregation in Berlin for his coreligionists' failure to reduce intra-German antagonisms sufficiently to spare them the humiliation inflicted by a rowdy gang of storm troopers. But he also petitioned the German government to commute the death sentence imposed on Nazi murderers of a Communist in the Silesian village of Potempa. In both instances Albrecht's conduct was guided by the same all-embracing love Quakers felt for all humanity: for Jews who did not share his Christian beliefs and for Nazis who violently opposed his vision of human brotherhood.

Shocked by the terrifying consequences of Hitler's investiture as head of the German government, Corder Catchpool instituted a network of agents who fed him eyewitness accounts of terrorist acts that he transmitted to Friends House in London. But then his own arrest—far from confirming the soundness of his partisanship—suddenly brought home to him that he had strayed from the path of conciliation and was about to take sides in a German civil war. He reconsidered and decided that he could be a peacemaker only if he gave each side the benefit of his understanding.

Although Catchpool's posture was not immediately embraced by every Friend, he persevered in this new equipoisal stance that was in tune with traditional Quaker practice. Carl Heath and Bertha Bracey might fleetingly disagree with him, and his American successor, Albert Martin, would never be able to work in the same evenhanded spirit, but the collective Quaker response to challenges facing domestic peace in Germany and harmony between nations in Europe supported Catchpool's position in the long run.

Quakers continued to succor the deprived without questioning their religious, moral, or ideological credentials. They were equally solicitous for suffering Socialists, Communists, Jews, and Christians. They worked to free Nazi activists from Lithuanian prisons and remained willing, though not able, to aid families of Nazi internees in Austria. The fact that their child-feeding enterprises in the Sudetenland turned them into potential partners of German expansionism did not deter them from pursuing their humanitarian course in that depressed region. In order to save German Jews in the aftermath of the Night of Broken Glass, they did not hesitate to enlist Gestapo aid to reach that—ultimately unattainable— goal. Nor did their disheartening engagement in darkest Germany keep most of them from opposing, with every resource at their command, a second European descent into universal conflict within the memory of one generation. Until 1939 Catchpool and Horace Alexander strove to keep contending parties at the negotiating table and, when that failed, to bring them back, even after the guns had spoken. When the war continued, Quakers, once again, devoted time and resources to the benefit of German internees and prisoners of war. As soon as the coming of peace permitted, they returned to Germany, where they once again refused to distinguish between former victims and former Nazis. All could count on the help of Friends.

Quakers appeared to have history on their side, as Margarethe Lachmund thought she discovered at the Quaker World Conference at Swarthmore College in 1937; there she learned how John Woolman had converted slaveholders among Friends into abolitionists by approaching them as fellow children of God, rather than as adversaries. It was this history lesson that made her also realize that she must approach National Socialists in the same charitable spirit.[33]

Yet history is more often enigmatic oracle than explicit teacher. Lachmund's forbearance saved her husband's career, but at the heavy price of his long incarceration after the war. It also saved some friends and associates from Nazi vengeance. Beyond that, Woolman's example was of limited use to Friends facing Nazis. The German Society of Friends as well as the foreigners working at the Berlin Center were, after all, not laboring to spread toleration of political opponents of the Hitler regime, or of Jews, in their own ranks, but were trying to persuade adversaries—impervious to the moral force of their example—to treat these groups in a humane and civil fashion. In that endeavor, success depended not on converting unbelievers but rather on persuading them that acceding to Quaker requests was to their advantage. To that extent Friends succeeded in some degree. Nazis, mindful that Quakers had fed many of them after World War I, performed occasional acts of kindness: one such saved Leonhard Friedrich's life at Buchenwald. Nazi authorities, at the same time, used Quaker benevolence to advance their own interests, as shown in Austria, in the Sudetenland, as well as in Germany. Even in Britain, Quaker commitment to the preservation of peace abetted German expansion on the Continent and could therefore count on a friendly reception of its representatives in Berlin.

But in the end, the Nazis were not swayed from their pitiless course or influenced by the generous example set by these emulators of Christ. Corder Catchpool might seek to understand them, but the pleas from Friends House to close concentration camps fell on deaf ears, and a variety of efforts to free individual prisoners ended more often than not in failure. Even so committed a Friend as Lord Noël-Buxton finally came to believe in 1939 that there remained no peaceful way of stopping the Nazis.

If British and American Friends could claim no converts from National Socialism, their German comrades had even less success with these forces of nihilism. Olga Halle might represent "the only ray of hope" left to the inhabitants of the Piaski Ghetto, but she could save neither their lives nor the twenty-eight "unhelped" cases at her office that haunted her to the end of her life. Thanks to an adversary that knew no pity, her ultimate reward was a stricken conscience. Manfred Pollatz saved many a Jewish child, but his son had to die to save the father and the refuge the parents maintained in Haarlem. At Eerde, Kurt Neuse opened a new life to many youngsters from Germany by teaching them English, but he could not save the group destined for extinction; his own reward was lifelong exile from the country of his birth.

Another burden the crusading Quaker had to bear was what we today call the search for priorities. Although converting others to their mode of believing and living concerned them far less in our time than it had in the seventeenth and eighteenth centuries, some of them, throughout the 1930s, remained uneasy that the dispensation of material charity was absorbing most of their energies and alone accounted for the high respect with which the rest of the world continued to view them. People came to them for bread, not for enlightenment. At Pendle Hill in 1942, the German Social Democrat Wilhelm Sollmann saw all too clearly that "the impressive relief work of the Society of Friends in Germany . . . and certain other territories under dictatorship, has been possible only because [it has] *for the time being wisely limited its activities to charity.* A word against militarism, conscription or conquest would result in . . . the immediate suppression of the Society of Friends."[34] Hans Albrecht would have agreed, as would have many other Friends, both foreign and German, whose service in Germany had repeatedly put the Sollmann contention to the test. The exceptions were the Heritage Pamphlets of the German Yearly Meeting, which succeeded only because no Nazi seems to have taken the trouble to read them. The one time one of these tracts came to official attention, Marie Sturm, the compiler, was condemned to two years in prison.

The retreat from a spiritual mission, no matter how much Gilbert MacMaster repeatedly deplored it, was a prerequisite for a continued Quaker presence in Nazi Germany and Nazi Europe. In the end, such compromise extended to violence on an even broader scale. If Anna Halle could feel liberated in May 1945; if Hans Albrecht could resume planning Quakerism's future in Germany; if Mary Friedrich could again dispose of the Pyrmont Quaker Meeting House without approval by the local police; and if Eerde's surviving denizens could rejoice when their Canadian liberators rolled up the drive in a tank, then this meant that a diversity of Friends had tacitly accepted that such happy endings had been ensured by guns and tanks. One wonders whether their happiness was tempered by the realization that they could now resume their healing course only because others had refused to conciliate an intolerant and intolerable adversary and had taken to arms to topple Hitler.

This contradiction has kept many men and women of goodwill from joining the Society of Friends. These hesitant admirers of Quakerism have felt bound to ask whether a Nazi victory would not have doomed Friends on the Continent, along with Jews, Gypsies, and any other groups these victors might have chosen to destroy. Would the purity and selflessness of Quaker conduct have been sufficient to stay the hand of their conquerors?

The past fifty years have left Friends little leisure to consider this question. Since 1945 they have moved on from healing the wounds of the recent past to coping with a world in which the crimes of Europe's dictators are being endlessly repeated. Since an American demographer conjured up the catastrophic consequences of a Jewish exodus from Europe in 1939, the refugee tide throughout the world has continued to rise to the point where "curbing the flow" has become the only practical—if distressingly elusive—solution.[35] The wholesale slaughter of human beings likewise continues. The discovery that you deal with your enemies by exterminating them threatens to become the most pervasive legacy of our century.[36]

Amid this orgy of murder, rapine, and suffering, Quakers continue to defy failure and hopelessness: in Haiti and Mozambique, on the Gaza Strip, in Yugoslavia, in San Salvador, and among the victims of Mississippi floods.[37] In the end, they always succeed in saving some of God's children, but never more than a minority of the afflicted. Still, what they attempt and what they achieve cannot be measured by an accountant's balance sheet of success and failure. Violence triumphs everywhere, but they will not follow its persuasive example. Evil persists, but they will never abet it. That also remains the abiding lesson of their encounter with Nazism. No matter what forces may assail them, they stand their ground. Stephen G. Cary, until 1990 the clerk of the Board of the AFSC, described in these words the example Friends continue to set: "Even though we are tiny, and even though there is a vast world to mend, it's important that we keep witnessing to what love can do." How much more it could do depends on the rest of mankind.[38]

Notes

Preface

1. Roon, *Protestants Nederland en Duitsland 1933–1941*, 12. I am indebted for the membership figures to Miep Lieftinck of the Dutch Yearly Meeting.
2. Quote from Ronald C. D. Jasper, *George Bell, Bishop of Chichester*, 137.
3. Schmitt, *Lucky Victim: An Ordinary Life in Extraordinary Times*, notably chapters 4, 5, 6, and 8.

Introduction: Quakers Seeking God, Peace, and an End to Human Suffering

1. D. Elton Trueblood, *The People Called Quakers*, 7.
2. Henry T. Gillett, *The Spiritual Basis of Democracy*, 3.
3. Lester M. Jones, *Quakers in Action: Recent Humanitarian and Reform Activities of the American Quakers*, 9.
4. Howard H. Brinton, *Friends for 300 Years*, 34, 40; Gillett, *Spiritual Basis*, 39.
5. See Brinton, *Friends for 300 Years*, 108–9.
6. Leonard W. Levy, *Blasphemy: Verbal Offense against the Sacred from Moses to Salman Rushdie* (New York: Knopf, 1993), 168–80.
7. This paragraph is indebted to two recent biographies: H. Larry Ingle, *First among Friends: George Fox and the Creation of Quakerism*, and Bonnelyn Young Kunze, *Margaret Fell and the Rise of Quakerism*.
8. Quote from Horace G. Alexander, *The Growth of the Peace Testimony of the Society of Friends*, 4.
9. Brinton, *Friends for 300 Years*, 164.
10. Peter Brock, *The Quaker Peace Testimony, 1660 to 1914*, 35.
11. Sydney D. Bailey, *Peace Is a Process*, 19–31; Arthur J. Mekeel, *The Relation of the Quakers to the American Revolution*, 325 and passim.
12. Brinton, *Friends for 300 Years*, 151–52.
13. Hans A. Schmitt, *The Path to European Union* (Baton Rouge: Louisiana State University Press, 1962), 4; Bailey, *Peace Is a Process*, 70–75.
14. Brock, *Quaker Peace Testimony*, 142–80, 263.
15. Elizabeth Fox Howard, *Midstream: A Record of Many Years*, 37.
16. Catchpool, *Letters of a Prisoner for Conscience Sake*, 81–89, 163, and *On Two Fronts: Letters of a Conscientious Objector*, 80, 95–97, 137–48. Catchpool's testimony should be supplemented by two useful, but far from definitive, biographical studies: Jean Corder Greaves, *Corder Catchpool*, and William R. Hughes, *Indomitable Friend: The Life of Corder Catchpool, 1883–1952*.
17. See Arthur Marwick, *Clifford Allen: The Open Conspirator*, 45–56.
18. Howard, *Midstream*, 42–45.
19. L. M. Jones, *Quakers in Action*, 16–17; Willis H. Hall, *Quaker International Work in Europe since 1914*, 63–71.

20. Quote from Howard, *Midstream*, 27.

21. Elizabeth Fox Howard, *Downstream: Records of Several Generations*, 19–20; John O. Greenwood, *Friends and Relief*, 1–17.

22. Helen E. Hatton, *The Largest Amount of Good: Quaker Relief in Ireland, 1654–1921*, 248–63.

23. Greenwood, *Friends and Relief*, 25–40.

24. Ibid., 41–46.

25. William K. Sessions, *They Chose the Star*, 14–73; Greenwood, *Friends and Relief*, 50–52.

26. Sessions, *They Chose the Star*, 77–93; Greenwood, *Friends and Relief*, 81–85.

27. Greenwood, *Friends and Relief*, 97–140; J. Russell Elkinton, "Quakers and Dukhobors," 19.

28. Greenwood, *Friends and Relief*, 149–60; Hope H. Hewison, *Hedge of Wild Almonds: South Africa, the Pro-Boers and the Quaker Conscience, 1890–1910*.

29. Quote from Howard, *Midstream*, 27.

30. Ibid., 68–81; Greenwood, *Friends and Relief*, 165–214.

31. Mary Hoxie Jones, *Swords into Ploughshares: An Account of the American Friends Service Committee, 1917–1937*, 42–44, 139–40. For some of the controversy about Quaker work in Soviet Russia, see David W. McFadden, "The Haines-Watts Mission and the Quaker Role in the Origins of Western Relief in Soviet Russia, 1920–1921" (paper presented to the 1994 Meeting of Quaker Historians and Archivists, Guilford College, N.C., June 25, 1994).

32. L. M. Jones, *Quakers in Action*, 18–34; M. H. Jones, *Swords into Ploughshares*, 7–20. For greater detail, see J. William Frost, " 'Our Deeds Carry Our Message': The Early History of the American Friends Service Committee," and Rufus M. Jones, *A Service of Love in Wartime: American Friends Relief Work in Europe, 1917–1919*.

33. Brinton, *Friends for 300 Years*, 173.

34. *Quaker Embassies: A Survey of Friends' Service in Europe since 1919*, 5; Elbert Russell, *The Quaker Challenge in a World of Force*, 9.

1. Quakers and Germans, 1919–1932

1. Huxley, *Crome Yellow*, 163.

2. Figures from Germany. Statistisches Reichsamt, *Statistisches Jahrbuch für das Deutsche Reich* (Berlin: Reimar Hobbing, 1932), 15.

3. Karl Wilhelm Dahm, *Pfarrer und Politik. Soziale Position und politische Mentalität des deutschen evangelischen Pfarrerstandes zwischen 1918 und 1933* and the English summary "German Protestantism and Politics, 1918–1939." A larger perspective is offered by Adelheid Bullinger, "Das Ende des landesherrlichen Kirchenregiments und die Neugestaltung der evangelischen Kirche," and Gerhard Anschütz, "Wandlungen der deutschen evangelischen Kirchenverfassung."

4. Hermann Greive, *Theologie und Ideologie. Katholizismus und Judentum in Deutschland und Österreich 1918–1935*.

5. Ingle, *First among Friends*, 267–85; Wilhelm Hubben, *Die Quäker in der deutschen Vergangenheit*, 20–104, 156–57; Heinrich Otto, *Werden und Wesen des Quäkertums und seine Entwicklung in Deutschland*, 184–204. See also C. E. Stansfield, "Die Mindener Quäker am Ende des 18. Jahrhunderts," *Mitteilungen für die Freunde des Quäkertums in Deutschland* (1931): 147–49; and Paul Helbeck, "Deutsche Kriegsdienstverweigerer vor hundert Jahren."

6. Trueblood, *The People Called Quakers*, 247–55.
7. Italics added.
8. Frederick J. Tritton, *Carl Heath, Apostle of Peace*, 12–22, and *The World Community of Friends*, 15, for the second quote; *Quaker Embassies*, 5–16; *Friends' Service in Germany*, 2–4; Bailey, *Peace Is a Process*, 85–89. For an account from the American side, see Charles E. Strickland, "American Aid to Germany, 1919 to 1921."
9. Joan Mary Fry, *Offener Brief an die Frankfurter Zeitung*, 1–4.
10. Anonymous and undated memorandum "Als Führer der Quäker in der Ruhr kommen in Frage," and text of a letter sent to a variety of individuals, July 22 and 24, 1919, both in Evangelisches Zentralarchiv Berlin (EZA), Quäker und Friedenskirchen, 51, Q, b 1.
11. Joan Mary Fry, *In Downcast Germany 1919–1933*, 8–23. On Elisabeth Rotten, see Otto, *Werden und Wesen*, 212.
12. J. M. Fry, *In Downcast Germany*, 61–64, 68.
13. Ibid., 35; A. Ruth Fry, *A Quaker Adventure: The Story of Nine Years' Relief and Reconstruction*, viii.
14. Hubben, *Die Quäker*, 169–74; Francis L. Carsten, "Die Quäker in Deutschland 1919–1924," 741–50. For details on the fight against tuberculosis, see Hertha Kraus, *International Relief in Action, 1914–1943*, 76–79.
15. Dr. von Bentheim, "Bericht über die Quäkerspeisungen," appendix of "Bericht über die Tätigkeit der Mittelstelle für Quäkerarbeit in Deutschland" (December 1922): EZA, 51, Q 1, b 2.
16. Greenwood, *Friends and Relief*, 225–31.
17. Rudolf Schubert, "Memoirs," 49, an incomplete manuscript of seventy-six typewritten pages, in private hands; Gilbert MacMaster, "Diary," 62, American Friends Service Committee Archives, Philadelphia (AFSC).
18. Anneliese Herwig, *Ein Lebensbild von Gilbert MacMaster (1869–1967) und seiner Lebensgefährtin Marga (1879–1967) nach seinen eigenen Aufzeichnungen*, 13–15; M. H. Jones, *Swords into Ploughshares*, 82–84.
19. Hubben, *Die Quäker*, 107–20, 132–50.
20. Otto, *Werden und Wesen*, 230–51.
21. Friedrich Siegmund-Schultze, "Von den Quäkern. Zusammenkunft der deutschen Freunde der Quäker in Dillenburg (17.-19. September)."
22. Mimeographed circular "An die Teilnehmer der Dillenburger Konferenz . . ." and "Bericht über die Tätigkeit der Mittelstelle für Quäkerarbeit in Deutschland," EZA, 51, Q 1, b 1 and 2, respectively.
23. Various conference reports of the *Mittelstelle*, ibid., loc. cit.
24. Otto, *Werden und Wesen*, 255–57; J. M. Fry, *In Downcast Germany*, 86–87.
25. "Gründungsbeschluss" reprinted in the special issue *50 Jahre Deutsche Jahresversammlung* of *Der Quäker*, July 1975; Michael Seadle, "Quakerism in Germany: The Pacifist Response to Hitler," 50.
26. Hubben, *Die Quäker*, 177.
27. Hans Albrecht, *Was ist uns Quäkertum?* Vortrag auf der fünften Deutschen Jahresversammlung der Freunde, 7–16 and passim. See also Rufus M. Jones, *Studies in Mystical Religion* (London: MacMillan, 1909), and *Spiritual Reformers of the 16th and 17th Centuries* (Boston: Beacon, 1959), 348–49, which anticipate Albrecht's contention.

28. Hans Albrecht, *Was bedeutet Mitgliedschaft bei den Quäkern?* Vortrag in der 6. Jahresversammlung der deutschen Freunde am 22. Juli 1931 in Hellerau, 1–12.

29. *Mitteilungen für die Freunde des Quäkertums in Deutschland* (1925): 113.

30. A copy of this report, dated November 30, 1929, in AFSC, Foreign Service (FS), Germany, 1930. See also Benjamin Heinrich Unruh, *Fügung und Führung im Mennonitischen Welthilfswerk 1920–1933. Humanität in christlicher Sicht.*

31. Hans Albrecht to Clarence E. Pickett, August 23, 1930, AFSC, FS, Germany, 1930.

32. For the letter to the Jewish congregation, see *Monatshefte der Deutschen Freunde* (1931): 303–5, the text of the appeal to the Churches in EZA, 51, Q 1, c. Responses are recorded in *Der Quäker* (1932): 106–9, 163–65, 190.

33. "Mitteilungen," *Der Quäker* (1932): 252–53; "Beschlüsse der 7. Jahresversammlung in Bad Pyrmont, 24.-28. August, 1932," copy in AFSC, FS, Germany, German Yearly Meeting (GYM), 1932. On the Potempa events, see Otis C. Mitchell, *Nazism and the Common Man: Essays in Germany History (1929–1939)*, 35–36. The Potempa murderers were still alive when Hitler became chancellor. They were released under a general amnesty for imprisoned Nazis.

34. "Ein Gutachten abgegeben in der Verhandlung gegen den Kunstmaler GEORG [sic] GROSZ wegen Gotteslästerung vor der Strafkammer des Landesgerichts Berlin am 3. Dezember 1930," and Albrecht's report to the GYM *Arbeitsausschuss*, March 28–29, 1931, AFSC, FS, Germany 1930 and 1931 respectively. For a sample of the press coverage, see *Berliner Tageblatt*, December 16, 1930.

35. I have summarized my own skepticism about the scapegoating of the Treaty of Versailles in "The Treaty of Versailles: Mirror of Europe's Post-War Agony." For a careful vindication of the "war guilt" thesis by a German scholar, see Hermann Kantorowicz, *Gutachten zur Kriegsschuldfrage 1914*, edited with an introduction by Immanuel Geiss, published forty years after it was written. For Hans Albrecht's views on this subject, as set forth in 1931, see the copy of his report as transmitted to Philadelphia on January 7, in AFSC, FS, Germany, 1931.

36. Copies ibid., GYM, 1931.

37. Copies ibid., loc. cit., 1932 and Alfons Paquet, "Politik im Unscheinbaren," reprinted in *Der Quäker* (1975): 188–90.

38. Anna S. Halle, "Ein altes Buch-heute noch lebendig (Aus Protokollen der Berliner Quäkergruppe 1920–1939)," 202–3.

39. See English 1921 tr. of Alfons Paquet, *The Quakers*.

40. Hans Martin Elster, "Alfons Paquet, Leben und Werk," in Paquet's *Gesammelte Werke*, (Stuttgart: 1970), 1:5–30; Otto Doderer, "Alfons Paquet"; and Vera Niebuhr, "Alfons Paquet. Rheinischer Dichter und Verfechter des Internationalismus."

41. Emil Fuchs, *Mein Leben*, 1:72. On Naumann's social patriotism cf. Elisabeth Fehrenbach, *Wandlungen des deutschen Kaisergedankens 1871–1918*, 200–216.

42. Fuchs, *Mein Leben*, 1:100–271.

43. Ibid., 309–23; ibid., 2:10–58, 121–29; and Herbert Trebs, *Emil Fuchs*, 11–25.

44. Fuchs, *Mein Leben*, 2:140–210. Schleswig-Holstein, of which Kiel was the largest city, was the only Prussian province, or comparable German jurisdiction, the Nazis carried in the July 1932 parliamentary elections.

45. *Schleiermachers Religionsbegriff und religiöse Stellung zur Zeit der ersten Ausgabe der Reden (1799–1806)*, Theologische Schriften und Kritiken, 76 (Berlin: R. Hobbing, 1901); *Vom Werden dreier Denker. Was wollten Fichte-Schelling-*

Schleiermacher in der ersten Periode ihrer Entwicklung? (Tübingen: Mohr, 1904); "Von Friedrich Schleiermacher zu Karl Marx," *Zeitschrift für Religion und Sozialismus*, 1:1929, cited here from its reprint, Emil Fuchs, *Von Schleiermacher zu Marx*, 133–48.

46. Gertrude Birke, "Rudolf Schlosser, his life and work," copy of a typescript, written shortly after World War II, in AFSC, FS, Germany, Berlin Center, 1941 [*sic*].

47. Käte Tacke, ed., *Lebensbilder deutscher Quäker während der NS Herrschaft 1933–1945. Sammlung von Schicksalen aus der Erinnerung, aus Briefen, Zeitungsartikeln und anderen Dokumenten.* 61–62. The quotes are from Wilhelm Mensching, *Conscience*, 20–27.

48. Biographical data from Max Schwartz, *MdR, Handbuch der Reichstage*, 757; *Deutsches Biogaphisches Archiv* on microfiche, NF, 1197, and the contemporary study by Kurt Zielenziger, *Gerhart von Schulze-Gävernitz, eine Darstellung seines Werkes und seines Wirkens.* On his political career, see Jürgen Bertram, *Die Wahlen zum Deutschen Reichstag vom Jahre 1912*, Beiträge zur Geschichte des Parlamentarismus und der politischen Parteien, 28 (Düsseldorf: Droste, 1964), 142, 186; and C. Hess, *"Das ganze Deutschland soll es sein." Demokratischer Nationalismus in der Weimarer Republik am Beispiel der Deutschen Demokratischen Partei*, Kieler Historische Studien, 24 (Stuttgart: Kohlhammer, 1978), 93, 216. See also the report on the German-Polish conference of 1927 in *Die Eiche* 7 (1927): 822–23 and the text of his 1930 Swarthmore Lecture, published by Allen and Unwin that same year.

49. The terminology of that quote anticipates Fehrenbach, *Wandlungen*, especially 158–70. For the date of the imperial visit, see Mathilde von Keller, *Vierzig Jahre im Dienste der Kaiserin* (Leipzig: Koehler und Amelang, 1925), 231.

50. In 1900 Krefeld was a city of slightly more than one hundred thousand inhabitants and the center of Germany's silk and velvet industry. Catholics outnumbered Protestants by a ratio of eight to seven, but the population also included Old Catholics, Mennonites, and about eighteen hundred Jews.

51. William Hubben, *Exiled Pilgrim*, 33–228. On his difficulties with Catholic superiors in Krefeld, see also J. M. Fry, *In Downcast Germany*, 96.

52. Her parents spelled her first name "Herta," but the Bryn Mawr Archives head the collection of her papers "Hertha Kraus," and I have followed their lead.

53. Kraus curriculum vitae, Bryn Mawr College, Hertha Kraus Papers, Box 4, Folder 9.

54. Alois Kraus, "Lebenserinnerungen," ibid., loc. cit., Box 4, Folder 1, also Minutes of an ad hoc meeting in Cologne, February 11, 1932, AFSC, FS, Germany, Reports, 1932. On Hertha's trip to Chicago, see *Der Quäker* (1932): 158.

55. Minutes of *Arbeitsausschuss* meeting, March 28–29, 1931, AFSC, FS, Germany, GYM, 1931.

56. Albrecht to AFSC, May 19, 1930, AFSC, FS, Germany, 1930. A surviving copy of the GYM budget for 1930 tells a similar story, Friends House Library (FH), Foreign Service Committee (FSC), GE 12; on the subsidy in the 1932 budget, see ibid., loc. cit.

57. Albrecht to Pickett, September 16, 1931, AFSC, FS, Germany, GYM, 1931.

58. Pickett to Albrecht, AFSC, FS, Germany, GYM, 1931.

59. Otto, *Werden und Wesen*, 291–92; J. M. Fry, *In Downcast Germany*, 218–20.

60. Seadle, "Quakerism in Germany," 58–59.

61. Richard M. Kelly, *Thomas Kelly: A Biography*, 21–54.

62. Herwig, *Gilbert MacMaster*, 7–14; MacMaster, "Diary," 5–34, 68–82, 93–128.
63. MacMaster, "Diary," 90; Herwig, *Gilbert MacMaster*, 14–16.
64. Albrecht to Pickett, August 23, 1930, AFSC, FS, Germany, 1930; Willis H. Hall, *Quaker International Work in Europe since 1914*, 104–10, 158–59.
65. Copy of Mary Friedrich's report, AFSC, FS, Germany, 1930; Brenda Bailey, *A Quaker Couple in Nazi Germany*, 7–29.
66. Dorothy Henkel to Friends House, January 29, 1932, FH, FSC, GE 10; Seadle, "Quakerism in Germany," 73; Richard Cary, "Le foyer-cantine français de Berlin." Jean-Baptiste Joly, "L'Assistance des Quaker," in Gilbert Badia, *Les bannis de Hitler. Accueil et lutte des exilés allemands en France 1933–1939*, 106–7.
67. Pickett to Ellen L. Goddard, October 22, 1930, AFSC, FS, Germany, 1930; same to William B. Harvey, November 13, 1931, ibid., loc. cit., GYM, 1931.
68. Otto, *Werden und Wesen*, 297–99.
69. Philip P. Hallie, *Lest Innocent Blood Be Shed*, especially 124–37, details Trocmé's association with Friends while hiding Jews in occupied France.
70. Gerhard Halle, "Wortlaut des am. 20., 21., und. 22.5.1932 in Douai, Sin-Le-Noble und Fives-Lille gehaltenen Vortrags," and "Eine Versöhnungsfahrt mit Corder Catchpool," typescripts in the possession of Anna Halle. The contents are recapitulated in "Kriegsdienst und Gewissen." See also Seadle, "Quakerism in Germany," 69–72.
71. For the context, see Ernst-Albrecht Plieg, *Das Memelland 1920–1939*, 72–89, and Hans Hopf, "Auswirkungen des Verhältnisses Litauens zu seinen Nachbarn auf das Memelgebiet. Zur Vorgeschichte des deutsch-litauischen Staatsvertrages vom 22. März 1939." On the Quaker role: Theodor Spiro to Albrecht, April 14, 1932, Albrecht to Pickett, April 22, 1932; Richard Cary, "Trip to Memel and Kowno," undated, all in AFSC, FS, Germany, GYM, and German Reports, 1932.
72. Albrecht, "To All Friends," August 25, 1929, AFSC, FS, Germany, 1930; Hubben, *Die Quäker*, 178.
73. Notes on Anna Branson's visits to various Friends centers and the GYM, AFSC, FS, Germany, GYM, 1931.
74. Albrecht to Pickett, May 30, 1932, ibid., loc. cit., 1932; Dorothy Henkel to FSC, January 12, 1933, FH, FSC, GE 10, Frankfurt 1932–1939.

2. The Trials of Revolution

1. This as late as 1937, cf., Germany, Foreign Office, *Documents on German Foreign Policy*, Series D, 1:55–56.
2. Quote from Eugen Weber, *Varieties of Fascism: Doctrines of Revolution in the Twentieth Century* (Princeton: Van Nostrand, 1964), 153.
3. Jeremy Noakes, "The Development of Nazi Policy toward the German-Jewish 'Mischlinge,'" 293–95; Jochen-Christoph Kaiser, "Protestantismus, Diakonie und 'Judenfrage' 1931–1941," 680–82.
4. Cf. Werner G. Jeanrod, "From Resistance to Liberation Theology: German Theologians and the Non/Resistance to the National Socialist Regime"; Ernst-Wolfgang Böckenförde, "Der deutsche Katholizismus im Jahre 1933. Eine kritische Betrachtung"; John Jay Hughes, "The Reich Concordat 1933: Capitulation or Compromise?"; Greive, *Theologie und Ideologie*, 201–10, on the "malicious invention," and Lutz-Eugen Reutter, *Katholische Kirche als Fluchthelfer im Dritten Reich. Die Betreuung von Auswanderern durch den St. Raphaels-Verein*, 40–58.

5. Shelley Baranowski, "From Rivalry to Repression: The German Protestant Leadership, Anti-Leftism and Anti-Semitism." Readers without access to German should also read Victoria Barnett's *For the Sake of the People: Protestant Protest against Hitler.* Another useful introduction is Hans-Joachim Kraus's "Die evangelische Kirche," esp. 264–68.

6. The most solid account of Confessional Church failure on this issue remains Wolfgang Gerlach, *Als die Zeugen schwiegen. Bekennende Kirche und die Juden,* 37–110. See also Richard Gutteridge, *Open Thy Mouth for the Dumb: The German Evangelical Church and the Jews, 1879–1950,* 129–32. On Pechmann, see the quote on 167–68 of Friedrich Wilhelm Kantzenbach, ed., *Widerstand und Solidarität der Christen in Deutschland 1933–1945. Eine Dokumentation zum Kirchenkampf aus den Papieren des D. Wilhelm Freiherrn von Pechmann.* A courageous contemporary protest was Gerhard Jasper, *Die evangelische Kirche und die Judenchristen;* for the statement emphasized here, see 18–20. On the 1934 and 1935 synods, see Günther van Norden, "Die Barmer theologische Erklärung und die Judenfrage," in *Das Unrechtsregime. Internationale Forschung über den Nationalsozialismus,* ed. Ursula Büttner, 1:315–30; while Marga Meusel's report can be found in Wilhelm Niemöller, ed., *Die Synode zu Steglitz. Geschichte-Dokumente-Berichte,* 29–58. The last quote is from Hermann Maas to Friedrich Siegmund-Schultz, October 19, 1935, EZA, 51, H II, c 6.

7. Karl Zehrer, *Evangelische Freikirchen und das "Dritte Reich,"* 35–36 and passim; Roland Blaich, "Religion under National Socialism: The Case of the German Adventist Church"; Christine E. King, "Strategies for Survival: An Examination of the History of Five Christian Sects in Germany, 1933–1945."

8. Friedrich Zipfel, *Kirchenkampf in Deutschland 1933–1945,* 176–203; Michael H. Kater, "Die ernsten Bibelforscher im Dritten Reich."

9. Quote from Eberhard Röhm and Jörg Thierfelder, *Juden-Christen-Deutsche,* 1:255.

10. To Harvey E. Perry, Bryn Mawr Library, Hertha Kraus Papers, Box 4, Folder 7. Italics added.

11. Seadle, "Quakerism in Germany," 2, 134–35.

12. "Membership lists of the German Yearly Meeting, October 1, 1933 and September 1, 1934," AFSC, FS, GYM, 1935.

13. Text in FH, FSC, GE 12, GYM, 1935 [*sic*].

14. Bracey to Albrecht, April 3, 1933, FH, FSC, G 7, Special Germany Papers, 1933; MacMaster, "Diary," 137; MacMaster to Pickett, April 17, 1933, Jack Sutters, ed., *American Friends Service Committee,* 2 vols. I, Doc. 8, 17–21, and Mahlon Harvey's undated report to the AFSC, received April 25, 1933, ibid., Doc. 9, 22–24. This source will hereafter be cited *AFSC,* with document and volume number.

15. Albrecht, *Die Begegnung mit der geistigen Situation in Deutschland,* 4, 10–16. On the Yearly Meeting, see *Der Quäker* (October 1933): 225–46. For Albrecht's explanation of the GYM position to the government, see copy of Albrecht to *Regierungspräsident* Hannover, July 13, 1933, in FH, FSC, G 12, GYM, 1927–34.

16. Decision of the Executive Committee, Nov. 25–26, 1933; Albrecht circular to German Friends, December 14, 1933, FH, FSC, GE 12, GYM, 1935.

17. See, for example, Grace E. Rhoads to Rebecca Pugh Lyon, July 3, 1934, citing reports of a visit to Germany by Clarence Pickett in *AFSC,* I, Doc. 28, 82–83.

18. The list of new members for the period 1933–1945 excludes Friends who died or left the Society before 1960. I owe this information to the generous help of Gerhard Wieding. For the accurate estimate that one-fourth of German Friends in 1933 were teachers, see Anna S. Halle, "Bemerkungen zu den Erbgutheften," copy of ms. dated September 15, 1989. Another list of thirty-three dismissed teachers, without date of dismissal, may be found in Tacke, ed., *Lebensbilder deutscher Quäker*, 5–6. For additional information on Quaker teachers, see also Lutz van Dick, *Oppositionelles Lehrerverhalten 1933–1945. Biographische Berichte über den aufrechten Gang von Lehrerinnen und Lehrer*, Veröffentlichungen der Max-Träger-Stiftung, 6 (Weinheim: Juventa, 1990), 130, 218–25.

19. Alois Kraus, "Lebenserinnerungen," Bryn Mawr College, Hertha Kraus Papers, Box 4, Folder 1, 100. Biographical data and obituary of Gertrude Schulz, ibid., loc. cit., Folder 8.

20. Fuchs, *Mein Leben*, 2:228–39; Herwig, *Gilbert MacMaster*, 18.

21. Birke, "Rudolf Schlosser," 4–5.

22. Hubben, *Exiled Pilgrim*, 235–60; see also MacMaster to Pickett, April 17, 1933 in *AFSC*, I, Doc. 8, 17–20.

23. Tacke, *Lebensbilder deutscher Quäker*, 83; Catchpool to Bracey, March 27 and 29, 1933, FH, FSC, G 7, Special Germany Papers, 1933.

24. Elisabeth Rotten to Fr. Siegmund-Schultze, May 21, 1933, EZA, H II, 1.

25. Bernard Kossmann and Monika Richter, eds., *Alfons Paquet (1881–1944), Begleitheft zur Ausstellung der Stadt- und Universitätsbibliothek Frankfurt am Main, 10. September–7. Oktober 1981* (Frankfurt: Stadtbibliothek, 1981), 21–38.

26. Rolf Helbeck to writer, August 27, 1994; Anneliese Becker to same, November 9, 1994. I am grateful for the gracious and detailed response both Helbeck descendants gave to my inquiry.

27. FH, FSC, G 7, Special Germany Papers, 1933.

28. Howard E. Yarnall, "The Spring Meeting of the *Arbeitsausschuss* in Pyrmont, Easter 1934," confidential, AFSC, FS, GYM, 1934.

29. For recent analyses of this malignant confection, see Hans Speier, *The Truth in Hell and other Essays on Politics and Culture* (New York and Oxford: Oxford University Press, 1989), 279–93, and Sergio Romano, *I falsi protocolli. Il 'complotto' ebraico dalla Russia di Nicola II a oggi*, 18–47.

30. Catchpool notes on *Arbeitsausschuss* session March 31–April 1, 1934, FH, FSC, GE 12, GYM, 1935.

31. Decision of the Executive Committee, November 24–25, 1934, AFSC, FS, GYM, 1935.

32. See report of 1934 German Yearly Meeting, AFSC, FS, Germany, GYM, 1934.

33. MacMaster, "Diary," 135.

34. Text in FH, FSC, GE 12, GYM, 1935.

35. Copy of letter from General von Vietinghoff to Religious Society of Friends, April 11, 1935, AFSC, FS, GYM, 1935.

36. "Betrifft Gesellschaft der Freunde (Quäker)," dated April 25 and June 26, 1935, Bundesarchiv Potsdam (BAP), Zentrales Archiv der SED, Reichssicherheitshauptamt (ZASED, RSHA), Abt. IV, St. 3/408.

37. *Biblische Lebensbilder* (Bad Pyrmont, Quäker Verlag, 1933). The German title of the French pamphlet was *Zur Unterdrückung des Verbrechens Krieg* (n.p.: 1932), tr. Ludwig Hecker.

38. Tacke, *Lebensbilder deutscher Quäker*, 63–66; Halle, "Erbguthefte," loc. cit. I am indebted to Anna Halle for a set of these pamphlets, from which all quotations are taken.

39. My copy of this songbook is also a gift of Anna Halle.

40. J. M. Fry, *In Downcast Germany*, 140–41; Catchpool to Bracey, June 15, 1934, FH, FSC, GE 5, 1933–34; Anna S. Halle, *"Die Gedanken sind frei . . ." Eine Jugendgruppe der Berliner Quäker 1935–1941*, 5–13; Anna S. Halle, "Ein altes Buch-heute noch lebendig (Aus Protokollen der Berliner Quäkergruppe 1920–1939)," 204, which also indicates that the Berlin protocols were in 1933 purged of passages that might aid the Secret Police. Also see Käte Tacke and Friedrich Huth, "Das Berliner Quäkerbüro," *Der Quäker* (1989): 178, and Olga Halle to H. J. Weider, reprinted ibid., (1973): 133.

41. Reports "Gesellschaft der Freunde und Jungfreundkreis," May 25 and June 3, 1935, BAP, ZASED, RSHA, IV, St. 3/408.

42. Louisa M. Jacob, "Notes from Nuremberg," January to March 6, 1933, and to Bracey, May 15, 1933, FH, FSC, GE 14, From Nuremberg, 1923–36; Bailey, *Quaker Couple*, 44–54. On the Friedrichs' move, see Leonhard Friedrich's unpublished obituary of Hans Albrecht, 1956, copy of which was provided by Brenda Bailey.

43. Ockel to Siegmund-Schultze, April 19, 1933, EZA, H II, 1, also report of *Arbeitsausschuss* meeting, Nov. 24–25, 1934, AFSC, FS, Germany, GYM, 1935, and Tacke, *Lebensbilder deutscher Quäker*, 67–73.

44. Elisabeth Rotten circular to German members of the Fellowship of Reconciliation, April 7, 1933, EZA, H II, 1.

45. Margarethe Lachmund's recollections of this episode are reprinted in Heinrich Carstens, ed., *Margarethe Lachmund zum 80. Geburstag*, 8, and accurately summarized in Seadle, "Quakerism in Germany," 86–90. On Hans Lachmund, see Horst S. Sassin, *Liberale im Widerstand. Die Robinsohn-Strassmann-Gruppe 1934–1942*, 30, 41, 98–99, 116, 139–40.

46. Copy of this letter from the collection of Quaker papers, preserved by Anna Halle.

47. Quote from Anna S. Halle, "Quäkerhaltung und -handeln im nationalsozialistischen Deutschland" (unpublished ms. in possession of the author).

48. Roger Carter, "The Quaker International Center in Berlin, 1920–1942," 22.

49. "Betrifft die Quäkersekte," June 25, 1935, BAP, ZASED, RSHA, IV, St. 3/408.

50. Mary G. Gary's undated report "The present situation in Germany, and the Quaker attitude," AFSC, FS, Germany, Letters from, 1934.

51. A. J. Sherman, *Island Refuge: Britain and Refugees from the Third Reich, 1933–39*, especially 35–39 (incidentally, this book is mainly a study of government policy); Barbara McDonald Stewart, *United States Government Policy on Refugees from Nazism, 1933–1940*, 48–53.

52. Richard Breitmann and Alan M. Kraut, *American Refugee Policy and European Jewry, 1933–1945*, 9–24.

53. See Marion Berghahn, *German Jewish Refugees in England: The Ambiguities of Assimilation*, 183–86; Doron Niederland, "Areas of Departure from Nazi Germany and the Social Structure of the Emigrants"; John Fox, "British Attitudes to Jewish Refugees from Central and Eastern Europe in the Nineteenth and Twentieth Centuries," 471–72, 483; Louise London, "British Reactions to the Jewish Flight from Europe," 57–58, 68. Also noteworthy in this context, Arnd

Bauerkämper, *Die 'radikale Rechte' in Grossbritannien*, Kritische Studien zur Geschichtswissenschaft, 93 (Göttingen: Vandenhoeck & Ruprecht, 1991), 204–18. On the United States see especially David S. Wyman, *Paper Walls: America and the Refugee Crisis*, 4–25, 226 n. 4, and Myron I. Scholnick, *The New Deal and Anti-Semitism in America*, 20–112.

54. Haim Genizi, *American Apathy: The Plight of German Refugees from Nazism*.
55. Ronald Stent, "Jewish Refugee Organizations," 578–80; Norman Bentwich, *They Found Refuge: An Account of British Jewry's Work for Victims of Nazi Oppression*, 7–24; Peter Ludlow, "The Refugee Problem in the 1930s: The Failures and Successes of Protestant Relief Programmes," 565–73; Jean-Baptiste Joly, "L'Assistance des Quaker," in Badia's *Les bannis de Hitler*, 107–11. On Dutch Quaker hospitality, see "Ons tehuis voor de duitsche Vluchtelingen," *De Vriendenkring* (November 1933).
56. Gerhard Hirschfeld, "A 'High Tradition of Eagerness,' British Non-Jewish Organizations in Support of Refugees"; London, "British Reactions," 61–63; Jasper, *George Bell, Bishop of Chichester*, 102–37.
57. Italics added.
58. Lawrence Darton, "An Account of the Work of the Friends Committee for Refugees and Aliens, first known as the German Emergency Committee of the Society of Friends," 3–6, 7–20, 34–39, hereafter cited as Darton, "An Account." Brenda Bailey, "Centenary of Bertha Bracey, 1893–1989: Bertha's Work for German Jewish Refugees," 5–13. I thank the author for providing me with a copy of her paper. "Report of Emergency Gathering of Friends on the Situation in Germany," March 27, 1933, FH, FSC, G7, Special Germany Papers, 1933; German Emergency Committee (GEC) minutes of March 27, April 12, April 25, June 8, July 3, August 21, and October 17, 1933. On appeals to the German embassy on behalf of political prisoners, also see Minutes of July 24 and August 8. All in FH, GEC, 1933–35.
59. Minutes of November 13 and 24, 1933, ibid., loc. cit.
60. Darton, "An Account," 31–39; Minutes, October 1, 1934, and undated "Memorandum to be laid before the Secretary of State for Foreign Affairs by a joint deputation from Society of Friends, German Emergency Committee, Refugee Professionals Committee, Save the Children Fund, Trades Union Council," ibid., loc cit.
61. Darton, "An Account," 38.
62. For the budget figures, see FH, FSC, GE 9, 1933–36, also Bracey to Catchpool, October 17, 1935, ibid., loc cit. On the uncertainties of American contributions for 1935, see Catchpool to Bernard Lawson and John Hargreaves, January 10 and 12, 1935, Lawson to Catchpool, January 16, and MacMaster to Lawson, June 29, 1935, all ibid., G 5, 1935.
63. Genizi, *American Apathy*, 41.
64. M. H. Jones, *Swords into Ploughshares*, 204–40.
65. Seadle, "Quakerism in Germany," 93.
66. Cary to Pickett, July 23, 1933, *AFSC*, I, Doc. 14, 32–34.
67. M. H. Jones, *Swords into Ploughshares*, 305–6.
68. Ibid., 647–48; Rhoads to Helen W. Dixon, July 18, 1934, AFSC, FS, Germany, GYM, 1934.
69. Quote from Rhoads to Cornelius Cruse, a Middletown, Conn., Friend and veteran of World War I relief, April 10, 1934; circular "to all Yearly Meetings in America,"

May 1934, AFSC, FS, General, 1934; Rhoads to Willis H. Hall, July 19, 1934, ibid., loc. cit.; Letters to England, 1934.

70. See, for instance, Rhoads to Alfred G. Garrett, February 25, 1934; Pickett to Edith M. Pye, August 23, 1935; an undated, unsigned memo "Service Abroad," reviewing 1934; "We" to William C. Biddle, October 30, 1935, all in AFSC, FS, German Refugees, General, 1935. Also AFSC to Jewish Joint Distribution Committee, October 1933, Pickett to Bracey, November 23, 1934, and Norman Bentwich to Charles [sic] E. Pickett, May 14, 1935, all in *AFSC*, I, Docs. 17, 36, 42, 49, 112–13, and 159 respectively. Finally Pickett to MacMaster, May 27, 1935, and Rhoads to same, June 4, 1935, AFSC, FS, Germany, Letters to, 1935.

71. For a summary of Cary's activities at the time of his death, see AFSC to Jewish Distribution Committee, *AFSC*, I, Doc. 17, 39–42.

72. MacMaster, "Diary," 134–58, for the years immediately following his return to Germany; also Seadle, "Quakerism in Germany," 108–11.

73. Rose Neuse, "Student Club Report," December 15, 1933, and letter to Bracey, same date, FH, FSC, GE 9, Corder Catchpool file, 1934. Praise of her "quiet and capable way" in Catchpool to Bracey, December 16, 1933, ibid., GE 5, 1933–1934.

74. Bracey to Catchpool, May 30, 1934, and Fred Tritton to same, September 27, 1935, ibid., GE 9, 1933–1936.

75. E. A. Otto Peetz and Margarethe Lachmund, "*. . . Allen Bruder sein . . .*" *Corder Catchpool (1883–1952), Ein englischer Freund in deutscher Not*, 55–56.

76. Corder Catchpool, "The Brown Reichskanzler: A Pen Picture from Berlin."

77. See the "Zeugenbericht von Rosa Dukas [one of Catchpool's informants] . . . aufgezeichnet . . . in Oktober/November 1940," in Yad Vashem Archives, 01/299. Rosa Dukas's sister Helene was Albert Einstein's private secretary.

78. The most detailed account, including the text of the letter of denunciation, in Peetz and Lachmund, "*Allen Bruder sein,*" 28–32. Much of this work is based on Hughes, *Indomitable Friend*. On the restraining order concerning arrests of foreigners, see Minister of the Interior Wilhelm Frick to State Governments, January 9, 1934 in *Bundesarchiv Koblenz and Freiburg*, Doc. 38, 264–65.

79. Quote from Hughes, *Indomitable Friend*, 91–92. On Catchpool's sympathies for German grievances, see also Siegmund-Schultze's plea on his behalf to the Vice President of the Evangelical Church Council of Prussia, D. Burghart, April 6, 1933, EZA, H II, b 1–2.

80. Greaves, *Corder Catchpool*, 24, from which this quote is taken.

81. Lawson reporting to Carl Heath on the Berlin situation, April 14, 1934, FH, FSC, GE 9, Corder Catchpool, 1934; Corder Catchpool, "Reflections on our Attitude towards the National Socialist Revolution" dated London, Whit-Monday, 1933, copy provided by Roger Carter.

82. Seadle, "Quakerism in Germany," 114–15, who cites an interview with Bertha Bracey, more than forty years after these events. Seadle did not have access to Friends House archives for this period, where I have found no such criticism of Catchpool over Bracey's signature.

83. Carl Heath to Catchpool, August 17, and September 12, 1933, FH, FSC, GE 9, to and from Corder Catchpool, 1933–1938. On the discussion of Catchpool's report, see GEC Minutes, September 11, 1933.

84. Robert Dell, *Germany Unmasked*, 17–18.

85. On Catchpool's modus operandi: Peetz and Lachmund, *"Allen Bruder sein,"* 36–39, and Pickett to Heath, November 16, 1934, AFSC, FS, England, Letters to, 1934.

86. Rufus Jones to Pickett, November 19, 1934, ibid., Austria, 1934.

87. Heath to Pickett, December 1, 1934, ibid., England, Letters from, 1934; Jones to Pickett from Rome, December 23, 1934, in ibid., Travel to Europe, 1934.

88. Bracey to Catchpool, February 17, 1933, FH, AFSC, GE 9, 1933–1936; copy of Albrecht circular to members of various GYM committees, January 16, 1935, and MacMaster to Pickett, October 12, 1935, AFSC, FS, Germany, GYM, 1935.

89. Pickett to Jones, February 19, 1935, and Jones to Pickett, "March 1935," ibid., loc. cit.

90. For example, see Minutes of the International Secretariat Berlin, March 23, 1934, FH, FSC, GE 9, Corder Catchpool, 1934; Catchpool to Myrtle Wright, June 15, 1935, ibid., G 5, 1935.

91. Catchpool to Bracey, February 24, 1934, FH, FSC, GE 9, Corder Catchpool, 1934; MacMaster, "Diary," 159.

92. From a ten-page manuscript in FH, FSC, GE 9, Corder Catchpool, 1934.

93. Graham Wootton, *An Official History of the British Legion,* 178–86; Richard Griffiths, *Fellow Travellers for the Right: British Enthusiasm for Nazi Germany, 1933–39,* 129–32.

94. Peetz and Lachmund, *"Allen Bruder sein,"* 52–53.

95. For a general survey of all three activities, see Seadle, "Quakerism in Germany," 138–73.

96. Catchpool to FSC, March 1933, in *AFSC,* I, Doc. 4, 9–10.

97. Catchpool to FSC, March 13, 1933, FH, FSC, GE 7, Special Germany Papers, 1933. Eyewitness Reports; MacMaster, "Diary," 135–58, and MacMaster to Rhoads, writing from Switzerland, September 11, 1934, AFSC, FS, Germany, 1934.

98. MacMaster, "Diary," 153–54. On Schönaich, who served again as president of the German Peace Society from 1946 to 1951, see also Dieter Riesenberger, *Geschichte der Friedensbewegung in Deutschland. Von den Anfängen bis 1933,* 220–22, 232–36, 248, and Stefan Appelius, *Pazifismus in Westdeuschland 1945–1968,* 2:743–44.

99. MacMaster, "Diary," 161–68. On Seger, see also Max Schwarz, *MdR, Biographisches Handbuch der Reichstage,* 759, and on his concentration camp stay: *Oranienburg. Erster authentischer Bericht eines aus dem KZ Geflüchteten* (Karlsbad: Graphia, 1934).

100. MacMaster, "Diary," 173–75; Schwarz, *MdR,* 762, indicates that Peter died in Augsburg on June 25, 1944. MacMaster was under the impression that he was again arrested during the war and died in Dachau. See also MacMaster to Pickett, February 12, 1934, *AFSC,* I, Doc. 20, 58–59. On the precise date of Peter's release, see W. R. Hughes report on his visit to Dachau, February 20, 1935, ibid., Doc. 46, 144.

101. MacMaster, "Diary," 175.

102. Hans G. Lehmann, "Ernst Reuter's Entlassung aus dem Konzentrationslager"; Elizabeth Fox Howard to Pickett, February 5, 1935, *AFSC,* I, Doc. 45, 142–43. On Heilmann, see MacMaster, "Diary," 176, Schwarz, *MdR,* 665, and David A. Hackett, *The Buchenwald Report,* 170–71. On Seger, Neubauer, Heilmann, and

Schumacher, see also Martin Schumacher, *M. d. R. Die Reichstagsabgeordneten der Weimarer Republik in der Zeit des Nationalsozialismus. Politische Verfolgung, Emigration und Ausbürgerung, 1933–1945,* 177, 322–23, 338, 451–53.

103. Berlin Center Committee Minutes, March 1, 1934, FH, FSC, GE 9, Corder Catchpool, 1934.
104. Cary to Bracey, September 7, 1933, FH, FSC, GE 5, 1933–34; Catchpool to Lawson, March 25; Gerhard and Olga Halle to Bracey, February 8, 1934; and Catchpool to Bracey, same date, ibid., G9, Corder Catchpool, 1934. Also, Bracey to Pickett, December 17, 1934, *AFSC,* I, Doc. 39, 118–20.
105. Catchpool to Hargreaves, June 28, 1935, FH, FSC, G 5, 1935, and Tritton to Albrecht, January 28, 1935, ibid., GE 12, to the GYM, 1925–1939.
106. It should be noted that a Gestapo report on the Society of Friends, dated April 25, 1935, accused Catchpool of leading a Quaker effort encouraging young Friends to refuse to do military service, BAP, ZASED, RSHA, IV, St. 3/408. MacMaster to Pickett, January 1935, *AFSC,* I, Doc. 42, 129–36; Catchpool memorandum (in German) to Hauptmann der Schutzpolizei Frohdin about his interrogation, August 21, 1935, FH, FSC, G 5, 1935.
107. For example, Hughes's notes on internment camps, July 24, 1935, *AFSC,* I, Doc. 30, 86–87, and his reports to GEC, December 31, 1934, and February 25, 1935, FH, GEC Minutes, 1933–35.
108. Paul Sturge to Göring, September 1934; Hughes to Grundtmann, October 22, 1934; Himmler to Göring, December 6, 1934, all in Prussian State Archive Dahlem, P1253/34. I am grateful to Anna Halle for locating these documents for me.
109. Hughes to Grundtmann, November 2, 1934, ibid., loc. cit. The emphasis was added in pencil, presumably by the recipient. On Grundtmann's position with Göring, and in the Prussian hierarchy, see David Irving, *Göring: A Biography* (London: MacMillan, 1989), 117, 136–37, and Alfred Kube, *Pour le mérite und Hakenkreuz-Hermann Göring im Dritten Reich* (Munich: R. Oldenbourg, 1986), 60–61.
110. Catchpool to Tritton, January 17, 1935, FH, FSC, GE 5, 1935; "Report from W. R. Hughes on a visit to Lichtenburg Concentration Camp. Confidential. Not for publication," in *AFSC,* I, Doc. 25, 73–76; Hughes's report on his visit to Dachau, February 20, 1935, ibid., Docs. 46 and 47, 144–53. German documents on these visits, beginning with Sturge's letter to Göring, February 25, 1935, and concluding with Catchpool to Hans Thomsen, April 16, 1935, in BAK, RK, R 43 II/1433a.
111. MacMaster to Pickett, April 29, 1935, *AFSC* I, Doc. 48, 156–58.
112. MacMaster to Pickett, January 1935, written in Berlin but taken abroad by an anonymous courier, *AFSC,* I, Doc. 42, 129–36. Hans Thomsen was subsequently German chargé d'affaires in Washington from 1939 to 1941, and after 1941 Hitler kept him in reserve for future important missions; see *Hitler's Secret Conversations, 1941–1944* with an introduction by H. R. Trevor-Roper (New York: Farrar, Strauss and Young, 1953), 396–97.
113. MacMaster to Pickett, Saarbrücken, January 24, 1935, *AFSC,* I, Doc. 41, 125–28; MacMaster, "Diary," 190; Gestapo Report on "Gesellschaft der Freunde," February 1935, BAP, ZASED, RSHA, IV, St. 3/408; MacMaster to Tritton, February 25, 1935, FH, FSC, G 5, 1935.
114. "Betrifft Organisatorischen Aufbau der Friedensbewegung (Einheitsfront) innerhalb der religiösen Gesellschaft der Freunde (Quäker)," BAP, loc. cit.

115. "Betrifft: Illegale Tätigkeit der religiösen Gesellschaft der Freunde," June 26, 1935, BAP, loc. cit.
116. "Betr. Illegale Tätigkeit der Internationalen Gesellschaft der Freunde (Quäker)," June 29, 1935. Munich. Bayerisches Hauptstaatsarchiv, Akten des Bayerischen Staatsministeriums des Innern, 79632.
117. "Betrifft: Quäkersekte," June 25, 1935, BAP, loc. cit.
118. Otto, *Werden und Wesen*, 304; *Friends Service in Germany*, 5–6; Howard, *Downstream*, 57–62. For the quote from the recollections of one of the guests see [Hilde Koch], *Refugee*, 199–200. I want to thank Prof. Heinz F. Koch, Ithaca College, for drawing my attention to this source. See also Darton, "An Account," 7–9; Albrecht to Bracey, October 30, 1934, showing the awareness of German Friends, FH, FSC, GE 12, GYM, 1935, and Gestapo report of June 18, 1935, in BAP, loc. cit.
119. Howard, *Across Barriers*, 92–103, and Gestapo to *Reichskanzlei* "Betr. die englische Staatsangehörige und Quäker Mitglied Elizabeth Fox Howard," August 16, 1935, BAP, loc. cit.
120. Copy of Paul Sturge to members of the Germany Emergency Committee, August 30, 1935, in AFSC, FS, General 1935, Letters from England.

3. Quakers and Nazis beyond Germany's Borders

1. Brinton, *Friends for 300 Years*, 149. For other contributions to the historiography of Quaker education, see the same author's *Quaker Education in Theory and Practice*, especially 45–69, 77–86; Walter Joseph Homan, *Children and Quakerism*, 83–136; W. A. Campbell Stewart, *Quakers and Education: As Seen in Their Schools in England*, 24–159, 232–75; Rufus Jones, *The Later Period of Quakerism*, 1:669–79; and Leonard S. Kenworthy, *Quaker Education: A Source Book*, especially 8–64.
2. Wilhelm Hubben, *Die Quäker*, 143–65, and on the Minden school and its curriculum, Friedrich Schmidt and Christian Schelp's unpublished chronicle "Geschichte der Gesellschaft der Freunde in und bey Minden . . . ," passim. I am indebted to Dr. F. Rasche of Minden for a typed transcription of that source.
3. Cf. Hermann Lietz, *Lebenserinnerungen*, 138, 192–94.
4. Ibid., 186–87, 266. On the reason for Lietz's break with Wyneken and Geheeb's "romantically sentimental all-inclusive humanitarianism," see Alfred Andreesen's *Hermann Lietz. Der Schöpfer der Landerziehungsheime*, 66–68, 131–35, an attempt to depict the subject as a precursor of National Socialist education. For a view that minimizes Lietz's ethnic exclusivism, see Hildegard Feidel-Mertz and Jürgen P. Krause, *Der andere Hermann Lietz. Theo Zollmann und das Landwaisenheim Veckenstedt*, which emphasizes Lietz's efforts to make his schools accessible to poor children. Another nationalist slant on the *Landschulheime* emerges from Kurt Hahn, "Die nationale Aufgabe der Landerziehungsheime."
5. Werner Köppen, *Die Schule Schloss Salem*, 32–37; Dennis Shirley, *The Politics of Progressive Education: The Odenwaldschule in Nazi Germany;* Walter Schäfer, *Paul Geheeb. Mensch und Erzieher*. The quote is from Klaus Mann, *Der Wendepunkt. Ein Lebensbericht* (Frankfurt: S. Fischer, 1966), 101.
6. "Gedanken über Quäkererziehung," *Mitteilungen für die Freunde des Quäkertums in Deutschland* (May 1924): 33–35; Berta [sic] Bracey, "Die Erziehung der Kinder der Quäker," ibid. (September 1925): 137–38; W[ilhelm] H[ubben], "Vom heutigen Geschichtsunterricht in Europa," ibid. (February 1926): 28–29; Otto

Buchinger, "Eindrücke aus Woodbrooke," *Monatshefte der deutschen Freunde* (April 1928): 113–15; "Erziehung unserer Jugend," ibid. (September–October 1929): 208–9.

7. Elisabeth Rotten, "Durch welche Schulen könnten pädagogisch und sozial die Aufgaben einer quäkerischen Erziehung verwirklicht werden?" ibid. (June–July 1930): 131–39, 169–76, also published separately. Finally, Johann Schwager, "Religionsunterricht in der Quäkererziehung," ibid. (September 1930): 201–5.

8. "Notes on Anna J. Branson's visits to various Friends Centers and the German Yearly Meeting," AFSC, FS, Germany, GYM, 1931.

9. "Report of School Committee," October 31–November 1, 1931, ibid., loc. cit. See also Wilhelm Hubben, "In einem amerikanischen Landschulheim," describing his stay as an exchange teacher in an American Quaker school and emphasizing the strength of a community most of whose students did not come from Quaker homes.

10. Cary to Pickett, November 4, 1931, ibid., Germany, 1930 [*sic*]. See also Pickett to Albrecht, October 24, 1931, ibid., Germany, GYM, 1931.

11. Quoting Hubben to *Arbeitsausschuss*, October 1931, ibid., loc. cit., 1932.

12. Schlosser to Bracey, December 6, 1933, in Sammlung Politisch Pädagogische Emigration, Prof. Hildegard Feidel-Mertz (HFM), which includes an apparently complete collection of the founders' correspondence of the Quaker school Eerde, cited as "Vorgeschichte." See also Feidel-Mertz's "Zur Vorgeschichte der Gründung der Internationalen Quäkerschule in Schloss Eerde b. Ommen/Holland." Mss. in possession of author. I am deeply indebted to Professor Feidel-Mertz for unlimited access to these sources. For other discussions of the school as a refuge for unemployed German teachers, see Jim Lieftinck to Hertha Kraus, May 15, 1933, HFM, Vorgeschichte, and Minutes, November 7, 1933, FH, GEC, 1933–1935.

13. Howard E. Yarnall, "The Spring Meeting of the *Arbeitsausschuss* in Pyrmont, Easter 1933," AFSC, FS, GYM, 1934.

14. Lieftinck to Bracey, May 15, 1933, HFM, Vorgeschichte.

15. On the Pallandt family and Eerde, see A. L., "Het huis Eerde," *Buiten* (January 1 and 8, 1916): 4–5, 16–17. On Krishnamurti, see Mary Lutyens, *Krishnamurti: The Years of Fulfillment* (London: J. Murray, 1983), 8–19, and the same author's *The Life and Death of Krishnamurti* (London: St. Martin's Press, 1990), 36–82.

16. Lutyens, *Life and Death*, 74, and my conversation with Erin Oudshoorn-van Pallandt on May 24, 1933. I am grateful for Mevr. Oudshoorn's help and hospitality.

17. See Piet Kappers, "Bericht über die Ausführbarkeit des Planes der Gründung einer Quäkerschule in Holland für deutsche Kinder," October 11, 1933, HFM, Vorgeschichte.

18. On the school's scope, see various drafts of a school prospectus by Wilhelm Mensching, Albrecht, Schlosser and Kappers. On the finances Bracey's undated memorandum to Albrecht, Schlosser and Kappers, and on the eventual German acceptance of Eerde as an international rather than German school, Albrecht's circular to "Liebe Freunde," March 26, 1934, all ibid., loc. cit.

19. Minutes, March 20, 1934, FH, GEC, 1933–35; Albrecht to Petersen, March 18, 1934, Schlosser to Kappers, March 20, 1934, HFM, Vorgeschichte; Peter Budde, "Katharina Petersen und die Quäkerschule Eerde. Eine Dokumentationscollage."

20. For the quote, see Schlosser to Bracey, January 19, 1934. On the importance of having at least one English staff member, Bracey to Catchpool, March 26,

1934, FH, FSC, GE 9, Corder Catchpool, 1934. For other comments on the Neuse appointment: Copy of MacMaster to Pickett, February 12, 1934, ibid., loc. cit.; Schlosser to Albrecht, March 1, 1934, Bracey to Schlosser, Telegram March 7, 1934, and finally, a more positive assessment, after meeting the candidate, by Kappers to "Freunde," March 25, 1934, HFM, Vorgeschichte.

21. Between 1935 and 1937, according to a chronological DYM membership list provided me by Miep Lieftinck. Katharina Petersen joined the DYM in 1937 and remained a member until her death in 1970.

22. For accounts of schools where children of religious Jews found at least temporary refuge, see Lucie Schachne, *Erziehung zum geistigen Widerstand. Das jüdische Landschulheim Herrlingen 1933 bis 1939*, Pädagogische Beispiele, Institutionesgeschichte in Einzeldarstellungen, 3 (Frankfurt: dipa Verlag, 1985); Hildegard Feidel-Mertz and Andreas Paetz, *Ein verlorenes Paradies. Das Jüdische Kinder- und Landschulheim Caputh (1931–1938)*, Pädagogische Beispiele, 8 (Frankfurt: dipa Verlag, 1994); Michael Daxner, " "Die private Jüdische Waldschule Keliski in Berlin," in *Jews in Nazi Germany, 1933–1943*, ed. Arnold Pauker, 249–57, and Ernst Papanek, *Out of the Fire.*

23. On the school's religious practices, see the prospectus drafts in HFM, Vorgeschichte, and Katharina Petersen, "The new Quakerschool in Holland"; Rudolf Schlosser, "Ob unsere Schule in Ommen eine Quäkerschule sei." Unpub. Memorandum, HFM, Vorgeschichte, and Kurt Neuse, "Quakerschool Eerde," in "Eerde 1934–1939" a mimeographed brochure celebrating the school's fifth anniversary. For a student's view of the Sunday meetings, Schmitt, *Lucky Victim*, 102–4. On the persistence of the quandary of Quaker schools with a minority of Quaker teachers and students, see the instructive *Faith and Practice in Friends Schools* (Philadelphia: AFSC, 1989), 1–4, 7, 9–10.

24. Johannes Lüdecke has set down his recollections in a manuscript that he has kindly shared with me. The main source on these beginnings remains "Tagebuch der Quäkerschule Eerde bei Ommen, eröffnet am 5.4.34," kept by Katharina Petersen, HFM, hereafter simply cited as "Eerde Diary."

25. These figures are derived from a detailed, chronological list of the student body reconstructed by Peter Budde, to date the author of the only substantial history of Eerde: "Die Internationale Quäkerschule in Eerde/Holland. Im Geiste praktischer Nächstenliebe und kraftvoller Toleranz." Herr Budde kindly furnished me a copy of this list. For other accounts of Eerde's beginnings, see Darton, "An Account," 29–32; the anonymous "Bericht over het eerste halfjaar," *De Vriendenkring*, December 1934, and the account of a visiting English teacher, S. F. Maltby, "A Significant Experiment."

26. On his road to Eerde, Werner Hermans to writer, June 14, 1993. Ron Chernow, *The Warburgs: The 20th Century Odyssey of a Remarkable Jewish Family*, 114, 120–21, 205–6, includes useful information on Max Adolph. The quote is from p. 509. On his father, see Ernst Gombrich, *Aby Warburg: An Intellectual Biography* (London: Warburg Institute, 1970). On the expectations attached to Max Adolph's employment, see Albrecht to "Liebe Freunde," March 29, 1934, HFM, Vorgeschichte, on the financially disappointing reality, Charlotte Esther Shalmon to writer, February 11, 1994. Max Adolph's popularity with students and the audience of his slide lectures is documented by the "Eerde Diary," October 30, November 14, and 30, 1934. For the quote from Josepha Einstein, see *Der Quäker*, November 1934.

27. "Eerde Diary," September 23, 1934. The enrollment figures from Budde's list of students. For the government decree that precipitated the crisis, Germany, *Reichsgesetzblatt*, September 11, 1934.

28. An official version of Germany currency policy is Helmut Wohlthat, "Devisenbewirtschaftung und zwischenstaatlicher Zahlungsverkehr," in *Grundlagen, Aufbau und Wirtschaftsordnung des nationalsozialistischen Staates*, vol. 3, 1938; Beitrag 54, notably 5–12. The chronicle of the clearing accord can best be traced through the minutes of the GEC, October 29, November 19, December 3, 1934, January 14 and April 1, 1935; Schlosser to Bracey, January 9, 1935, FH, FSC, GE 10, Frankfurt, 1932/39; the March and April correspondence between Catchpool and MacMaster in Berlin, and John E. Hargreaves and Bernard Lawson in London, ibid., GE 5, 1935, and GE 9, 1933–36, and finally in "Eerde Diary," November 1, 21, 25, 26, 1934, and March 19, 1935. For a text of the agreement, see the translation in AFSC, FS, Netherlands, Eerde School, Ommen, 1939. Its effect on school finances was explained to me by Rose Neuse during interviews on October 27 and 28, 1992. At the time sixty Dutch cents was the equivalent of one mark, forty U.S. cents, and one shilling, 7 pence. The U.S. minimum wage was thirty-five cents per hour.

29. On Boost's controversial tenure—he was the only faculty member, before World War II, whose contract was not renewed—see "Eerde Diary," April 4, 1936; Nettie Galjart-Witmer to writer, December 10, 1993, and Schmitt, *Lucky Victim*, 85–89. An appreciation of Kurt Neuse's educational leadership is Max A. Warburg's "Kurt Neuse," in the special issue of the *Eerde Herald* "20 jaar Quakerschool," (Easter 1954), 47–49. Dutch authorities were initially unimpressed by the level of Dutch instruction, see Van Andel to Minister of Education, July 4, 1936, in Netherlands. Ministerie van Onderwijs en Wetenschappen, Inspecteur van Het Gymnasial en Middelbaar Onderwijs. Parents of Dutch children felt differently, viz. M. de Boer-Brouwer, "Waarom ik mijn kinderen naar Eerde stuurde," and R. E. D. Tilanus-deKanter, "5 jaar," *Eerde Herald*, loc. cit., 5–7.

30. "Eerde Diary," March 5 and 6, 1935, and June 6, 1936.

31. "Eerde Diary," January 28, February 5, 23, 1935; Hilsley's own account of his first interview with Katharina Petersen in his memoirs, *When Joy and Pain Entwine: Reminiscences*, 11–21. More on his teaching in Schmitt, *Lucky Victim*, 89–92. On the performance of *Orfeo*, the testimony of Kurt Weingarten, who sang the part of Eros, in his unpublished diary, HFM, and Marianne Josephs to writer, undated [1937] in Schmitt Papers, 1935–1940, in private hands.

32. On the beginning of that supervisory role, "Eerde Diary," March 15, 1935. More on student government in Schmitt, *Lucky Victim*, 100–102, and Otto Edgar Rosenstern, "Mitarbeiter und Schüler," in "Eerde 1934–1939."

33. Particularly instructive in that context is the surviving correspondence between Elisabeth Schmitt, one of the housemothers, and her husband: on homesick children, August 9 and October 19, 1935; on the controversial Jan Boost, July 2, 1935; on Petersen's unpopularity, August 6 and November 2, 1935; Schmitt Papers, the latter an interesting corrective to Budde, "Katharina Petersen."

34. Franz Werfel, *Barbara oder die Frömmigkeit* (Berlin: P. Zsolnay, 1929), especially 409–21, and the same author's prologue to an English collection of his novellas dealing with the Vienna of the 1920s, *Twilight of a World*, trans. H. T. Lowe-Porter (New York: Viking Press, 1937), 4.

35. See Emma Cadbury's obituary in *The Friend*, March 26, 1965.

36. Keith Spalding, *33 - alles umsteigen* (Lübeck: Outline, 1993), 111; Karl Thieme, "Deutsche Katholiken," 279–81.

37. For the quote on Innitzer, Rufus Jones to Pickett, November 19, 1934, and on Protestant fears, Headley Horsnaill to Pickett, August 26, 1934, AFSC, FS, Austria, 1934.

38. Emma Cadbury to Henry Cadbury, February 26, 1934, ibid., loc. cit.

39. Greenwood, *Friends and Relief*, 232–33; see also successive accountings of the number of families helped in various locations, dated April 12, May 8, and October 1, 1934, AFSC, FS, Vienna, Financial Statements, 1934, and Tritton to MacMaster, September 1934, ibid., England, Letters from, 1934, concerning the politically neutral administration of funds. As late as August, the AFSC addressed the Washington office of the American Federation of Labor because its promised contribution had not been received: Pickett to Margaret Scattergood, August 6, 1934, ibid., Austria, 1934.

40. On the events of July 25 and their aftermath, see Ulrich Eichstätt, *Von Dollfuss zu Hitler. Geschichte des Anschlusses Österreichs 1933–38*, Veröffentlichungen des Instituts für europäische Geschichte, Mainz, 10 (Wiesbaden: Steiner, 1955), 50–55, and the undated "Notes of Fred J. Tritton," copy AFSC, FS, Austria, 1934.

41. On Unruh's career, see James Irwin Lichti, "The German Mennonite Response to the Dissolution of the Rhoen-Bruderhof," 12–15, to whom I am also indebted for his several patient responses to my questions about Mennonite history. On Mennonites in Nazi Germany, the standard work is Diether Götz Lichdi, *Mennoniten im Dritten Reich. Dokumentation und Deutung*. Unruh's connection with the Foreign Office was kindly explained to me by his son, who is currently preparing a biography of his father, cf., Heinrich Unruh to writer, January 25, 1993. On Unruh's mission to the United States, see *Oberkirchenrat* Wahl to *Legationsrat* Freudenberg, July 28, 1934, Germany, Auswärtiges Amt, Politisches Archiv, Kultus VI A, Evangelische Angelegenheiten, Vol. 6. In preparation of his mission Unruh apparently sent an open letter to Rufus Jones, setting forth an officially acceptable version of Nazi church policy, but I have not been able to locate that letter in the Rufus Jones Papers at Haverford College or at the AFSC archives in Philadelphia.

42. For MacMaster's version of the meetings see his "Statement to Friends from England, Germany and Austria at Prague Conference," August 27, 1934, and copy of B. H. Unruh to MacMaster, September 6, 1934, both in AFSC, FS, Austria, 1934.

43. "Undated Notes by Fred J. Tritton," and Horsnaill to Pickett, August 26, 1934, ibid., loc cit.

44. The quote from Tritton to MacMaster, September 7, 1934, FH, FSC, GE 9, 1933–36. The conditions under which help was to be extended were laid down in near-identical decisions by the GEC, Minutes, September 3, 1934, and AFSC's FSS, Minutes, September 27, 1934. Emma Cadbury's instructions are recapitulated in Tritton to Rhoads, September 7, 1934, ibid., England, Letters from, 1934.

45. Horsnaill to Pickett, August 26, 1934, ibid., Austria, 1934.

46. Rufus Jones to AFSC, September 3, 1934, ibid., loc. cit.; Pickett to Carl Heath, September 13, 1934, ibid., England, Letter to, 1934; Pickett Memorandum to FSS, September 17, 1934, ibid., Vienna, 1934.

47. Rufus Jones to Pickett, November 12, 1934, ibid., Travels to Europe, 1934; Rufus Jones to Herbert Hoover, November 14, 1934, ibid., Austria, 1934.

48. Telegram Pickett to Rufus Jones, December 13, 1934, ibid., Vienna, 1934; Jones to Pickett, December 23, 1934, ibid., Travels to Europe, 1934; Pickett to Oswald Garrison Villard, December 28, 1934, ibid., Austria, 1934; FSS Minutes, December 27, 1934, January 24, and February 26, 1935, and Catchpool to Tritton, February 19, 1935, FH, FSC, G 5, 1935.
49. Cf., Eichstätt, *Von Dollfuss zu Hitler*, 59–60.
50. On Catchpool's visit, see E. A. Otto Peetz and Margarethe Lachmund, *"Allen Bruder sein,"* 151–53; Pickett to Letitia Moon Conard, September 19, 1935, AFSC, FS, General, 1935.
51. Ernst-Albrecht Plieg, *Das Memelland 1920–1939*, 95–135; Hans Hopf, "Auswirkungen des Verhältnisses Litauens," 251–55. See also "Aufzeichnungen des Legationssekretärs von Halem," August 7, 1935, in *Akten zur deutschen auswärtigen Politik 1918–1945* (ADAP), Series C, VI, 1, 537–40.
52. Catchpool to Paul Sturge, July 15, to Tritton, September 27 and 28, 1935, all in FH, FSC, G 5, 1935. Catchpool had already helped secure the services of Alexander Lawrence, R. C., "to represent 126 arrested leaders of the German minority in Memel." Cf., D. C. Watt, "Influence from Without: German Influence on British Opinion, 1933–38, and the Attempt to Counter It," 129. On British interest in a German-Lithuanian rapprochement, see also Gerhard L. Weinberg, *The Foreign Policy of Hitler's Germany. Starting World War II* (Chicago and London: University of Chicago Press, 1980), 301–2.
53. Catchpool to Tritton, November 1, 1935, FH, FSC, G 5, 1935. Catchpool, "Visit to Memelland and Lithuania," with letter of transmittal to Clifford Allen, Lord Hurtwood, July 16, 1935, at University of South Carolina, Thomas Cooper Library, Hurtwood Papers. See also Catchpool to Hans Thomsen, November 7, 1935, enclosing Catchpool's letter to President Smetona, BAK, RK, R43 II/1433a.
54. Catchpool, "Report on the Prisons of Lithuania," November 1935, and Corder Catchpool to President Smetona, pleading for the release of five sick prisoners, November 5, 1935 and February 8, 1936, FH, FS, G 5. See also Catchpool to Bracey, January 8, 1936, counseling discretion on publicizing the trip. On the second journey "Visit to Memelland and Lithuania," 18th and 28th September 1936," in Hurtwood Papers, loc. cit.
55. Ibid., loc. cit.
56. Catchpool, "The Political Situation in Memelland," September 28, 1938, Hurtwood Papers. The diplomatic parallels are illuminated by a Memorandum of a conversation between Konstantin von Neurath and the British Ambassador, December 12, 1935, Neurath to Erich Wilhelm Zechlin (German Minister to Lithuania), February 7, 1935, and Ribbentrop's *Aufzeichnung*, March 17, 1938, ADAP, C, II, 885–86; C, IV, 2, 1090; and D, V, 362. The idea of compensating Poland for the surrender of Danzig and the Corridor at Lithuania's expense seems to have occurred to Heinrich Brüning as early as 1932. See Stephen S. Schuker, "Ambivalent Exile: Heinrich Brüning and America's Good War," in *Zerrissene Zwischenkriegszeit. Wirtschaftshistorische Beiträge Knut Borchardt zum. 65. Geburtstag*, ed. Christoph Buchheim, Michael Hutter, and Harold James, (Baden-Baden: Nomos, 1994), 353.
57. "The political situation in Memelland"; and "Visit to Memelland and Lithuania," Hurtwood Papers.

4. From Nuremberg to Danzig

1. Götz Aly and Karl Heinz Roth, *Die restlose Erfassung. Volkszählen, Identifizieren, Aussondern im Nationalsozialismus,* 7–8, 14–18.
2. Herwart Vorländer, *Die NSV: Darstellung und Dokumentation einer nationalsozialistischen Organisation,* supplemented, but not superseded, by Eckhard Hansen, *Wohlfahrtspolitik im NS Staat. Motivationen, Konflikte und Machtstrukturen im 'Sozialismus der Tat' des Dritten Reiches;* and Christoph Sachsse and Florian Tennstedt, *Der Wohlfahrtsstaat im Nationalsozialismus.*
3. Gestapo Circular, August 9, 1937, *Bundesarchiv of the Federal Republic of Germany, Koblenz and Freiburg,* Doc. 140, 285; Rudolf Pechel, *Deutscher Widerstand* (Erlenbach/Zürich: E. Rentsch, 1947), 11.
4. Rudolf Schubert, "Why I left Germany," May 1938, typescript in private hands. I am indebted to Christof N. Schubert of Charlottesville, Va., for access to his father's papers.
5. Siegele-Wenschkewitz, "Universitätstheologie," in Günter Brakelmann and Martin Rosowski, eds., *Antisemitismus. Von religiöser Judenfeindschaft zur Rassentheologie,* 166–67.
6. Karl Zehrer, *Evangelische Freikirchen und das "Dritte Reich,"* 54–59.
7. Forell to Ritchie, January 10, 1936, *AFSC,* I, Doc. 108, 317–18.
8. Cf., Ethel Mary Tinneman, "The German Catholic Bishops and the Jewish Question: Explanation and Judgment," 57. For the most detailed appreciation of Lichtenberg, see Otto Ogiermann, *Bis zum letzten Atemzug. Das Leben und Aufbegehren des Priesters Bernard Lichtenberg.*
9. Klaus Drobisch and Gerhard Fischer, eds., *Widerstand aus Glauben. Christen in der Auseinandersetzung mit dem Hitlerfaschismus,* 180–81.
10. Kurt Meier, *Kirche und Judentum. Die Haltung der evangelischen Kirche zur Judenpolitik des Dritten Reiches,* 188–89.
11. Aly and Roth, *Die restlose Erfassung,* 8.
12. See the report of Friedrich Siegmund-Schultze to the International Committee for the Christian Appeal for German Refugees in London, January 31, 1936, EZA, 51/H II, c 11.
13. AFSC, Clarence Pickett's Journal of a Trip to Europe, 1934.
14. Forell to Siegmund-Schultze, December 12, 1935, EZA, 51/H II, c 11.
15. David Kramer, "Jewish Welfare Work under the Impact of Pauperization," 176–87; Bruno Blau, "The Jewish Population of Germany, 1939–1945," 168; Robert D. Yarnall diary, December 7–24, 1938, of the visit of three American Friends to Berlin in FH, FSC, GE 5, 1937/38, based on figures provided by Cora Berliner. On Berliner, see Esriel Hildesheimer, "Cora Berliner. Ihr Leben und Wirken."
16. Elkinton to Anne Martin, December 1938 in *AFSC,* I, Doc. 148, 441–43.
17. Gestapo circular, December 8, 1938 in *Bundesarchiv,* Doc. 105, 292.
18. Reinhard Rürup, "Das Ende der Emanzipation: Die anti-jüdische Politik in Deutschland von der Machtergreifung bis zum zweiten Weltkrieg," 98–99, as trenchant a summary of Nazi Jewish policy as one is likely to find in the large literature on the subject.
19. Undated [1936?] copy of a Memorandum "Zur Lage der christlichen Nichtarier," in FH, FSC, GE 9, To and from Corder Catchpool, 1933–38; Noakes, "Development of Nazi Policy," 320–28, and Ursula Büttner, "The Persecution of Christian Jewish Families in the Third Reich," 267–89.

20. *Statistisches Jahrbuch für das Deutsche Reich,* 1939–1940: 74.
21. William Hagen, "Before the Final Solution: Toward a Comparative Analysis of Political Antisemitism in Interwar Germany and Poland," Working paper 37. European Society and Culture Research Group. Center for German and European Studies, University of California, Berkeley, 1993, 29.
22. Herbert A. Strauss, "Jewish Emigration from Germany: Nazi Policies and Jewish Responses," 354–55. On the concomitantly slow acceleration of the rates of departure of professionals, see Niederland, "The Emigration of Jewish Academics and Professionals from Germany in the First Years of Nazi Rule," 285–300.
23. Quoted by Mark Wischnitzer, "Jewish Emigration from Germany, 1933–1938," 42.
24. I am in this case drawing on Carlota Jackisch, *El Nazismo y los refugiados alemanes en la Argentina, 1933–1945,* 78–80, to draw attention to an exceedingly well-researched and contextually sound case study.
25. Yehoyakim Cochavi, "The 'Hostile Alliance': The Relationship between the Reichsvereinigung of Jews in Germany and the Regime," 241–54. See also Elkinton to Yarnall, February 3, 1939, AFSC, FS, Refugee Services, Germany, Berlin, 1939.
26. Martha and Robert Balderston to Hertha Kraus, March 1, 1939, *AFSC,* I, Doc. 200, 574. On the pressure exerted by Swiss Nazis and anti-Semites in the Swiss bureaucracy, see Ralph Weingarten, "Juden in der Schweiz," 89–93. The official history of Swiss migration policy is set forth, often with commendable candor, by Carl Ludwig, *Die Flüchtlingspolitik der Schweiz seit 1933 bis zur Gegenwart (1957),* especially 52–151. For an aggressively critical view of Swiss immigration policies see Monica Imboden and Brigitte Lustenberger in Carsten Goehrke and Werner G. Zimmermann, eds., *"Zuflucht Schweiz." Der Umgang mit Asylproblemen im 19. und 20. Jahrhundert.* Die Schweiz und der Osten, 3 (Zürich: Hans Rohr, 1994), 257–308. See also Alfred G. Frei, " 'In the End I Just Said O.K.': Political and Moral Dimensions of Escape at the Swiss Border," 61–81, and Nettie Sutro, *Jugend auf der Flucht 1933–1948. Fünfzehn Jahre im Spiegel des Schweizer Hilfswerks für Emigrantenkinder,* 69–73.
27. Barbara Vormeier, "La république française et les réfugiés et immigrés d'Europe centrale. Accueil, séjour, droit d'asile (1919–1939); Ralph Schor, "L'Opinion française et les réfugiés d'Europe centrale (1933–1939)"; Cathérine Nicault, "L'Accueil des Juifs d'Europe centrale par la communauté juive française (1933–1939)"; Pierre Bolle, "Les réfugiés d'Europe centrale et les protestants français (1933–39)"; and René Bédarida, "Les Catholiques français face aux réfugiés allemands et autrichien (1933–39)"; all in Karel Bartosek et al., eds., *De l'éxile à la résistance, Réfugiés et immigrés d'Europe Centrale en France 1933–1945,* 14–20, 27–41, 53–59, 61–65, 67–74. Vicki Caron, "The Politics of Frustration: French Jewry and the Refugee Crisis in the 1930s," 313–49, sheds a more favorable light on French Jewry's efforts on behalf of their European coreligionists than do earlier assessments. For a confirmation of the facts and figures contained in the French literature, see Walter F. Petersen, "Die deutschen politischen Emigranten in Frankreich 1933–1940. 'Die selben Debatten wie zu hause?' "
28. See report of the Paris Conference Liaison Committee, June 19, 1939, in *AFSC,* I, Doc. 210, 609–10.
29. This story has been told in several monographs, among them Bob Moore, *Refugees from Nazi Germany in the Netherlands, 1933–1940;* J. Baert, *De Vluchteling*

in Nederland, Met een overzicht van het aantal en de aard der vluchtelings-comités (Assen: Van Gorcum, 1938), especially 13–24; D. J. Lambooy, "Les Bays-Bas et le problème de réfugiés," 25–52, reflecting the official position; David Cohen, *Zwervend en dolend. De Joodse vluchtelingen in Nederland in de jaren 1933–1940;* Ivo Schoffer, "Die Niederlande und die Juden in den dreissiger Jahren in historischer Perspektive"; Dan Michmann, "Die jüdische Emigration und die niederländische Reaktion zwischen 1933 und 1940"; Dan Michmann and Ursula Langkai Alex, "Chronologische Übersicht wichtigster Fakten zur niederländischen Flüchtlingspolitik"; all in Kathinka Dittrich and Hans Würzner, eds., *Die Niederlande und das deutsche Exil 1933–1940,* 61–72, 73–85, 87–90. On the aid of Dutch Jews for refugees, see Dan Michmann, "The Committee for Jewish Refugees in Holland (1933–1940)"; and Gertrude van Tijn, "Werkdorp Nieuwesluis."

30. See the Perry Report of a trip to Poland, July 20–27, 1939, and the Perrys' letter to Clarence Pickett, June 23, 1939, both in *AFSC,* I, Doc. 202, 585–97, and Doc. 215, 618–22, as well as Steven Koblik, *The Stones Cry Out: Sweden's Response to the Persecution of the Jews.*

31. Ralph Weingarten, *Die Hilfeleistung der westlichen Welt bei der Endlösung der deutschen Judenfrage. Das 'Intergovernmental Committee on Political Refugees' (IGIC) 1938–1939,* Europäische Hochschulschriften, III, Geschichte, 157 (Berne, Frankfurt, Las Vegas: Lang, 1981). On prospects in Cuba and Mexico, see Pickett to Mary van Kleeck, March 29, 1939 and Hertha Kraus to Luise Lieftinck, March 21, 1939, in *AFSC,* I, Doc. 230, 648, and Doc. 233, 652–53; Leonardo Senkman, "Argentina's Immigration Policy during the Holocaust (1938–1945)," 155–66. On the British Dominions, see Suzanne Rutland, "Australian Government Policies to Refugee Migration, 1933–1939," 224–38; Michael Blakeney, *Australia and the Jewish Refugees, 1933–1948;* Gerald E. Dirks, *Canada's Refugee Policy: Indifference or Opportunism?;* Irving Abella and Harold Troper, *None Is Too Many: Canada and the Jews of Europe, 1933–1948.*

32. Quoted by Rita Thalmann, "L'Antisemitisme en Europe occidentale et les réactions face aux persécutions nazies pendant les anneés trente," 148.

33. London, "British Reactions," 65–66, as well as sources illustrating individual efforts such as Joshua B. Stein's *Our Great Solicitor Josiah B. Wedgwood* (Selinsgrove, Penn.: Susquehanna, 1992), especially 103–4; Herbert Pollock's report of Capt. Foley's generous support of despairing Jews at the embassy in Berlin, in Yad Vashem Archives, 01/7; and Judith Taylor, "The Kitchener Transmigration Camp at Richborough," *Yad Vashem Studies* 14 (1981): 233–46, describing a facility accommodating three thousand refugees for whom passport and visa regulations had been waived.

34. Sherman, *Island Refuge,* 75–78, 238–40. The quote is from Martin Gilbert, "British Government Policy towards Jewish Refugees (November 1938–September 1939)," 144.

35. Amy Zahl Gottlieb, Introduction to *Archives of the Central British Fund for World Jewish Relief, 1933–1960: A Listing and Guide to the Research Publication Microfilm Collection,* 11–25; Doris Bader Whitman, *The Uprooted: A Hitler Legacy: Voices of Those Who Escaped before the "Final Solution,"* especially 139–64; Karen Gershon, ed., *We Came as Children,* 21–22; and Barry Turner, . . . *And the Policeman Smiled,* 34–104.

36. Hitler paid tribute to American racial and sterilization policies in *Mein Kampf*, 17th ed. (Munich: Franz Eher, 1943), 99. See also Stefan Kühl, *The Nazi Connection: Eugenics, American Racism and German National Socialism*, especially 46–76; Philip E. Reilly, *The Surgical Solution: A History of Involuntary Sterilization in the United States*, notably 75–103. For the broader constitutional implications of these practices, see Henry J. Abraham, *Freedom and the Court: Civil Rights and Liberties in the United States*, 124–29.

37. Leonard Dinnerstein, *Antisemitism in America*, notably 106–15; Haim Genizi, *American Apathy: The Plight of German Refugees from Nazism*, 137–45, on the Catholic response; Myron I. Scholnick, *The New Deal and Anti-Semitism in America*, 63–148. The AFSC pamphlet was *Refugee Facts: A Study of the German Refugee in America* (Philadelphia: AFSC, 1938). On Protestant responses, see also Robert W. Ross, *So It Was True: The American Protestant Press and the Nazi Persecution of the Jews,* and the case study by Jack R. Fischel, "The North American Mennonites' Response to Hitler's Persecution of the Jews." John Peter Horst Grill and Robert L. Jenkins, "The Nazis and the American South in the 1930s: A Mirror Image," conclude that "instead of exploiting what appeared to be a natural connection with the South, *Nazi representatives attempted unsuccessfully to capture the mass support of ethnic Germans in the region"* (italics mine).

38. On diplomatic reluctance to issue immigration visas, see Shlomo Shafir, "American Diplomats in Berlin (1933–1939) and Their Attitude to the Nazi Persecution of the Jews."

39. Cf., Wischnitzer, "Jewish Emigration," 38–39; Strauss, "Jewish Emigration," 354–55.

40. One such cliché, "world-Jewry," was discredited by the U.S. Consulate in Buenos Aires, which found that refugees "consider themselves, Italians, Spanish, Belgians, etcetera, but *not* Jews" (italics in original). John Mendelsohn, ed., *The Holocaust: Selected Documents in Eighteen Volumes,* 5:216.

41. Walter Adams, "Extent and Nature of the World Refugee Problem," 35.

42. Naomi Shepherd, *A Refuge from Darkness: Wilfred Israel and the Rescue of the Jews,* 118–19; Jasper, *George Bell,* 117–18, 137–38; see also 1938 Report of High Commissioner for Refugees from Germany on the plight of non-Jewish refugees, EZA, 5, H II, c 6.

43. Cf., Tritton to Schlosser, January 15, 1935, FH, FSC, G 7, to Frankfurt, 1930–1938.

44. Bracey to R. G. Roesel, Anglo-German Information Service, May 3, 1935, FH, Germany and Holland Committee Minutes, 1935–1940.

45. See her letters to Corder Catchpool, January 7, and March 5, 1936, FH, FSC, GE 9, 1933–36, and to Pickett, June 29, 1937 in *AFSC,* I, Doc. 95, 298–99.

46. Bracey to Pickett, March 14, 1937, ibid., Doc. 91, 266–75; Tritton to Elkinton, February 10, 1939, FH, FSC, GE 8, To Berlin, 1937–38; Brenda Bailey, "Centenary of Bertha Bracey, 1893–1989: Bertha's Work for German Jewish Refugees," and Bracey to Sir Herbert Emerson, July 31, 1939, *AFSC,* I, Doc. 119, 507–9. The day of the signing of the German-Soviet nonaggression pact she sent a similar proposal to Rufus Jones, Haverford College, Quaker Collection, Rufus Jones Papers, Box 40/2516.

47. Roger Carter to writer, March 16, 1994; Hedwig Born, "Vertreibung und Flucht," in Gesellschaft der Freunde in Deutschland, *Begegnung mit dem Judentum. Ein*

Gedenkbuch (Bad Pyrmont: Quäker Verlag, 1962), 15–17. For the accomplishments of the Germany and Holland Committee in 1939, see Darton, "An Account," 61–64.

48. On Paula Kurgass, "Dictionary of Quaker Biography," FH, and the Quaker effort in France in general, Jean-Baptiste Joly, "L'Assistance des Quaker," 105–16.

49. Roon, *Protestants Nederland*, 30–32. See also "Memorandum on the desirability of establishing a Central Office for the Emigration of Non-Aryan Christians, submitted to the Comité voor Niet Arische Christen, Dec. 1938." I owe a copy of this document to J. Roger Carter, together with other material that he kindly sent me. Everything from this source will hereafter be identified by the acronym RCP. For AFSC contributions, see Pickett to Balderston, May 22, 1939, AFSC, FS, Netherlands, 1939.

50. Edith M. Pye to Pickett, October 1, 1935, *AFSC*, I, Doc. 53, 166–67.

51. Cf., Pickett to Caroline Norment, November 21, 1938, AFSC, FS, Germany, General, 1938.

52. Pickett to Yarnall, November 14, 1935, AFSC, FS, Refugees, 1935.

53. Frank Ritchie, "German Refugees and American Christians," undated, *AFSC*, I, Doc. 55, 170–74, and his report to his own committee, December 9, 1935, ibid., Doc. 60, 190–93; Pickett to Ritchie, October 7, 1935, ibid., Doc. 58, 181–82, and Ritchie to Pickett, December 14, 1935, Doc. 62, 196. On Ritchie's own expectations, see also his letter to Siegmund-Schultze, November 11, 1935, EZA, H II, 1.

54. Pickett to Martin, October 15, 1936, AFSC, Germany, Correspondence to Germany, 1936; Copy Frank Ritchie to Martin, January 25, 1938, FH, FSC, GE 5, 1937–38 and Anne Martin to Bracey, March 31, and Bracey to Martin, May 10, 1938, ibid., GE 8, Berlin, 1937–39.

55. M. H. Jones, *Swords into Ploughshares*, 352–53, 357–58.

56. See Hertha Kraus, curriculum vitae in Bryn Mawr College Library, Hertha Kraus Papers, Box 4, Folder 9. Announcement of her appointment, Mildred Fairchild to Marion Hathaway, May 21, 1936, and college news release, June 16, 1936, ibid., loc. cit., 5/5; Pickett to Martin, April 6, and May 20, 1937, AFSC, Germany, Letters to, 1937, and Kraus' undated [1937?] memo to Pickett, "Cases of German Refugees," ibid., Refugee Service Statistics, 1938.

57. See summary of operating expenditures, 1936, and Hargreaves to Martin, January 8, 1937, FH, FSC, GE 8, To Berlin, 1937–39; Pickett to both Martins, May 26, 1937, *AFSC*, I, Doc. 99, 290–92; M. H. Jones, *Swords into Ploughshares*, 359.

58. Pickett diary excerpt in *AFSC*, I, Doc. 188, 387, and the Refugee Committee's 1938 Report, ibid., Doc. 153, 456–60.

59. "1938 Thanksgiving Appeal to the Churches thruout [*sic*] the U.S." and the "Appeal to Every Monthly Meeting in the United States and Canada, to be read at Meeting on Sunday, November 20, 1938." AFSC, FS, Refugee Services, 1938.

60. Pickett to Caroline Norment, November 21, 1936, AFSC, FS, Germany, General, 1938. See also "Memorandum giving gist of conversation between Dr. Hans Thomsen, Counselor to the German Embassy and Chargé d'affaires and Clarence E. Pickett," November 25, 1938, ibid., Delegation to Germany, 1938.

61. This account rests on Robert Yarnall's "Factual Notes on German Trip, December 7–December 24, 1938," a copy of which I found in FH, FSC, GE 5, 1937/38. Rufus Jones's account of the meeting at the Gestapo appeared as "Our Day in the

German Gestapo," *The American Friend,* June 10, 1947. For other evidence, see Rufus Jones to Pickett, December 13, and to his wife Elizabeth, December 16, 1938, HC, QC, Rufus Jones Papers, Box 58/364 & 366d. On Raymond Geist, see Barbara McDonald Stewart, *United States Government Policy on Refugees from Nazism, 1933–1940,* 187–88. Hilgenfeldt's habit of lying about the NSV's treatment of non-Aryans is documented in Vorländer, *Die NSV,* 247, 425, and by Noakes, "Development of Nazi Policy," 328. A good summary of the visit of the three Friends to Berlin can also be found in Elizabeth Gray Vining, *Friend of Life: The Biography of Rufus H. Jones,* 282–93.

62. Yarnall, "Factual Notes," cited above.

63. Ibid., loc. cit.

64. *The Friend,* December 1938; *The Christian Century,* January 18, 1939.

65. Pickett to Joseph C. Hyman, January 4, 1939; to Paul Baerwald, January 20, 1939; Tel. Baerwald to Pickett, January 21, 1939; Frank Aydelotte to Herbert Maass, January 12, 1939; Bernard Flexner to Frank Aydelotte, all in *AFSC,* I, Doc. 155, 158–60. Also Robert Yarnall to Pickett, January 5, 1939, ibid., Doc. 180, 510–11, and Rufus Jones' report to South China Meeting, HC, QC, Rufus Jones Papers, Box 58/368.

66. See in *AFSC,* Louis J. Taber to Pickett, April 25, 1939, I, Doc. 165, 481; Robert A. Taft to the head of Jewish War Veterans of the United States, May 10, 1939, Doc. 166, 482–83; Pickett to Taft, May 31, 1939, Doc. 167, 484–85, and Pickett to Walter H. McKenna, October 17, 1939, Doc. 172, 495–96.

67. Luise Lieftinck was equally dissatisfied with Dutch performance on this score, regardless of what she claimed on its behalf in her correspondence with Pickett. This is confirmed by her stormy correspondence with the Dutch Protestant Aid Committee's chairman V. H. Rutgers, which ended in her resignation from the committee on December 16, 1939. See Amsterdam. Rijksinstituut voor Oorlogs-documentatie, 181/I1. Luise Lieftinck to Pickett, June 14, 1939, and Pickett's response, June 29, 1939, AFSC, FS, Netherlands, 1939.

68. *The Christian Century,* January 18, 1939.

69. See AFSC, FSS, Minutes, September 26, 1935, and ibid., Board of Directors, Minutes, October 2, 1935. For Martin's acceptance by Berlin Friends, see Sturge to Pickett, October 11, 1935, FH, FSC, GE 9, 1933–36. The suggestion that Henry Gillett played a role in his appointment may be found in Albert P. Martin, "An Autobiography," a twenty-nine-page typescript, composed in 1978. I owe this source and other information about the family and its Berlin sojourn to the kindness of Martin's two sons from his first marriage, Joseph Haines and Richard Slater Martin.

70. Albert P. Martin Personnel File, Brown University Archives, provided me by Martha L. Mitchell, Brown University Archivist.

71. Martin, "Autobiography," 9, 17, 23–23c.

72. Ibid., 31a; Martin Personnel File; *Brown Daily Herald,* December 9, 1935; Seadle, "Quakerism in Germany," 117–19, exaggerates the financial worries resulting from Martin's resignation from Brown, where his junior position offered no opportunities for advancement. Martin's in-laws supported the family during a brief period of unemployment, following their return to the United States in 1938. See also Richard S. Martin to writer, March 30, 1994, and by the same "The German Years," undated eight-page manuscript.

73. Catchpool to Bracey, March 3, 1936, FH, FSC, G 5, 1936, and Bracey to Catchpool, ibid., GE 9, 1933–36.

74. Catchpool to Bracey, January 7, March 3, and April 9, 1936, ibid., loc. cit.; Peetz and Lachmund, *Allen Bruder sein*, 50–62.

75. Catchpool to Frank Ritchie ("Dear Friend"), July 7, 1936, *AFSC*, I, Doc. 71, 212–20.

76. Catchpool to Sturge, March 12, 1936, FH, FSC, G 5, 1936.

77. "Dictionary of Quaker Biography," FH; Margaret B. Collyer to Bracey, March 12, 1937, ibid., G 5, 1937–38.

78. Martin to Bracey, August 7, October 16, 1936, ibid., loc. cit., 1936.

79. On MacMaster's concerns, see his letter to Pickett, December 9, 1936, in his "Diary," and Martin to Hugh Moore, November 7, 1936, *AFSC*, I, Doc. 78, 236–37, also Seadle, "Quakerism in Germany," 120–22.

80. For example, Anne Martin to Bracey, May 5, 1937, FH, FSC, GE 5, 1937–38; Gestapo to the Berlin Center, May 11, 1937, ibid., GE 12, from the GYM, 1936–39; also Albert Martin to Pickett, March 9, 1938, AFSC, FS, Germany, Correspondence from, 1936 [*sic*].

81. Martin to Pickett, August 12, 1936, ibid., loc. cit.; June 10, 1937, ibid., loc. cit., December 5, 1937, *AFSC*, I, Doc. 107, 311–13, and March 9, 1938, AFSC, FS, Germany, Correspondence from, 1938.

82. Martin, "The German Years," 6.

83. Käte Tacke and Friedrich Huth, "Das Berliner Quäkerbüro: Von seiner Entstehung und seiner Arbeit," *Der Quäker*, June–July 1989, 139.

84. On Ossietzky, see Irwin Abrams, *The Nobel Peace Prize and the Laureates*, 125–29; Charmian Brinson and Marian Malet, eds., *Rettet Ossietzky! Dokumente aus dem Nachlass von Rudolf Olden*, 9–28, 87–88, 178–80, 194–95, 221–22, and Elke Suhr, *Carl von Ossietzky. Eine Biographie*, 220–22. Quaker involvement is documented by Helen Bentwich to Otto Lehmann-Russbueldt, May 15, 1934, in "Betr: Information über die gegen Deutschland tätigen Emigrantenkreise in London," Dahlem. Preussiches Geheimes Staatsarchiv, Rev. 90p, 58, H 1; Catchpool to Bracey, November 8, 1933, FH, FSC, GE 5, 1933–34; Catchpool to Bracey, April 17, 1934, ibid., GE 9, 1934, and Martin to Bracey & Pickett, Copenhagen, November 14, 1936, *AFSC*, I, Doc. 80, 240–41. A copy of Albert Martin to the head of the Westend Hospital, Werner Schultz, November 8, 1936, detailing Ossietzky's medical needs, survives in Gestapo Archives, BAK, R 58/1135.

85. Hurtwood's letter to the *Times*, December 8, 1936, and to Bracey, March 5, 1937, as well as Ernst Toller to Bracey, May 23, 1939, thanking Friends for their assistance, in Brinson and Malet, *Rettet Ossietzky!* 107, 117, 378. Letter of the Germany and Holland Committee to Propaganda Ministry and Secret Police, January 11, 1937, BAK, R 58/1135.

86. On continued Quaker efforts for political prisoners, GEC Minutes, May 26, 1936; Minutes of the Berlin Secretariat, February 11–12, 1937, FH, FSC, G 5, 1937–38. Richard Albrecht, *Der militante Sozialdemokrat Carlo Mierendorff 1897 bis 1943. Eine Biographie*. 185–87. On Schubert, see Henry T. Cadbury to Rudolf Schubert, July 29, 1939, Schubert Papers. Also [Hilda Koch], *Refugee*. On Sollmann, see Felix E. Hirsch, "William Sollmann: Wanderer Between two Worlds," especially 207, 217–28, and Albrecht Ragg, "The German Socialist Emigration in the United States," 121. On continuing efforts on behalf of Neubauer

and other political victims, see Gestapo reports December 21, 1936, February 14, February 27, April 16, November 5, and November 15, 1937, in BAK R58/1135. As to Niemöller, see Martin to Bracey, March 8, 1938 and Catchpool to Sturge, February 20, 1939, FH, FSC, GE 9, To and from Corder Catchpool, 1933–38.

87. Martin, "The German Years," 7; Martin, "Autobiography," 37–37c; Martin to Bracey, April 12, and Martin to Sturge, June 18, 1938, FH, FSC, GE 9, Unnumbered from Berlin, 1938–39.

88. *Elmira (New York) Star Gazette,* December 14, 1938; Martin, "Autobiography," loc. cit.

89. "Dictionary of Quaker Biography," FH; Bracey to Martin, April 26, 1938; Pickett to Martin, April 3, and Barbara Cary to Martin, June 21, 1938, AFSC, Germany Correspondence, Letters to, 1938.

90. Anne Martin to Bracey, August 15, 1938, FH, FSC, GE 5, 1937–38.

91. Tritton to Elkinton, February 17, 1939, ibid., GE 8, To Berlin.

92. Memorandum, "A Proposal for the Quäker Büro Berlin," July 27, 1939, AFSC, FS, Refugee Section, Germany, 1939. On the staff additions, Minutes of Berlin Secretariat, May 7, 1939, FH, FSC, GE 5, 1939, and Roger Carter to writer, December 15, 1993.

93. See "Report on the work of the Berlin Secretariat," August 31, 1938, signed by Carter with a postscript by Elkinton, AFSC, FS, Germany, General, 1938.

94. Catchpool to Bracey, November 2, 1935, FH, FSC, GE 5, 1935; Catchpool to Pickett, October 26, and November 28, 1935, AFSC, Germany, Letters from, 1935, and January 8 and January 22, 1936, ibid., Letters from, 1936.

95. Martin to Pickett and Bracey, Copenhagen, June 9, September 8, 1937, AFSC, Germany, Correspondence from, 1937; Anne Martin to Bracey, March 25, 1938, FH, FSC, GE 8, To [sic] Berlin, 1937–1939.

96. William R. Hughes, "Report of a visit to Germany, November 26 to December 14, 1938," December 16, 1938, *AFSC,* I, Doc. 141, 418–22. For a useful view of Eisenach's Nazi establishment, see John Connelly, "The Uses of Volksgemeinschaft: Letters to the NSDAP Kreisleitung Eisenach, 1939–1940," *Journal of Modern History* 68 (1996): 923–28.

97. Elkinton to Pickett, Ommen, December 22, 1938, *AFSC,* I, Doc. 146, 435–40.

98. On Grüber, see his memoirs, *Erinnerungen aus sieben Jahrzehnten,* more reliable than some of his critics claim, also Evangelische Hilfsstelle für ehemals Rassenverfolgte in Berlin, *An der Stechbahn. Erlebnisse und Berichte aus dem Büro Grüber in den Jahren der Verfolgung,* 12–29, and under the same auspices *Das "Büro Pfarrer Grüber" 1938–1940,* 9–16; Eberhard Röhm and Jörg Thierfelder, *Juden-Christen-Deutsche,* 2:2, 259–67.

99. Harald von Königswald, *Birger Forell. Leben und Wirken in den Jahren 1933–1938,* 123–32; Hilde and Will Völger, "Birger Forell," in *Durchkreuzter Hass. Vom Abenteuer des Friedens. Berichte und Selbstdarstellungen,* ed. Rudolf Weckerling, 123–32; Laura Livingstone, "Aus Deutschlands dunklen Tagen," in ibid., 41–46. Grüber's letters to the Dutch Aid Committee for Racial and Religious Refugees are preserved in Rijksinstituut voor Oorlogsdokumentatie, 181, 11, especially his plea of September 18, 1939, to make Holland a bridge to salvation and to see to it that Protestant efforts matched those of Catholic and Jewish organizations. The work of some of his associates across Germany is detailed in Anneliese Feurich et al., eds., *Juden und Christen, Kinder eines Vaters. Beiträge zur Pogromnacht*

9/10 November 1938, 59–71, a source to which Roger Carter drew my attention; Helmut Baier, "Zwischen Anpassung und Widerstand. Evangelisches kirchliches Leben," 161–81; Eckhart Marggraf, "Hermann Maas. Evangelischer Pfarrer und 'stadtbekannter Judenfreund,'" 71–82, and Jörg Thierfelder, "Hermann Maas und die badische Landeskirche im Dritten Reich," in *Das Land zwischen Rhein und Odenwald,* ed. Uwe Uffelmann (Villingen/Schwenningen: Neckar Verlag, 1987), 158–71.

100. Elkinton to Pickett, June 14, 1939 from Ommen, AFSC, Refugee Services, Germany, Berlin, 1939. But note also the judgment of the visiting James Vail, who feared that "Father Grübler's [*sic*] poor judgment" might some day lead to the closing of his office "and its workload accrue to Friends." Vail to Pickett, March 27, 1939, *AFSC,* I, Doc. 188, 523–33.

101. Reutter, *Katholische Kirche als Fluchthelfer,* 89–130. See particularly the *Verein*'s report of May 4, 1939, transmitted to Gestapo via Büro Grüber in "Dokumenten-auswahl zur Tätigkeit beim Bischöflichen Ordinariat Berlin," Diözesanarchiv Berlin, 024194, obtained for me by Anna Halle.

102. Röhm and Thierfelder, *Juden-Christen-Deutsche,* 2:2, 251–54, 269–70; Werner Cohn, "Bearers of a Common Fate? The 'Non-Aryan' Christian 'Fate Comrades' of the Paulus Bund."

103. Evangelische Hilfsstelle, *Büro Pfarrer Grüber,* 14–16, and Roger Carter to Otto Hirsch, June 21, 1939, RCP. A copy of this document is in FH, FSC, GE 5, 1939.

104. Vail to Pickett, March 6, 1939, *AFSC,* I, Doc. 185, 521–27.

105. Carter to Hirsch as cited in fn. 103.

106. See Minutes of German Committee for Non-Aryan Christian Children, June 15, 1939; Copy, Reichsvereinigung der Juden in Deutschland, Abt. Wanderung, Rundschreiben A 274 "Betr. Beratung und Betreuung nichtarischer Christen," July 13, 1939, Diözesanarchiv Berlin, 024196; Roger Carter Memorandum on the relief work of the Quäkerbüro, August 9, 1939, FH, FSC, GE 5, 1939.

107. See the testimonials in Harald Roth, ed., *Es tat weh nicht mehr dazu zu gehören. Kindheit und Jugend im Exil,* Ravensburger junge Reihe (Ravensburg: Otto Maier, 1989), especially 33–43, and Erna Philipp, "Experiences of a Welfare Worker in Rhineland Westphalia," Yad Vashem Archives, 02/20.

108. Reutter, *Katholische Kirche als Fluchthelfer,* 188–89; Evangelische Hilfsstelle, *Büro Pfarrer Grüber,* 7; Peter W. Ludlow, "The Refugee Problem in the 1930s: The Failures and Successes of Protestant Relief Programmes," 602–3, puts the number of Grüber rescues at eleven hundred; Kaiser, "Protestantismus, Diakonie und 'Judenfrage' 1931–1941," 709–11; Roger Carter, "Die Religiöse Gesellschaft der Freunde zur Zeit der NS-Diktatur," 372–73 (as quoted), and by the same, "Das Internationale Quäkerbüro Berlin 1920–1942." Bailey, *Quaker Couple,* 97–100. I first encountered the figure 1,135 in Seadle, "Quakerism in Germany," 239, who cites Darton's "An Account" as his authority, but without page reference. Anna S. Halle, "Quäkerhaltung und -handeln im nationalsozialistischen Deutschland," Unpub. paper, 7, also accepted it, but by the time the second part of her essay appeared as "The German Quakers in the Third Reich," she had dropped it as entirely unreliable. See also her letter to Roger Carter, August 21, 1993, of which she kindly sent me a copy. Much source material remains to be sifted, including twenty thousand AFSC case files at the Balch Institute in Philadelphia, before this issue can be put *ad acta.*

109. For example, Minutes, March 15, 1939, FH, Germany and Holland Committee, 1935–40.

110. Roger Carter, "Report on the position of the Berlin Quaker Centre," August 24, 1939, FH, FSC, G 5, 1939.

111. Elkinton to Pickett, September 1, 1939, AFSC, FS, Refugee Service, 1939.

112. Quoted in her "German Quakers," 235.

113. On Alfons Paquet, MacMaster to Pickett, March 1, 1937, *AFSC*, I, Doc. 89, 262–63; on the Schulze-Gävernitz son, Jürgen Heideking, "Gero von Schulze-Gävernitz. Deutscher Patriot im amerikanischen Geheimdienst," 281–90; Bailey, *Quaker Couple*, 75; Margarethe Lachmund, *With Thine Adversary in the Way: A Quaker Witness for Reconciliation*, 17, and Tacke, *Lebensbilder deutscher Quäker*, 38–40.

114. MacMaster to Pickett, December 9, 1936, *AFSC*, I, Doc. 86, 250–56; Kraus to Pickett, April 16, 1937, AFSC, FS, Refugees, 1937; Pickett to Martin, January 22, 1937, ibid., Germany, Letters to, 1937; Martin to Pickett and Kraus, June 23, 1937, in *AFSC*, I, Docs. 100–101, 293–95, and Bracey to Carter, January 14, 1939, FH, FSC, GE 9, Unnumbered to and from Berlin, 1938–40. On the rescue of Jewish Friends, see the list of cases in Bailey, *Quaker Couple*, 97–100, and on the case of Herta Israel at the Berlin Center, Carter to Ida Witworth, June 18, 1939, and Carter to writer, June 27, 1995, RCP.

115. Minutes, November 18, 1936, FH, Germany and Holland Committee, 1935–1940; Bracey to the GYM, November 20, 1936, and Albrecht to Bracey, December 1, 1936, ibid., GE 12, from the GYM, 1936–39.

116. See, for example, Martin to Pickett and Hugh Moore, October 16, 1936, AFSC, Germany, Correspondence, Letters from, 1936; Bracey to T. Arthur Leonard, December 31, 1936, FH, FSC, GE 12, from the GYM [*sic*], 1936–39.

117. Undated note (December 1936?), Sturge to Bracey, ibid., loc. cit.; Pickett to Albrecht, January 15, 1937, AFSC, FS, Germany, GYM, 1937. See also the anonymous and undated "Notes on the German Yearly Meeting," in AFSC, FS, GYM, 1936.

118. Unsigned letter to Pickett from London, March 1, 1936, ibid., Germany, Correspondence [*sic*], Letters from, 1936.

119. See, for example, Henrietta Jordan, "Meine Erfahrungen mit deutschen Quäkern in den Jahren schwerster Bedrängnis," *Der Quäker* (June 1975): 238.

120. Halle, "Quäkerhaltung," 22.

121. Luther to German Foreign Office, September 20, 1935; Bismarck to same, September 11, 1936, BAK, RK, R 4311; Albrecht to Pickett, New York, October 13, 1937, AFSC, FS, Germany, GYM, 1937. I am indebted to Thomas Conrad for photocopies of the German diplomatic correspondence.

122. On Otto Weis and Gerhard Wieding, see Tacke, *Lebensbilder deutscher Quäker*, 114–15, 117–19. On Halle, see his *Otto Lilienthal. Der erste Flieger* (Berlin: VDI Verlag, 1936), and the following items from the Halle family archives: Anna Halle's "Bemerkungen zur Publikationsgeschichte der ersten wissenschaftlichen Biographie über Otto Lilienthal von Gerhard Halle," September 18, 1990; Gerhard Halle to Lilienthal Gesellschaft für Luftfahrtforschung, September 6, 1938, and his letter to his local air-raid warden, February 23, 1939. On Lachmund, see her *With Thine Adversary*, 19–22, and Sassin, *Liberale im Widerstand*, 169–70.

123. Geheime Staatspolizei Berlin to Stapostelle Hannover, July 25, 1936, and Stapostelle Hannover to Gestapo Berlin, August 21, 1936, BAK, R58/1135. This file includes Albrecht's request for permission to hold the yearly meeting in 1937, dated July 7, 1937, reporting that 40 foreign Friends were expected.
124. Stapoleitstelle Frankfurt/Oder to Stapoleitstelle Magdeburg, January 27, 1938; report of Stapoleitstelle Frankfurt/Oder, same date; Guben police report to Stapoleitstelle Frankfurt/Oder, February 19, 1938, and report of Section II a 2, Berlin on Guben Quaker meetings, dated December 9, 1938, ibid., loc. cit.
125. The text of the 1938 address in Hans Albrecht, *Die Grundlagen der Gemeinschaft,* while the 1939 address in paraphrased by Anneliese Herwig in her obituary of Hans Albrecht in *Der Quäker* (July 1975): 209–10.
126. "Notes on the German Yearly Meeting," undated, AFSC, FS, GYM, 1936; on the admission of new members, Bailey, *Quaker Couple,* 103.
127. Seadle, "Quakerism in Germany," 182–88; Pickett to Henry Tatnall Brown, November 15, 1937, AFSC, FS, Germany, General, 1937; Gestapo Berlin to German Foreign Office, February 26, 1938, BAK, R58/1135.
128. Anna Halle to writer, January 8, 1994; Eva Gordon to writer, April 8, and 20, 1994, as quoted, as well as the essay on one of the youth's group members, Katherina Provinzki, in Tacke, *Lebensbilder deutscher Quäker,* 87–91.
129. Cf., Rudolf Schlosser to Elsie F. Howard, December 1, 1938, translation of Rudolf Schlosser report "Old Peoples Home and Infirmary for Jews in Germany," February 6, 1939, FH, FS, GE 10, Frankfurt, 1932–39; Minutes of February 15, 1939, ibid., Germany and Holland Committee, 1935–40, and Schlosser memo "Einige Erfahrungen und Wünsche zur Auswanderungsberatung," February 24, 1939, AFSC, FS, Refugee Service, Germany, Frankfurt, 1939.
130. Confidential report from Anne Martin, July 1936, *AFSC,* I, Doc. 72, 221–27.
131. On Ockel, see Tacke, *Lebensbilder deutscher Quäker,* 70–72, on the others: Leiter der SD Aussenstelle Guben to Guben Police, March 15, 1937; Stapostelle Frankfurt/Oder to Guben Police, September 15, 1937; Report of Section II 2, Berlin, December 9, 1938, all in BAK, R58/1135.
132. Minister of War to Gestapo, July 11, 1936, ibid., loc. cit.
133. Undated report of Douglas M. Steere (September 1937?), AFSC, FS, Germany, General, 1937.
134. Elkinton to Pickett from Ommen, November 24, 1938, ibid., Germany, Correspondence, Letters from, 1938.
135. Albrecht to Helen W. Dixon, January 30, 1939, FH, FSC, GE 9, Unnumbered to and from Berlin, 1938–39.
136. Roger Carter to writer, March 16, 1994.
137. A list of these men and women was attached to Roger Carter's letter to Otto Hirsch, June 21, 1939, RCP. Their names are also listed in Bailey, *Quaker Couple,* 94–95.
138. Marianne Josephs to writer, January 19, 1938. Schmitt Papers.
139. Minutes, April 21, 1937, January 19 and March 16, 1938, FH, Germany and Holland Committee, 1935–40. For the quote, see *Eerder Berichtsblätter,* March 1938. (A set of this mimeographed school paper is part of HFM.) Katharina Petersen to Else Cappel, September 17, and November 22, 1938, Cappel Papers in private hands; Petersen to writer, May 20, 1938, Schmitt Papers, and Minutes of Eerde Board meeting, May 13, 1938, Amsterdam, Internationaal Instituut vor Sociale Geschiedenis (IISG), Quakers 14. For a contemporary assessment of

Petersen's stewardship, see Piet Kappers, "Eerde's erste Leiterin," "Eerde 1934–1939," HFM.

140. On Frommel and his circle's "danger to National Socialism," see Chef des Sicher-heitshauptamtes to Information Office of German Labor Front, April 4, 1936, and Gestapo report on the subversive nature of his writings, June 22, 1936, both in BAK, R 58/751. On Frommel's impact in Eerde, Hanna Glücksmann to writer, October 13, 1937, Schmitt Papers. I learned of the differences between Kappers and Neuse during my interview with Rose Neuse, October 27, 1992. Posthumous appreciations of Frommel include Wolf van Cassel, "Wolfgang Frommel, poeta et amicus"; Richard Bregenzer, "Erinnerungen an Wolfgang Frommel." Manuel R. Goldschmidt, "Ernst Morwitz im Gespräch mit Wolfgang Frommel. Aufzeich-nungen und Erinnerungen," and Paul Otto Drescher, "Assistent in Frankfurt. Mit Wolfgang Frommel am Rundfunk 1933." The latter includes an account of Frommel's "midnight lectures," notably his disquisition on Sparta, a devastating putdown of the Nazi revolution.

141. "Verslag van de Quakerschool Eerde," HFM; Schlosser to Bracey, August 22, 1936, FH, FSC, GE 10, Frankfurt, 1932–1939.

142. These figures are based on Peter Budde's "Schülerliste" and his "Die Interna-tionale Quäkerschule in Eerde/Holland. Im Geist praktischer Nächstenliebe und kraftvoller Toleranz." Elkinton to Pickett, March 8, 1939, AFSC, FS, Netherlands, Eerde School, 1939, puts the number of students at 130.

143. These transactions are documented in the files of Friends House, and less com-pletely in the archives of AFSC.

144. Undated circular by Pickett, AFSC, FS, Holland, Quakerschool Ommen, 1936. Context provided by other AFSC correspondence establishes late 1938 or early 1939 as the likely date.

145. But note Elkinton to Pickett, March 8, 1939, AFSC, FS, Netherlands, Eerde School, Ommen, 1939, who continued to worry that the preponderance of German Jewish students made the school disproportionately dependent on the clearing. He recommended a continued search for "extra-German patronage."

146. *Eerder Berichtsblätter*, February and April 1939.

147. See especially Josi Einstein, "Zin en karakter van de feesten op Eerde," *De Vriendenkring* (November 1937); by the same, "Winter op Eerde," ibid., June 1938, and "De vrienden van de Quakerschool," ibid., March 1939.

148. M[ollie] Swart, "Medewerkers onder elkaar," and Otto Edgar Rosenstern, "Mitar-beiter und Schüler," "Eerde 1934–1939," 15, 18–19.

149. *Eerder Berichtsblätter*, April 1939.

150. Robert Balderston's report on agricultural school, undated; same to Piet Kappers, March 17, 1939; Meeting of the School Committee, 25/26 March, 1939, in Hanover, and Minutes of meeting between Robert and Martha Balderston, with Kurt and Rose Neuse and Werner Hermans from the Quaker school Eerde, Mr. M. Brusse, director of the Quaker agricultural school, Baron Ph. van Pallandt and Piet A. Kappers; Kurt Neuse to Kappers, July 8, 1939, all in AFSC, FS, Netherlands, Eerde School, Ommen, 1939; *Eerde Berichtsblätter*, May 1939; *De Vriendenkring*, February 1939. For an earlier German venture of this kind, intended to prepare young German Jews for a career in farming, see Werner T. Angress, "Auswandererlehrgut Gross-Breesen," highlighting the difficulties at-tending what was often a drastic transformation of students' aspirations and values.

151. Kurt Neuse, "Punkte f. Behandlung auf der Sitzung des Executive Committees [*sic*]," August 27, 1939, IISG, Quaker 14; *De Vriendenkring*, February 1939.

152. Mary Champney to Pickett, September 16; Telegram Elkinton to AFSC, from Copenhagen, September 15; Bernard G. Lawson to Mary Hoxie Jones, November 3, all 1939, and Neuse to Pickett, January 15, 1940, all in AFSC, FS, Netherlands, Eerde School, Ommen, 1939.

153. Lichdi, *Mennoniten im Dritten Reich*, 122–35. The author does not give any source for his description of Unruh's position, and there appear to exist no figures on Mennonite service in the German army.

154. Catchpool to Tritton, August 28, September 1, September 5, 1934, FH, FSC, G 5, 1934; Peetz and Lachmund, *Allen Bruder sein*, 66–67, gives the impression that Quaker involvement began in 1935; M. H. Jones, *Swords into Ploughshares*, 353, gives April 24, 1935, as the date of definite commitment.

155. Bracey to Catchpool, April 17, 1936, Benjamin Unruh to Catchpool, April 20, 1936, FH, FSC, GE 5, 1933–36; Pickett to Bracey, September 15, 1936, ibid., loc. cit.

156. The most comprehensive account of the entire operation is Catchpool's confidential "Child Feeding Scheme in the Sudeten Area of Czechoslovakia, known as Quäkerhilfe (Quaker Relief)," dated January 12, 1938, in University of South Carolina, Thomas Cooper Library, Clifford Allen Papers. On the collision with Alfred Martin, see Martin to Bracey, May 26, 1937 ("I have about abandoned all hope of ever trying to work with Corder."), FH, FSC, GE 5, 1937–38; Sturge to Catchpool, May 28, 1937, ibid., GE 9, To and from Corder Catchpool, 1933–38, and Bracey to Martin, May 30, 1937, ibid., GE 8, To Berlin, 1937–39, expressing "great regret . . . that this matter has not been more tactfully handled." On Martin's and Catchpool's joint inspection trip through Czechoslovakia, Anne Martin to Bracey, November 19, 1937, ibid., GE 5, 1937–38.

157. Greaves, *Corder Catchpool*, 27, and Heinrich Unruh to writer, January 25, 1993, quoting the German Foreign Office report.

158. Carter to Tritton, August 16 and 19, 1939, FH, FSC, GE 5, 1939, Jan.–Sept.

159. Tritton to Carter, August 18 and 21, 1939, ibid., GE 8, To Berlin, 1937–39.

160. Headley Horsnaill, "Refugee Relief, Vienna Center, January–March 1937," *AFSC*, I, Doc. 92, 276; Same to Sturge, July 19, 1937, ibid., Doc. 104, 302–4, and Anon, "Christian Refugee Situation in Austria," April 7, 1937, ibid., Doc. 93, 277–78.

161. Radomir V. Luža, *Austro-German Relations in the Anschluss Era*, 215–20. For documentation on German policy and its implementation, see Edith Klamper, ed., *Dokumentationsarchiv des österreichischen Widerstands*, for example, Joseph Bürckel to all party and government officials in Austria, August 20, 1938, Doc. 106, 232; Report to the head of the Gestapo, Vienna, no date (after the Kristallnacht), Doc. 111, 240; as a case study of an individual Jewish expulsion, Gestapo Innsbruck to Bezirkshauptmann Innsbruck, November 19, 1938, Doc. 118, 249–50, and Gestapo Vienna to Reich Commissioner for the re-unification [*sic*] of Austria with the German Reich, June 1, 1939, Doc. 127, 262–63.

162. Wischnitzer, "Jewish Emigration from Germany, 1933–1938," 30–33.

163. Anne Martin to Pickett, May 12, 1938, *AFSC*, I, Doc. 116, 337–43; D. Robert Yarnall's "Factual notes on German trip, December 7–December 24, 1938," and Roger Carter's "Confidential report on the situation of the Vienna group of the Society of Friends," both in FH, FSC, GE 5, 1937–38.

164. Eichstätt, *Von Dollfuss zu Hitler,* 433–34; Radomir V. Luža, *The Resistance in Austria, 1938–1945,* 11.

165. See Klamper's introduction to *Dokumentationsarchiv des österreichischen Widerstands,* xvi; the "Report from Vienna of a representative of the Nederlandsch Kinder Comité," January 7, 1939, *AFSC,* I, Doc. 195, 559–62, and Gildemeester to Vienna Gestapo, November 21, 1939, *Dokumentationsarchiv,* Doc. 137, 275–76.

166. Koblik, *The Stones Cry Out,* 90–95; Ludlow, "Refugee Problem in the 1930s," 599–600.

167. Truus Wijsmuller-Meyer, *Geen Tijd voor Tranen,* 43–108; "Report of the Children's Department of the Friends Center," Vienna, Nov. 1938–Sept. 1939," *AFSC,* I, Doc. 197, 564–69.

168. Florence Barrow to Pickett, May 19, 1938; John Reich to same, April 1, 1938; Clarence Pickett Diary, September 21, 1938, and Yarnall to Pickett, July 23, 1938, all in *AFSC,* I, Doc. 114, 335, Doc. 117, 344–48, Doc. 123, 363–65, Doc. 128, 379–83, and MacMaster, "Diary," 178–82, 169, 210.

169. These recollections are reprinted in Hubert Butler, *The Children of Drancy,* 197–207. I am grateful to my Virginia colleague David Levin for drawing my attention to this source.

170. Ibid., 200; MacMaster to Pickett, November 10, 1938, *AFSC,* I, Doc. 126, 370–73. See also Gestapo report on "Gesellschaft der Freunde in Wien I, Singerstrasse 16," June 1, 1938, BAK, R 58/1135.

171. MacMaster to Pickett, as cited above, and Roger Carter to writer, March 16, 1994.

172. Tessa Cadbury (née Rowntree) to writer, January 9, 1995.

173. "Statistics of the Emigration Movement from 15.3.1938–28.8.1939"; "Statistics re emigration of non-Aryan children"; Graphic "Society of Friends, Wien, Kinder-Aktion, Nichtarische Kinder ins Ausland"; and "Report of the Children's Department of the Friends' Center, Vienna, November 1938–September 1939," all in *AFSC,* FS, Refugee Services, Austria, International Center, Vienna, 1939. On the Graz operation, see Stapostelle Graz, June 17 and 18, 1938, BAK, R 58/1135, whose terms also seem to confirm that Quakers in Graz had also fed some Nazi families. For Jewish emigration totals, see Bruce F. Pauley, *From Prejudice to Persecution: A History of Austrian Anti-Semitism,* 294.

174. Käte Neumayer to Pickett, August 29, 1939, *AFSC,* FS, Refugee Services, Austria, International Center, Vienna, 1939.

175. Tessa Rowntree, "From Prague to London," *The Friend* (May 4, 1939), copy by the same "Some memories of Germany, Austria, and Czechoslovakia, February 1938–March 1939," written for Brenda Bailey, January 2, 1990, who quotes it extensively in her *Quaker Couple,* 87–88, and Tessa Cadbury to writer, March 31, 1994. I am very grateful to this last surviving veteran of the Vienna and Prague efforts, now the widow of the American Friend Jack Cadbury, for sending me this material and for answering my questions.

176. Tessa Rowntree to Richard Wood, April 22, 1939, *AFSC,* I, Doc. 209, 667–68, and to writer, March 31, and June 14, 1994.

5. British Friends and the Appeasement of Nazi Germany

1. For example, Secretary of State von Bülow to Head of Reich Chancellory Meissner, January 10, 1935, requesting that Hitler receive Lord Hurtwood, ADAP, Series C, III, 2, 778–79.

2. D. C. Watt, "Christian Essay in Appeasement," 30–31, including the quote on Corder Catchpool; Marwick, *Clifford Allen;* Martin Gilbert, *Plough My Own Furrow: The Story of Lord Allen of Hurtwood as Told through his Writings and Correspondence;* Mosa Anderson, *Noël-Buxton: A Life;* Victoria de Bunsen, *Charles Roden Buxton: A Memoir;* George Lansbury, *My Pilgrimage for Peace,* 219–20. Margarete Gärtner, *Botschafterin des guten Willens. Aussenpolitische Arbeit, 1914–1950;* Watt, "Influence from Without"; Griffiths, *Fellow Travellers for the Right,* 110–12. On Berber, see his report of a meeting of the Christian World Student Union in *Die Eiche* 9 (1921): 372–73; his own *Die völkerrechtliche Lage Deutschlands,* passim, and his memoirs *Zwischen Macht und Gewissen. Lebenserinnerungen,* ed. by Ingrid Strauss.

3. Anderson, *Noël-Buxton,* 127; Minutes on the conversation between the führer and Lord Allen of Hurtwood, January 25, 1935, ADAP, C, III, 2, 853–56.

4. Martin Gilbert, *The Roots of Appeasement,* 164–65, and his *Plough My Own Furrow,* 358–60, 368–69; also Marwick, *Clifford Allen,* 161–70.

5. Quoted in Gilbert, *Plough My Own Furrow,* 359, 362–63.

6. Marwick, *Clifford Allen,* 163–72; Gilbert, *Plough My Own Furrow,* 378–79. The last quote is from Griffiths, *Fellow Travellers for the Right,* 151 (italics mine).

7. Corder Catchpool, "Last chance." Copy of memorandum written March 7, 1936 in University of South Carolina, Thomas Cooper Library, Hurtwood Papers; Charles Roden Buxton, *The Alternatives to War,* 167–71.

8. Greaves, *Corder Catchpool,* 27; Peetz and Lachmund, *Allen Bruder sein,* 68–69. The quote is from Lansbury's letter to Lord Hurtwood, May 11, 1937, in Gilbert, *Plough My Own Furrow,* 381.

9. Corder Catchpool, "Report on visit to Germany, January 2–January 20, 1939," copy in University of South Carolina, Thomas Cooper Library, Hurtwood Papers; Peetz and Lachmund, *Allen Bruder sein,* 69–76; Anderson, *Noël-Buxton,* 135–39. The quote is from Hughes, *Indomitable Friend,* 147.

10. Philip Gibbs, *Across the Frontiers,* 355–56. On Gibbs also Angelika Schwarz, *Die Reise ins Dritte Reich. Britische Augenzeugen im nationalsozialistischen Deutschland (1933–39),* 135, 232–33, 248–49, 274, 307, 345–50, 358, 369. On Corder Catchpool's contributions to *Across the Frontiers,* see Peetz and Lachmund, *Allen Bruder sein,* 54.

11. Copies of Corder Catchpool to Horace G. Alexander, February 4 and 17, 1938, Swarthmore College, Swarthmore Peace Collection, Alexander Papers.

12. Anderson, *Noël-Buxton,* 140, Corder Catchpool, "Note on present situation in Czechoslovakia," June 22, 1938, FH, FSC, GE 9, To and from Corder Catchpool, 1933–38.

13. Marwick, *Clifford Allen,* 173–76, 179–81; Gilbert, *Plough My Own Furrow,* 403–8, including the quotes from Hurtwood's House of Lords speech.

14. On Hurtwood's impressions of his August 10 interview with Ribbentrop, see Tel. Mr. Newton (Prague) to Viscount Halifax, August 13, 1938, E. L. Woodward et al., eds., *Documents on British Foreign Policy, 1919–1939,* Series 3, II, 1938, 88; Gilbert, *Plough My Own Furrow,* 410–24; Marwick, *Clifford Allen,* 182–89.

15. Alexander, *Growth of the Peace Testimony,* passim.

16. Carter to Bracey, October 3, 1938, FH, FSC, GE 9, Unnumbered to and from Berlin, 1938–39.

17. Catchpool to Alexander, February 20, and June 6, 1939, Swarthmore College, Swarthmore Peace Collection, Alexander Papers; Corder Catchpool, "Confidential Conversation [with Fritz Berber] on current questions of international politics (June 1–3, 1939)," in University of South Carolina, Thomas Cooper Library, Hurtwood Papers; Greaves, *Corder Catchpool*, 31–32; Peetz and Lachmund, *Allen Bruder sein*, 60–61.

18. Carter to Tritton, April 12, 21, July 7, 13, and his "Some notes on a visit to the Free City of Danzig, June 23, 1939," all in FH, FSC, GE 5, 1939; Carter to writer, June 27, 1995.

19. Carter's "Account of a conversation with F. B. on Friday, July 28, 1939," FH, FSC, GE 5, 1939.

20. Herbert von Dirksen, *Moscow-Tokyo-London: Twenty Years of German Foreign Policy*, 224–28.

21. Heinrich Unruh to writer, January 25, 1993. Unruh claims to know more details of the conversations Buxton and Catchpool had at the Wilhelmstrasse, but did not wish to divulge them before the appearance of his biography of his father. See also Roger Carter, "Report on the Position in the Berlin Quaker Center," August 24, 1939, FH, FSC, GE 9, 1939; Carter to writer, March 16, 1994, and Gärtner, *Botschafterin des guten Willens*, 371–75, 380–86.

22. Anderson, *Noël-Buxton*, 148; Greaves, *Corder Catchpool*, 33; Charles Roden Buxton, *The Case for Early Peace* (London: Friends Peace Committee, 1940), and Friedrich Berber's introduction to *Europäische Politik 1933–1938 im Spiegel der Prager Akten*, 15.

23. Alex Bryan, *Corder Catchpool: A Hero Who Never Made Heroic Gestures*, 16, quoting Catchpool on the preventability of World War II.

6. Quaker Work in Time of War

1. On the few exceptional cases of emigration permits granted, mostly to Jews outside of Germany, between 1941 and 1944, see Ruth Zariz, "Officially Approved Emigration from Germany after 1941: A Case Study."

2. Noakes, "Development of Nazi Policy," 331–54.

3. These generalizations are among others illustrated by the following evidence: Anna Jastrow, widow of Leopold von Ranke's prize pupil, Ignaz Jastrow (1856–1934), to Gerhard Halle, September 28, 1941, in possession of Anna Halle; Heinrich Spiero's letters to his daughters, November 28, December 3, 4, 15, 1940, October 30, November 14, December 5, 1941, University of Virginia, Alderman Library, Spiero Papers, and Sabine Gova, "Heinrich Spiero—ein Gedenkwort zu seinem fünfundachzigsten Geburtstag," *Deutsche Rundschau*, n.s., 87 (1961): 250–54. I am grateful to Maria Warburg-Mills for entrusting her grandparents' letters to me.

4. Blau, "Jewish Population," 171; Doris L. Bergen, "Catholics, Protestants and Anti-Semitism in Nazi Germany," 349. For some Christian exceptions, see Wilhelm von Pechmann to Bishop Hans Meiser, November 8, 1941, in Kantzenbach, ed., *Widerstand und Solidarität*, 314–15, and Wolfgang See and Rudolf Weckerling, *Frauen im Kirchenkampf. Beispiele aus der Bekennenden Kirche Berlin-Brandenburg 1933 bis 1945*, 148.

5. This view surfaced in Heinrich Unruh to writer, January 25, 1993. On the actual plan, see Christopher R. Browning, *The Path to Genocide*, 18–20, 23; B. A. Sijes,

Studies over Jodenvervolging, 53–60, and Rolf Vogel, *Ein Stempel hat gefehlt*, 163–73, 313–35; Christof Dipper, "The German Resistance and the Jews"; on the protest of the wives, Abraham Pisarek and Hazel Rosenstrauch, eds., *Aus Nachbarn wurden Juden. Ausgrenzung und Selbstbehauptung 1933–1942*, 178–80.

6. Thierack to Bormann, October 13, and Bormann to Thierack, October 18, 1942, in Henry Friedlander and Sybil Milton, eds., *Bundesarchiv of the Federal Republic of Germany, Koblenz and Freiburg*, Doc. 50, 157–79.

7. Dated October 20, 1939 in Rudolf Morsey, ed., "Zwei Gestapo-Berichte zur Geschichte der Kirchenkampfes in den Jahren 1938 und 1939."

8. Elkinton to Pickett, September 11, 1939, AFSC, FS, Refugee Services, Germany, Berlin, 1939; Morris Diaries, October 8, 1939, AFSC, Diaries, Letters and Memoranda of Homer L. Morris and Edna W. Morris as Commissioners to Germany for the AFSC, 1939, hereafter cited as AFSC, Morris Diaries.

9. The bare outline of this story has been told by Hal Elliot Wert, "U.S. Aid to Poles under Nazi Domination, 1939–1940." I thank Jack Sutters for bringing this article to my attention.

10. Homer Morris to Pickett, Copenhagen, September 22, 1939, AFSC, FS, Refugee Services, Germany, Berlin, 1939.

11. Report by Homer and Edna Morris from Amsterdam, September 14–October 27, 1939, *AFSC*, I, Doc. 191, 541–51; Entries October 5–23, 1939, AFSC, Morris Diaries; Tel. Homer Morris to AFSC, October 24, 1939, and copy of Morris Memorandum to Hilgenfeldt, October 26, 1939, AFSC, FS, Poland, 1939.

12. Morris Report, *AFSC*, I, Doc. 191, 548–51; Entry October 14, 1939, AFSC, Morris Diaries; "Summary of the Case Work Service of the Quakerbüro Berlin during November 1939," *AFSC*, I, Doc. 194, 556–58.

13. Rufus Jones to Herbert Hoover, January 9, 1940, Haverford College, Quaker Collection, Rufus Jones Papers, Box 58, 376.

14. *The Friend*, May 16, 1940.

15. Elkinton to Pickett, June 6, 1940, and Copy of Elkinton to Albrecht, July 15, 1940, AFSC, FS, Germany, Letters from, 1940.

16. Leonard S. Kenworthy, *Worldview: The Autobiography of a Social Studies Teacher and Quaker*, 1–77.

17. Ibid., 59–61, 61–68. Also Margaret Hope Bacon, *Let This Life Speak: The Legacy of Henry Joel Cadbury*, 127, 237–43.

18. Entries, July 18, September 19, October 7, October 15, November 24, December 3, 1940, AFSC, Kenworthy Diary; on Lehmann's mission, also James Lichti to writer, January 26, 1994. On the number of emigrants cleared for departure: Leonard S. Kenworthy, *An American Quaker Inside Nazi Germany: Another Dimension of the Holocaust*, 32, and his *Worldview*, 66–68.

19. Kenworthy's Berlin Center report, November 17, 1940–January 31, 1941, AFSC, FS, Berlin Center, 1941; Minutes February 3, March 3, 20, May 5, 22, 1941, AFSC, FSS Personnel Committee, 1941; Meeting of the Directing Committee for Berlin and Vienna, March 16, 1941, and Kenworthy Berlin Center report, February 1–April 12, 1941, ibid., Berlin Center, 1941.

20. Ernst Wiechert, *Von den treuen Begleitern* (Hamburg: H. Ellermann, 1937), passim.

21. Entries June 4, 6, 10, 14, 22, 1941, AFSC, Kenworthy Diary.

22. Douglas Steere to Mary Hoxie Jones, October 21, 1940, ibid., Berlin Center, 1940.
23. Steere to Elkinton, October 7, 1940, ibid., Letters from Germany, 1940.
24. On the state of German-American relations, see Manfred Jonas, *The United States and Germany: A Diplomatic History*, 254–57. Elkinton to Mary Hoxie Jones, June 1, 1941, AFSC, FS, Germany, Berlin Center, 1941; Minutes June 25, 1941, ibid., FSS, reflecting reports by Elkinton and Kenworthy.
25. Grüber, *Erinnerungen aus sieben Jahrzehnten*, 142–98; Evangelische Hilfsstelle, *Büro Pfarrer Grüber*, 13–18; see also See and Weckerling, *Frauen im Kirchenkampf* (on Margarethe Grüber), 148–52; Bruno Theek, "Mein Kamerad Werner Sylten," in Drobisch and Fischer, eds., *Widerstand aus Glauben*, 221–23; Werner Oehme, *Märtyrer der evangelischen Christenheit 1933–1945*, 100–105, 120–24, 136–46, 235–41, 247–48; Reutter, *Katholische Kirche als Fluchthelfer*, 180–82; Otto Ogiermann, *Bis zum letzten Atemzug. Das Leben und Aufbegehren des Priesters Bernhard Lichtenberg*, 123–226.
26. Elkinton to Pickett, October 14, 1941, AFSC, FS, Germany, Berlin Center, 1941.
27. Olga Halle and Martha Roehn to Mary Hoxie Jones, November 27, 1941, ibid., Germany, Berlin Center, 1941; Anne Halle, "Quäkerhaltung und-handeln im nationalsozialistischen Deutschland," Unpub. paper, 8–10; Minutes, November 13, 1941, AFSC, FSS; Pickett to Albrecht, November 18, 1941, ibid., Germany, Berlin Center, 1941.
28. The preceding is an attempt to summarize a copious correspondence in AFSC archives, in the files containing letters from Germany 1939 to 1941, and the Vienna correspondence for the same time span.
29. Entries October 7, 1939 and June 15, 1940, ibid., Morris Diaries, and reports from Margaret Jones, ibid., Letters from Margaret Jones, 1940; Kenworthy, *American Quaker*, 32. Berber, *Zwischen Macht und Gewissen*, 118. For a late sample of his propagandistic writings, see "Epochen europäischer Gesamtordnung," *Donaueuropa* 2 (1942): 729–38.
30. Douglas V. Steere, "Quaker Life in Germany in the Autumn of 1940." "Not for publication," dated February 1, 1941. I owe a copy of this report to Anne Halle.
31. Kenworthy, *Quaker in Nazi Germany*, 58–66, 89.
32. Albrecht to his daughter Etta, January 1, 1941, in possession of Etta Mekeel.
33. Reported by Kenworthy to Etta and Arthur Mekeel, July 16, 1941, in possession of the recipients.
34. Copy of translation of a letter to Isabell Grubb, October, 1943, ibid., loc. cit.
35. "Liste an die Freunde zur Mitarbeit bei der Kriegsgefangenenhilfe des Quäkerbüros in Verbindung mit der Internationalen YMCA," presumably circulated in 1941. Provided by Anna Halle.
36. MacMaster to Tritton, November 30, 1942, and to Mary Hoxie Jones, March 10, 1945, in private hands; Bailey, *Quaker Couple*, 171–80.
37. This paragraph rests on, sometimes contradictory, recollections of surviving members: Anna S. Halle, *"Die Gedanken sind frei . . ." Eine Jugendgruppe der Berliner Quäker, 1935–1941*, 20–22; Hans Lüdecke, "Über die Gruppe der jungen Leute bei den Quäkern," mss., and letter to writer January 31, 1994; Eva Gordon to writer, April 8, 1994 and February 7, 1995 with a useful list of members and their fate for the years 1936–1942. For recollections about the split in the group, I am indebted to Isi Fischer-Sperling's "Erinnerungen zur Quäker-Jugendgruppe der Berliner Gruppe der Freunde ab etwa 1941" and her letter to

writer, April 12, 1995. I am grateful for all of these individuals for sharing their recollections.

38. Tacke, *Lebensbilder deutscher Quäker*, 109–10.
39. Ibid., 11–16; Sassin, *Liberale im Widerstand*, 181, 459; Kurt Grossmann, *Die unbesungenen Helden. Menschen in Deutschlands dunklen Tagen*, 85–93.
40. Eva Fogelmann, *Conscience and Courage: Rescuers of Jews during the Holocaust*, 74–75.
41. Tacke, *Lebensbilder deutscher Quäker*, 92–95.
42. Ibid., 66; Else Rosenfeld and Gertrud Luckner, eds., *Lebenszeichen aus Piaski*, 20–24; Thomas Schnabel, "Gertrud Luckner. Mitarbeiter der Caritas in Freiburg," in *Der Widerstand im deutschen Südwesten, 1933–1945*, ed. Michael Bosch and Wolfgang Niess, 117–28.
43. Tacke, *Lebensbilder deutscher Quäker*, 40–43; Sassin, *Liberale im Widerstand*, 193, 222–25, 491–92; Rosenfeld and Luckner, *Lebenszeichen aus Piaski*, 10, 43, 58, 129–31, 135–48. For evidence that Lachmund also participated in the support of Jewish Germans at Gurs, see her brief report about Gurs for German Friends, dated January 15, 1941, in possession of Anna Halle.
44. For a long time postwar Germany chose to forget the heroism of its conscientious objectors during World War II. The pioneering study of Albrecht Hartmann and Heidi Hartmann, *Kriegsdienstverweigerung im Dritten Reich*, has now been superseded by Karsten Bredemeier's *Kriegsdienstverweigerung im Dritten Reich. Ausgewählte Beispiele*, (which, despite its subtitle, is more wide ranging and more solidly documented), and Norbert T. Haase and Paul Gerhard, eds., *Die anderen Soldaten* (Frankfurt: Fischer, 1995). A number of interesting documents about Catholic refusers are included in Klamper, ed., *Dokumentationsarchiv des österreichischen Widerstands*, 363–65, 398–401, and reflected in Klemens von Klemperer, "The Solitary Witness: One More Footnote to Resistance Studies," 129–39, and Gordon C. Zahn, *German Catholics and Hitler's War: A Study in Social Control*, 54–55, 147. In addition to studies on Jehovah's Witnesses, already cited, see also Manfred Koch, "Julius Engelhard, Drucker, Kurier und Organisator der Zeugen Jehovah's," in Bosch and Niess, eds., *Widerstand im deutschen Südwesten*, 94–103, and Brian Dunn, "Jehovah's Witnesses in the Holocaust Kingdom."
45. Hermann Stöhr, *So half Amerika. Die Auslandshilfe der Vereinigten Staaten 1812–1930* (Stettin: The Author, 1936).
46. The most detailed account in Eberhard Röhm, *Sterben für den Frieden: Hermann Stöhr (1898–1940), und die ökumenische Friedensbewegung*. Pages 166–242 deal with the last year of Stöhr's life. Helmut Gollwitzer, "Krieg und Christen in unserer Generation," in Weckerling, *Durchkreuzter Hass*, 230–41, claims him as a Quaker. Tacke, *Lebensbilder deutscher Quäker*, lists him among Quakers victimized by the Third Reich, but that list includes friends of Friends. The quote is from Hartmann and Hartmann, *Kriegsdienstverweigerung*, 14–15.
47. Interviews with Inge Pollatz, May 20, 1993, and Rose Neuse, October 27/28, 1992.
48. Olga Halle, "Ein Quäker verweigert den Wehrdienst im Zweiten Weltkrieg—ein Gedächtnisprotokoll," *Der Quäker* (July 1975): 205–7, paraphrased in Hartmann and Hartmann, *Kriegsdienstverweigerung*, 37–40; Gerhard Halle to Wehrbezirkskommando Berlin VIII, April 26, 1937; Wehrbezirkskommando Berlin VIII to Gerhard Halle, June 2 (1944?), copies in possession of Anna Halle.
49. Gerhard Halle to Herr Tittelbach, September 9, 1940, ibid., loc cit.

50. Gerhard Halle to Heinz Weber, May 26, 1942, and to Martha Roehn, January 3, 1943, ibid., loc cit.
51. Tacke, *Lebensbilder deutscher Quäker*, 5–6, 38–39, 45–50.
52. Ibid., 79–82; Sigrid Jacobeit and Lieselotte Thoms-Heinrich, *Kreuzweg Ravensbrück. Lebensbilder antifaschistischer Widerstandskämpferinnen*, 135–46.
53. Schnabel, "Gertrud Luckner," in *Der Widerstand im deutschen Südwesten, 1933–1945*, ed. Bosch and Niess, 123–24.
54. Tacke, *Lebensbilder deutscher Quäker*, 29–30.
55. Bailey, *Quaker Couple*, 140–55, 195–208; Leonhard Friedrich, "Als Gast bei Adolf Hitler in Buchenwald," *Der Quäker* (July 1975): 193–200, in English translation "Buchenwald and After," *Quaker Monthly* (November 1979): 201–3; Copy of Hans Albrecht to *Regierungsrat* Hagenbuch, August 7, 1942, in Anna Halle's possession.
56. Otto, *Werden und Wesen*, 350–53; Tacke, *Lebensbilder deutscher Quäker*, 30–31, 99–100; Bailey, *Quaker Couple*, 136–226; Birke, "Rudolf Schlosser," copy in AFSC, FS, Germany, Berlin Center, 1941; Heinrich Carstens, "Nachruf für Rose Bartsch," *Der Quäker* (November 1984); "Mitteilung," dated October 1, 1945, one of the three lists of Quaker survivors sent to me by Brenda Bailey.
57. Albrecht to Dr. Drinkuth, May 4, 1944, original in possession of Anna Halle. For a chronicle of British protests against massive bombing of German cities, see Vera Brittain, *Testament of Experience* (London: Virago Press, 1979), 296–99 and passim.
58. Hans Albrecht, "Tagebuch über den Kampf um Berlin und die ersten Wochen der Besatzung durch die Russen (ab April 21, 1945)," entries for April 29 and May 2, 1945, in possession of Etta Mekeel: Olga Halle to Frau Goehring in Anna Halle, "Systematisch ausgewählte Briefzitate zur materiellen z. T. auch politischen Lage der Bevölkerung in Berlin 1945–50," mss.
59. Klaus Schwabe, "Hans Lachmund-Lebensbild eines Demokraten," 51–53, a citation I owe to my Virginia colleague Angelika Powell; also Sassin, *Liberale im Widerstand*, 243–44.
60. G. A. Kooy, *Het Echec van een 'Volkse' Beweging, Nazi- en Denazificatie in Nederland 1931–1945*, especially 285–96, 336–41, 345–46. See also Gerhard Hirschfeld, *Fremdherrschaft und Kollaboration. Die Niederlande unter deutscher Besatzung 1940–1945*, 157–88.
61. Kooy, *Het Echec*, 293–94.
62. Louis de Jong, *Het Koninkrijk der Nederlanden in de Tweede Wereldoorlog*, 4:2, 824–49; Werner Warmbrunn, *The Dutch under German Occupation, 1940–1945*, 133–36; Konrad Kwiet, *Reichskommissariat Niederlande. Versuch und Scheitern nationalsozialistscher Neuordnung*, 92–138; Hirschfeld, *Fremdherrschaft und Kollaboration*, 45–59. Through a misunderstanding the program of Netherlands Union was inserted in *De Vriendenkring*, September 1940, from which the quote is taken. On the German response to the internment of Germans in the Netherlands East Indies, see "Berichte über die Dienstbesprechungen bei Generalkommissar Schmidt," July 17, 1940–January 1, 1941, in Rijksinstituut voor Oorlogsdocumentatie (ROD), HSSPF, 54 a.
63. Hirschfeld, *Fremdherrschaft und Kollaboration*, 18–39, 107–16. See also C. Sleeswijk, "On the Famine in Holland in the Spring of 1945," mss. furnished by Mevr. Erin Oudshoorn-van Pallandt.

64. Michael R. Marrus, "Reflections on the Historiography of the Holocaust," *Journal of Modern History* 66 (1994): 106; Warmbrunn, *The Dutch*, 167–70; Hirschfeld, *Fremdherrschaft und Kollaboration*, 24–39; Pinkas Hakehillot, *Geschiedenis van de Joodse Gemeenschap in Nederland*, 162–65, 173, 228–29; Raul Hilberg, *Perpetrators, Victims, Bystanders: The Jewish Catastrophe, 1933–1945*, 78–80, 210–11, 132–35, on the dilatory execution of German edicts in the Netherlands; *Statistiek der Bevolking van Joodschem Bloed in Nederland*, Introduction, Tables I, IV, XII, E; Sijes, *Studies over Jodenvervolging*, 128; Israel Tauber, "The Persecution of Jews in Holland," Jewish Survivors Report, Documents of Nazi Guilt, 2, Archives of the Central British Fund for World Jewish Relief (1933–1960), Reel 14/75; Joseph Michman, "Planning for the Final Solution against the Background of Developments in Holland in 1941." For the record of life in Westerbork, see J. Presser, ed., *In Dépôt. Dagboek uit Westerbork van Philip Mechanicus*, and Jacob Boas, *Boulevard des Misères. The Story of Transit Camp Westerbork.*

65. This dilemma and its destructive consequences are at the heart of André Stein, *Quiet Heroes: True Stories of the Rescue of Jews by Christians in Nazi-occupied Holland.*

66. The most comprehensive treatment of the Dutch Protestant responses to the Nazi phenomenon in Germany remains Roon, *Protestants Nederland.* The following are other useful accounts: J. M. Snoek, *De Nederlandse Kerken en de Joden 1940–1945. De Protesten bij Seyss-Inquart, Hulp aan joodse Onderduikers, de Motieven voor Hulpverleening*, 31, 74–75, and A. F. Manning, "The Dutch Catholics under German Occupation," 196–98.

67. Snoek, *Nederlandse Kerken*, 75–77; Manning, "Dutch Catholics," 199–223; Karl Josef Hahn (himself a Catholic refugee from Nazism in the Netherlands), "Katholischer Widerstand gegen den Nationalsozialismus in den Niederlanden."

68. Warmbrunn, *The Dutch*, 160–63; Minutes of the Protestant Aid Committee, April 11, April 24, June 17, 1940, ROD, 181, I, 1; H. C. Touw, *Het Verzet der Hervormde Kerk*, passim; Snoek, *Nederlandse Kerken*, 88–97, 113–31, and an extensive documentary appendix. The critical observations that the churches could have saved more lives conclude Ger van Roon's "Les Protestants Hollandais pendant la IIe guerre mondiale," *Miscellania Historiae Ecclesiasticae* 9 (1984): 224–39.

69. Miep Lieftinck to writer, September 11, 1993; Minutes, Dutch Yearly Meeting, May 13 and 14, 1939. I owe access to this source to the late clerk of the DYM, Mien Schreuter.

70. Champney to Pickett, October 2, 1939; Pickett to Kappers, November 10, 1939; Kappers Memoranda on operations of Amsterdam Center, December 5 and December 26, 1939, all in AFSC, FS, Netherlands, 1939; Homer and Edna Morris diaries, November 10 and 17, 1939, ibid., loc. cit.

71. Champney to Tritton, December 27, 1939; Collyer to same, January 22, 26, February 16, March 27, 1940; Tel. Sturge to Collyer, April 9, 1940; Collyer to FSC, April 10 (?), 1940, all in FH, FSC, H 1, From Holland, 1939–1947. FSC Minutes June 2, 1944 indicate that Amsterdam Center remained open in 1941. The AFSC *Annual Report* for 1942 merely states: "No information is available for the Amsterdam Center."

72. Minutes, Dutch Yearly Meeting, September 29, 1940; Minutebook, Landescommissie, October 9, 1941, July 12, 1942, January 20, May 22, and May 30, 1944;

Minutes, Amsterdam Monthly Meeting, July 7, 1940, November 11, 1942, and May 22, 1944; *De Vriendenkring*, November 1940. The papers of SS and Police Chief Hanns Albin Rautter, preserved at ROD, contain no evidence of any contact with Friends, nor any response to their communications.

73. Minutes, Amsterdam Monthly Meeting, November 11, 1942; Touw, *Verzet der Hervormde Kerk*, 1939; *De Vriendenkring*, June and December 1943; Report on Dutch Friends by Frits Philipp, Paris, March 8, 1945, *AFSC*, II, Doc. 418, 543–44; Interview with Miep Lieftinck, May 19, 1993.

74. Quaker archives contain a host of scattered indicators of individual contributions to the Pollatz refuge, without, however, revealing exactly what it cost to maintain it and where all of its funds originated. Bracey to Catchpool, February 7, 1936, regrets "the reluctance of Manfred and Lilli Pollatz to budget and estimate in the way most people do." The Dutch Protestant Aid Committee considered assisting them, viz. Luise Lieftinck to A. H. Rutgers, December 19, 1938, ROD, 181, I, 1. Contributions also came from the United States, see Mary Hoxie Jones to Champney, October 5 and November 10, 1939, AFSC, FS, Netherlands, 1939, and at the end of 1939 FSC formed a committee to look after the Pollatzes and their children, Germany and Holland Committee Minutes October 18, December 20, 1939, April 24, 1940, FH, FSC. As late as 1941 Lilli thanked Philadelphia for contributions of $200 and $375, AFSC, FSS, Minutes 1941, and copy of Kappers to Anna Spakler, January 31, 1941, ibid., Holland, Amsterdam Center, 1941.

75. For example, Report by Elizabeth Shipley, August 1, 1934, *AFSC*, I, Doc. 32, 101–2; similarly, Catchpool to Bracey, January 31, 1936, FH, FSC, G 5, 1936.

76. Collyer to Tritton, March 27 and April 1, 1940, ibid., H 1, From Holland, 1939–1947. Italics mine.

77. Elkinton to Pickett, January 19, 1939, AFSC, FS, Netherlands, 1939. See also the announcement in *De Vriendenkring*, September–October 1934: "The school is German and wishes to remain so."

78. Cf., Lilli Pollatz's report on some of the school's methods "Zur Frage der quäkerischen Erziehung. Ein praktischer Versuch als Beitrag," *Der Quäker* (November 1935): 297–98.

79. This is the gist of my interviews with Inge Pollatz, May 20, Chris Hollaender, a retired Dutch school inspector, May 25, and Peter Barns, an English businessman, May 31, 1993. I am very grateful to all three for their willingness to share these recollections and for their generous hospitality.

80. In addition to sources already cited, the section on Manfred and Lilli Pollatz rests on Copy of Letter from Lilli Pollatz, May 20, 1945, *AFSC*, II, Doc. 419, 545–46, "Lebenslauf von Erwin Manfred Pollatz" furnished me by Inge Pollatz, and Manfred Pollatz's petition for Dutch citizenship, June 14, 1946, ROD, II, 362 A. On Karl-Heinz's military career, see Champney to Henry Cadbury, May 29, 1941, AFSC, FS, Holland, Amsterdam Center, 1941; Testimonial by H. Barentsz, July 12, 1945, and an obituary of Manfred (1964), ROD, loc. cit. Both of the latter claim that he served as a physician in the SS. My colleague Charles W. Sydnor, Jr., found no trace of him in the SS officer files at the Berlin Document Center.

81. Kenworthy Diary, December 5, 1940, January 23, 1941, AFSC; Elisabeth to Julius Schmitt, November 15, 1940, Schmitt Papers; Interview with Rose Neuse, October 28, 1992; Minutes of Eerde Finance Committee, October 3, 1941 and September 10, 1942, IISG, Quaker 14.

262   Notes

82. "Schulveranstaltungen," accounts by various students preserved in HFM. Elisabeth to Julius Schmitt, July 12, 1940, loc. cit.
83. Kurt Neuse to Elkinton, September 6, 1941, AFSC, FS, Holland, Ommen, 1941; Kappers to AFSC, November 24, 1941, ibid., Amsterdam Center, 1941. MacMaster to Tritton, Basel, November 1942 copy in possession of Etta Mekeel; Report on Dutch Friends by Frits Philipp, Paris, March 8, 1945, *AFSC*, II, Doc. 418, 543–44; undated report "Friends in Holland," FH, FSC, H. 1. On Wimmer, see N.K.C.A. In't Veld, ed., *De SS in Nederland, Documenten uit SS Archieven 1935–1945*, biographical data, 463–65. Rautter's assessment to Himmler, May 12, 1942, 720–22, concludes a.o. that Wimmer "is pan-German but strongly rooted in Catholicism." See also Kwiet, *Reichskommissariat Niederlande*, 79; *Onderdrukking en Verzet, Nederland in Oorlogstijd*, 4 v. (Arnhem & Amsterdam, n.d.), I, 350–51; Jong, *Koninkrijk der Nederlanden*, 6:99–101. On Wimmer's acquaintance with Piet Kappers: Werner Hermans to writer, April 21, 1993.
84. Point 4 in an open letter by Clemens Brühl to Werner Hermans and a number of other individuals and concerned groups, expressing 14 objections to Hermans' reminiscences "Velen zijn niet meer teruggekomen," *The E.U.R.O.P.A. Herald*, #1, Spring/Summer, 1979, in ROD II, 1360; Richard Schmitt to writer, July 2, 1992 and December 22, 1993; Hermans to writer, April 21, 1993.
85. On Kappers's threat to Frommel, see Claus Bock, *Untergetaucht unter Freunden. Ein Bericht 1942–1945*, 41; Manuel Goldschmidt, "Nu gaan we lezen," in Almar Tjepkema and Jaap Walvis, eds., *"Ondergedoken,"* 59; Miep Lieftinck to writer, March 13, 1995; Robert Wolf to writer, April 4, 1994; Sigmund Lippmann (a student at the castle) to writer, February 23, 1994. On the delivery to Westerbork of individuals caught in hiding, see Presser, *In Dépôt*, 85, 95, 162, 242, and on the continuing illusions about the destination of the deported: Boas, *Boulevard des Misères*, 67, and Louis de Jong, "The Netherlands and Auschwitz," 45–47, 50–53.
86. On precarious existences in Frommel's hideout, Bock, *Untergetaucht*, passim. On other aspects covered in this section: Robert Wolf to writer, April 4, 1994; E[lisabeth] S[chmitt], "Huis 'de Esch' (Pallandthuis) 1941–1943," typescript in AFSC, Case Record of Ursula Bein #18404. On the fate of one of the legal absentees, Otto Edgar Rosenstern, Herbert J. Rosenstern to writer, February 20, 1994, enclosing his brother's last letter, dated June 9, 1941. The fate of the nine deported children is recorded at ROD, Oorlogsgravenstichting, *In Memoriam*, V/91, VI/16, XV/220, 383, XIX/107, XXI/101, XXIII/16, 188, XXV/103, XXX/193. A record of life at segregated De Esch, as seen by the youngest deportee, survives in *Die Tagebücher des Klaus Seckel. Das letzte Stückchen Eerde*. The last entry is dated April 4, 1943, 101–2. See the reviews by Horst Nachmann, "Ich nahm das Kreuz . . . Die Geschichte eines Jungen der nicht mehr leben durfte weil er Jude war," *Frankfurter Rundschau* (March 11, 1961), and Herman B. Besselaer, "De Zeven Dagboeken van Eerde's Ondergang," *Algemeen Handelsblad* (April 29, 1961). Alfred Cohn to writer, April 5, 1994, for the account of Hermann Isaac at Auschwitz. The letters the children wrote are in my possession, and will be deposited in the University of Virginia archives.
87. Minutes of the Eerde Finance Committee, November 30, 1943, IISG, Quaker 14; on Otto Reckendorf, copy of his letter to his sister Angelika, August 19, 1945, sent me by Verena Borton. The fate of the Warburgs is detailed in Chernow, *The Warburgs*, 509–11, and Josi Warburg's letter to American relatives, July 22,

1945, Max Adolph Warburg Papers, kindly furnished by Maria Warburg-Mills. On life at Eerde in the last year of the war, Elisabeth Schmitt to Richard Schmitt, February 15, 18, 21, March 6, 28, April 3, 1945, Schmitt Papers; Richard Neuse to writer, October 21, 1992, and interview with Rose Neuse, October 27, 1992.

88. Roger C. Wilson, *Quaker Relief: An Account of the Relief Work of the Society of Friends, 1940–1948*, 127–28, 167, and Howard Elkinton's "Report on my Third Journey for AFSC," July 10, 1941, AFSC, FS, Relief in various German-occupied countries, 1941; on the Nîmes Committee see Donald A. Lowrie, *Hunted Children*, 82–94 (which, despite its title, deals mostly with hunted adults); Anne Grynberg, *Les camps de la honte. Les internés juifs des camps français (1939–1944)*, 214–59; report "Refugee Problems in Unoccupied France," *AFSC*, II, Doc. 314, 211–13; C. Bleuland van Oordt to John F. Rich, ibid., Doc. 306, 206–7. On Trocmé and his wife's part in the rescue of Jews: Philip P. Hallie, *Lest Innocent Blood Be Shed*. The text of Boegner's appeal to Pétain may be found in *AFSC*, II, Doc. 351, 323–24. For its consequences, see Donald A. Lowrie to Tracy Strong, ibid., Doc. 346, 312–17, and Jacques Adler, "The Changing Attitude by the 'Bystanders' toward the Jews in France, 1940–1943," in Milfull, ed., *Why Germany? National Socialist Anti-Semitism and the European Context*, 178. On the Belgian negotiations, see Hans Thomson to "German agencies concerned," January 8, 1941, introducing James G. Vail; Baron Hoysingen-Huene to Vail, n.d.; Report by Harold Evans and James G. Vail on negotiations with the German government, January–February 1941, all in AFSC, FS, Reports on negotiations with British and German governments, 1941.

89. Wilson, *Quaker Relief*, 181–82, also Clarence Pickett to Epiganio Penetta, September 26, 1941, *AFSC*, II, Doc. 326, 262. On Casablanca, see Lawrence Darton, "An Account," 117 and the exchange between Leslie O. Heath and Robert D. Murphy, January 25, and February 8, 1943, *AFSC*, II, Doc. 376–77, 398–402, 403.

90. Henry P. Thornton, "Report on Miranda and the condition of Refugees in Spain," July 27, 1943, ibid., Doc. 393, 451–54; Pickett to "His Excellency the Ambassador of Spain," April 28, 1944, ibid., Doc. 401, 500–505; Statistical Report from the Madrid Office to Lisbon, January 13, 1945, and Blickenstaff to Lisbon Offices, January 4, 1945. I owe copies of the last two documents to Thomas Conrad.

91. On Quaker activity on behalf of refugees in Japan, see *AFSC*, II, Docs. 333–39, 280–91, and Caroline Cherry's unpublished paper, "Edith Sharpless and the Survival of the Society of Friends in Japan, 1940–1943," presented to the biannual meeting of Quaker archivists and historians at Guilford College, N. C., June 25, 1994. I am grateful to Ms. Cherry for providing me with a copy of her paper.

92. Bailey, "Centenary of Bertha Bracey, 1893–1989," 20, and Bertha Bracey, "Europe's Displaced Persons and the Problems of Relocation," AFSC Refugee Section Report 1941, *AFSC*, II, Doc. 340, 292, and Mary Rogers to Committee for Christian Refugees on conditions in a refugee camp in upstate New York, ibid., Doc. 341, 295–96.

93. Howard, *Midstream*, 122–30. The last quote is taken from the same author's *Across Barriers*, 118.

94. Bailey, "Centenary of Bertha Bracey," loc. cit.

7. The Year 1945 and All That

1. Wilson, *Quaker Relief*, 102–15; Greenwood, *Friends and Relief*, 302, 319.
2. Wilson, *Quaker Relief*, 130–33, 223–73; Stanley Johnson, *Quaker Work for Prisoners of War in South-West France, 1945–1948* (York: Sessions, 1990); Magda Kelber

(herself a refugee from Nazi Germany), *Quäkerhilfswerk Britische Zone 1945–1948*, 11–13; Greenwood, *Friends and Relief,* 317; on conditions in Belsen, see also John Eryl Hall Williams, *A Page of History in Relief: London, Antwerp, Belsen, Brunswick, 1944–1946*, 26–32, 104–6; John W. Perry, "Working among German Prisoners," *The Wayfarer* (October 1945), and reports by William P. Hughes and Elizabeth Fox Howard in *The Friend,* July 20, 1945.

3. Greenwood, *Friends and Relief,* 313, 317. On how the Quaker got their uniforms, and cooperation with military authorities, Wilson, *Quaker Relief,* 116–18, 223.

4. Achim von Borries, "Die Quäker-'Wenig Reden viel—tun,'" 71. On AFSC work in the French zone, see the recently published letters of Joel Carl Welty, *The Hunger Year in the French Zone of Divided Germany, 1946–1947*, passim.

5. Margaret McNeill (an Irish Friend), *By the Rivers of Babylon: A Story of Relief Work among the Displaced Persons of Europe*, 7–9.

6. Kelber, *Britische Zone,* 33.

7. Kelber, *Britische Zone,* 19–21, 33, 38–40; Greenwood, *Friends and Relief,* 320–21, 324; McNeill, *By the Rivers of Babylon,* 85–106.

8. Kelber, *Britische Zone,* 108–11; Greenwood, *Friends and Relief,* 320–22. For a list of volunteers, see Wilson, *Quaker Relief,* 356–73.

9. Welty, *Hunger Year,* 4–7, 9, 19, 71, 308.

10. Welty, *Hunger Year,* 167; Greenwood, *Friends and Belief,* viii, 323, 337; Borries, "Die Quäker," 72–73; Bailey, *Quaker Couple,* 241–42; Joan Hewitt, *Lending a Hand in Holland in 1945–1946*, 1–18 (from which the first quote is taken), and Irwin Abrams, "The Quaker Peace Testimony and the Nobel Peace Prize," in *The Pacifist Impulse in Historical Perspective*, ed. Harvey L. Dyck (Toronto: University of Toronto Press, 1996), 210–16.

11. Tacke, *Lebensbilder deutscher Quäker,* 52–53; "Die Bühnenbildnerin Hanna Jordan. Ein Film von Anna Linsel." I thank Ms. Linsel for lending me a video of her film, made for West German television in 1991. Katharina Petersen, "Das Internierungslager Sandbostel," *Der Quäker* (July–August, 1947): 153–56.

12. Henny Ludewig to Etta Mekeel, January 8, 1947, lent me by the recipient.

13. Anna Halle, "Persönliches zum 8. May 1945," *Die Mahnung* (May 1995); Bailey, *Quaker Couple,* 223–25; Basil Reckitt, *Diary of Military Government in Germany 1945* (Ilfracombe: Elms Court, 1989), 62; Hans Albrecht, "Berlin Diary," June 15, 1945; Albrecht to Pickett, October 9, 1945, in possession of Etta Mekeel.

14. Bailey, *Quaker Couple,* 226–27, 231–35, 240–41, 244.

15. Hans Albrecht Circular to German Friends, August 1946 and Hans Albrecht, "Einige Gedanken über Quäkerschulen in Deutschland," both in possession of Etta Mekeel. For other scant information on re-admissions: Anna Halle to writer, March 19, 1995, and Gerhard Wieding to writer, March 20, 1995. On the October 1946 meeting of the Executive Committee, see *Der Quäker,* September–October 1946: 46–48, 62–63, including the quote (italics mine).

16. See Leonhard Friedrich's unpublished obituary of Hans Albrecht, which I owe to Brenda Bailey.

17. On Fuchs between 1945 and 1947, see Douglas Steere to Margaret Jones, October 12, 1947, on the American interlude: Fuchs' correspondence with Hertha Kraus, especially his letter from Pendle Hill, December 1, 1948, all in Bryn Mawr College Library, Hertha Kraus Papers, Box 5, Folder 4. Also Norman Moss, *Klaus Fuchs, the Man Who Stole the Atom Bomb,* 125–26; Robert Chadwell Williams, *Klaus Fuchs, Atom Spy,* 102–4.

18. Moss, *Klaus Fuchs*, 182–83; Robert Jungk, *Brighter than a Thousand Suns: A Personal History of the Atomic Scientists*, 18–19.
19. *Ruf und Antwort*. Festgabe für Emil Fuchs zum 90. Geburtstag (Leipzig: Köhler & Amelang, 1964), 151, for the summary of Clarence Pickett's contribution. On other distinctions the DDR conferred on him, see Trebs, *Emil Fuchs*, 3–4, 28.
20. Isi Fischer-Sperling, "Und warum hatten die Russen meinen Vater verhaftet?" Copy of mss., provided by the author; Albrecht, "Berlin Diary," May 14, May 20, May 27, June 2–3, June 15.
21. Lachmund, *With Thine Adversary*, 5–6; Karl Wilhelm Fricke, *Politik und Justiz in der DDR. Zur Geschichte der politischen Verfolgung 1945–1968-Berichte und Dokumentation*, 205–15.
22. On the role of non-Marxist parties in the political structure of the DDR, see Hans A. Schmitt, "Men and Politics in East Germany," 236–37. Much of the information in this paragraph is drawn from three *Mitteilungsblätter* that Leonhard Friedrich managed to run off and distribute in October and December 1945, and April 1946. (I owe the copies to Brenda Bailey) and Steere to Jones, October 12, 1947, Bryn Mawr, Hertha Kraus Papers, Box 5/4. The quote is from Hertha Kraus, "Among Friends in Germany," *The Friend* (March 27, 1947). Petersen's OBE was announced in *Der Quäker* (1959): 33.
23. Greenwood, *Friends and Relief*, 325; Rudi Boeck to Hans-Geerd Albrecht, September 12, 1956, in possession of Etta Mekeel. Wilson, *Quaker Relief*, 293, describes joint meetings of worship of Quaker relief workers and Viennese Friends without allusions to the divisive past.
24. Lilli Pollatz to AFSC, *AFSC*, II, Doc. 419, 546–47; interview with Inge Pollatz, May 20, 1993; "Lebenslauf von Herbert Erwin *Manfred* Pollatz," ROD, II, 362 a.
25. AFSC, FS, Holland, 1946 includes a membership list; Copy of "Epistle of Netherlands Yearly Meeting, received 12th June, 1945," FH, FSC, H 1, From Holland, 1939–1947; Interview with Mien Schreuter, May 18, 1993. The Reformed Church also wrestled with this dilemma during the occupation, but many of its pastors decided to help Jews by issuing forged baptismal certificate because it was "God's command to lie in the service of truth," according to J. J. Buskes, Jr., *Waar stond de Kerk? Schets van het kerkelijk Verzet*, 89.
26. *Vriendenkring*, November 1945, March and June 1946. For a resume of the 1945/46 interim: H. Wild, "Eerde again a childrens' home," *Eerde Herald* (April 2, 1946). On the reopening, ibid., March and April, 1946, and Minutes of the Board, June 21, 1946, IISG, Quaker 14; Werner Hermans to writer, April 21, 1993.
27. Writer to Florence A. Schmitt, June 16, September 23, 1945, Schmitt Papers; Rose Neuse to FSC, May 15, and June 4, 1945, and *FSC News Bulletin*, #16, July 1945.
28. Werner Hermans to Klaus Friedeberger, September 9, 1945, copy in possession of Hanna Jordan; Werner Hermans to writer, April 21, 1993; Guusta Veldman, *Knackers achter Prikkeldraat. Kamp Erika bij Ommen*. Thè most comprehensive works on the context of postwar purges of Dutch Nazis, are A. D. Belinfante, *In Plaats van Bijltjesdag. De Geschiedenis van de bijzondere Rechtspleging na de Tweede Wereldoorlog*, and Peter Ronijn, *Snel, Streng en Rechtvaardig. Politiek Beleid inzake de Bestraffing en Reclassering van "foute" Nederlanders, 1945–1955*.
29. The postwar history of Eerde is quite well documented in the Anna Spakler papers at IISG, to whose existence Peter Budde drew my attention. See especially Spakler

to Petersen, October 12, 1948, and Petersen to Spakler, October 29, 1948, IISG, Quaker 12.

30. On Beverweerd, "Quaker School in a Castle," *The Friend* (September 12, 1958).
31. The quote is from the last paragraph of Eliot's *Middlemarch*. Since 1970 Quaker membership in developing countries has risen from 49,000 to 177,000, while membership in North America and Europe has declined. Bolivia, for instance, has slightly more members than Great Britain: Wallace Cayrd, "Dramatic Changes in World Quaker Membership," *Friends Journal* (December 1995): 14.
32. For example, Myrtle Wright to Grace Rhoads, January 20, 1934, AFSC, FS, General, 1934.
33. Carstens, *Margarethe Lachmund*, 37. Woolman's exemplary conversion of Quaker slaveholders still exercises a wider appeal; see the editorial "The Woolman Approach," *The Christian Science Monitor* (March 10, 1995).
34. F. W. Sollmann, *Religion and Politics*, 16–17 (italics mine).
35. Cf., David D. Newsom, "The Flow of Refugees and the World's Response," *The Christian Science Monitor* (December 23, 1992), and Ben Barber, "World's Refugees Told: 'Go Back Home' as West Cringes before a Flood," ibid., August 18, 1994.
36. One among countless examples: Mary Anne Weaver, "Annals of Political Terror: Burying the Martyrs," *The New Yorker* (December 28, 1992–January 4, 1993).
37. American Friends Service Committee, *Annual Report, 1994*.
38. *"An infinite Ocean of Light."* An Address . . . to the Annual Gathering of the American Friends Service Committee, November 17, 1960 (Philadelphia, n.d.), 15.

Bibliography

Unpublished Sources

Amsterdam. Internationaal Instituut voor Sociale Geschiedenis, Quakers 12–14.

Amsterdam. Rijksinstituut voor Oorlogsdocumentatie, 181, I and II, 1, 362A, 1360; HSSPF, 54a.

Bailey, Brenda. "Centenary of Bertha Bracey, 1893–1989: Bertha's Work for German Jewish Refugees." Lecture given at Armscate (Warwickshire) General Meeting, August 8, 1993.

Bayerisches Hauptstaatsarchiv München. Akten des Bayerischen Staatsministeriums des Innern, 76932.

Brown University Archives: Personnel Record of Albert P. Martin.

Bryn Mawr College Library: Hertha Kraus Papers.

Bundesarchiv Koblenz: Reichskanzlei R43; Gestapo R 58/751 and 1135.

Bundesarchiv Potsdam: Zentrales Partei Archiv der SED, Reichssicherheitshauptamt, Abt. IV St. 3/408.

Central British Fund for World Jewish Relief 1933–60: Archives on Microfilm available from Research Publications Ltd., Reading, U.K.

Cherry, Caroline, "Edith Sharpless and the Survival of the Society of Friends in Japan, 1940–1943." Unpub. paper, presented to the biannual meeting of Quaker archivists and historians at Guilford College, N.C., June 25, 1994.

Darton, Lawrence, "An Account of the Work of the Friends Committee for Refugees and Aliens, First Known as the German Emergency Committee of the Society of Friends." London, mimeographed and issued by the Friends Committee for Refugees and Aliens, 1954.

Diözesenarchiv Berlin: Dokumentenauswahl zur Tätigkeit des Hilfswerks beim Bischöflichen Ordinariat: Including correspondence with Büro Grüber and Gestapo, 024194.

Evangelisches Zentralarchiv Berlin: H II and Q, b, 51: Quäker und Friedenskirchen 1919–1927, all part of Friedrich Siegmund-Schultze Papers.

Germany. Auswärtiges Amt: Politisches Archiv, Kultus VI A, Evangelische Angelegenheiten, Vol. 6.

Halle, Anna S. "Quäkerhaltung und -handeln im nationalsozialistischen Deutschland." Unpublished ms. in possession of the author.

Haverford College, Quaker Collection: Rufus Jones Papers.

London. Friends House, Friends Service Committee: GE 5–14, H. 1.

Philadelphia. American Friends Service Committee Archives. Foreign Service Section: Germany 1919–1947; Austria 1934–1942; Netherlands 1931–1947; Kenworthy diary; MacMaster diary; Morris diary; letters from Margaret Jones

Preussisches Geheimes Staatsarchiv, Dahlem: Rep. 90 P, Nr. 58, I.

Sammlung Politisch-Pädagogische Emigration, Professor Hildegard Feidel-Mertz, University of Kassel.

Swarthmore College, Swarthmore Peace Collection: Horace G. Alexander Papers.

University of South Carolina, Thomas Cooper Library: Hurtwood Papers.

University of Virginia, Alderman Library: Heinrich Spiero Papers.

Yad Vashem Archives: 01/17, 01/299, 01/220.

Papers in Private Hands

Hans Albrecht

Else Cappel

Roger Carter

Halle family

Albert P. Martin

Schmitt family

Rudolf Schubert

Hans-Ludwig Waiblinger, "Erinnerungen seiner vier Jahre in Eerde," written at Christmas 1942.

Interviews

Peter Barns. May 31, 1993.

Chris Hollaender. May 15, 1993.

Miep Lieftinck. May 19, 1993.

Rose Neuse. October 27 and 28, 1992.

Erin Oudshoorn-van Pallandt. May 22, 1993.

Inge Pollatz. May 20, 1993.

Mien Schreuter. May 18, 1993.

Correspondents

Brenda Bailey

Anneliese Becker

Verena Borton

Tessa Cadbury-Rowntree

Roger Carter

Alfred Cohn

Isi Fischer-Sperling

Nettie Galjart-Witmer
Eva Gordon
Anna S. Halle
Rolf Helbeck
Werner Hermans
Hanna Jordan
James Lichti
Miep Lieftinck
Sigmund Lippmann
Johannes Lüdecke
Joseph Haines Martin
Richard Slater Martin
Maria Mills-Warburg
Richard Neuse
Erin Oudshoorn-van Pallandt
Herbert J. Rosenstern
Richard G. Schmitt
Esther Charlotte Shalmon-Warburg
Heinrich Unruh
Gerhard Wieding
Robert Wolf

Published Sources

Albrecht, Hans. *Die Begegnung mit der geistigen Situation in Deutschland.* Bad Pyrmont: Quäker Verlag, 1933.

————. *Die Grundlagen der Gemeinschaft.* Bad Pyrmont: Quäker Verlag, 1939.

————. *Was bedeutet Mitgliedschaft bei den Quäkern?* Berlin-Lübars: Quäker Verlag, 1931.

————. *Was ist uns Quäkertum?* Berlin-Lübars: Quäker Verlag, 1930.

Alexander, Horace G. *The Growth of the Peace Testimony of the Society of Friends.* London: Friends Peace Committee, 1939.

Auswärtiges Amt. *Akten zur deutschen auswärtigen Politik 1918–1945.* Series C and D. Baden-Baden: Imp. Nationale, 1951.

Bentwich, Norman. *They Found Refuge: An Account of British Jewry's Work for Victims of Nazi Oppression.* London: Crescent Press, 1956.

Berber, Friedrich. *Europäische Politik 1933–1938 im Spiegel der Prager Akten.* Veröffentlichungen des Deutschen Instituts für Aussenpolitische Forschung, VIII. Essen: Essener Verlagsanstalt, 1942.

————. *Die völkerrechtspolitische Lage Deutschlands.* Schriften der Deutschen Hochschule für Politik, I: Idee und Gestalt des Nationalsozialismus, 21. Berlin: Junker & Dünnhaupt, 1936.

————. *Zwischen Macht und Gewissen. Lebenserinnerungen.* Ed. Ingrid Strauss. Munich: C. H. Beck, 1986.

Boberach, Heinz, ed. *Berichte des SD und der Gestapo über Kirchen und Kirchenvolk in Deutschland 1934–1944.* Veröffentlichungen der Kommission für Zeitgeschichte, A, 12. Mainz: Matthias Grünewald Verlag, 1971.

Bock, Claus. *Untergetaucht unter Freunden. Ein Bericht 1942–1945.* Castrum Peregrini, 166–67. Amsterdam: Castrum Peregrini, 1985.

Brinson, Charmian, and Marian Malet, eds. *Rettet Ossietzky! Dokumente aus dem Nachlass von Rudolf Olden.* Schriftenreihe des Fritz-Küster Archivs. Oldenburg: Universität Oldenburg, 1990.

Butler, Hubert. *The Children of Drancy.* Mullingar: Lilliput Press, 1988.

Buxton, Charles Roden. *The Alternative to War: A Programme for Statesmen,* London: Allen and Unwin, 1936.

Catchpool, Corder. "The Brown Reichskanzler: A Pen Picture from Berlin." *The Friend* (February 10, 1933).

————. *Letters of a Prisoner for Conscience Sake,* London: Allen and Unwin, 1941.

————. *On Two Fronts: Letters of a Conscientious Objector.* The Garland Library of War and Peace. New York and London: Garland, 1972.

Dell, Robert. *Germany Unmasked.* London: Martin Hopkinson, 1934.

Dirksen, Herbert von. *Moscow-Tokyo-London: Twenty Years of German Foreign Policy.* Norman: University of Oklahoma Press, 1952.

Erkens, Rainer, and Horst R. Sassin, eds. *Dokumente zur Geschichte des Liberalismus in Deutschland 1930–1945.* Schriften der Friedrich-Naumann Stiftung-Liberale Texte. Sankt Augustin: COMDOK Verlag, 1989.

Evangelische Hilfsstelle für ehemals Rassenverfolgte in Berlin. *An der Stechbahn. Erlebnisse und Berichte aus dem Büro Grüber in den Jahren der Verfolgung.* East Berlin: Evangelische Verlagsanstalt, 1951.

Friedlander, Henry, and Sybil Milton, eds. *Bundesarchiv of the Federal Republic of Germany, Koblenz and Freiburg.* Archives of the Holocaust, 20. New York and London: Garland, 1993.

Fry, A. Ruth. *A Quaker Adventure: The Story of Nine Years' Relief and Reconstruction.* London: Nisbet, 1926.

Fry, Joan Mary. *In Downcast Germany 1919–1933.* London: James Clarke, 1944.

————. *Offener Brief an die Frankfurter Zeitung.* Frankfurt: Frankfurter Societäts Druckerei, n.d.

Fuchs, Emil. *Mein Leben.* 2 vols. Leipzig: Koehler & Amelang, 1957.

————. *Von Schleiermacher zu Marx.* East Berlin: Union Verlag, 1969.

Gärtner, Margarete. *Botschafterin des guten Willens. Aussenpolitische Arbeit, 1914–1950.* Bonn: Athenäum Verlag, 1955.

Gibbs, Philip. *Across the Frontiers.* London: Michael Joseph, 1938.

————. *The Pageant of the Years: An Autobiography.* London: Heinemann, 1946.

Goldschmidt, Manuel R. "Ernst Morwitz im Gespräch mit Wolfgang Frommel. Aufzeichnungen und Erinnerungen." *Castrum Peregrini* 213 (1994): 7–46.

Grüber, Heinrich. *Erinnerungen aus sieben Jahrzehnten.* Cologne: Kiepenheuer & Witsch, 1968.

Hackett, David A. *The Buchenwald Report.* Boulder, Colo: Westview, 1995.

Halle, Anna Sabine. *"Die Gedanken sind frei . . ." Eine Jugendgruppe der Berliner Quäker, 1935–1941.* Beiträge zum Widerstand, 14. Berlin: Gedenkstätte Politischer Widerstand, 1990. Published first in an English translation by Mary E. B. Feagins as Pendle Hill Pamphlet, 265, Wallingford, Pa., 1985.

Hewitt, Joan. *Lending a Hand in Holland in 1945–1946.* York: William Sessions, 1990.

Hilsley, William. *When Joy and Pain Entwine: Reminiscences.* Werkhoven: International School Beverweerd, n.d.

Howard, Elizabeth Fox. *Across Barriers.* London: Friends' Service Council, 1941.

————. *Downstream: Records of Several Generations.* London: Friends' Home Service Committee, 1955.

————. *Midstream: A Record of Many Years.* London: Friends' Book Center, 1945.

————. *Upstream: A Family Scrapbook.* London: Friends' Book Center, 1944.

Hubben, William. *Exiled Pilgrim.* New York: Macmillan, 1943.

In't Veld, N.K.C.A., ed. *De SS in Nederland, Documenten uit SS Archieven 1935–1945.* Rijksinstituut voor Oorlogsdocumentatie, Bronnenpublicaties, Documenten, 2. The Hague: Martinus Nijhoff, 1976.

Jasper, Gerhard. *Die evangelische Kirche und die Judenchristen.* Göttingen: Vandenhoeck & Ruprecht, 1934.

Jones, Rufus M. *A Service of Love in Wartime: American Friends Relief Work in Europe, 1917–1919.* New York: Macmillan, 1920.

Kantorowicz, Hermann. *Gutachten zur Kriegsschuldfrage 1914.* Frankfurt: Europäische Verlagsanstalt, 1967.

Kantzenbach, Friedrich Wilhelm, ed. *Widerstand und Solidarität der Christen in Deutschland 1933–1945. Eine Dokumentation zum Kirchenkampf aus den Papieren des D. Wilhelm Freiherrn von Pechmann.* Einzelarbeiten aus der Kirchengeschichte Bayerns, 5. Neustadt/Aisch: Degener, 1971.

Kenworthy, Leonard S. *An American Quaker Inside Nazi Germany: Another Dimension of the Holocaust.* Kennett Square, Pa.: Quaker Publications, 1982.

————. *Quaker Education: A Source Book.* Kennett Square, Pa.: Quaker Publications, 1987.

————. *Worldview: The Autobiography of a Social Studies Teacher and Quaker.* Richmond, Ind.: Friends' United Press, 1977.

Klamper, Edith, ed. *Dokumentationsarchiv des österreichischen Widerstands.* Archives of the Holocaust, 19. New York and London: Garland, 1991.

[Koch, Hilde]. *Refugee.* New York: Prentice-Hall, 1940.

Lachmund, Margarethe. *With Thine Adversary in the Way: A Quaker Witness for Reconciliation.* Pendle Hill Pamphlet, 228. Wallingford, Pa.: Pendle Hill Publications, 1979.

Lansbury, George. *My Pilgrimage for Peace.* New York: Henry Holt, 1938.

Lietz, Hermann. *Lebenserinnerungen,* ed. with letters and reports by Alfred Andreesen. Weimar: Hermann Lietz Verlag, 1935.

————. *Von Leben und Arbeit eines deutschen Erziehers.* Veckenstedt a/H: Verlag des Landwaisenheimes, n.d.

Mendelsohn, John, ed. *The Holocaust: Selected Documents in Eighteen Volumes.* Vols. 5 and 6. New York and London: Garland, 1982.

Mensching, Wilhelm. *Conscience.* Pendle Hill Pamphlet, 117. Wallingford, Pa.: Pendle Hill Publications, 1980.

Morsey, Rudolf, ed. "Zwei Gestapo Berichte zur Geschichte des Kirchenkampfes in den Jahren 1938 und 1939." *Wichmann Jahrbuch* 17/18 (1963/1964): 3–23.

Netherlands. Bevolkingsregisters. Rijksinspektie Statistiek. *Statistiek der Bevolking van joodschem Bloede in Nederland.* The Hague: Algemene Landsdrukkerij, 1942.

Niemöller, Wilhelm, ed. *Die Synode zu Steglitz. Geschichte-Dokumente-Berichte.* Arbeiten zur Geschichte des Kirchemkampfes, 21. Göttingen: Vandenhoeck & Ruprecht, 1975.

Papanek, Ernst. *Out of the Fire.* New York: Morrow, 1975.

Paquet, Alfons. *The Quakers.* Leominster: The Orphans' Printing Press, 1921? Translation of an article that originally appeared in the *Frankfurter Zeitung,* June 27, 1920.

Presser, J., ed. *In Dépôt. Dagboek uit Westerbork van Philip Mechanicus.* Amsterdam: Polak & Van Gennep, 1964.

Rosenfeld, Else, and Gertrud Luckner, eds. *Lebenszeichen aus Piaski.* Munich: Biederstein Verlag, 1968.

Rotten, Elisabeth. *Durch welche Schulen könnten pädagogisch und sozial die Aufgaben einer quäkerischen Erziehung verwirklicht werden?* Berlin-Lübars: Quäker Verlag, 1930.

Schmitt, Hans A. *Lucky Victim: An Ordinary Life in Extraordinary Times.* Baton Rouge: Louisiana State University Press, 1989.

Schulze-Gävernitz, Gerhart von. *Democracy and Religion: A Study in Quakerism.* Swarthmore Lecture, 1930. London: Allen & Unwin, 1930.

Sutters, Jack. *American Friends Service Committee.* Archives of the Holocaust, 2, in two parts. New York and London: Garland, 1993.

Tacke, Käte, ed. *Lebensbilder deutscher Quäker während der NS Herrschaft 1933–1945. Sammlung von Schicksalen aus der Erinnerung, aus Briefen, Zeitungsartikeln und anderen Dokumenten.* Quäkerhaltung im 20 Jahrhundert, 1. Bad Pyrmont: Quäker Verlag, 1992.

Die Tagebücher des Klaus Seckel. Das letzte Stückchen Eerde. Assen: Van Gorcum, 1961.

Tjepkema, Almar, and Jaap Walvis, eds. *"Ondergedoken."* Weesp: De Haan, 1985.

Welty, Joel Carl. *The Hunger Year in the French Zone of Divided Germany, 1946–1947.* Beloit, Wis.: Beloit College, 1993.

Wijsmuller-Meyer, Truus. *Geen Tijd voor Tranen.* Amsterdam: P. N. van Kampen en Zoon, [1963?].

Woodward, E. L. et al., eds. *Documents on British Foreign Policy, 1919–1939.* Series 3, II. London: HMSO, 1938.

Secondary Works

Abella, Irving, and Harold Troper. *None Is Too Many: Canada and the Jews of Europe, 1933–1948.* Toronto: Lester and Orpen Dennys, 1982.

Abraham, Henry J. *Freedom and the Court: Civil Rights and Liberties in the United States.* 5th ed. Oxford and New York: Oxford University Press, 1988.

Abrams, Irwin. *The Nobel Peace Prize and the Laureates.* Boston: G. K. Hall, 1988.

Adam, Uwe Dietrich. *Judenpolitik im Dritten Reich.* Tübinger Schriften zur Sozial- und Zeitgeschichte, 1. Düsseldorf: Droste Verlag, 1972.

Adams, Walter. "Extent and Nature of the World Refugee Problem." *Annals of the American Academy of Political and Social Science* 203 (1939): 26–36.

Adler, Jacques. "The Changing Attitude by the 'Bystanders' toward the Jews in France, 1940–1943." In *Why Germany? National Socialist Anti-Semitism and the European Context,* ed. John Milfull. Providence and Oxford: Berg, 1993.

Albrecht, Richard. *Der militante Sozialdemokrat Carlo Mierendorff 1897 bis 1943. Eine Biographie.* Berlin and Bonn: Dietz Nachf, 1987.

Alexander, Horace G. *The Growth of the Peace Testimony of the Society of Friends.* London: Friends Peace Committee, 1939.

Aly, Götz, and Karl Heinz Roth. *Die restlose Erfassung. Volkszählen, Identifizieren, Aussondern im Nationalsozialismus.* Berlin: Rotbuch Verlag, 1984.

Anderson, Mosa. *Noël-Buxton: A Life.* London: Allen and Unwin, 1952.

Andreesen, Alfred. *Hermann Lietz. Der Schöpfer der Landerziehungsheime.* Munich: J. F. Lehmann, 1934.

Angress, Werner T. "Auswandererlehrgut Gross-Breesen." *Leo Baeck Institute Year Book* 10 (1965): 168–87.

Anschütz, Gerhard. "Wandlungen der deutschen evangelischen Kirchenverfassung." *Zeitschrift für öffentliches Recht* 20 (1940): 231–44.

Appelius, Stefan. *Pazifismus in Westdeuschland 1945–1968.* 2 vols. Aachen: G. Mainz, 1991.

Bacon, Margaret Hope. *Let This Life Speak: The Legacy of Henry Joel Cadbury.* Philadelphia: University of Pennsylvania Press, 1987.

Badia, Gilbert. *Les bannis de Hitler. Accueil et lutte des exilés allemands en France 1933–1939.* Paris: Presses Universitaires de Vincennes, 1984.

Baier, Helmut. "Zwischen Anpassung und Widerstand. Evangelisches kirchliches Leben." In Centrum Industriekultur, *Unterm Hakenkreuz. Alltag in Nürnberg 1933–1945.* Munich: Hugenduber, 1983.

Bailey, Brenda. *A Quaker Couple in Nazi Germany.* York: William Session, 1994.

Bailey, Sydney D. *Peace Is a Process.* Swarthmore Lecture 1993. London: Quaker Home Service, 1993.

Baranowski, Shelley. "From Rivalry to Repression: The German Protestant Leadership, Anti-Leftism and Anti-Semitism, 1933." *Holocaust Studies Annual* 2 (1986): 28–44.

Barnett, Victoria. *For the Soul of the People: Protestant Protest against Hitler.* New York: Oxford University Press, 1992.

Bartosek, Karel et al., eds. *De l'éxile à la résistance, Réfugiés et immigrés d'Europe Centrale en France 1933–1945.* Saint Denis: Presses Universitaires de Vincennes, 1989.

Baumann, Arnulf H., ed. *Ausgegrenzt. Schicksalswege 'nichtarischer' Christen in der Hitlerzeit.* Hanover: Lutherisches Verlagshaus, 1992.

Belinfante, A. D. *In Plaats van Bijltjesdag. De Geschiedenis van de bijzondere Rechtspleging na de Tweede Wereldoorlog.* Assen: Van Gorcum, 1978.

Bentz, Wolfgang, ed. *Die Juden in Deutschland 1933–1945. Leben unter nationalsozialistischer Herrschaft.* Munich: C. H. Beck, 1988.

Berber, Friedrich. "Epochen europäischer Gesamtordnung." *Donaueuropa* 2 (1942): 729–38.

Bergen, Doris L. "Catholics, Protestants and Anti-Semitism in Nazi Germany." *Central European History* 27 (1994): 329–48.

Berghahn, Marion. *German Jewish Refugees in England: The Ambiguities of Assimilation.* New York: St. Martin's Press, 1984.

Blaich, Roland. "Religion under National Socialism: The Case of the German Adventist Church." *Central European History* 26 (1993): 255–80.

Blakeney, Michael. *Australia and the Jewish Refugees, 1933–1948.* Sydney: Croom Helm, 1985.

Blau, Bruno. "The Jewish Population of Germany, 1939–1945." *Jewish Social Studies* 12 (1956): 161–72.

Boas, Jacob. *Boulevard des Misères. The Story of Transit Camp Westerbork.* Hamden, Conn.: Shoe String Press, 1985.

Böckenförde, Ernst-Wolfgang. "Der deutsche Katholizismus im Jahre 1933. Eine kritische Betrachtung." *Hochland* 53 (1960/1961): 215–39.

Borries, Achim von. "Die Quäker—'Wenig reden—viel tun.'" In vol. 6 of *Der Friedens-Nobelpreis von 1901 bis Heute.* Zug: Edition Pacis, 1987.

Boyens, Armin. *Kirchenkampf und Ökumene 1933–1939.* Munich: Chr. Kaiser, 1969.

Bracey, Bertha. "Europe's Displaced Persons and the Problem of Relocation." *International Affairs* 20 (1944): 225–42.

Bracher, Karl Dietrich. "Kirche in der Diktatur: Die deutsche Erfahrung von 1933/34." In vol. 1 of *Das Unrechtsregime: Internationale Forschung über den Nationalsozialismus,* ed. Ursula Büttner. Hamburg: Hans Christians, 1986.

Brakelmann, Günter. "Die Bochumer Bekenntnisse des Jahres 1933. Ein Meilenstein auf dem Weg nach Barmen." In vol. 1 of *Das Unrechtsregime: Internationale Forschung über den Nationalsozialismus,* ed. Ursula Büttner. Hamburg: Hans Christians, 1986.

Brakelmann, Günter, and Martin Rosowski, eds. *Antisemitismus. Von religiöser Judenfeindschaft zur Rassentheologie.* Göttingen: Vandenhoeck & Ruprecht, 1989.

Bredemeier, Karsten. *Kriegsdienstverweigerung im Dritten Reich. Ausgewählte Beispiele.* Baden-Baden: Nomos, 1991.

Bregenzer, Richard. "Erinnerungen an Wolfgang Frommel." *Castrum Peregrini* 202 (1992): 32–50.

Breitmann, Richard, and Alan M. Kraut, *American Refugee Policy and European Jewry, 1933–1945.* Bloomington: University of Indiana Press, 1987.

Brinton, Howard H. *Friends for 300 Years.* Wallingford, Pa.: Pendle Hill Publications, 1965.

———. *Quaker Education in Theory and Practice.* Rev. ed. Pendle Hill Pamphlet, 9. Wallingford, Pa.: Pendle Hill Publications, 1949.

Brock, Peter. *The Quaker Peace Testimony, 1660 to 1914.* York: Sessions Book Trust, 1990.

Browning, Christopher R. *The Path to Genocide.* Cambridge: Cambridge University Press, 1992.

Bryan, Alex. *Corder Catchpool: A Hero Who Never Made Heroic Gestures.* London: Quaker Home Service, 1982.

Budde, Peter. "Die Internationale Quäkerschule in Eerde/Holland. Im Geiste praktischer Nächstenliebe und kraftvoller Toleranz." In *Schulen im Exil. Die verdrängte Pädagogik nach 1933,* ed. Hildegard Feidel-Mertz. Einbeck/Hamburg: Rohwolt, 1983.

———. "Katharina Petersen und die Quäkerschule Eerde. Eine Dokumentationscollage." In *Aufklärung als Lernprozess,* ed. Monika Schumann and

Hermann Schnorbach. Festschrift für Hildegard Feidel-Mertz. Frankfurt: dipa Verlag, 1992.

Bullinger, Adelheid. "Das Ende des landesherrlichen Kirchenregiments und die Neugestaltung der evangelischen Kirche." *Zeitschrift für evangelisches Kirchenrecht* 19 (1967): 73–105.

Bunsen, Victoria de. *Charles Roden Buxton: A Memoir.* London: Allen and Unwin, 1948.

Buskes, J. J., Jr. *Waar stond de Kerk? Schets van het kerkelijk Verzet.* De Volkspaedagogische Bibliotheek, 3. Amsterdam: Uitgeverij Vrij Nederland, 1947.

Büttner, Ursula. "The Persecution of Christian-Jewish Families in the Third Reich." *Leo Baeck Institute Year Book* 35 (1989): 267–89.

Caron, Vicki. "The Politics of Frustration: French Jewry and the Refugee Crisis in the 1930s." *Journal of Modern History* 65 (1993): 311–56.

Carsten, Francis L. "Die Quäker in Deutschland 1919–1924." In vol. 2 of *Deutschland und Europa in der Neuzeit,* ed. Ralph Melville et al., eds. Festschrift für Karl Otmar Freiherr von Aretin zum 65. Geburtstag. Wiesbaden: Steiner, 1988.

Carstens, Heinrich, ed. *Margarethe Lachmund zum 80. Geburtstag.* Vienna: Sensen Verlag, 1976.

Carter, Roger. "Das Internationale Quäkerbüro Berlin 1920–1942." *Der Quäker* (July–August 1995): 160–69.

———. "The Quaker International Center in Berlin, 1920–1942." *The Journal of the Friends' Historical Society* 56 (1990): 15–31.

———. "Die Religiöse Gesellschaft der Freunde zur Zeit der NS-Diktatur." *Ökumenische Rundschau* 34 (1985): 370–73.

Cary, Richard. "Le foyer-cantine français de Berlin." *L'Echo des Amis* (January 1933): 4–5.

Cassel, Wolf van. "Wolfgang Frommel, poeta et amicus." *Castrum Peregrini* 184/5 (1988): 16–26.

Chernow, Ron. *The Warburgs: The 20th Century Odyssey of a Remarkable Jewish Family.* New York: Random House, 1993.

Cochavi, Yehoyakim. "The 'Hostile Alliance': The Relationship between the Reichsvereinigung of Jews in Germany and the Regime." *Yad Vashem Studies* 22 (1992): 241–54.

Cohen, David. *Zwervend en dolend. De Joodse vluchtelingen in Nederland in de jaren 1933–1940.* Haarlem: Erven F. Bohn, 1955.

Cohn, Werner. "Bearers of a Common Fate? The 'Non-Aryan' Christian 'Fate-Comrades' of the Paulus Bund, 1933–1939." *Leo Baeck Institute Year Book* 33 (1980): 327–66.

Commissie voor Demografie der Joden in Nederland. *De Joden in Nederland na de Tweede Wereldoorlog.* Amsterdam: Joachimsthal's Uitgeverij, 1961.

Dahm, Karl Wilhelm. "German Protestantism and Politics, 1918–1939." *Journal of Contemporary History* 3 (1968): 29–49.

————. *Pfarrer und Politik. Soziale Position und politische Mentalität des deutschen evangelischen Pfarrerstandes zwischen 1918 und 1933.* Dortmunder Schriften zur Sozialforschung, 29. Cologne: Kiepenheuer & Witsch, 1965.

Dinnerstein, Leonard. *Antisemitism in America.* New York and Oxford: Oxford University Press, 1994.

Dipper, Christof. "The German Resistance and the Jews." *Yad Vashem Studies* 17 (1984): 51–93.

Dirks, Gerald E. *Canada's Refugee Policy: Indifference or Opportunism?* Montreal and London: McGill-Queen's University Press, 1977.

Dittrich, Kathinka, and Hans Würzner, eds. *Die Niederlande und das deutsche Exil 1933–1940.* Königstein i. T.: Athenäum, 1982.

Doderer, Otto. "Alfons Paquet." In vol. 3 of *Nassauische Lebensbilder.* Veröffentlichungen der Historischen Kommission für Nassau, X. Wiesbaden: Historische Kommission, 1948.

Drescher, Paul Otto. "Assistent in Frankfurt. Mit Wolfgang Frommel am Rundfunk 1933." *Castrum Peregrini* 213 (1994): 47–59.

Drobisch, Klaus, and Gerhard Fischer, eds. *Widerstand aus Glauben. Christen in der Auseinandersetzung mit dem Hitlerfaschismus.* East Berlin: Union Verlag, 1985.

Dunn, Brian. "Jehovah's Witnesses in the Holocaust Kingdom." *Holocaust Studies Annual* 2 (1986): 155–72.

Eichstätt, Ulrich. *Von Dollfuss zu Hitler. Geschichte des Anschlusses Österreichs 1933–1938.* Veröffentlichungen des Instituts für europäische Geschichte, Mainz, 10. Wiesbaden: Franz Steiner, 1955.

Elkinton, J. Russell. "Quakers and Dukhobors." *Friends Journal* (November 1995): 16–19.

Evangelische Hilfsstelle für ehemals Rassenverfolgte. *Das "Büro Pfarrer Grüber" 1938–1940.* Berlin: EHR, 1988.

Fehrenbach, Elisabeth. *Wandlungen des deutschen Kaisergedankens 1871–1918.* Studien zur Geschichte des neunzehnten Jahrhunderts, 1. Munich and Vienna: R. Oldenbourg, 1969.

Feidel-Mertz, Hildegard, and Jürgen P. Krause, *Der andere Hermann Lietz. Theo Zollmann und das Landwaisenheim Veckenstedt.* Pädagogische Beispiele. Institutionsgeschichte in Einzeldarstellungen, 6. Frankfurt: dipa-Verlag, 1989.

Feurich, Anneliese et al., eds. *Juden und Christen, Kinder eines Vaters. Beiträge zur Pogromnacht 9/10 November 1938.* Dresden: Kirchliche Bruderschaft Sachsens, 1988.

Fischel, Jack R. "The North American Mennonites' Response to Hitler's Persecution of the Jews." *Holocaust Studies Annual* 2 (1986): 141–54.

Fogelmann, Eva. *Conscience and Courage: Rescuers of Jews during the Holocaust.* New York: Anchor, 1992.

Fox, John. "British Attitudes to Jewish Refugees from Central and Eastern Europe in the Nineteenth and Twentieth Centuries." In *Second Chance: Two Centuries of German-Speaking Jews in the United Kingdom,* ed. W. E. Mosse et al. Tübingen: Mohr, 1991.

Frei, Alfred G. "'In the End I Just Said O.K.': Political and Moral Dimensions of Escape at the Swiss Border." *Journal of Modern History* 64 (supplement, 1992): 68–81.

Fricke, Karl Wilhelm. *Politik und Justiz in der DDR. Zur Geschichte der politischen Verfolgung 1945–1968-Berichte und Dokumentation.* Cologne: Berend, 1979.

Friends' Service in Germany. London: Friends Service Council, 1937.

Frost, J. William. "'Our Deeds Carry Our Message': The Early History of the American Friends Service Committee." *Quaker History* 81 (1992): 1–52.

Genizi, Haim. *American Apathy: The Plight of German Refugees from Nazism.* Ramat Gen: Bar-Ilan University, 1983.

———. "American Non-Sectarian Refugee Relief Organizations (1933–1945)." *Yad Vashem Studies* 11 (1976): 164–220.

Gerlach, Wolfgang. *Als die Zeugen schwiegen. Bekennende Kirche und die Juden.* Berlin: Institut Kirche und Judentum, 1987.

Gershon, Karen, ed. *We Came as Children.* London: Papermac, 1989.

Gesellschaft der Freunde in Deutschland. *Begegnung mit dem Judentum. Ein Gedenkbuch.* Bad Pyrmont: Quäker Verlag, 1962.

Gilbert, Martin. "British Government Policy towards Jewish Refugees (November 1938–September 1939)." *Yad Vashem Studies* 13 (1979): 127–67.

———. *Plough My Own Furrow: The Story of Lord Allen of Hurtwood as Told through his Writings and Correspondence.* London: Longmans, Green, 1965.

———. *The Roots of Appeasement.* New York: New American Library, 1966.

Gillett, Henry T. *The Spiritual Basis of Democracy: The Living Way.* Oxford: Basil Blackwell, 1952.

Greaves, Jean Corder. *Corder Catchpool.* London: Friends Home Service, 1953.

Greenwood, John O. *Friends and Relief.* Vol. 1 of *Quaker Encounters.* York: William Sessions, 1975.

Greive, Hermann. *Theologie und Ideologie. Katholizismus und Judentum in Deutschland und Österreich 1918–1935.* Heidelberg: Lambert Schneider, 1969.

Griffiths, Richard. *Fellow Travellers for the Right: British Enthusiasm for Nazi Germany, 1933–39.* London and New York: Oxford University Press, 1983.

Grill, John Peter Horst, and Robert L. Jenkins. "The Nazis and the American South in the 1930s: A Mirror Image." *The Journal of Southern History* 58 (1992): 667–94.

Grossmann, Kurt R. *Die unbesungenen Helden. Menschen in Deutschlands dunklen Tagen.* 2nd ed. Frankfurt: Ullstein, 1961.

Grynberg, Anne. *Les camps de la honte. Les internés juifs des camps français (1939–1944).* Paris: Editions de la Découverte, 1991.

Gutteridge, Richard. *Open Thy Mouth for the Dumb: The German Evangelical Church and the Jews, 1879–1950.* Oxford: Blackwell, 1976.

Hahn, Karl Josef. "Katholischer Widerstand gegen den Nationalsozialismus in den Niederlanden." *Hochland* 57 (1964/1965): 232–53.

Hahn, Kurt. "Die nationale Aufgabe der Landenziehungsheime." *Die Eiche* 19 (1931): 319–34.

Hakehillot, Pinkas. *Geschiedenis van de Joodse Gemeenschap in Nederland.* Amsterdam: Ede, 1992.

Hall, Willis H. *Quaker International Work in Europe since 1914.* Chambéry (Savoie): Imprimeries Réunies, 1938.

Halle, Anna S. "Ein altes Buch-heute noch lebendig (Aus Protokollen der Berliner Quäkergruppe 1920–1939)." *Der Quäker* (July 1975): 201–5.

———. "The German Quakers in the Third Reich." *German History* 11 (1993): 222–36.

Halle, Gerhard. "Kriegsdienst und Gewissen." *Der Quäker* (August 1932): 215–23.

Hallie, Philip P. *Lest Innocent Blood Be Shed.* New York: Harper and Row, 1979.

Hansen, Eckhard. *Wohlfahrtspolitik im NS Staat. Motivationen, Konflikte und Machtstrukturen im 'Sozialismus der Tat' des Dritten Reiches.* Beiträge zur Sozialpolitik-Forschung, 6. Augsburg: Maro Verlag, 1991.

Hartmann, Albrecht, and Heidi Hartmann. *Kriegsdienstverweigerung im Dritten Reich.* Frankfurt: Haag and Herchen, 1986.

Hatton, Helen E. *The Largest Amount of Good: Quaker Relief in Ireland, 1654–1921.* Kingston and Montreal: McGill-Queen's University Press, 1993.

Heideking, Jürgen. "Gero von Schulze-Gävernitz. Deutscher Patriot im amerikanischen Geheimdienst." In *Der Widerstand im deutschen Südwesten, 1933–1945,* ed. Michael Bosch and Wolfgang Niess. Stuttgart: Kohlhammer, 1984.

Helbeck, Paul. "Deutsche Kriegsdienstverweigerer vor hundert Jahren." *Die Eiche* 11 (1924): 171–77.

Herwig, Anneliese. *Ein Lebensbild von Gilbert MacMaster (1869–1967) und seiner Lebensgefährtin Marga (1879–1967) nach seinen eigenen Aufzeichnungen.* Bad Pyrmont: Quäkerhaus, 1969.

Hewison, Hope H. *Hedge of Wild Almonds: South Africa, the Pro-Boers and the Quaker Conscience, 1890–1910.* Portsmouth, N.H.: Heinemann, 1989.

Hilberg, Raul. *Perpetrators, Victims, Bystanders: The Jewish Catastrophe, 1933–1945.* New York: Harper Collins, 1992.

Hildesheimer, Esriel. "Cora Berliner. Ihr Leben und Wirken." *Leo Baeck Institute Bulletin* 67 (1984): 41–70.

Hirsch, Felix E. "William Sollmann: Wanderer between Two Worlds." *The South Atlantic Quarterly* 52 (1953): 207–27.

Hirschfeld, Gerhard. *Fremdherrschaft und Kollaboration. Die Niederlande unter deutscher Besatzung 1940–1945.* Studien zur Zeitgeschichte, 25. Stuttgart: DVA, 1984.

———. "A 'High Tradition of Eagerness,' British Non-Jewish Organizations in Support of Refugees." In *Second Chance: Two Centuries of German-Speaking Jews in the United Kingdom,* ed. W. E. Mosse et al. Tübingen: Mohr, 1991.

Holmes, Colin. *John Bull's Island: Immigration and British Society 1871–1971.* London: Macmillan, 1988.

Homan, Walter Joseph. *Children and Quakerism.* Reprint. New York: Arno Press, 1972.

Hopf, Hans. "Auswirkungen des Verhältnisses Litauens zu seinen Nachbarn auf das Memelgebiet. Zur Vorgeschichte des deutsch-litauischen Staatsvertrages vom 22. März 1939." *Jahrbuch der Albertus-Universität zu Königsberg/Pr.* 12 (1962): 235–70.

Hubben, Wilhelm. "In einem amerikanischen Landschulheim." *Pädagogische Warte* (July 15, 1931): 617–19.

———. *Die Quäker in der deutschen Vergangenheit.* Leipzig: Quäker Verlag, 1929.

Hughes, John Jay. "The Reich Concordat 1933: Capitulation or Compromise?" *The Australian Journal of Politics and History* 20 (1974): 161–71.

Hughes, William R. *Indomitable Friend: The Life of Corder Catchpool, 1883–1952.* London: Allen and Unwin, 1956.

Huxley, Aldous. *Crome Yellow.* London: Phoenix Library, Chatto and Windus, 1928.

Ingle, H. Larry. *First among Friends: George Fox and the Creation of Quakerism.* New York and Oxford: Oxford University Press, 1994.

Jackisch, Carlota. *El Nazismo y los refugiados alemanes en la Argentina, 1933–1945.* Buenos Aires: Fundacion Editorial de Belgrano, 1989.

Jacobeit, Sigrid, and Lieselotte Thoms-Heinrich. *Kreuzweg Ravensbrück. Lebensbilder antifaschistischer Widerstandskämpferinnen.* Frankfurt: Röderberg Verlag, n.d.

Jasper, Ronald C. D. *George Bell, Bishop of Chichester.* London: Oxford University Press, 1973.

Jeanrod, Werner G. "From Resistance to Liberation Theology: German Theologians and the Non/Resistance to the National Socialist Regime." *Journal of Modern History* 64 (supplement, 1992): 187–203.

Jonas, Manfred. *The United States and Germany: A Diplomatic History.* Ithaca: Cornell University Press, 1984.

Jones, Lester M. *Quakers in Action: Recent Humanitarian and Reform Activities of the American Quakers.* New York: Macmillan, 1929.

Jones, Mary Hoxie. *Swords into Ploughshares: An Account of the American Friends Service Committee, 1917–1937.* Reprint, Westport, Conn.: Greenwood, 1971.

Jones, Rufus. *The Later Period of Quakerism.* 2 vols. London: Macmillan, 1921.

Jong, Louis de. *Het Koninkrijk der Nederlanden in de Tweede Wereldoorlog.* 13 vols. The Hague: Nijhoff, 1969–1991.

———. "The Netherlands and Auschwitz." *Yad Vashem Studies* 7 (1968): 45–53.

Jungk, Robert. *Brighter than a Thousand Suns: A Personal History of the Atomic Scientists.* New York: Harcourt, Brace, Jovanovich, 1958.

Kaiser, Jochen-Christoph. "Protestantismus, Diakonie und 'Judenfrage' 1931–1941." *Vierteljahrshefte für Zeitgeschichte* 37 (1989): 673–714.

Kater, Michael H. "Die ernsten Bibelforscher im Dritten Reich." *Vierteljahrshefte für Zeitgeschichte* 17 (1969): 181–218.

Kelber, Magda. *Quäkerhilfswerk Britische Zone 1945–1948.* Bad Pyrmont: Leonhard Friedrich, 1949.

Kelly, Richard M. *Thomas Kelly: A Biography.* New York: Harper and Row, 1966.

King, Christine E. "Strategies for Survival: An Examination of the History of Five Christian Sects in Germany, 1933–1945." *Journal of Contemporary History* 14 (1979): 211–34.

Klemperer, Klemens von. "The Solitary Witness: One More Footnote to Resistance Studies." In *Contending with Hitler: Varieties of German Resistance in the Third Reich,* ed. David Clay Large. New York: Cambridge University Press, 1991.

Koblik, Steven. *The Stones Cry Out: Sweden's Response to the Persecution of the Jews.* New York: Holocaust Library, 1988.

Königswald, Harald von. *Birger Forell. Leben und Wirken in den Jahren 1933–1938.* Witten and Berlin: Eckart Verlag, 1962.

Kooy, G. A. *Het Echec van een 'Volkse' Beweging. Nazi- en Denazificatie in Nederland 1931–1945.* Assen: Van Gorcum, 1964.

Köppen, Werner. *Die Schule Schloss Salem.* Heidelberger Studien zur Erziehungswissenschaft. Ratingen nr. Düssseldorf: A. Henn, 1967.

Kramer, David. "Jewish Welfare Work under the Impact of Pauperization." In *The Jews in Nazi Germany, 1933–1945,* ed. Arnold Paucker. Leo Baeck Institute, Schriftenreihe wissenschaftlicher Arbeiten, 45. Tübingen: Mohr, 1986.

Kraus, Hans-Joachim. "Die evangelische Kirche." In *Entscheidungsjahr 1932,* ed. W. E. Mosse and Arnold Paucker. Tübingen: Mohr, 1966.

Kraus, Hertha. "Among Friends in Germany." *The Friend* (March 27, 1947): 22–24.

———. *International Relief in Action, 1914–1943.* Scottsdale, Pa.: Herald Press, 1944.

Kühl, Stefan. *The Nazi Connection: Eugenics, American Racism and German National Socialism.* New York and Oxford: Oxford University Press, 1994.

Kunze, Bonnelyn Young. *Margaret Fell and the Rise of Quakerism.* London: Macmillan, 1994.

Kwiet, Konrad. *Reichskommissariat Niederlande. Versuch und Scheitern nationalsozialistischer Neuordnung.* Schriften der Vierteljahrshefte für Zeitgeschichte, 17. Stuttgart: DVA, 1968.

Lambooy, D. J. "Les Bays-Bas et le problème des réfugiés." *Annuaire Grotius* (1939): 25–52.

Lawson, Bernard G. *The Overseas and International Service of British and Irish Friends in the 20th Century (to 1961).* Beaconsfield, England: The Author, 1962.

Lehmann, Hans G. "Ernst Reuter's Entlassung aus dem Konzentrationslager." *Archiv für Sozialgeschichte* 13 (1973): 483–508.

Lichdi, Diether Götz. *Mennoniten im Dritten Reich. Dokumentation und Deutung.* Schriftenreihe des Mennonitischen Geschichtsvereins, 9. Weierhof/Pfalz: Mennonitischer Geschichtsverein, 1977.

Lichti, James Irwin. "The German Mennonite Response to the Dissolution of the Rhoen-Bruderhof." *Mennonite Life* (June 1991): 10–17.

London, Louise. "British Reactions to the Jewish Flight from Europe." In *Britain and the Threat to Stability in Europe, 1918–1945,* ed. Peter Catterall. London and New York: Leicester University Press, 1993.

Lowrie, Donald A. *The Hunted Children.* New York: W. W. Norton, 1963.

Ludlow, Peter. "The Refugee Problem in the 1930s: The Failures and Successes of Protestant Relief Programmes." *English Historical Review* 90 (1975): 564–603.

Ludwig, Carl. *Die Flüchtlingspolitik der Schweiz seit 1933 bis zur Gegenwart (1957).* Bern: Herbert Lang, 1966.

Luža, Radomir V. *Austro-German Relations in the Anschluss Era.* Princeton: Princeton University Press, 1975.

———. *The Resistance in Austria, 1938–1945.* Minneapolis: University of Minnesota Press, 1984.

Maltby, S. F. "A Significant Experiment." *The New Era in Home and School* (March 1935): 82–83.

Manning, A. F. "The Dutch Catholics under German Occupation." *Miscellania Historiae Ecclesiasticae* 9 (1984): 196–223.

Marggraf, Eckhart. "Hermann Maas. Evangelischer Pfarrer und 'stadtbekannter Judenfreund.'" In *Der Widerstand im deutschen Südwesten, 1933–1945,* ed. Michael Bosch and Wolfgang Niess. Stuttgart: Kohlhammer, 1984.

Marwick, Arthur. *Clifford Allen: The Open Conspirator.* Edinburgh and London: Oliver and Boyd, 1964.

McNeill, Margaret. *By the Rivers of Babylon: A Story of Relief Work among the Displaced Persons of Europe.* London: Bannisdale Press, 1950.

Meier, Kurt. *Kirche und Judentum. Die Haltung der evangelischen Kirche zur Judenpolitik des Dritten Reiches.* Halle: VEB Max Niemeyer, 1968.

Mekeel, Arthur J. *The Relation of the Quakers to the American Revolution.* Washington, D.C.: University Press of America, 1979.

Michmann, Dan. "The Committee for Jewish Refugees in Holland (1933–1940)." *Yad Vashem Studies* 14 (1981): 205–32.

Michmann, Joseph. "The Controversial Stand of the *Joodse Rad* in the Netherlands: Lodewijk E. Visser's Struggle." *Yad Vashem Studies* 10 (1974): 9–68.

———. "Planning for the Final Solution against the Background of Developments in Holland in 1941." *Yad Vashem Studies* 17 (1986): 145–80.

Mikovits, Martine. "Die jüdische Emigration von Österreich nach Amerika zwischen März 1938 und September 1939." Master's thesis, University of Vienna, 1992.

Milfull, John, ed. *Why Germany? National Socialist Anti-Semitism and the European Context.* Providence and Oxford: Berg, 1993.

Mitchell, Otis C. *Nazism and the Common Man: Essays in German History (1929–1939).* Minneapolis: Burgess, 1972.

Mitteilungen für die Freunde des Quäkertums in Deutschland, 1924–1927.

Monatshefte der Deutschen Freunde, 1927–1931.

Moore, Bob. *Refugees from Nazi Germany in the Netherlands, 1933–1940.* Studies in Social History, 9. Dordrecht and Boston: Nijhoff, 1986.

Moss, Norman. *Klaus Fuchs, the Man Who Stole the Atom Bomb.* London: Grafton Books, 1987.

Mosse, George L. "Die deutsche Rechte und die Juden." In *Entscheidungsjahr 1932,* ed. W. E. Mosse and Arnold Paucker. Tübingen: Mohr, 1966.

Mosse, W. E., and Arnold Paucker, eds. *Entscheidungsjahr 1932.* Tübingen: Mohr, 1966.

Nachmann, Horst. "'Ich nahm das Kreuz . . .' Die Geschichte eines Jungen der nicht mehr leben durfte weil er Jude war." *Frankfurter Rundschau* (March 11, 1961).

Newsom, David D. "The Flow of Refugees and the World's Response." *Christian Science Monitor* (December 23, 1992).

Niebuhr, Vera. "Alfons Paquet: The Development of His Thought in Wilhelmian and Weimar Germany." Ph.D. diss., University of Wisconsin, 1977.

———. "Alfons Paquet. Rheinischer Dichter und Verfechter des Internationalismus." *Archiv für Frankfurts Geschichte und Kunst* 57 (1980): 219–42.

Niederland, Doron. "Areas of Departure from Nazi Germany and the Social Structure of the Emigrants." In *Second Chance: Two Centuries of German-Speaking Jews in the United Kingdom,* ed. W. E. Mosse et al. Tübingen: Mohr, 1991.

———. "The Emigration of Jewish Academics and Professionals from Germany in the First Years of Nazi Rule." *Leo Baeck Institute Year Book* 33 (1988): 285–300.

Noakes, Jeremy. "The Development of Nazi Policy toward the German-Jewish 'Mischlinge.'" *Leo Baeck Institute Year Book* 35 (1989): 291–354.

Oehme, Werner. *Märtyrer der evangelischen Christenheit 1933–1945.* East Berlin: Evangelische Verlagsanstalt, 1979.

Ogiermann, Otto. *Bis zum letzten Atemzug. Das Leben und Aufbegehren des Priesters Bernhard Lichtenberg.* Leutesdorf: Johannes Verlag, 1985.

Otto, Heinrich. *Werden und Wesen des Quäkertums und seine Entwicklung in Deutschland.* Vienna: Sensen Verlag, 1972.

Paucker, Arnold, ed. *Jews in Nazi Germany, 1933–43.* Schriftenreihe wissenschaftlicher Abhandlungen des Leo Baeck Instituts, 45. Tübingen: Mohr, 1986.

Pauley, Bruce F. *From Prejudice to Persecution: A History of Austrian Anti-Semitism.* Chapel Hill: University of North Carolina Press, 1992.

Peetz, E. A. Otto, and Margarethe Lachmund. *". . . Allen Bruder sein . . ." Corder Catchpool (1883–1952), Ein englischer Freund in deutscher Not.* Stimmen der Freunde, 3. Bad Pyrmont: Religiöse Gesellschaft der Freunde in Deutschland, 1963.

Perry, John W. "Working among German Prisoners" *The Wayfarer* (October 1945).

Petersen, Katharina. "The New Quakerschool in Holland" *The Friend* (July 13, 1934).

Petersen, Walter F. "Die deutschen politischen Emigranten in Frankreich 1933–1940. 'Die selben Debatten wie zu hause?'" In vol. 2 of *Deutschland und Europa in der Neuzeit,* ed. Ralph Melville et al., eds. Festschrift für Karl Otmar Freiherr von Aretin zum 65. Geburtstag. Wiesbaden: Steiner, 1988.

Pisarek, Abraham, and Hazel Rosenstrauch, eds. *Aus Nachbarn wurden Juden. Ausgrenzung und Selbstbehauptung 1933–1942.* Berlin: Transit, 1983.

Plieg, Ernst-Albrecht. *Das Memelland 1920–1939.* Würzburg: Holzner Verlag, 1962.

Der Quäker, 1931–1942, 1946–.

Quaker Embassies: A Survey of Friends' Service in Europe since 1919. London: Friends Service Council, 1934.

Ragg, Albrecht. "The German Socialist Emigration in the United States." Ph.D. diss., Loyola University of Chicago, 1977.

Reilly, Philip E. *The Surgical Solution: A History of Involuntary Sterilization in the United States.* Baltimore: Johns Hopkins University Press, 1991.

Reutter, Lutz-Eugen. *Katholische Kirche als Fluchthelfer im Dritten Reich. Die Betreuung von Auswanderern durch den St. Raphaels-Verein.* Recklinghausen and Hamburg: Paulus Verlag, 1971.

Rieber, Wilhelm. "Zum Gedenken an Hans Albrecht." *Der Quäker* (March 1957).

Riesenberger, Dieter. *Geschichte der Friedensbewegung in Deutschland. Von den Anfängen bis 1933.* Göttingen: Vandenhoeck & Ruprecht, 1985.

Röhm, Eberhard. *Sterben für den Frieden. Spurensicherung: Hermann Stöhr (1898–1940), und die ökumenische Friedensbewegung.* Stuttgart: Calwer Verlag, 1985.

Röhm, Eberhard, and Jörg Thierfelder. *Juden-Christen-Deutsche.* 2 vols. in 3 parts. Stuttgart: Calwer Verlag, 1990–1992.

Romano, Sergio. *I falsi protocolli. Il "complotto" ebraico dalla Russia di Nicola II a oggi.* Milan: Corbaccio, 1992.

Ronijin, Peter. *Snel, Streng en Rechtvaardig. Politiek Beleid inzake de Bestraffing en Reclassering van "foute" Nederlanders, 1945–1955.* Weesp: De Haan, 1989.

Roon, Ger van. *Protestants Nederland en Duitsland 1933–1941.* Utrecht & Antwerp: Het Spectrum, 1973.

Ross, Robert W. *So It Was True: The American Protestant Press and the Nazi Persecution of the Jews.* Minneapolis: University of Minnesota Press, 1980.

Ruf und Antwort. Festgabe für Emil Fuchs zum 90. Geburtstag, Leipzig: Koehler & Amelang, 1964.

Rürup, Reinhard. "Das Ende der Emanzipation: Die anti-jüdische Politik in Deutschland von der Machtergreifung bis zum zweiten Weltkrieg." In *The Jews in Nazi Germany, 1933–1945,* ed. Arnold Paucker. Leo Baeck Institute, Schriftenreihe wissenschaftlicher Arbeiten, 45. Tübingen: Mohr, 1986.

Russell, Elbert. *The Quaker Challenge in a World of Force.* Philadelphia: American Friends Literature Council, 1921.

Rutland, Suzanne. "Australian Government Policies to Refugee Migration, 1933–1939." *Journal of the Royal Australian Historical Society* 69 (1984): 224–38.

Sachsse, Christoph, and Florian Tennstedt. *Der Wohlfahrtsstaat im Nationalsozialismus.* Geschichte der Armenfürsorge in Deutschland, 3. Stuttgart: Kohlhammer, 1992.

Sassin, Horst S. *Liberale im Widerstand. Die Robinsohn-Strassmann-Gruppe 1934–1942.* Hamburg: Hans Christians, 1993.

Sauer, Paul. "Otto Hirsch (1885–1941), Director of the Reichsvertretung." *Leo Baeck Institute Year Book* 32 (1987): 341–68.

Schäfer, Walter. *Paul Geheeb. Mensch und Erzieher.* Aus den deutschen Landerziehungsheimen, 4. Stuttgart: Ernst Klett, [1959?].

Schlosser, Julie. *Freundschaft mit einem englischen Quäker.* Hamburg: Furche Verlag, 1956.

Schmitt, Hans A. "Men and Politics in East Germany." *Current History* 52 (1967): 232–37.

———. "Quaker Efforts to Rescue Children from Nazi Education and Discrimination: The International Quakerschool Eerde." *Quaker History* 85 (1996): 45–57.

———. "The Treaty of Versailles: Mirror of Europe's Post-War Agony." In *The Treaty of Versailles: The Shaping of the Modern World,* ed. James Lott. Blacksburg, Va.: Virginia Tech, 1989.

Scholnick, Myron I. *The New Deal and Anti-Semitism in America.* New York: Garland, 1990.

Schumacher, Martin. *M. d. R. Die Reichstagsabgeordneten der Weimarer Republik in der Zeit des Nationalsozialismus. Politische Verfolgung, Emigration und Ausbürgerung, 1933–1945.* Düsseldorf: Droste, 1994.

Schwabe, Klaus. "Hans Lachmund—Lebensbild eines Demokraten." *Stier und Greif, Blätter zur Kultur- und Landesgeschichte in Mecklenburg-Vorpommern* 5 (1995): 50–53.

Schwarz, Angelika. *Die Reise ins Dritte Reich. Britische Augenzeugen im nationalsozialistischen Deutschland (1933–39).* Göttingen: Vandenhoeck & Ruprecht, 1993.

Schwarz, Max. *MdR, Biographisches Handbuch der Reichstage.* Hanover: Verlag für Litteratur & Zeitgeschehen, 1965.

Seadle, Michael. "Quakerism in Germany: The Pacifist Response to Hitler." Ph.D. diss., University of Chicago, 1977.

See, Wolfgang, and Rudolf Weckerling. *Frauen im Kirchenkampf. Beispiele aus der Bekennenden Kirche Berlin-Brandenburg 1933 bis 1945.* Berlin: Wichern Verlag, 1984.

Senkman, Leonardo. "Argentina's Immigration Policy during the Holocaust (1938–1945)." *Yad Vashem Studies* 21 (1991): 155–88.

Sessions, William K. *They Chose the Star.* Rev. ed. York: Sessions Book Trust, 1991.

Shafir, Shlomo. "American Diplomats in Berlin (1933–1939) and Their Attitude to the Nazi Persecution of the Jews." *Yad Vashem Studies* 9 (1973): 71–104.

Shepherd, Naomi. *A Refuge from Darkness: Wilfred Israel and the Rescue of the Jews.* New York: Pantheon Books, 1984.

Sherman, A. J. *Island Refuge: Britain and Refugees from the Third Reich, 1933–39.* Berkeley and Los Angeles: University of California Press, 1973.

Shirley, Dennis. *The Politics of Progressive Education: The Odenwaldschule in Nazi Germany.* Cambridge: Harvard University Press, 1992.

Siegmund-Schultze, Friedrich. "Von den Quäkern. Zusammenkunft der deutschen Freunde der Quäker in Dillenburg (17.-19. September)." *Die Eiche* 9 (1921): 373–74.

Sijes, B. A. *Studies over Jodenvervolging.* Assen: Van Gorcum, 1974.

Snoek, J. M. *De Nederlandse Kerken en de Joden 1940–1945. De Protesten bij Seyss-Inquart, Hulp aan joodse Onderduikers, de Motieven voor Hulpverleening.* Kampen: J. H. Kok, 1990.

Sollmann, F. W. *Religion and Politics.* Pendle Hill Pamphlet, 14. Wallingford, Pa.: Pendle Hill Publications, 1942.

Stein, André. *Quiet Heroes: True Stories of the Rescue of Jews by Christians in Nazi-occupied Holland.* Toronto: Lester Orpen Dennys, 1988.

Stent, Ronald. "Jewish Refugee Organizations." In *Second Chance: Two Centuries of German-Speaking Jews in the United Kingdom,* ed. W. E. Mosse et al. Tübingen: Mohr, 1991.

Stewart, Barbara McDonald. *United States Government Policy on Refugees from Nazism, 1933–1940.* New York and London: Garland, 1982.

Stewart, W. A. Campbell. *Quakers and Education: As Seen in Their Schools in England.* London: Epworth Press, 1953.

Strauss, Herbert A. "Jewish Emigration from Germany: Nazi Policies and Jewish Responses." *Leo Baeck Institute Year Book* 25 (1980): 313–61.

Strickland, Charles E. "American Aid to Germany, 1919 to 1921." *Wisconsin Magazine of History* 45 (1961): 256–70.

Suhr, Elke. *Carl von Ossietzky. Eine Biographie.* Cologne: Kiepenheuer & Witsch, 1988.

Sutro, Nettie. *Jugend auf der Flucht 1933–1948. Fünfzehn Jahre im Spiegel des Schweizer Hilfswerks für Emigrantenkinder.* Zurich: Europa Verlag, 1952.

Thalman, Rita. "L'Antisémitisme en Europe occidentale et les réactions face aux persécutions nazies pendant les années trente." In Colloque de l'Ecole des Hautes Etudes en Sciences Sociales, *L'Allemagne nazie et le génocide juif.* Paris: Le Seuil, 1985.

Thieme, Karl. "Deutsche Katholiken." In *Entscheidungsjahr 1932,* ed. W. E. Mosse and Arnold Paucker. Tübingen: Mohr, 1966.

Tijn, Gertrude van. "Werkdorp Nieuwesluis." *Leo Baeck Institute Year Book* 14 (1969): 182–99.

Tinneman, Ethel Mary. "The German Catholic Bishops and the Jewish Question: Explanation and Judgment." *Holocaust Studies Annual* 2 (1986): 55–86.

Touw, H. C. *Het Verzet der Hervormde Kerk.* The Hague: Boekencentrum, 1946.

Trebs, Herbert. *Emil Fuchs.* Reihe Christ in der Welt, 4. East Berlin: Union Verlag, 1965.

Tritton, Frederick J. *Carl Heath, Apostle of Peace.* London: Friends Home Service Committee, n.d.

———. *The World Community of Friends.* London: Friends World Committee for Consultation, [1941?].

Trueblood, D. Elton. *The People Called Quakers.* New York: Harper and Row, 1966.

Turner, Barry. . . . *And the Policeman Smiled.* London: Bloomsbury Publishing, 1991.

Unruh, Benjamin Heinrich. *Fügung und Führung im Mennonitischen Welthilfswerk 1920–1993. Humanität in christlicher Sicht.* Schriftenreihe des Mennonitischen Geschichtsvereins, 8. Karlsruhe: Heinrich Schneider, 1966.

Veldman, Guusta. *Knackers achter Prikkeldraat. Kamp Erika bij Ommen.* Utrecht: Matrijs, 1993.

Vining, Elizabeth Gray. *Friend of Life: The Biography of Rufus H. Jones.* Philadelphia: Lippincott, 1958.

Vogel, Rolf. *Ein Stempel hat gefehlt.* Munich and Zurich: Droemersche Verlagsanstalt, 1977.

Voigt, Klaus. "Refuge and Persecution in Italy, 1933–1945." *Simon Wiesenthal Center Annual* 4 (1987): 3–64.

———. *Zuflucht auf Widerruf. Exil in Italien 1933–1945.* Stuttgart: Klett-Cotta, 1989.

Vorländer, Herwart. *Die NSV: Darstellung und Dokumentation einer nationalsozialistischen Organisation.* Schriften des Bundesarchivs, 35. Boppard: Harald Boldt, 1988.

De Vriendenkring, 1930-.

Warmbrunn, Werner. *The Dutch under German Occupation, 1940–1945.* Stanford: Stanford University Press, 1963.

Watt, D. C. "Christian Essay in Appeasement." *Wiener Library Bulletin* 14 (1960): 30–31.

———. "Influence from Without: German Influence on British Opinion, 1933–38, and the Attempt to Counter It." In *Personalities and Politics: Studies in the Formulation of British Foreign Policy in the Twentieth Century,* ed. D. C. Watt. South Bend, Ind.: Notre Dame University Press, 1965.

Weckerling, Rudolf, ed. *Durchkreuzter Hass. Vom Abenteuer des Friedens. Berichte und Selbstdarstellungen.* Heinrich Grüber zum Siebzigsten Geburtstag. 2nd ed. Berlin: Käthe Vogt, 1961.

Weingarten, Ralph. "Juden in der Schweiz." In *Minderheiten in der Schweiz. Toleranz auf dem Prüfstand*, ed. Alfred Cattani and Alfred A. Häsler. Zurich: Verlag Neue Zürcher Zeitung, 1984.

Wert, Hal Elliot. "U.S. Aid to Poles under Nazi Domination, 1939–1940." *The Historian* 27 (1995): 511–24.

Whitman, Doris Bader. *The Uprooted: A Hitler Legacy: Voices of Those Who Escaped before the "Final Solution."* New York and London: Plenum Press, 1993.

Williams, John Eryl Hall. *A Page of History in Relief: London, Antwerp, Belsen, Brunswick, 1944–1946*. York: Sessions Book Trust, 1993.

Williams, Robert Chadwell. *Klaus Fuchs, Atom Spy*. Cambridge: Harvard University Press, 1987.

Wilson, Roger C. *Quaker Relief: An Account of the Relief Work of the Society of Friends, 1940–1948*. London: Allen and Unwin, 1952.

Wischnitzer, Mark. "Jewish Emigration from Germany, 1933–1938." *Jewish Social Studies* 2 (1940): 23–44.

Wootton, Graham. *An Official History of the British Legion*. London: MacDonald and Evans, 1936.

Wyman, David S. *Paper Walls: America and the Refugee Crisis*. New York: Pantheon Books, 1985.

Zahn, Gordon C. *German Catholics and Hitler's War: A Study in Social Control*. Notre Dame: University of Notre Dame Press, 1989.

Zariz, Ruth. "Officially Approved Emigration from Germany after 1941: A Case Study." *Yad Vashem Studies* 18 (1987): 275–91.

Zehrer, Karl. *Evangelische Freikirchen und das "Dritte Reich."* Arbeiten zur Geschichte des Kirchenkampfes, Ergänzungsreihe, 13. Göttingen: Vandenhoeck & Ruprecht, 1986.

Zielenziger, Kurt. *Gerhart von Schulze-Gävernitz, eine Darstellung seines Werkes und seines Wirkens*. Bio-bibliographische Beiträge zur Geschichte der Rechts- und Staatswissenschaften, 4. Berlin: P. L. Prager, 1926.

Zipfel, Friedrich. *Kirchenkampf in Deutschland 1933–1945*. Veröffentlichungen der Historischen Kommission zu Berlin, 11. Berlin: De Gruyter, 1965.

Index